MW00779191

MACHIAVELLI

MACHIAVELLI

THE CHIEF WORKS AND OTHERS

TRANSLATED BY ALLAN GILBERT

VOLUME THREE

Non in exercitu, nec in robore . . .

Duke University Press   Durham and London   1989

© 1958, 1961, 1963, 1965, 1989 by Allan H. Gilbert
Library of Congress Catalogue Card number 64-16192
Cloth 0-8223-0922-x
Paper 0-8223-0947-5
Cloth 3-vol. set 0-8223-0913-0
Paper 3-vol. set 0-8223-0931-9

Printed in the United States of America
on acid-free paper ∞

TABLE OF CONTENTS

VOLUME ONE

VOLUME TWO

VOLUME THREE   Page

ILLUSTRATIONS

frontispiece

Terra cotta bust of Machiavelli by an unknown artist, in the Societa Columbaria, Florence. (Alinari photograph)

facing page 136

San Leo in 1957

facing page 546

Serravalle

following page 726

Plates illustrating the ART OF WAR

facing page 876

The expulsion of the devil from one possessed

facing page 1114

Bags from which the names of Florentines who were to hold public office were drawn.

TEXTS USED IN TRANSLATING

TUTTE LE OPERE STORICHE E LETTERARIE DI NICCOLÒ MACHIAVELLI, *a cura di Guido Mazzoni e Mario Casella, Firenze 1929.*

TUTTE LE OPERE *di Niccolò Machiavelli, a cura di Francesco Flora e di Carlo Cordiè, 1959, 1960 (to be completed).*

LE OPERE DI NICCOLÒ MACHIAVELLI, *per cura di P. Fanfani e di L. Passerini e di G. Milanesi, Firenze 1873-77 (incomplete).*

OPERE DI NICCOLÒ MACHIAVELLI, *Italia 1813.*

OPERE MINORI DI NICCOLÒ MACHIAVELLI, *con note di F. L. Polidori, Firenze 1852.*

IL PRINCIPE DI NICCOLÒ MACHIAVELLI, *Firenze (Giunta) 1532.*

IL PRINCIPE DI NICCOLÒ MACHIAVELLI, *Rome (Blado) 1532.*

DISCORSI DI NICCOLÒ MACHIAVELLI, *Firenze (Giunta) 1531.*

LIBRO DELLA ARTE DELLA GUERRA DI NICCOLÒ MACHIAVELLI, *Firenze (Giunta) 1524.*

COMEDIA DI CALLIMACO & DI LUCRETIA, *[Firenze ?] [1524 ?].*

MANDRAGOLA, *a cura di S. Debenedetti, Strasburgo (Bibliotheca Romanica).*

NICCOLÒ MACHIAVELLI, ISTORIE FIORENTINE, *per cura di Plinio Carli, Firenze 1927.*

Niccolò Machiavelli, LETTERE FAMILIARI *pubblicate per cura di Edoardo Lisio, Firenze 1883.*

Niccolò Machiavelli, LETTERE FAMILIARI, *a cura di Gerolamo Lazzeri, Milano 1923.*

Machiavelli, LETTERE, *[a cura di Giuseppe Lesca], Firenze 1929.*

Niccolò Machiavelli, LETTERE, *a cura di Franco Gaeta, Milano 1961.*

Oreste Tommasini, LA VITA E GLI SCRITTI DI NICCOLÒ MACHIAVELLI, *vol. 2, parte 2, Appendice, Roma 1911.*

Pasquale Villari, NICCOLÒ MACHIAVELLI . . . *illustrati con nuovi documenti, Milano 1912-1914.*

VOLUME THREE

THE HISTORY OF FLORENCE

List of Books

[*Late in the year 1520 Machiavelli received from Pope Leo X (Gio-vanni de' Medici) a commission to write the* HISTORY OF FLORENCE. *Eight books were presented to Pope Clement VII in 1525; no others were completed.*

Machiavelli announces dissatisfaction with the historians of Florence acces-sible to him, in that they dealt inadequately with the internal affairs of the city, though they were satisfactory for external matters, such as warfare. From his own attempt to treat those internal affairs, however, he allowed himself to be turned aside, partly through his interest in the Sforza wars in Lombardy, partly because all Italian activities were of import for his city. Moreover, Machiavelli did not spend his life in archives. But an archival attempt would have demanded that he be ahead of his age, and would have occupied time far longer than the four years and a half he gave to the HISTORY. *What could one man hope to do with the uncalendared records of the city of Florence? The latter part of his work and the notes for its continuation do indicate documentary study. Yet part of the* HISTORY *is only a compilation, not to be used, as historians did until an astonishingly recent time, as a source for facts. Still there is in it truth enough to serve as a basis for Machiavelli's observations on man as a political animal.*

One of the chief of these is that government exists for the common good. To forgetfulness of this truism is to be charged the long list of Florentine troubles, where political changes were made for the benefit of a party, not for that of the city as a whole. The city was continually torn by divisions, not united for the happiness of the citizens. On this internal strife Machiavelli often remarks, handling his material to emphasize it. For example, the story of Michele di Lando, not for the most part unreliable in fact, is that of a man who in his unselfish virtue thought of the city as a whole, and for his patriotism suffered ingratitude inspired by party spirit.

Avowedly fictitious are the frequent orations in the Thucydidean manner of the Florentine historians before Machiavelli. These are developed beyond dramatic requirements into expositions of social and political truths suggested by Florentine events. Incidentally, these orations enabled Machiavelli to deal with the problem of the Medici. They were de facto *rulers of Florence, and her only possible rulers. For a wise patriot the clear path was to accept them, hoping for a better future. So Machiavelli did. He writes of the family up to the death of Lorenzo, where his history ends, with a frankness that shows his courage or his knowledge of the good sense of the living Medici. Yet one of his friends, Donato Giannotti, reports that Niccolò often said to him:*

> I cannot write this history from the time when Cosimo took over the government up to the death of Lorenzo just as I would write it if I were free from all reasons for caution. The actions will be true, and I shall not omit anything; merely I shall leave out discussing the universal causes of the events. For instance, I shall relate the events and the circumstances that came about when Cosimo took over the government; I shall leave untouched any discussion of the way and of the means and tricks with which one attains such power; and if anyone nevertheless wants to understand Cosimo, let him observe well what I shall have his opponents say, because what I am not willing to say as coming from myself, I shall have his opponents say.

Yet even in such speeches, Machiavelli sometimes substituted for his first draft softer second thoughts. For example, a speech by Rinaldo degli Albizzi is changed from direct to indirect discourse, and the following is bolder than the final form:

> Union and prosperity are impossible while Cosimo de'Medici lives in this city, because his way of living surpasses what is proper for a citizen; his excessive wealth makes him bold; with it he has bribed all the heads of the common people and many other citizens, in such a way that in all the councils and magistracies of the city he can do what he wants to; our soldiers are all his partisans, because he employs whom he likes, whom he likes he gets rid of . . . . He lacks nothing of being prince but the title. It is the duty therefore of a good citizen to find a remedy for this, to call the people to the Public Square, and to take over the government, in order to restore to the republic her liberty. [Cf. bk. 4, chap. 28.]

That even a weakened form of this stood in the manuscript put in the hands of Giulio de'Medici, Pope Clement VII, is astonishing enough, a tribute to Machiavelli's desire to write a history that would inspire all lovers of the common good of man in whatever age or nation.]

THE HISTORY OF FLORENCE

TO THE MOST HOLY AND BLESSED FATHER OUR RULER CLEMENT VII, HIS HUMBLE SERVANT NICCOLÒ MACHIAVELLI

Since Your Holiness, Most Blessed and Most Holy Father, when you were still occupying a lower position, charged me to write out what has been done by the Florentine people, I have used all the industry and skill given me by nature and bestowed on me by experience to satisfy you. And since, in writing, I have come to those times which, through the death of the Magnificent Lorenzo de' Medici, changed Italy's condition, and since the events occurring afterward have been loftier and greater, and must be set forth with a loftier and greater spirit, I have thought it well that all I have written up to those times should be assembled in one volume and presented to Your Most Blessed Holiness, in order that in some measure you may now enjoy the fruits of your seeds and my toils.

As you read then, Your Holiness will first see, beginning with the time when the Roman Empire lost her power in the West, with how many disasters and under how many princes Italy for centuries suffered change in her governments; you will see that the Papacy, the Venetians, the Kingdom of Naples, and the Duchy of Milan took the first places and the chief authority in the land; you will see that your native city, withdrawing as a result of internal division from her allegiance to the Emperors, continued to be divided until her government came under the protection of your house. And because Your Blessed Holiness especially charged and required me to write in such a way of the things done by your ancestors that I should be far from all flattery (because however much it pleases you to hear men's true praises, to the same extent fictitious praises and those described with special favor displease you), I greatly fear lest, as I describe the probity of Giovanni, the wisdom of Cosimo, the kindness of Piero, and the high-mindedness and prudence of Lorenzo, I may seem to Your Holiness to be disobeying your orders. Of that transgression I clear myself before you and before anybody whom such descriptions displease as inaccurate, because finding how full of their praises were the accounts of those who at various times have written of them, I was obliged either to write of them just what I found or, as hostile, to be silent about them. And if underneath their excellent works was concealed any ambition which, as some say, was opposed to the common good, I who do not recognize it in them am not obliged to write of it; indeed in all my narratives I have never permitted a dishonorable deed to be defended with an honorable reason nor a praiseworthy deed, as though done for an opposite purpose, to be blackened.

But how far I am from flattery can be observed in all the parts of my history, and especially in the public speeches and private conversations, both quoted and reported, which in their ideas and arrangement preserve what is fitting to the temperament of the person who speaks without any reservation. Yet I avoid, in all places, offensive terms, as unnecessary to the dignity and truth of history. So nobody who rightly examines my writings can rebuke me as a flatterer, especially when he sees that I have said little on the achievement of Your Holiness' father. The cause of this was his short life, in which he had no opportunity to make himself known, nor have I with my writings been able to make him glorious. Nevertheless great and splendid enough were his deeds, since he begot Your Holiness—an act that far outweighs all those of his ancestors and will give him more ages of fame than the malice of Fortune took from him years of life. I have then striven, Most Holy and Blessed Father, in these writings of mine, without defacing the truth, to satisfy everybody; and perhaps I have not satisfied anybody, and if this should be so, I shall not be astonished by it, because I judge it impossible, without angering many, to write on the affairs of their own times. Nevertheless, I come cheerfully into the field, hoping that, as by the kindness of Your Holiness I am honored and supported, so by the armed legions of your most sacred judgment I shall be aided and protected; and with the same spirit and confidence in which I have written up to now, I am going to continue my undertaking, if life does not desert me and Your Holiness does not forsake me.

PREFACE

It was my purpose, when I first decided to write of the things done at home and abroad by the Florentine people, to begin my narrative with the year of the Christian era 1434, the date when the Medici family, through the abilities and laudable deeds of Cosimo and Giovanni his father gained more power than any other in Florence, because I considered that Messer Lionardo d'Arezzo and Messer Poggio, two very good historians, had told in detail all the things that happened before that time. But later carefully reading their works, in order to see with what ruling ideas and methods they carry on their writing, so that, by imitating them, I might make my history more acceptable to readers, I found that in description of the wars fought by the Florentines with foreign princes and peoples they are very careful, but as to civil strife and internal hostilities, and the effects these have produced, about one part of them they are wholly silent, and the other part they describe so briefly that their readers can get no profit or pleasure. The cause of their doing so is either that they considered these affairs so paltry as to be unworthy of preserva⁄ tion in writing, or that they feared to offend the descendants of those whom, in such narratives, they would have to calumniate.[1] These two causes (with all respect to them) appear to me wholly unworthy of great men, because if anything in history delights or teaches, it is what is presented in full detail. If any reading is useful to citizens who govern republics, it is that which shows the causes of the hatreds and factional struggles within the city, in order that such citizens having grown wise through the sufferings of others, can keep them⁄ selves united.

If the experiences of any republic are moving, those of a man's own city, when he reads about them, are much more moving and more useful; and if in any republic internal dissensions were ever worth noting, in that of Florence they are especially noteworthy, because most of the other republics of which there is any record have been content with one sort of factional struggle, with which, according as it has happened, they have sometimes expanded, sometimes ruined their cities. But Florence, not content with one sort of factional quarrel, has had many. In Rome, as everybody knows, after the kings were driven out, there was disunion between the nobles and the people, which continued in the city until her fall. So it did in Athens, and in all the other republics that flourished in those days. But in Florence first there were factions among the nobles, then

1. *To descendants, the truthful historian seems to calumniate ancestors when he relates their evil deeds.*

factional struggles between the nobles and the middle class, finally between the middle class and the masses. Many times it happened that one of these parties, having conquered the others, was itself divided into two factions. From these dissensions resulted as many deaths, as many exiles, as many ruined families as ever were known in any city of which we have record.

Certainly, according to my judgment, nothing shows so well the vigor of our city as does the quality of these dissensions, which had might enough to destroy the greatest and most powerful of cities. Nevertheless ours seemed always to grow stronger. Such was the ability of those citizens and the power of their intelligence and spirit to make themselves and their native city great, that as many as re-mained superior to so many ills could do more to exalt her with their ability than the evil influence of those events that might have weak-ened her could do to depress her. And beyond doubt if Florence had had the good fortune, when she freed herself from the Empire, to take a form of government that would have kept her united, I do not know what republic, modern or ancient, would have been superior to her—with such ability in arms and in peaceful arts she would have abounded. She expelled such numbers of the Ghibellines that they filled Tuscany and Lombardy. Yet the Guelfs and those who remained within her walls, when they fought against Arezzo, a year earlier than the battle of Campaldino, raised among the citizens of their party twelve hundred men-at-arms and twelve thousand infan-try. Later, in the war fought against Filippo Visconti Duke of Milan, when she had to put to the test her economic ability and not her own arms (which by then had disappeared), we see that in the five years while that war lasted the Florentines spent three million five hundred thousand florins. When that was ended, being dis-contented with peace, in order to show further the power of their city, they besieged Lucca.

I cannot, therefore, see any reason why these divisions do not deserve to be fully described. And if those very noble writers held back in order not to injure the memory of those whom they were going to discuss, they deceived themselves and showed that they did not understand the ambition of men and the desire they have to perpetuate the names of their ancestors and themselves; these historians did not remember that many who have not had opportunity to gain fame with praiseworthy deeds have striven to gain it with blameworthy actions, nor did they consider that conspicuous actions such as those of government and state, however they are carried on or whatever outcome they have, are always looked upon as bringing their doers honor rather than censure.

These things, when I had considered them, made me change my plan, and I determined to begin my history with the origin of our city. And because it is not my intention to fill the places of others, I shall describe in detail, up to 1434, only the things that happened inside the city, and of those outside I shall say nothing else than what is necessary for understanding of those inside. Then, when I have passed the year 1434, I shall write in detail of both sorts. Besides this, in order that this *History* may at all times be better understood, before I deal with Florence I shall describe by what means Italy came under those powers which at that time ruled her. All these things, both Italian and Florentine, will be completed in four books. The first will tell in brief all the events that happened in Italy from the decline of the Roman Empire to 1434; the second will carry its narrative from the origin of the city of Florence to the war that, after the expulsion of the Duke of Athens, was fought against the Pope; the third will end in the year 1414, with the death of King Ladislas of Naples; and with the fourth I shall come to the year 1434. From that time on, I shall present, with many details, the things that happened in Florence and outside, up to our present times.

BOOK ONE

CHAPTER 1
[Barbarian invasions. 375-439]

The peoples who live in the northern countries beyond the Rhine and the Danube, being born in a prolific and healthful region, often have increased to such a multitude that part of them were forced to leave their native places and seek new lands to dwell in. The method they used when one of those districts wished to get rid of some of its inhabitants was to divide its people into three parts, assigning every man in such a way that every part was equally provided with nobles and commoners, rich and poor. Then the part on which the lot fell went to seek its fortune, and the other two parts, freed from the burden of the third, remained behind to enjoy their ancestral goods. The groups which left home were the multitudes that destroyed the Roman Empire. Opportunity to do so was given them by the Emperors who, by abandoning Rome, the ancient seat of the Empire, and living in Constantinople, made the western part of the Empire weaker, since by watching it less carefully, they left it exposed to plunder by their officials and their enemies. And certainly for the overthrow of so great an empire, founded on the blood of so many able men, the fitness of things demanded that the rulers should not be less sluggish than they were, or the officials less disloyal, or the attackers weaker and less persistent. Actually, not one multitude but many joined forces for her destruction.

The first who came against the Empire from these northern regions after the Cimbri (whom Marius, a Roman citizen, defeated) were the Visigoths, whose name in their language means nothing more than Western Goths in ours. After some combats on the borders of the Empire, for a long time, by grant of the Emperors, they occupied territory on the Danube River. Although for various reasons and at various times they frequently assailed the Roman provinces, nonetheless the Emperors' power always kept them in check. The last who gloriously defeated them was Theodosius. Being brought under his authority, they never again established a king over themselves but, contented with the pay granted them, lived and fought under the Emperor's control and under his ensigns.

But after Theodosius died and his sons Arcadius and Honorius were left heirs of his Empire, but not of his ability and Fortune, with their rule conditions changed. Theodosius had appointed over the three parts of his empire three deputies: Rufinus over the East; over the West, Stilicho; and Gildo over Africa. All of these, after the death of the monarch, determined not to act as deputies in their provinces but to occupy them as princes. Gildo and Rufinus were crushed very early, but Stilicho, knowing better how to conceal his purpose, sought to gain the confidence of the new Emperors and nevertheless so to shake their power that it would then be easier for him to seize it. In order to make the Visigoths hostile, he advised the Emperors no longer to give those barbarians their accustomed subsidies. Besides this, since he believed that to shake the Empire these enemies would not be enough, he arranged that the Burgun-dians, Franks, Vandals and Alans, they too northern peoples and already beginning to seek new lands, should attack the Roman provinces. Thereupon the Visigoths, deprived of their subsidies, in order to be better organized to revenge that injury, made Alaric their king and, attacking the Empire, at last plundered Italy and took and sacked Rome. After that victory Alaric died and was succeeded by Ataulfus, who took as his wife Placidia, sister of the Emperors. Because of that marriage he agreed to go to the rescue of Gaul and Spain, provinces that the Vandals, Burgundians, Alans and Franks, for the reasons given above, had attacked. The result was that the Vandals, who had taken that part of Spain called Baetica, being hard pressed by the Visigoths and unable to resist, were invited by Boniface, who was ruling Africa for the Empire, to invade his province because, having rebelled, he feared that the Emperor would punish his transgression. For the reasons given, the Vandals gladly undertook that expedition and under their king Genseric made them-selves masters of Africa. Meanwhile the Empire had descended to Theodosius the son of Arcadius; since he paid little attention to things in the West, the Vandals believed they could keep what they had gained.

CHAPTER 2

[*Barbarian conquests. 440–600*]

And so the Vandals ruled Africa, the Alans and the Visigoths Spain; and not merely did the Franks and the Burgundians conquer Gaul, but the regions they inhabited were called by their name, so that one region is called France and the other Burgundy. Their success roused new multitudes to the destruction of the Empire, and another people, called Huns, conquered Pannonia, a province on the other shore of the Danube, which today, having taken the name of those Huns, is called Hungary. To these troubles others were added because the Emperor, seeing himself attacked from so many sides, in order to have fewer enemies, made truces, now with the Vandals, now with the Franks. These things increased the authority and the might of the barbarians but diminished that of the Empire.

Nor was the island of Britain, which today is called England, safe from such great destruction, because the Britons, fearing those people who had seized France and not seeing how the Emperor could protect them, called to their aid the Angles, people of Germany. Under Vortiger their king, they undertook the expedition; at first they protected the Britons, but later drove them from the island and remained there themselves to live, and from their own name called it England. But the earlier inhabitants, being deprived of their native land, of necessity became courageous and decided that though they had not been able to defend their own country, they were able to conquer that of others. They therefore with their families crossed the sea and conquered the region nearest to the shore, and after their own name called that land Brittany.

CHAPTER 3

[*Italy invaded. 452–476*]

The Huns, who, as we said above, had taken Pannonia, uniting with other peoples called Zepidi, Heruli, Thuringi, and Ostrogoths (for so in that language the eastern Goths are called), set out to seek new lands. And since they could not enter France, which was defended against the barbarian forces, they came into Italy under Attila, their king, who a little earlier, in order to be sole ruler in the king-dom, had killed Bleda, his brother. Since he had thereby become very powerful, Andaricus King of the Zepidi, and Velamir King of the Ostrogoths were subject to him. Coming into Italy, then, Attila invested Aquileia, where he remained without any hindrance for two years; and in besieging it, he laid waste all the region round about and dispersed all its inhabitants. This, as we shall tell in its place, brought about the founding of the city of Venice. After the capture and destruction of Aquileia and of many other cities, he turned toward Rome; from her destruction he refrained on the request of the Pope, for whom Attila had so much respect that he left Italy and retired to Austria, where he died. After his death, Velamir, King of the Ostrogoths, and the leaders of the other nations took up arms against Eric and Uric, his sons; they killed one and forced the other, with the Huns, to recross the Danube and return into their own country. The Ostrogoths and the Zepidi then settled in Pan-nonia, and the Heruli and the Thuringi remained near the Danube on the other side of the river. After Attila had left Italy, Valentini-anus, the Western Emperor, determined to bring back prosperity; to be better situated for defending Italy against the barbarians, he left Rome and made Ravenna his capital.

These troubles in the Western Empire were the reason why the Emperor, who lived in Constantinople, many times granted its possession to others, as a matter of great danger and expense. And many times also the Romans without his permission, seeing that they were abandoned, set up for themselves an emperor who would defend them, or someone on his own authority usurped the Empire, as happened in those times when the Roman Maximus seized it after Valentinianus' death; he forced Eudoxia, who had been the latter's wife, to take him as her husband. Eager to revenge such an injury since, being sprung from imperial blood, she could not endure mar-riage with a private citizen, Eudoxia secretely encouraged Genseric, king of the Vandals and master of Africa, to come into Italy, showing him the ease and the value of conquering it. Allured by the hope of booty, that king came at once and, finding Rome abandoned, plun-dered the city, remaining there fourteen days. He also took and plundered many other cities in Italy, and having loaded himself and his army with booty, returned to Africa. When the Romans were back in Rome, since Maximus was dead, they made Avitus, a Roman, Emperor.

Then, after many events in Italy and outside her, and after the deaths of many emperors, the control of Constantinople came to Zeno and that of Rome to Orestes and Augustulus his son, who seized the Empire by trickery. And while they planned to hold it by force, the Heruli and the Thuringi, who after the death of Attila placed themselves, as I said, on the other side of the Danube near the river, made a league and under Odoacer, their general, came into Italy. And into the regions they left vacant, the Longobards entered, led by their king, Godogus—they too a northern people who, as we shall tell in its place, were the final plague of Italy. So, having come into Italy, Odoacer defeated and killed Orestes near Pavia, and Augustulus fled. After that victory, in order that Rome might change her title with her power, Odoacer, abandoning the name of the Empire, had himself called King of Rome. He was the first, among the leaders of peoples who then were overrunning the world, who settled down to live in Italy, because the others, either through fear that they could not hold her because she could easily be assisted by the Eastern emperor, or for some other hidden reason, had plundered her and then sought other countries in which to make their abode.

CHAPTER 4

[*Theodoric in Italy. 476–526*]

So in those days the ancient Roman Empire was under these leaders: Zeno, reigning in Constantinople, controlled all the Eastern Empire; the Ostrogoths ruled Moesia and Pannonia; the Visigoths, Suevi, and Alani held Gascony and Spain; the Vandals, Africa; the Franks and the Burgundians, France; the Heruli and the Thuringi, Italy. The Kingdom of the Ostrogoths had come to Theodoric, the grandson of Velamir, who, being friendly with Zeno, the Eastern Emperor, wrote to him that his Ostrogoths believed it unjust, since they were superior in vigor to all the other peoples, that they should be inferior in dominion, and that it was impossible to keep them confined within the boundaries of Pannonia. Hence, since he was forced to let them take arms and seek new lands, he wished first to inform the Emperor of his intention, in order to enable him to provide for it, by granting them some country where with his favor they could live more honorably and in greater ease. Hence Zeno, partly through fear, partly that he hoped to drive Odoacer out of Italy, gave Theodoric permission to march against him and take possession of the land. Theodoric at once departed from Pannonia, where he left the Zepidi, people friendly to him; having come into Italy, he killed Odoacer and his son and after his example took the title of King of Italy. He established his capital in Ravenna, moved by the same reasons that once made the Emperor Valentinianus dwell there.

Now Theodoric was a man very able in war and in peace, so that in the first he was always conqueror, in the second he greatly benefited his cities and his people. He scattered the Ostrogoths and their leaders through his lands, so that in war he could control them and in peace could govern them. He enlarged Ravenna, he rebuilt Rome, and, except for military discipline, he restored to the Romans every other dignity. He kept within their boundaries, without any of the disturbance of war, by his authority alone, all the barbarian kings who were occupying the Empire. He built towns and fortresses between the head of the Adriatic Sea and the Alps, to hinder more easily the passage of new barbarians who might attempt to attack Italy. And if near the end of his life so many virtues had not been defaced by cruelties caused by various suspicions about his kingdom, such as the deaths of Simmacus and of Boethius, very holy men, his memory would have been altogether worthy of every sort of honor; because, by means of his ability and his goodness, not merely Rome and Italy but all the other parts of the Western Empire, freed from the continual attacks by so many floods of barbarians that for many years they had been enduring, showed new life, and attained good order and a very happy condition.

CHAPTER 5

[Changes in Italy in barbarian times. 395–493]

And truly, if any times ever were miserable in Italy and in these provinces overrun by the barbarians, they were those extending from Arcadius and Honorius up to Theodoric. For if one will consider what a damage it may be to a republic or to a kingdom to change its prince or government, not through any external force but merely because of internal discords (by which we see that through little changes all republics and all kingdoms, even though very powerful, are overthrown), one can then easily imagine how much in those times Italy and the other Roman provinces suffered, for they not merely changed their government and their prince, but their laws, their customs, their way of living, their religion, their speech, their dress, their names. Individually and still more in total these things when merely thought about and not seen or suffered, are enough to terrify the firmest and steadiest mind. From this came the destruction, the origin, and the expansion of many cities. Among those destroyed were Aquileia, Luni, Chiusi, Popolonia, Fiesole and many others. Among those for the first time built were Venice, Siena, Ferrara, Aquila and many other cities and fortified towns that for brevity are omitted. Small towns that became big were Florence, Genoa, Pisa, Milan, Naples and Bologna. To all these are to be added the destruc- tion and the rebuilding of Rome and of many others that were variously torn down and rebuilt.

Among these ruins and these new peoples originated new tongues, as appears in the languages now used in France, in Spain, and in Italy; these are mixtures of the native languages of these new peoples and of the ancient Roman, that make a new sort of speech. Besides this, not merely have the provinces changed their names, but so have the lakes, the rivers, the seas, and the men, for France, Italy, and Spain are full of names that are new and wholly unlike the ancient ones; for example, omitting many others, the Po, Garda, the Archi- pelago are known by names unlike the ancient. The men, too, instead of Caesars and Pompeys, are now Pieri, Giovanni, and Mattei.

But among all these changes, of not less importance was that in religion because, in fighting the established habits of the ancient faith with the miracles of the new, there sprang up very serious troubles and enmities between men. And if indeed the Christian religion had been united, it would have caused slighter disturbances, but since the Greek, the Roman, and the Ravenna churches were fighting among themselves, and in addition the heretical beliefs were fighting with the catholic ones, in many ways they afflicted the world. Of this a witness is Africa, since she endured many more distresses because of the Arian sect, believed in by the Vandals, than because of their avarice or natural cruelty. Living, then, in the midst of so many persecutions, men bore written in their eyes the terror of their spirits, because in addition to the countless ills they suffered, a good part of them lacked the power to flee for aid to God, in which all the wretched are wont to hope, because the greater part of them, uncertain to what god they ought to turn, destitute of all aid and all hope, died wretchedly.

CHAPTER 6

[*Italy in Justinian's time. 493–555*]

No little praise therefore is due to Theodoric as the first who allayed so many evils. During the thirty-eight years of his reign he brought Italy to such greatness that the ancient afflictions were no more to be seen in the land. But when he died and left on the throne Atalaric, the son of his daughter Amalasiunta, Italy in a short time, since Fortune was not yet satisfied, returned to her ancient distresses. Soon after his grandfather's death, Atalaric died, and the kingdom was left to his mother; she was betrayed by Theodatus, whom she had summoned to aid her in ruling the kingdom. By killing her and making himself king, he incurred the hatred of the Ostrogoths. This encouraged the Emperor Justinian to believe that he could drive Theodatus from Italy, so he appointed Belisarius leader of an expedition for the purpose; this man had already conquered Africa, driven out the Vandals and restored that province to the Empire. Belisarius conquered Sicily, passed thence into Italy and took Naples and Rome. After this defeat the Goths killed Theodatus their king as its cause and in his stead chose Vitigetes; after some combats Belisarius besieged and captured him in Ravenna. But before Belisarius had completed his conquest, Justinian recalled him and put in his place Joannes and Vitales, completely unlike him in ability and conduct, so that the Goths regained their courage and chose as their king Ildovrado, governor in Verona.

After he was killed, the kingdom came to Totila, who defeated the Emperor's soldiers, regained Tuscany and Naples, and pushed the imperial generals almost out of the provinces Belisarius had regained. Justinian therefore decided to send Belisarius back to Italy. Returning with weak forces, he lost the reputation gained from his earlier deeds instead of gaining more. For when he was with his soldiers at Ostia, Totila captured Rome before his eyes, but since Totila could neither abandon nor hold her, for the most part he destroyed her, drove away the people, and took the Senators off with him. Making little account of Belisarius, he led his army into Calabria to meet soldiers who had come from Greece to aid that general. So Belisarius, seeing Rome abandoned, undertook a noble enterprise: entering the Roman ruins with the utmost speed, he rebuilt the city walls and called back the inhabitants. But Fortune opposed this praiseworthy enterprise because Justinian, at that time attacked by the Parthians, recalled Belisarius. In obedience to his master, he abandoned Italy, and the province remained in the power of Totila, who again took Rome. But he did not treat the city with the same cruelty as before, because at the request of St. Benedict, who in those days had a lofty reputation for holiness, he chose rather to rebuild her.

Justinian meanwhile, having made a truce with the Parthians and planned to send new soldiers for the relief of Italy, was hindered by the Slavs, a new northern people who had crossed the Danube and attacked Illyria and Thrace; hence Totila conquered almost all Italy. But as soon as Justinian had overcome the Slavs, he sent his armies into Italy under Narses the eunuch, a man most excellent in war, who, arriving in Italy, defeated and killed Totila. The Goths who survived that defeat gathered in Pavia, where they made Teia their king. Narses, on the other hand, after his victory took Rome, and at last fought with Teia near Nocera and killed and defeated him. Through this victory he wholly destroyed the name of the Goths in Italy, where, from King Theodoric to Teia, they had ruled seventy years.

CHAPTER 7

[*The exarchate of Ravenna. 565–568*]

But as soon as Italy was free from the Goths, Justinian died, and there was left as his successor Justin his son, who, on the advice of his wife Sofia, recalled Narses from Italy and sent there Longinus as his successor. Longinus followed the plan of the others, by living in Ravenna. And besides this he gave Italy a new form, because he did not set up governors of provinces, as the Goths had done, but established in all the cities and regions of importance leaders whom he called Dukes. In this arrangement he did not honor Rome more than other cities because, taking away the Consuls and the Senate, names until that day preserved there, he put her under a Duke who was sent annually from Ravenna, and she was called the Roman Dukedom. And to the official stationed at Ravenna who ruled all Italy for the Emperor, Longinus gave the name of Exarch. This division made easier the destruction of Italy and more quickly gave opportunity for the Longobards to conquer her.

CHAPTER 8
[*The Longobards. 568–756*]

Narses was very angry with the Emperor for taking away from him the government of that province which he had gained with his ability and his blood, since it was not enough for Sofia to injure him by recalling him but she added words full of insult, saying that she wished to have him return to spin with the other eunuchs. Hence Narses, bursting with anger, persuaded Alboin king of the Longo-bards, who then ruled in Pannonia, to invade Italy. As I showed above, the Longobards had entered those regions near the Danube which the Heruli and Thuringi abandoned when their king Odoacer led them into Italy. After the Longobards had been there some time and their kingship had come to Alboin, a bold and savage man, they crossed the Danube and fought with Commundus king of the Zepidi, who was ruling Pannonia, and defeated him. Finding among the spoil Rosmunda, Commundus' daughter, Alboin took her as his wife and made himself master of Pannonia. In harmony with his savage nature, he made from Commundus' skull a cup from which he drank in memory of that victory. When he was summoned into Italy by Narses, with whom he had been allied in the war with the Goths, leaving Pannonia to the Huns, who re-turned to their country after Attila's death, as we have said, Alboin came into Italy. Finding that province divided into many parts, he at once seized Pavia, Milan, Verona, Vicenza, all Tuscany, and the larger part of Flaminia, today called Romagna.

In the belief that through so many sudden conquests he now was victorious in Italy, Alboin held in Verona a splendid banquet, and being made rash by much drinking and Commundus' skull being full of wine, he had it presented to Queen Rosmunda, who was at table opposite him, saying in a loud voice, which she heard, that in such prosperity he wished her to drink with her father. Those words were like a stab in that lady's breast. Deciding on revenge and knowing that Almachild, a noble and fiery Longobard youth, loved her handmaid, she planned with her a secret arrangement for Almachild to sleep with the queen instead of the maid. Almachild, coming into a dark place according to her plan and believing he was with the maid, lay with Rosmunda. She then revealed herself, showing him that it was in his choice either to kill Alboin and always enjoy her and the kingdom, or to be killed by Alboin as the violator of his wife. Almachild decided to kill Alboin. But when they had killed him, since they had not succeeded in seizing the kingdom but on the contrary feared that the Longobards who loved Alboin would kill them, they fled with all the royal treasure to Ravenna, where Longinus honorably received them.

In the midst of these disturbances, the Emperor Justin died; Tiberius was crowned in his place. Occupied with wars against the Parthians, he could give Italy no attention. Hence Longinus thought he had a good opportunity to become king of the Longobards and of all Italy by means of Rosmunda and her treasure. He discussed this plan with her, and urged her to kill Almachild and to take himself as her husband. She accepted this and prepared a cup of poisoned wine which with her own hand she gave to Almachild when, thirsty, he had come out of the bath. When he had drunk half of it, feeling his vitals disturbed and realizing the cause, he compelled Rosmunda to drink the rest. So in a few hours both of them died, and Longinus was deprived of his hope of becoming king.

The Longobards, meanwhile, gathering in Pavia, which they had made the chief seat of their kingdom, chose Clefi as their king. He rebuilt Imola, which had been destroyed by Narses, and took Rimini and almost every city as far as Rome, but in the course of his victories he died. This Clefi was so cruel not merely to foreigners but also to his own Longobards that, frightened by the royal power, they no longer wished to set up kings, but chose among themselves thirty dukes to govern the rest. This plan was the reason why the Longobards never could conquer all Italy, and why their kingdom did not go beyond Benevento, and why Rome, Ravenna, Cremona, Mantua, Padua, Monselice, Parma, Bologna, Faenza, Forlì, Cesena partly protected themselves for a time, partly were never conquered. Not to have a king made them less ready for war, and when they did again establish one, after having been free for a time, they were less obedient and more prone to dissensions among themselves. This state of things first impeded their victory, then at last drove them from Italy. When the Longobards were in this condition, the Romans and Longinus made an agreement with them that everyone should lay down his arms and enjoy what he was occupying.

CHAPTER 9
[*The Popes. 4th–16th Centuries*]

In these times the popes attained greater authority than ever before. The first after St Peter, because of their holy lives and their miracles, were respected by the people. Their examples so strengthened the Christian religion that the princes were obliged, to get rid of the great disorder then existing in the world, to adopt that religion. When the Emperor became a Christian and left Rome for Constantinople, the Roman Empire fell more quickly, as we said in the beginning, and the Roman church grew more rapidly. Nevertheless up to the coming of the Longobards, since all Italy was subject either to emperors or kings, the pontiffs of those times obtained no other power than was given them through respect for their habits and their teaching. In secular things they obeyed the emperors and the kings, and sometimes were killed by them or employed as their servants in their administration. But Theodoric king of the Goths brought the popes greater importance in the affairs of Italy when he established his seat in Ravenna; since Rome was without a prince, the Romans for their protection began to render more submission to the pope. Yet this did not much increase the popes' strength; it only caused the Church of Rome to be put over that of Ravenna. But when the Longobards came and Italy was divided into several parts, the pope had reason for making himself more active; since he was almost ruler in Rome, the Emperor of Constantinople and the Longobards respected him; by means of the pope, the Romans entered into an alliance—not as subjects but as equals—with the Longobards and with Longinus. And so the popes, continuing to be friends now with the Longobards, now with the Greeks, increased their dignity.

But later, after the ruin of the Eastern Empire (which came about in these times under the Emperor Heracleus, because the Slavic people, whom we mentioned above, again assailed Illyria, and when that was conquered called it, after their own name, Slavonia; and the other parts of the Empire were attacked first by the Persians, then by the Saracens, who under Mahomet came out of Arabia, and lastly by the Turks, and Syria, Africa, and Egypt were taken from it) the pope because of the Empire's weakness had no further possibilities for taking refuge with it in his difficulties. And on the other side, since the forces of the Longobards were growing, he decided that he must seek new help, and had recourse to France, to the kings there. Hence the many wars that were carried on by the barbarians in Italy after these times were for the most part caused by the popes, and the many barbarians that flooded her were usually summoned by them. This sort of thing has lasted even to our times; it has kept and now keeps Italy disunited and weak. So, in describing events from those times to ours, the fall of the Empire will no longer be shown—since it has struck bottom—but the growth of the pontiffs and those other princedoms which have ruled Italy from that time to the coming of Charles VIII. It will be evident that the popes, first with censures, and then with censures and arms at the same time, mixed with indulgences, excited fear and awe, and that through bad use of censures and arms they have wholly lost awe, and as to fear, they are in the power of others.

CHAPTER 10

[*Pope Gregory III.*[1] *731–741*]

But getting back to our subject, I say that Gregory III had now come to the papacy, and Astolfo to the kingdom of the Longobards; the latter, in violation of the treaties that had been made, took Ravenna and began war against the Pope. Because of that, Gregory, who, for the reasons given above, no longer relied on the Emperor of Constantinople, because he was weak, and did not wish to rely on the faith of the Lombards,[2] who many times had broken it, betook himself to France to Pepin II. The latter, at first Lord only of

1. *Misled by his source, the* DECADES *of Flavius Blondus, Machiavelli has attributed to Gregory III the actions of Stephen II.*
2. *The Longobards. Machiavelli changes to the modern form.*

Austrasia and Brabant, had become King of France, not so much through his own ability as through that of Charles Martel his father and Pepin his grandfather. Charles Martel, being ruler of the king-dom, inflicted a memorable defeat on the Saracens near Tours, on the River Loire, where more than two hundred thousand were killed. As a result, Pepin his son, through his father's reputation and ability, later became king of that kingdom. To him Pope Gregory, as has been said, sent for aid against the Longobards. Pepin promised to send it, yet wished first to see him and to do him honor in his presence.

So Gregory went to France, passing through the lands of the Lombards, his enemies, without hindrance—so great was their rever-ence for religion. Having come into France, Gregory was honored by that King and sent back with his armies into Italy; these besieged the Longobards in Pavia. Hence Astolfo, forced by necessity, en-tered into a treaty with the French; they made the treaty on account of requests by the Pope, who did not wish the death of his enemy but that he should be converted and live. In this treaty Astolfo promised to restore to the Church all the cities he had taken from her. But when Pepin's soldiers had returned to France, Astolfo did not keep the agreement. So the Pope again had recourse to Pepin, who sent a second army into Italy, conquered the Longobards and took Ra-venna. Against the wish of the Greek Emperor he gave that city to the Pope, with all the other cities in the Exarchate, and added to them the districts of Urbino and the March. But Astolfo died while still restoring those cities, and Desiderio, a Lombard who was duke of Tuscany, took up arms to seize the kingdom. He asked aid from the Pope, promising his friendship; since the Pope granted aid, the other princes gave up. Desiderio at first kept his promise and continued to restore the cities to the Pontiff, according to the agree-ment made with Pepin; moreover no longer did an exarch come from Constantinople to Ravenna, but the city was ruled according to the Pope's will.

CHAPTER 11

[*Charlemagne; the Pope's temporal power. 768–844*]

Pepin then died and was succeeded as king by his son Charles who, through the magnitude of the things he did, was called the Great. The papacy meanwhile had come to Theodore I. He got into strife with Desiderio and was beseiged by him in Rome. So the Pope applied for aid to Charles, who, having crossed the Alps, besieged Desiderio in Pavia, and captured him and his sons and sent them as prisoners into France. Then Charles visited the Pope in Rome, where he decreed that as Vicar of God, the Pope could not be judged by men. And the Pope and the Roman people made him Emperor. And so Rome again had its Emperor in the West; and whereas the Pope had according to custom been confirmed by the Emperors, the Emperor, for his election, now had need of the Pope; and the Empire kept on losing its offices and the Church gaining them. By these means continually there was an increase in her author‑ity over the temporal princes. By that time the Longobards, having been two hundred and thirty‑two years in Italy, no longer retained anything of the foreigner except the name. So when Charles set about reorganizing Italy, which he did in the time of Pope Leo III, he permitted them to live in those places where they had been brought up, and after their name that province was called Lombardy. And that they might hold the Roman name in respect, he decided that all that part of Italy near them, which was subject to the Exarchate of Ravenna, should be called Romagna. Besides this, he made his son Pepin King of Italy, with jurisdiction that extended as far as Bene‑vento; and all the rest was in the power of the Greek Emperor, with whom Charles had made an agreement.

In those times Paschal I came to the pontificate, and the parish priests of the Roman churches, being nearer the Pope and having a share in his election, began calling themselves cardinals, in order to adorn their power with a splendid title. And they arrogated so much authority, especially after they excluded the people of Rome from choosing the Pope, that seldom did the choice of him go outside their number. Thus, when Paschal died, Eugenius II was set up, from the titular church of Santa Sabina.

And Italy, when she was in the hands of the French, changed in part her form and organization, because in temporal matters the Pope had taken more authority, and they had brought into her the names of count and marquis, as earlier Longinus, exarch of Raven‑na, had established there the name of duke. At last, after several pontiffs, Osporco, a Roman, came to the papacy, who, because of the ugliness of his name, called himself Sergius. This was the be‑ginning of the change of name that the popes make on their election.

CHAPTER 12
[Berengar. 814–951]

Meanwhile Charles the Emperor died, and was succeeded by Louis his son. After Louis' death so many differences came up among his sons that, in the time of his grandsons, the house of France lost the Empire, which was moved to Germany, and the first German emperor was called Arnolfo. Not merely did Charles' family, through its dissensions, lose the Empire but also the Kingdom of Italy, for the Lombards regained their power and attacked the Pope and the Romans. Hence the Pope, seeing nobody to whom he could turn, of necessity chose as King of Italy Berengar Duke of the Friuli. These happenings gave courage to the Huns, who were in Pannonia, to attack Italy, and coming to conflict with Berengar, they were forced to return to Pannonia, or rather to Hungary, for so that province, after them, had come to be called.

Romanus was in those days the Emperor in Greece, for he had taken the Empire from Constantine, being prefect of his army. And because early in his reign Apulia and Calabria had rebelled (which, as we said above, were subject to his empire), angered by that rebellion, he permitted the Saracens to cross over into those places. When they had come and taken those provinces, they tried to capture Rome. But the Romans, because Berengar was busy defending himself from the Huns, chose as their general Alberico Duke of Tuscany, and by means of his valor saved Rome from the Saracens. The latter, leaving that siege, made a fortress on Mount Gargano, and from there ruled Apulia and Calabria, and continually raided the rest of Italy. And so Italy in those times came to be wonderfully distressed, being attacked on the side of the Alps by the Huns and on the side of Naples by the Saracens.

Thus Italy suffered these afflictions many years and under three Berengars, who succeeded one another. In that time the Pope and the Church were troubled every hour, having no place where they could turn, because of the disunion of the Western princes and the weakness of the Eastern ones. The city of Genoa and all its coastal territories in those times the Saracens laid waste. From that came the greatness of the city of Pisa, in which many people who were driven from their native cities found refuge. These things happened in the year of the Christian religion 931. But when the Empire came to Henry and Matilda's son, Otto Duke of Saxony, a prudent man and of high reputation, Agabitus the Pope decided to beg him to come into Italy and take it from under the tyranny of the Berengars.

CHAPTER 13

[*Affairs in the states of Italy. 951–1046*]

The states of Italy in these times were organized as follows: Lombardy was under Berengar III and his son Albert. Tuscany and Romagna were governed by an official of the Western emperor. Apulia and Calabria were partly under the Greek emperor, partly under the Saracens. In Rome there were set up each year two consuls from the nobility, who ruled it according to the ancient custom; there was added to this a prefect who administered justice to the people; they had a council of twelve men, who assigned the rulers each year to the cities subject to them. The Pope had more or less power in Rome and in all Italy according to the assistance of the emperors or of those who were most powerful in the land.

Otto the Emperor then came into Italy and took the kingdom away from the Berengars, who had reigned there fifty-five years, and restored his powers to the Pope. He had a son and a grandson each also named Otto, who, one after the other, succeeded him in the Empire. And in the time of Otto III, Pope Gregory V was driven out by the Romans; hence Otto came into Italy and put him back in Rome. And the Pope, to avenge himself on the Romans, took away from them authority to choose the Emperor and gave it to six princes of Germany: three bishops, Mayence, Treves and Cologne, and three princes, Brandenburg, Palatine and Saxony; this happened in 1002. After the death of Otto III, the Electors chose as Emperor Henry Duke of Bavaria, who, after twelve years, was crowned by Stephen VIII. The lives of Henry and Simeonda his wife were very holy, as is shown by the many churches endowed and built by them, among which was the church of San Miniato, near the city of Florence. Henry died in 1024. Conrad of Suevia succeeded him, and then Henry II. He came to Rome, and because three popes were causing schism in the Church, he deposed them all and caused the choice of Clement II, who crowned him Emperor.

CHAPTER 14

[The government of Italy. The Popes and the Roman people.
1046–1061]

Italy was then ruled partly by the people, partly by the princes, partly by the appointees of the Emperor; the chief of these, to whom all the others were subordinate, was called chancellor. Among the princes the most powerful were Gottfried and the Countess Matilda his wife, the daughter of Beatrice, sister of Henry II. She and her husband held Lucca, Parma, Reggio and Mantua, with all that today is called the Patrimony.

The popes at this time were strongly opposed by the ambition of the Roman people, who earlier had made use of papal influence to gain freedom from the Emperors. After the people had seized the rule of the city and reformed her as they thought best, they immedi' ately became hostile to the popes, who from that people received many more injuries than from any Christian prince. And in the times when the popes with their censures made all the West tremble, the Roman people were in rebellion against them, and neither of the two had any other intention than to take away the reputation and the authority of the other. On the assumption, then, of the papacy by Nicholas II, just as Gregory V took from the Romans the power to choose the emperor, so Nicholas took from them the power to share in choosing the pope, and assigned that choice to the cardinals only. Nor was he satisfied with this, because, having made an agreement with those princes who ruled Calabria and Apulia, for reasons that we shall soon report, he forced all the officials sent by the Romans, throughout the territory controlled by them, to render obedience to the Pope, and some of them he deprived of their offices.

CHAPTER 15

[Henry IV at Canossa; Robert Guiscard. 1061–1084]

After the death of Nicholas, there was a schism in the Church, because the clergy of Lombardy were not willing to obey Alexander II, chosen at Rome; so they made Cadolo of Parma antipope. Henry, who hated the power of the pontiffs, informed Pope Alex' ander that he must renounce the pontificate, and the cardinals that they must go into Germany to elect a new pontiff. As a result of this, he was the first prince to learn the great importance of spiritual wounds, because the Pope held a council at Rome and deprived Henry of the empire and of the kingdom. Some Italian states followed the Pope, and some Henry. This was the seed of the division into Guelfs and Ghibellines, so that Italy, when without the barbarian floods, might be torn in pieces with intestine wars. Henry then, being excommunicated, was obliged by his subjects to come to Italy, and barefoot, to kneel before the Pope and ask pardon. This happened in the year 1080. Nevertheless, a little later a new discord came up between the Pope and Henry, so that the Pope again excommunicated him; the Emperor sent an army to Rome with his son, also named Henry, and with the help of the Romans, who hated the Pope, besieged him in his fortress. So Robert Guiscard came from Apulia to rescue him, and Henry did not wait for him but returned into Germany. The Romans alone remained obstinate, so that Robert sacked Rome and put her again into the ancient ruins from which various pontiffs had earlier restored her. And because this Robert first organized the Kingdom of Naples, I think it not superfluous to tell in detail his actions and his origin.

CHAPTER 16

[*The Normans in Italy. 845–1520*]

When discord rose between the heirs of Charlemagne, as we have shown above, opportunity was given for new northern people, called Normans, to attack France, and they conquered the district that today is called Normandy. Of these people, one portion came into Italy in the times when that land was overrun by the Berengars, the Saracens, and the Huns, and took some cities in Romagna, where in the midst of those wars they vigorously sustained themselves. To Tancred, one of those Norman princes, several sons were born, among whom was William, called Iron-armed, and Robert, called Guiscard. The sovereignty had come to William, and the disturbances in Italy to some extent had stopped. Nevertheless the Saracens held Sicily and every day were raiding the shores of Italy. Because of this, William made an agreement with the princes of Capua and of Salerno and with Malochus, the Greek, who for the Emperor of

Greece was ruling Apulia and Calabria, to attack Sicily, and if they should gain the victory, they agreed among themselves that, of the booty and of the territory, each of them should have a fourth part as his share. The expedition was successful, and driving out the Sara- cens, they took possession of Sicily. After this victory, Malochus had soldiers come secretly from Greece and took possession of the island for the Emperor, and divided merely the spoil. At this William was discontented, but he waited until a more fitting time to show it, and departed from Sicily with the princes of Salerno and of Capua.

When they had left him to return home, William did not go back to Romagna, but led his army toward Apulia, and quickly took Melfi, and then in a short time, in spite of the forces of the Greek Emperor, he made himself master of almost all Apulia and Calabria. These provinces were ruled until the time of Nicholas II by Robert Guiscard his brother. And because he had many differences with his nephews about the inheritance of those states, he used the power of the Pope to settle them. This the Pope did gladly, for he was eager to gain Robert's support, so that the latter would protect him against the German emperors and against the arrogance of the Roman people; and so it turned out, according to what we have explained above, for on the urging of Gregory VII he drove Henry from Rome and sub- dued the people. Robert was succeeded by Roger and William, his sons, to whose possessions were added Naples and all the territory extending from Naples to Rome, and then Sicily, all of which were controlled by Roger. But when William went to Constantinople to receive the Emperor's daughter as his wife, his territory was attacked by Roger and taken from him. Made proud by such an acquisition, Roger first called himself King of Italy; later, satisfied with the title of King of Apulia and of Sicily, he was the first who gave name and organization to that kingdom, which even to this day keeps its ancient boundaries, though it has many times changed not merely family but nation, because when the stock of the Normans died out, that kingdom went to the Germans, from them to the French, from them to the Aragonese, and today is held by the Flemings.

CHAPTER 17

[*The Crusades. 1088–1192*]

By this time the papacy had come to Urban II, who was hated in Rome. And because he feared that on account of the discords in Italy he could not be secure, he turned to a noble undertaking, and went into France with all the clergy and brought together in Auvergne many people, to whom he made a speech against the infidels. By this he so much inflamed their spirits that they determined to make an expedition to Asia against the Saracens. This expedition and all the other similar ones were later called Crusades, because all those who went on them were marked on their arms and on their clothing with a red cross. The leaders of this expedition were Godfrey, Eustace and Baldwin of Bouillon—counts of Boulogne—and a Peter the Hermit, widely renowned for holiness and prudence. Many kings and many states joined in contributing money for it, and many individuals without any pay served as soldiers—so powerful then in the minds of men was religion, when they were moved by the examples of her leaders.

This expedition at the beginning was glorious, for all of Asia Minor, Syria, and part of Egypt came into the power of the Christians. By its means was founded the order of the Knights of Jerusalem, which even today rules and holds the island of Rhodes, now the sole obstacle to Mohammedan power. It caused the founding also of the order of the Templars, which as a result of their wicked conduct soon disappeared. There happened at various times various events, in which many nations and particular men were renowned. In support of that expedition, the King of France and the King of England crossed the sea; and the Pisans, Venetians and Genoese gained very great reputations; with varied fortune they carried on the war as late as the time of Saladin the Saracen. His ability and the dissensions among the Christians finally took from them all the renown that in the beginning they had gained, and after ninety years they were driven from the place that with such honor and good fortune they had regained.

CHAPTER 18
[*Frederick Barbarossa and the Antipope. 1088–1174*]

After the death of Urban, the next Pope installed was Paschal II, and Henry IV succeeded to the Empire. He came to Rome, pretending to be friendly with the Pope; then he put the Pope and all the clergy in prison and did not liberate them until they granted him power to manage the churches in Germany as he wished. In those days the Countess Matilda died and left the Church heir to all her territory.

After the death of Paschal and of Henry IV, there were many popes and emperors, until the papacy came to Alexander III, and the Empire to Frederick of Suevia, called Barbarossa. In those days the pontiffs had many troubles with the Roman people and with the emperors, which in the time of Barbarossa greatly increased. Frederick was a man of high ability in war, but of so much pride that he could not endure having to yield to the Pontiff. Nonetheless, on his election he came to Rome for the crown and peacefully returned into Germany. But for only a little while did he continue this policy, because he returned into Italy to master some cities in Lombardy that were not obeying him.

In that time it happened that the Cardinal of San Clemente, of Roman birth, separated himself from Pope Alexander, and by some of the cardinals was made pope. Frederick the Emperor was at this time besieging Crema. When Alexander complained to him about the antipope, he replied that both of them should visit him, and then he would decide which of them should be pope. Disliking this reply, Alexander excommunicated him, because he saw him inclined to favor the antipope, and fled to Philip King of France. Frederick, meanwhile, continuing the war in Lombardy, took and destroyed Milan. For this reason Verona, Padua and Vicenza united against him for their common defense. Meanwhile came the death of the antipope, so that Frederick set up in his place Guido of Cremona. The Romans, at this time, through the absence of the Pope and through the hindrances the Emperor found in Lombardy, had regained some authority in Rome, and continued to acknowledge the submission of those cities that had before been their subjects. And because the Tusculans did not wish to yield to their authority,

the whole population of Rome marched against them. The Tusculans were aided by Frederick, and defeated the army of the Romans
with such great slaughter that never afterward was Rome either
populous or rich. Meanwhile Pope Alexander had returned to
Rome, since he believed he would be secure, because of the hostility
of the Romans to Frederick, and because of the enemies the latter had
in Lombardy. But Frederick, putting aside all hesitation, marched
on Rome, where Alexander did not wait for him, but fled toWilliam
King of Apulia, who was heir to that kingdom after the death of
Roger. But Frederick, driven away by the plague, gave up the siege
of Rome and went back to Germany. And the cities of Lombardy
that were united against him, in order to be able to attack Pavia and
Tortona, which adhered to the imperial party, built a city to be their
headquarters in that war, which they named Alessandria, in honor of
Pope Alexander and in mockery of Frederick. Then Guido the
antipope died, and in his place was set up Giovanni da Fermo,
who with the help of the Emperor's party remained in Montefiasconi.

CHAPTER 19

[*St. Thomas of Canterbury. Death of Barbarossa. 1170–1190*]

Pope Alexander meanwhile had gone to Tusculum, summoned
by that people so that with his authority he would defend them from
the Romans. There ambassadors came to him from Henry King of
England to make plain to him that the King was without guilt in the
death of the blessed Thomas, bishop of Canterbury, though he had
been publicly censured for it. The Pope therefore sent two cardinals
to England to learn the truth of the matter. Although they did not
find the King plainly guilty, yet because he was generally reputed to
have sinned and because he had not honored Thomas according to
his deserts, they assigned to the King as penance that, summoning
all the barons of his realm, he should in their presence make apology
with an oath; and in addition that he should at once send two hundred soldiers to Jerusalem, paid for a year, and that he himself should
be under bond to go there in person, with the largest army he could
assemble, before three years had passed, and that he should annul
everything done in his kingdom in opposition of the Church's liberty, and that he should agree that any of his subjects could at will

appeal to Rome. All these things Henry agreed to. Thus so great a king subjected himself to that judgment which today a private citizen would be ashamed to submit to. Nonetheless, while the Pope had such great authority over distant princes, he could not make himself obeyed by the Romans, from whom he could not secure permission to stay in Rome, though he promised that he would not concern himself with other than churchly matters. So much more at a distance than nearby the things that make a show are feared.

At this time Frederick had returned into Italy, and when he prepared to wage another war against the Pope, all his prelates and barons gave him to understand that they would desert him if he were not reconciled with the Church, so he was forced to submit to the Pope at Venice, where they laid aside their hostility; in the agreement the Pope deprived the Emperor of all authority over Rome, and named William, King of Sicily and Apulia, as his ally. And Frederick, discontented when not making war, went off on an expedition into Asia, in order to vent on Mahomet the ambition that he had not been able to vent on the representatives of Christ. But having come to the River . . . ,¹ attracted by the clearness of the water, he bathed in it. As a result of that mistake, he died. And so the waters gave more aid to the Mahometans than did the excommunications to the Christians, because the latter bridled his pride and the former destroyed it.

1. *Left blank by Machiavelli.*

CHAPTER 20

[Frederick II, Emperor and King of Naples. 1190–1218]

On the death of Frederick, nothing was left for the Pope to do except to control the insolence of the Romans, and after many disputes over the election of the consuls, the two parties agreed that the Romans according to their custom should choose them, but that the consuls should not assume the magistracy unless they first took oath to keep their faith with the Church. This agreement caused Giovanni the antipope to flee to Mount Albano, where he soon after died. In these times, William King of Naples also died, and the Pope planned to take over that Kingdom, since the King left no other sons than Tancred his natural son; but the barons did not yield to the Pope, but decided that Tancred should be king. The Pope at that time was Celestine III, who, eager to get that Kingdom out of Tancred's hands, contrived that Henry, son of Frederick, should be made emperor, and promised him the Kingdom of Naples on condition that he should restore to the Church the cities that belonged to her. To make the thing easy he took Constance, the daughter of King William, from a cloister, and gave her to Henry as wife, though she was already old. Thus the Kingdom of Naples passed from the Normans, who had been the founders of it, to the Germans. Henry the Emperor, as soon as he had settled the affairs of Germany, came to Italy with his wife Constance and with a son four years old, named Frederick, and without much difficulty seized the Kingdom, because by that time Tancred was dead, and as his heir had left a little son named Roger.

After some time Henry died in Sicily and was succeeded in the Kingdom by Frederick, and in the Empire by Otto Duke of Saxony, chosen as a result of support by Pope Innocent III. But as soon as he had received the crown, against all expectations Otto became an enemy to the Pontiff; he occupied the Romagna and made arrangements for attacking the Kingdom. For that reason the Pope excommunicated him, so that he was abandoned by everybody, and the electors chose as emperor Frederick King of Naples. Frederick came to Rome for the crown, and the Pope did not wish to crown him, because he feared his power, and sought to get him out of Italy, as he had got rid of Otto. So Frederick in anger went to Germany and, making various wars against Otto, overcame him. Meanwhile Innocent died, who, as the greatest of his excellent works, built the hospital of Santo Spirito in Rome. His successor was Honorius III, in whose time originated the orders of Saint Dominic and of Saint Francis, in 1218. This Pontiff crowned Frederick. Then Giovanni, who was descended from Baldwin King of Jerusalem, and who was with the remnants of the Christians in Asia and still held that title, gave Frederick one of his daughters in marriage, and with the dower granted him the title of that kingdom; from this it comes that any king of Naples is called King of Jerusalem.

CHAPTER 21

[Frederick II as Emperor; Guelfs and Ghibellines. 1212–1243]

In Italy things were then going as follows. The Romans elected no more consuls, and in place of these, and with the same power, they set up sometimes one, sometimes more senators. The league made against Frederick Barbarossa by the cities of Lombardy was still in force; these were Milan, Brescia, Mantua, with the greater part of the cities of Romagna, and in addition, Verona, Vicenza, Padua and Treviso. On the side of the Emperor were Cremona, Bergamo, Parma, Reggio, Modena and Trent. The other cities and towns of Lombardy, of Romagna and of the March of Treviso favored, according to necessity, now this party, now that one. In the time of Otto III, a certain Ezzolino came into Italy and remained there; he had a son to whom was born another Ezzolino. The last, being rich and powerful, allied himself with Frederick II, who, as has been said, had become an enemy to the Pope. And coming into Italy, by means of the effort and aid of Ezzolino, Frederick took Verona and Mantua, destroyed Vicenza, seized Padua and defeated the army of the allied cities; then he went on toward Tuscany. Ezzolino meanwhile had subjugated all the March of Treviso. He was not able to capture Ferrara, because it was defended by Azzo da Este and by the soldiers the Pope had in Lombardy. Hence, when the besieging army had gone, the Pope gave that city in fief to Azzo da Este, from whom are descended those who today are its rulers.

Frederick fixed his seat at Pisa, in his eagerness to make himself master of Tuscany; and in paying off his friends and his enemies in that province, he sowed so much discord that it caused the ruin of all Italy, because the Guelf and Ghibelline parties increased, since those were called Guelfs who followed the Church, and those who followed the Emperor, Ghibellines; this name was first heard at Pistoia. After Frederick left Pisa, in many ways he attacked and laid waste the cities of the Church, so that the Pope, having no other resource, proclaimed a crusade against him, as his predecessors had done against the Saracens. And Frederick, in order that his soldiers might not suddenly desert him, as did those of Frederick Barbarossa and others of his ancestors, hired many Saracens; to attach them to himself and to make a barrier in Italy that would be solid against the Church, so that he need not fear papal curses, he gave them Nocera in the Kingdom, in order that, having a refuge of their own, they could with greater security serve him.

CHAPTER 22

[*Manfred King of Naples; Ezzolino; Charles of Anjou. 1243–1268*]

The papacy had now come to Innocent IV, who, fearing Frederick, went off to Genoa and thence to France, where he summoned a council at Lyons, to which Frederick determined to go. But he was kept away by the rebellion of Parma. Being repulsed in his expedition against her, he went off into Tuscany and from there into Sicily, where he died. And in Suevia he left his son Conrad, and in Apulia, Manfred, born of a concubine, whom he had made Duke of Benevento. Conrad came to take possession of the Kingdom, and when he reached Naples he died; he was survived by Conradin, a child, who was in Germany. Meanwhile Manfred, first as guardian of Conradin, took possession of all that state. Then, reporting that Conradin was dead, he made himself king, against the wish of the Pope and the Neapolitans, whom he forced to consent.

While these troubles were going on in the Kingdom, there were in Lombardy many disturbances between the Guelf and Ghibelline parties. On the Guelf side was a legate of the Pope; on the Ghibelline was Ezzolino, who possessed almost all Lombardy on the other side of the Po. And because, in the course of the war, Padua rebelled against him, he put to death twelve thousand Paduans; he himself, before the war ended, was killed, at the age of eighty years. After his death all the cities he possessed became free.

Manfred King of Naples continued hostilities against the Church in the manner of his ancestors, and kept the Pope, who was named Urban IV, in unceasing anxieties. Hence the Pontiff, in order to overcome him, proclaimed a crusade against him and went to Perugia to wait for soldiers. And when he realized that soldiers were coming in small numbers and were weak and behind time, he decided that in order to defeat Manfred he needed surer aid; so he turned for assistance to France, and appointed, as King of Sicily and Naples, Charles of Anjou, brother of Louis King of France, and summoned him into Italy to take that kingdom. But before Charles came to Rome, the Pope died, and in his place Clement IV was chosen. In this Pope's time, Charles came to Ostia with thirty galleys, and arranged that his other people should come by land. And during the visit he made to Rome, the Romans, to get his favor, made him senator. The Pope invested him with the King, dom, with the pledge that he would every year pay to the Church fifty thousand florins, and decreed that in the future neither Charles nor anybody else holding that Kingdom could be Emperor. And when Charles moved against Manfred, he defeated and killed him near Benevento, and became master of Sicily and of the Kingdom. But Conradin, to whom by the will of his father that state belonged, having gathered many soldiers in Germany, came into Italy against Charles, with whom he fought at Tagliacozzo. And he was first defeated and then, fleeing in disguise, was taken and killed.

CHAPTER 23
[*The beginning of papal nepotism. 1276–1281*]

Italy remained quiet until the papacy was assumed by Adrian V. Since Charles was at Rome and ruled it through the office of senator that he held, the Pope, unable to endure his power, went off to live at Viterbo, and urged Rudolph, the Emperor, to come into Italy against Charles. Thus the pontiffs, now through love for religion, now through their personal ambition, did not cease to provoke new dissensions in Italy and to stir up new wars, and when they had made a prince powerful, they repented of it and sought his ruin; thus that country which through their own weakness they could not hold, they did not permit any other to hold. Yet the princes were afraid of them, because they always won, either fighting or running away, if through some deception they were not defeated, as Boniface VIII and some others, who under the pretense of friendship were captured by the emperors. Rudolph never came into Italy, since he was kept away by his war with the King of Bohemia.

Meanwhile Adrian died, and the new pontiff chosen was Nicho, las III of the house of Orsini, a man bold and ambitious, who strove in every way to lessen the power of Charles. So he arranged that Rudolph the Emperor should complain because Charles was keeping a governor in Tuscany to support the Guelf party, which he had restored to that province after the death of Manfred. Charles yielded to the Emperor and took away his governor, and the Pope sent there a cardinal, his nephew, as governor for the Empire. Hence the Emperor, because of this honor shown him, restored to the Church the Romagna, which his predecessors had taken away from her, and the Pope appointed Bertoldo Orsini as Duke of Romagna. And since he believed he had become so strong that he could show a bold face to Charles, he deprived him of his office as senator and made a decree that nobody of royal blood should thereafter be a senator in Rome. He also formed the purpose of taking Sicily from Charles, and to this end carried on secret negotiations with Peter King of Aragon, which later, in the time of his successor, were put into effect. He planned also to set up two of his own house as kings, one in Lombardy, the other in Tuscany; their power was to defend the Church from Germans who might attempt to come into Italy and from the French who were in the Kingdom.

But in the midst of these plans he died. He was the first of the popes who openly revealed his personal ambition, and who attempted, under the pretext of aggrandizing the Church, to honor and assist his own relatives. As before this time no mention had ever been made of any pontiff's nephews or relatives, so in the future they will fill history; and at last we shall come to sons; and there is nothing left for the pontiffs to try except that, as up to our times they have planned to leave their sons as princes, in the future they may strive to leave them the popedom as hereditary. It is indeed true that up to now the princedoms they have established have had short lives, because most of the time the pontiffs, since they lived but a short while, either did not finish setting out their plants, or if they did set them out, left them with so few and so weak roots that, since the strength sustaining them was gone, at the first wind they withered away.

CHAPTER 24

[*Pope Martin IV: the Sicilian vespers. 1281–1285*]

This man's successor was Martin IV who, being French by nationality, favored Charles' party. To aid him, Charles sent his soldiers into the Romagna, which had revolted against the Pope. When they were besieging Forlì, Guido Bonatto, an astrologer, directed that the people should attack the French at a time he set; thus all the beseigers were captured or killed. At this time the plan made by Pope Nicholas with Peter King of Aragon was put into effect. As its result, the Sicilians killed all the French in that island, and Peter made himself lord of it, saying that it belonged to him because Manfred's daughter Constance was his wife. But Charles died while preparing for a further war by which to recover the island, leaving as his heir Charles II, who during the first war had been captured in Sicily. In order to gain his freedom, he promised to become a prisoner again if within three years he did not get the Pope to invest the royal family of Aragon with the Kingdom of Sicily.

CHAPTER 25
[Boniface VIII and the Colonna family. 1286–1303]

Rudolph the Emperor, instead of coming into Italy to restore the Empire's reputation there, sent an ambassador with authority to set free all those cities that would buy themselves off. Hence many cities did buy themselves off and with liberty changed their form of govern-ment. Adolph of Saxony succeeded to the Empire, and Peter of Morrone, as Pope Celestine, to the papacy. Being a hermit and altogether holy, after six months he renounced the papacy. The next elected was Boniface VIII.

The Heavens (knowing a time would have to come when the French and the Germans would abandon Italy and that land would remain entirely in the hands of the Italians) in order that the Pope, when he lacked opposition from beyond the Alps, might not make his power solid or enjoy it, raised up in Rome two very powerful families, the Colonna and the Orsini; with their power and their proximity these two were to keep the papacy weak. Hence Pope Boniface, who knew this, undertook to get rid of the Colonna; besides excommunicating them, he proclaimed a crusade against them. This, though it somewhat injured them, injured the Church still more, because that weapon which through love of the Faith he might have used effectively, when through personal ambition it was turned against Christians, began to stop cutting. Thus too great a desire to satisfy their own greed caused the popes, little by little, to disarm themselves.

Besides this, Boniface deprived two Colonna cardinals of their cardinalates. When Sciarra, the head of that house, fled in disguise, he was captured by Catalan pirates and put at the oar. But being recognized at Marseilles, he was sent to King Philip of France, whom Boniface had excommunicated and deprived of his kingdom. And Philip, thinking that in an open war against the popes he would either be the loser or would run many risks, turned to deceptions, and pretending that he wanted to make a truce with the Pope, he sent Sciarra into Italy secretly. This man, having come to Alagna, where the Pope was, brought his friends together at night and captured him. And though the people of Alagna soon set the Pope free, in his grief over that insult he died insane.

CHAPTER 26

[*Italy disturbed; Guelfs and Ghibellines. 1300–1322*]

Boniface founded the Jubilee in 1300 and planned that it should be celebrated every hundred years. In these times there were many troubles between the Guelf and the Ghibelline parties, and because Italy had been abandoned by the emperors, many cities became free and many were seized by tyrants. Pope Benedict restored their hats to the Colonna cardinals, and gave his blessing to Philip King of France. He was succeeded by Clement V, who, because he was French, took the papal court to France in the year 1305.

Meanwhile Charles II of Naples died, and was succeeded by Robert his son; and the empire was attained by Henry of Luxemburg, who came to Rome to be crowned, notwithstanding that the Pope was not there. As a result of his coming, there were various disturbances in Lombardy, because he put back into their cities all the exiles, whether they were Guelfs or Ghibellines. From this it followed that, since they fought each other, there was war throughout that region, which the Emperor with all his power could not prevent. Having left Lombardy, by way of Genoa, he came to Pisa. There he made efforts to take Tuscany from King Robert, but not having any success, he went on to Rome. There he remained only a few days, because he was driven out by the Orsini, with the aid of King Robert, and he returned to Pisa. In order more safely to make war on Tuscany, and to get her out of King Robert's control, he had him attacked by Frederick, King of Sicily. But while he hoped at the same time to conquer Tuscany and to take King Robert's territory, he died. He was succeeded in the Empire by Ludwig of Bavaria.

Meanwhile the papacy came to John XXII. In his time, the Emperor did not cease to harass the Guelfs and the Church, which for the most part was defended by King Robert and by the Florentines. Because of this, many wars were fought in Lombardy by the Visconti against the Guelfs, and in Tuscany by Castruccio of Lucca against the Florentines.

But because the family of the Visconti founded the dukedom of Milan, one of the five principalities that after that time ruled Italy, I shall begin at an earlier point an account of their situation.

CHAPTER 27
[*The Visconti. 1167–1450*]

After the Lombard cities mentioned above had formed a league to defend themselves from Frederick Barbarossa, Milan, as soon as her ruins were rebuilt, in the hope of revenging her injuries joined the league. It checked Barbarossa and for a time kept alive in Lombardy the Church party. During the disorders of the wars then waged, great power in Milan was gained by the Della Torre family, which always kept growing in influence, whereas in Lombardy the emperors had little power. But when Frederick II came into Italy and the Ghibelline party became powerful through the activity of Ezzolino, in every city a Ghibelline faction appeared. In Milan among those siding with the Ghibellines were the Visconti family, who drove the Della Torre family from the city. But not long had they remained outside when, through truces made between the Emperor and the Pope, they were brought back into their native place.

When the Pope with his court went into France, Henry of Luxemburg came into Italy to obtain the crown of Rome. In Milan he was received by Maffeo Visconti and Guido della Torre, who then were the heads of those families. Maffeo planned to make use of the Emperor in driving out Guido, judging the enterprise easy because the latter belonged to the party opposed to the Empire. He found his opportunity in the people's complaints about the insulting behavior of the Germans, and cautiously kept encouraging everybody, and persuading them to take arms and get rid of slavery under such barbarians. And when he saw he had arranged the affair to his advantage, he had one of his faithful followers stir up a riot, in which all the people took arms against the German race.

No sooner was the rebellion begun, than Maffeo with his sons and all his partisans were under arms. They ran to Henry, telling him that the uproar was caused by the Della Torre family who, not satisfied to remain in private life, had taken an opportunity to try to plunder him, in order to please the Guelfs of Italy and become princes of Milan. But they urged him to keep up his courage, for if he wished to be defended, they with their party were ready to rescue him in any circumstances. Henry believed everything Maffeo said was true, united his forces with those of the Visconti and attacked the Della Torre family, who had hurried into various parts of the city to end the riots; such of the Della Torre family as they could catch they killed, and the others, deprived of their property, they sent into exile.

So then Maffeo Visconti was like a prince in Milan; his heirs were Galeazzo and Azzo, and theirs were Luchino and Giovanni. Giovanni became archbishop in that city, and Luchino, who died before him, left as heirs Bernabò and Galeazzo. But when Galeazzo also died soon afterward, his heir was Giovan Galeazzo, called Count of Virtù. After the archbishop's death, he by trickery killed his uncle Bernabò and became sole prince of Milan. He was the first who had the title of Duke. His heirs were Filippo and Giovanmariagnolo. When the latter was killed by the people of Milan, the state was left to Filippo, who did not leave any male children. So that state was transferred from the house of the Visconti to that of the Sforza, in the way and for the reasons that in their place will be set forth.

CHAPTER 28

[The Emperor Ludwig; John, King of Bohemia. 1327–1334]

But going back to where I left off, Ludwig, the Emperor, in order to give reputation to his party and to take the crown, came into Italy. Being in Milan, in order to have a reason for getting money from the Milanese, he pretended to leave them free and put the Visconti in prison. Then, on the request of Castruccio of Lucca, he released them. Going on to Rome in order more easily to stir up Italy, he made Peter of Corvara antipope, since through his reputa- tion and through the power of the Visconti he planned to keep the opposing parties feeble in Tuscany and Lombardy. But when Cas- truccio died, his death at once caused Ludwig's ruin, for Pisa and Lucca rebelled against him, and the Pisans sent the antipope as a prisoner to the Pope in France; thereupon the Emperor, hopeless about affairs in Italy, returned to Germany.

No sooner was he gone than John King of Bohemia came into Italy, called by the Ghibellines of Brescia, and made himself master of that place and of Bergamo. Because he came with the Pope's permission, though he pretended the opposite, the papal legate in Bologna aided him, thinking this a good device for providing against the Emperor's return into Italy. As a result of this policy, Italy changed her situation, because the Florentines and King Robert, seeing that the Legate was aiding the undertakings of the Ghibel- lines, became enemies of all those to whom the Legate and the King of Bohemia were friends. And without paying any attention to Guelf or Ghibelline parties, many princes joined with them, among whom were the Visconti, the Della Scala, Filippo Gonzaga of Mantua, the Carrara, and the Este. Hence the Pope excommuni- cated them all. In fear of this league, the King went home in order to collect more forces, and though later he returned into Italy with more soldiers, nevertheless the enterprise proved too hard for him, so that, frightened, to the Legate's displeasure he returned into Bohe- mia. He left only Reggio and Modena garrisoned, and to Marsilio and Piero de' Rossi he committed Parma, since they were very powerful in that city. When he had gone, Bologna joined with the league, and the allies divided among themselves four cities that re- mained on the side of the Church; they agreed that Parma should go to the Della Scala family, Reggio to the Gonzaga, Modena to the Este, and Lucca to the Florentines. In the course of their attempts against these cities, many wars were started which for the most part the Venetians later settled.

Perhaps some will object because in the course of so many events that have happened in Italy, we have put off so long speaking of the Venetians, since theirs is a republic which for organization and power deserves above every other princedom in Italy to have her praises sounded. But that such bewilderment may be removed by

showing its cause, I shall go far back in time, in order that everybody
may learn what their origin was and why for so long a time they put
off intruding themselves into Italian affairs.

CHAPTER 29
[*Venice. 452–1520*]

When Attila King of the Huns was besieging Aquileia, the
inhabitants of the city, after they had defended themselves a long
time, in despair for their safety sought refuge as well as they could,
with their portable property, on many islands that lay uninhabited
at the end of the Adriatic. The Paduans also, seeing the fire near
them and fearing that when Aquileia was conquered Attila would
attack them, took their portable goods of most value into the same
sea at a place called Rivo Alto, to which they sent also their women,
their children, and their aged; their young men they kept in Padua
to defend her. Besides these, the people of Monselice, with the inhabitants of the hills round about, driven by the same fear, went to
the islands in the same sea. But after Aquileia was taken, and Attila
had destroyed Padua, Monselice, Vicenza, and Verona, the people
of Padua and the most powerful of the others continued to dwell in
the swamps around Rivo Alto. In the same way all the people
throughout that province anciently called Vinezia, driven by the
same events, retired into those swamps. So, forced by necessity, they
left pleasant and fertile places and took up their abode in those that
were barren, ugly, and lacking in every convenience.

And because many people were of a sudden brought together, in
a very short time they made those places not merely habitable but
delightful, and having established among themselves laws and customs, in the midst of such great catastrophes in Italy they were safe
and happy. In a short time they grew in reputation and power
because, in addition to the aforesaid dwellers, many from the cities
of Lombardy took refuge there, being driven out especially by the
cruelty of Clefi King of the Longobards. This brought no little
increase to that city, so that in the times of Pepin, King of France—
when through the request of the Pope he came to drive the Longobards out of Italy—it was stated in the agreements then made between
him and the emperor of the Greeks that the Duke of Benevento and

the Venetians were not to acknowledge subjection to either of them but, between them, were to enjoy their liberty. Besides this, since necessity had brought the Venetians to live in the midst of the waters, it also compelled them to consider—since they had no power on land—how they could live there honorably; and going with their ships through all the world, they filled their city with various sorts of merchandise; since these were needed by other men, large numbers necessarily visited that place. They did not consider for many years any other dominion than that which would facilitate their commerce; therefore they gained possession of many ports in Greece and in Syria; and as a result of the voyages that the French made to Asia, because much use was made of their ships, they received as payment the island of Candia.

While they lived in this manner, their name on the sea was formidable and on the Italian mainland highly honored. Hence, in all the disputes that arose they were most of the time the arbiters, as they were in the differences that rose among the allies over the cities they were to divide among themselves. Of these, when the case was referred to the Venetians, Bergamo and Brescia were left to the Visconti. But in time the Venetians, led on by their desire to rule, gained possession of Padua, Vicenza and Treviso, and later of Verona, Bergamo and Brescia, and many cities in the Kingdom and in Romagna. Thus they attained such a reputation for power that not merely to the Italian princes but to the kings beyond the Alps they gave cause for dread. Hence when these foreign rulers made a league against them, in one day the Venetians were deprived of the territory which in the course of many years they had gained with boundless expense.[1] And though in very recent times they have regained part of it, yet they have not regained either their reputation or their military strength. Hence like all Italian princes they now live in the power of others.

1. *At the battle of Vailà (Agnadello, Geradadda, Ghiaradadda). Cf.* PRINCE *12.*

CHAPTER 30
[Petty tyrants; Joanna of Naples. 1334–1348]

The papacy was now occupied by Benedict XII. Seeing that he had wholly lost power over Italy and fearing that Ludwig, the Emperor, would become her master, he decided to gain the friendship of all those who had usurped Italian cities that earlier had obeyed the Emperor; since they had reason to fear the Empire, they would join with himself in the defense of Italy. Hence he decreed that all the tyrants of Lombardy should retain the cities they had usurped, with legal titles. Soon after this grant Benedict died and Clement VI was made pope. The Emperor, seeing how liberally the Pontiff had given away the cities of the Empire and determining to be not less liberal than the Pope with other rulers' property, gave the cities they were ruling to all the tyrants who were in possession of cities belonging to the Church, so that these tyrants could retain them with imperial authorization.

In this way Galeotto Malatesti and his brother became lords of Rimini, Pesaro and Fano; Antonio da Montefeltro of the March and of Urbino; Gentile da Varano of Camerino; Guido da Polenta of Ravenna; Sinibaldo Ordelaffi of Forlì and Cesena; Giovanni Man-fredi of Faenza; Lodovico Alidosi of Imola; and in addition various others in many other cities, so that few of the numerous cities of the Church were left without a prince. This situation kept the Church weak until Alexander VI's time, but by ruining the successors of those tyrants, he restored her power. When the Emperor made this grant, he was at Trent, and he spread the report that he was going to cross into Italy. As a result, there were many wars in Lombardy, through which the Visconti made themselves masters of Parma.

At this time Robert King of Naples died. He was survived only by his two granddaughters, children of his son Charles who, dying some time before, left the elder, named Joanna, heir to the Kingdom, with directions that she should take for her husband Andrea, son of the King of Hungary, Charles' grandson. Andrea did not live with her long before she brought about his death. She then married another cousin of hers, the Prince of Taranto, named Lodovico. But Ludwig King of Hungary, Andrea's brother, led soldiers into Italy to revenge his death, and drove Queen Joanna and her husband out of the Kingdom.

CHAPTER 31
[*Tribunes at Rome. 1347–1354*]

At this time there happened in Rome a thing worthy of note: namely that a certain Niccolò di Lorenzo, chancellor in the Capitol, drove the senators from Rome and made himself head of the Roman republic, with the title of Tribune, and brought her back to her ancient form, with such fame for justice and vigor that not merely the neighboring cities but all Italy sent him ambassadors. Hence the ancient provinces, seeing how Rome was reborn, raised their heads and honored him, some of them moved by fear, some by hope. But Niccolò, in spite of his great reputation, lost his courage when he had hardly begun. Growing timid under so great a weight, without being pursued by anybody, he secretly fled to the court of Charles King of Bohemia, who had been elected Emperor by order of the Pope, in contempt of Ludwig of Bavaria. In order to please the Pope, Charles sent Niccolò to him as prisoner. It happened next, after some time, that in imitation of him a certain Francesco Baron-cegli seized the Tribunate in Rome and drove away the senators, so that the Pope, as the quickest means for checking him, took Niccolò out of prison and sent him to Rome and gave him the office of Tribune. So Niccolò again assumed the government and put Francesco to death. But since the Colonna became his enemies, he also not long after was put to death, and power restored to the senators.

CHAPTER 32
[*Queen Joanna; the Visconti; the Pope returns from Avignon; war between Genoa and Venice. 1342–1381*]

Meanwhile the King of Hungary, having driven out Queen Joanna, returned to his kingdom. But the Pope, who preferred to have the Queen near Rome rather than the King, handled affairs in such a way that the King consented to return her kingdom to her if only her husband Lodovico, content with the title of Taranto, should not be called King.

When the year 1350 came, the Pope decided that the Jubilee, planned by Pope Boniface VIII for every hundred years, could be celebrated every fifty years. After he had so decreed, the Romans as the result of the favor consented to let him send to Rome four cardinals to reform the government of the city and to let him appoint senators as he wished. The Pope also declared Lodovico of Taranto King of Naples. To repay this favor, Queen Joanna gave Avignon, part of her inheritance, to the Church.

In those times Luchino Visconti died, so that Giovanni, Archbishop of Milan, became sole lord of the city. He carried on many wars with Tuscany and with his neighbors, so that he became very powerful. On his death Bernabò and Galeazzo his nephews were left as his heirs; soon afterward Galeazzo died, leaving as his heir Giovan Galeazzo, who shared the duchy of Milan with Bernabò.

In these times the Emperor Charles was King of Bohemia, and the Pope was Innocent VI. The latter sent into Italy the Cardinal Egidio, a Spaniard by birth who, through his ability, not merely in Romagna and in Rome but in all Italy restored her reputation to the Church; he recovered Bologna, which the Archbishop of Milan had seized; he forced the Romans to accept a foreign senator, who every year was to be sent them by the Pope; he made an honorable peace with the Visconti; he defeated and captured John Hawkwood, the Englishman, who with four thousand English was campaigning for the Ghibellines in Tuscany. As a result, Urban V on assuming the papacy heard of so many victories that he determined to visit Italy and Rome; Charles the Emperor also came there; yet after a few months Charles returned to his kingdom, and the Pope to Avignon. After Urban's death, the next chosen was Gregory XI. Since Cardinal Egidio also was dead, Italy returned to her ancient dissensions, caused by those who were allied against the Visconti. So the Pope first sent a legate into Italy with six thousand Bretons, and then, in 1376, came in person and brought his court back to Rome after it had been in France for seventy-one years. Since he soon died, Urban VI was installed. Then a little later ten cardinals, who said Urban had not been properly elected, invested Clement VII at Fondi.

In these times the Genoese, who for many years had lived under Visconti rule, rebelled. Then they fought with the Venetians a very important war, which divided all Italy, over the island of Tenedos. In that war cannon, new instruments devised by the Germans, were first seen. Though the Genoese were for a time superior, for many months besieging Venice, nevertheless at the end of the war the

Venetians were winners; through the papacy peace was made in the year 1381.

CHAPTER 33

[*The Antipope; Giovan Galeazzo Visconti. 1381–1402*]

As we have said, there was schism in the Church, in which Queen Joanna favored the schismatic Pope. Hence Urban brought about an expedition into the Kingdom against her by Charles of Durazzo, a descendant of the kings of Naples. On arriving, he took away her power and made himself master of the Kingdom, and she fled to France. The King of France, angered by this, sent Louis of Anjou into Italy to gain back the Kingdom for the Queen, and to drive Urban from Rome and subject the city to the antipope. But Louis died in the middle of this enterprise, and his soldiers returned defeated to France. The Pope meanwhile went to Naples, where he put nine cardinals in prison because they had belonged to the party of France and of the Antipope. Then he got angry with the King because he refused to make one of his nephews Prince of Capua, but pretending not to care, he asked that Nocera be granted him for his dwelling; there he fortified himself and prepared to deprive the King of the Kingdom. The King therefore marched to besiege him, but the Pope fled to Genoa, where he put to death those cardinals he held as prisoners. From there he went to Rome, and in order to give himself reputation, appointed twenty-nine cardinals. At this time Charles, King of Naples, went to Hungary, where he was made King and a little later put to death; at Naples he left his wife, along with Ladislas and Joanna, his children.

At this time also Giovan Galeazzo Visconti killed Bernabò his uncle and seized all the territory of Milan; and since it was not enough for him to have become Duke of all Lombardy, he wished also to conquer Tuscany. But when he thought he was about to get control and then to be crowned King of Italy, he died. Urban VI's successor was Boniface IX. The antipope Clement VII also died in Avignon, and after him came Benedict XIII.

CHAPTER 34

[Mercenary soldiers; the Jubilee; the Visconti lose control of Lombardy. 1393–1405]

Many soldiers, English, German and Breton, were in Italy at this time, brought partly by princes who at various times came into Italy, partly sent by the popes when they were in Avignon. By means of these, all the Italian princes for a long time carried on their wars, until Lodovico da Conio appeared, a Romagnole, who gathered a company of Italian soldiers named after St. George. Its efficiency and discipline in a short time took away the reputation of the foreign soldiers and brought it back to the Italians, of whom afterward the princes of Italy, in their wars against each other, availed themselves.

The Pope on account of his quarrels with the Romans went to Assisi, where he lived until the Jubilee of 1400. At that time the Romans, so that he would return to Rome for the profit of that city, were willing again to receive from him a foreign senator and to let him fortify the Castle of St. Angelo. After he had returned under these conditions, he decreed, in order to make the Church richer, that when a benefice became vacant the appointee should pay a year's income to the Camera.

After the death of Giovan Galeazzo Duke of Milan, though he left two sons, Giovanmariagnolo and Filippo, that state was divided into many parts; in the troubles that followed, Giovanmaria was killed and Filippo remained for a time shut up in the castle of Pavia, where through the fidelity and vigor of the castelan he was safe. Among others who seized cities occupied by their fathers was Guglielmo della Scala, who, having been exiled, was in the hands of Francesco da Carrara the lord of Padua. Through him Guglielmo regained the state of Verona, where he remained but a short time, because, by the command of Francesco, he was poisoned and the city taken from him. Thereupon the people of Vicenza, who had lived in security under the banners of the Visconti, fearing the greatness of the lord of Padua, gave themselves over to the Venetians; for their sake the Venetians undertook war against Francesco and took from him first Verona and then Padua.

CHAPTER 35
[*Ladislas of Naples; Antipopes. 1404–1413*]

Meanwhile Pope Boniface died and Innocent VII was chosen. The people of Rome petitioned him to give back their fortresses and restore to them their liberty. To this the Pope did not consent. Hence the people called to their aid Ladislas, King of Naples. After that, having made an agreement with the King, the Pope returned to Rome, for in fear of the people he had fled to Viterbo, where he had made Lodovico his nephew Count of the March.

He died soon, and was followed by Gregory XII, who promised that he would renounce the papacy whenever the antipope also would renounce it. With the encouragement of the cardinals, in order to test whether the Church could reunite, Benedict the antipope came to Porto Venere, and Gregory to Lucca, where they discussed many things and did not decide any of them. Hence the cardinals of both Popes abandoned them, and as to the Popes, Benedict went into Spain and Gregory to Rimini. On the other hand the cardinals, with the aid of Baldassarre Cossa, Cardinal and legate of Bologna, held a council at Pisa, where they elected Alexander V. He at once excommunicated King Ladislas and invested Louis of Anjou with that kingdom. Uniting with the Florentines, the Genoese, the Venetians and Baldassarre Cossa the legate, the cardinals attacked Ladislas and took Rome away from him. But in the excitement of this war Alexander died, and the next pope was Baldassarre Cossa, who took the name of John XXIII. Leaving Bologna, where he was elected, and going to Rome, he found there Louis of Anjou, who had come with the army of Provence. Fighting a battle with Ladislas, they defeated him. But through the failure of their mercenary generals, they did not follow up the victory. Hence the King after a short time regained his strength and regained Rome; the Pope fled to Bologna and Louis to Provence. Then planning how he could diminish the power of Ladislas, the Pope managed to have Sigismund, King of Hungary, chosen Emperor; he then encouraged him to come to Italy and consulted with him at Mantua. They agreed to call a General Council in which the Church would be reunited, for if united she could easily resist the forces of her enemies.

CHAPTER 36

[*Three popes. 1414–1417*]

There were at that time three popes, Gregory, Benedict and John, who kept the Church weak and without reputation. The place chosen for the council was Constance, a city in Germany, against Pope John's intention. The death of King Ladislas had removed the Pope's reason for pushing the idea of a council; nonetheless, being pledged, he could not refuse to go. After a few months in Constance, realizing his error too late, he attempted to escape, but was put in prison and obliged to resign the papacy. Through an agent, Gregory one of the antipopes also resigned; and Benedict the other antipope, not consenting to resign, was condemned as a heretic. At the end, abandoned by his cardinals he too was forced to resign, and the council elected as pontiff Otto, of the house of Colonna, called Martin V. And so the Church was united, after forty years during which she had been divided among several popes.

CHAPTER 37

[*Filippo Visconti. 1412–1418*]

All through these times, as we have said, Filippo Visconti was in the castle of Pavia. But then Fazino Cane died, who in the confusion in Lombardy had made himself master of Vercelli, Alessandria, Novara and Tortona, and had got together great wealth. Having no children, he left as heir of his states Beatrice his wife, and arranged with his friends that they should have her marry Filippo. Becoming powerful through this marriage, Filippo regained Milan and all the state of Lombardy. Then, being thankful for great benefits, as princes almost always are, he accused Beatrice his wife of adultery and put her to death. Having meanwhile become very powerful, he was planning wars in Tuscany, in order to carry out the projects of Giovan Galeazzo his father.

CHAPTER 38

[*Queen Joanna of Naples; Sforza and Braccio. 1415–1425*]

When Ladislas, King of Naples, died, he left to Joanna his sister, in addition to the Kingdom, a great army led by the principal mercenary generals of Italy; among the chief of these was Sforza da Cotignuolo, who by the standards of such armies was considered very able. The Queen, to get rid of the disgrace of keeping a certain Pandolfello, whom she had brought up, took as her husband Jacopo della Marcia, a Frenchman of royal blood, with this condition: namely, he should be satisfied to be called Prince of Taranto and should leave to her the title of Queen and the control of the King-dom. But the soldiers, as soon as Jacopo arrived in Naples, called him King. Hence between the husband and the wife there were severe contests, in which many times one conquered the other. Yet at last the Queen remained in her position.

She later became an enemy to the Pontiff. Hence Sforza, in order to reduce her to necessity, so that she would have to throw her-self into his arms, gave up his contract, contrary to her expectation. Thus suddenly finding herself unarmed and having no other remedy, she went for help to Alfonso, King of Aragon and of Sicily, whom she adopted as her son. She also hired Braccio da Montone, who in military affairs had quite as high a reputation as Sforza; he was an enemy of the Pope through his seizure of Perugia and other cities of the Church. Then there followed peace between Queen Joanna and the Pope. But King Alfonso, who feared she would treat him as she had treated her husband, cautiously strove to make himself master of the fortresses; she, being astute, forestalled him and fortified her-self in the castle of Naples. The suspicions between the two then increased until they came to arms. With the aid of Sforza, who had returned to her service, the Queen defeated Alfonso, drove him from Naples, and deprived him of his adoption. She then adopted Louis of Anjou. This brought on a new war between Braccio, who had taken Alfonso's part, and Sforza, who aided the Queen. In the course of that war, Sforza was drowned when crossing the Pescara River. Hence the Queen was again unarmed and would have been driven from the Kingdom if Filippo Visconti, Duke of Milan, had not assisted her. He forced King Alfonso to return to Aragon.

Braccio, however, not frightened because Alfonso had given up, continued the campaign against the Queen. When he beseiged L'A-quila, the Pope, who thought Braccio's greatness not to the advantage of the Church, hired the military services of Francesco, the son of Sforza. Attacking Braccio at L'Aquila, Francesco defeated and killed him. Of Braccio's followers, Oddo his son remained alive. The

Pope deprived him of Perugia but left him the state of Montone. A little later he was killed while fighting in Romagna in the Florentine service. So of those who had fought under Braccio, Niccolò Piccino now had the highest reputation.

CHAPTER 39
[*A view of the Italian states. 1434*]

Because we have now come in our narrative close to the times that I had in mind, and because what is left to deal with concerns for the most part only the wars of the Florentines and the Venetians with Filippo Duke of Milan, which will be presented when we deal especially with Florence, I do not wish to go farther. I shall only bring briefly to memory the situation of Italy, both as to rulers and as to military power, in the times we have reached in our writing.

As to the chief states, Queen Joanna II held the Kingdom of Naples. In the March, the Patrimony and Romagna, part of the cities were subject to the Church, part controlled by their vicars or tyrants, for example, Ferrara, Modena and Reggio by the Este family; Faenza by the Manfredi; Imola by the Alidosi; Forlì by the Ordelaffi; Rimini and Pesaro by the Malatesti; and Camerino by the Varano family. As to Lombardy, part was subject to Duke Filippo, part to the Venetians, because all those who held individual states there had disappeared, except the house of Gonzaga, which ruled in Mantua. As to Tuscany, for the most part her rulers were the Florentines; only Lucca and Siena lived according to their own laws, Lucca under the Guinigi, Siena free. The Genoese, being sometimes free, sometimes subjects of the kings of France or of the Visconti, lived without honor and were to be counted among the lesser powers.

All these principal powers were, as to weapons of their own, unarmed. Duke Filippo, remaining shut up in his chamber and not letting himself be seen, directed his wars through his commissioners. The Venetians, when they turned to the land, laid aside those weapons that on the sea had made them famous and, following the habit of the other Italians, managed their armies with some outsider as general. The Pope, since weapons were unsuitable to him as an ecclesiastic, and Queen Joanna of Naples, since she was a woman, did of necessity what the others did by unwise choice. The Florentines also were subject to the same necessity, because by frequent dissensions that republic had destroyed her nobility and was in the hands of men brought up in trade; they therefore followed the methods and the Fortune of the others.

So the weapons of Italy were in the hands either of the lesser princes or of men without any territory. The lesser princes took up arms not induced by any love for renown, but in order to live more richly or more securely; the others, brought up to arms from infancy and not knowing how to carry on any other occupation, sought by means of military service to make themselves honored either through possessions or through power. Among the latter, the most renowned were Carmignuola, Francesco Sforza, Niccolò Piccino (Braccio's pupil), Agnolo della Pergola, Lorenzo and Micheletto Attenduli, Tartaglia, Jacopaccio, Ceccolino da Perugia, Niccolò da Tolentino, Guido Torello, Antonio dal Ponte ad Era and many others like them. With them were those rulers of whom I have spoken above, to whom are to be added the barons of Rome, the Orsini and Colonna, with other lords and gentlemen of the Kingdom and of Lombardy. Depending on war, these men made among themselves a compact and understanding, as it were, by which they turned war into a technique for so wasting time that when two states made war both of them generally lost. In the end these soldiers rendered war so abject that any average general in whom had been reborn some shadow of ancient efficiency would have put them to shame—to the astonishment of all Italy, who in her dearth of wisdom respected these mercenary generals. Of these slothful rulers and of these dastardly armies my history will be full.

But before I go to this matter, as I promised at the beginning I must deal with the origins of Florence, and let everybody fully understand the condition of the city in the times I have dealt with and how, in the midst of all the troubles that for a thousand years afflicted Italy, Florence reached it.

BOOK TWO

[THE ORIGIN AND EARLY HISTORY OF FLOR-ENCE, TO 1353]

CHAPTER 1

[The effects of cultivation on unhealthy regions]

One of the great and wonderful provisions of ancient republics and principalities which in these present times has vanished, was that for building at all times numbers of new cities and towns. Nothing is so worthy of an excellent prince or of a well-organized republic or so useful to a province as to build new towns where men can gather for convenient defense and farming. This the ancients could easily bring about through their habit of sending into conquered or empty countries new inhabitants whom they called colonies. Not only was this practice the cause for building new cities but it made a conquered province more secure for the conqueror, filled empty places with inhabitants, and kept men well distributed within the provinces. As a result of this process, since men lived more comfortably in such a province, they increased in number there and in attack were speedier and in defense more secure.

Since this custom, through the bad practice of republics and princes, has now vanished, its disuse causes the ruin and weakness of provinces, for only this method makes empires more secure and, as I have said, keeps countries thickly inhabited. Security results because a colony that a prince places in a newly conquered land is like a castle and a garrison to hold the others in loyalty. Without this, he cannot keep a province fully inhabited or make sure that the population is well distributed, because all the places in it are not productive or healthful. For this reason, there are in some places plenty of men but in others they are scarce; and if there is no way for taking them from where they are plentiful and putting them where they are scarce, a province in a short time is ruined, for one part of it, through its small number of inhabitants, becomes desert, and another, through their excess, becomes poor. And because nature cannot provide for this defect, diligence must provide for it. Countries that are unhealthful become healthful when a multitude of men all at once takes possession; for with cultivation they give health to the ground and with fires they cleanse the air—something Nature could never provide for. This is demonstrated by the City of Venice; though she is placed in a swampy and unhealthful site, yet the many inhabitants that at one time gathered there made it healthful. Pisa, too, because of the noxious air, was never full of inhabitants until Genoa and her shores were laid waste by the Saracens. This caused those people, driven from their native places, at one time to gather there in large numbers, which made her populous and powerful.

With the disappearance, however, of this method of sending colonies, conquered lands are harder to hold, empty lands do not fill up, and those that are too full are not relieved. Hence many parts of the world, and especially of Italy, have become, in comparison with ancient times, uninhabited. And all this has happened and is happening because princes have no desire for true glory, and republics no government that deserves to be praised. In ancient times, then, by virtue of these colonies, cities were often newly founded and those already begun flourished. Among these was the city of Florence, which had her origin from Fiesole and her growth from colonies.

CHAPTER 2

[*Florence to 1215*]

It is very true, as Dante and Giovanni Villani show, that the City of Fiesole, being situated on the summit of the mountain, in order that her markets might be more visited and merchants might more conveniently come there with their wares, arranged a place for them not on the height, but in the plain between the foot of the mountain and the Arno River. These markets I judge were the reason for the first buildings put up in those places, since the merchants were influenced by their wish to have convenient storehouses in which to put their goods, and these in time became solid buildings. Later, after the Romans, having conquered the Carthaginians, had made Italy secure from foreign wars, the number of these buildings was greatly multiplied. For men never continue in difficult conditions unless some necessity keeps them there. Hence, though fear of war makes them glad to live in strong and difficult places, yet when that has ceased, at the call of convenience they are more glad to live in comfortable and easily accessible spots. The security, then, that the reputation of the Roman Republic brought about in Italy was such that the dwellings near the Arno, already begun in the way I have mentioned, increased to such a number that they took the form of a town, which at first was called Villa Arnina.

Then there were civil wars in Rome, first between Marius and Sulla, then between Caesar and Pompey, and after that between the slayers of Caesar and those who attempted to revenge his death. So first by Sulla and later by those three Roman citizens, who, after taking vengeance for Caesar, divided the Empire, colonies were sent to Fiesole. Of these, either all or part made their dwellings in the plain, near the city already begun. Hence, because of this growth, that place became so full of buildings and of men and of everything else for well-ordered life that it could be counted among the cities of Italy.

About the derivation of the name of Florence there are various opinions. Some think she was named after Florinus, one of the leaders of the colony; some think that at first not Florentia but Fluentia was her name, because she was situated near the flowing [*fluente*] of the Arno; and they bring up as witness Pliny, who says: "The Fluentines are near the flowing Arno." This may be false, because Pliny in that passage explains where the Florentines were located, not what they were called, and that reading *Fluentini* must be corrupt, because Frontinus and Cornelius Tacitus, who wrote close to the time of Pliny, give the names of Florence and the Florentines. Already in Tiberius' time they were ruled in the manner of the other Italian cities, and Cornelius says that Florentine ambassadors came to the Emperor to ask that the water from the swamps of Chiana should not empty upon their land. Nor is it reasonable that this city at the same time should have two names. I believe, then, that she was always called Florence, whatever the reason for that name. And so, whatever the cause of her origin, she began under the Roman Empire, and writers spoke of her in the days of the early Emperors.

And when that Empire was harassed by the barbarians, Florence also was laid waste by Totila, King of the Ostrogoths, and two hundred and fifty years later Charlemagne rebuilt her. From that time until the year 1215 A.D. she was subject to the same Fortune as the rulers of Italy. In those times, the first to rule there were Charlemagne's descendants, then the Berengari, and finally the German emperors, as in our general treatment we have shown. In those times the Florentines could not expand or do anything worth re/cording because of the power of those in authority over them. Nonetheless, in 1010, on St. Romulus' day, a holiday at Fiesole, they took and ruined Fiesole; they did this either with the Emperors' permission, or in that time between the death of one and the election of another when everybody was freer than usual. But when the pontiffs got more power in Italy and the German emperors grew weak, all the cities of that region ruled themselves with less respect for the prince, until in 1080, in Henry III's time, Italy was openly divided between him and the Church. Notwithstanding this, the Florentines until 1215 kept themselves united, obeying the con/querors and seeking no other dominion than to live safely.

But as in our bodies, in proportion as illnesses are later they are the more dangerous and deadly, so in proportion as Florence was later in joining the parties of Italy, she was then more tortured by them. The cause of the first division is well known, because Dante and many other authors have related it, yet I shall briefly narrate it.

CHAPTER 3

[The Buondelmonti and Donati begin their feud with the Amidei and Uberti. 1215]

In Florence the most powerful families were the Buondelmonti and the Uberti; next to them were the Amidei and Donati. A rich widow of the Donati family had a very beautiful daughter. In her own mind she had planned to give her as wife to Messer Buondel/monte, a young aristocrat and head of the Buondelmonti family. Her plan, either through neglect or through believing she always had plenty of time, she had not yet revealed to anybody when Chance decreed that a daughter of the Amidei should be betrothed to Messer Buondelmonte. Though greatly displeased by the news, the widow yet hoped by means of her daughter's beauty to break the match off before the marriage was celebrated. So when she saw Messer Buon/delmonte coming alone toward her house, she went downstairs, asking her daughter to follow. Then as the man was passing, she said to him: "Truly I am very glad you have taken a wife, though I had reserved for you this daughter of mine." Opening the door, she had him look at her. Seeing the girl's unusual beauty and knowing her blood and her dower not inferior to those of the woman he had taken, the knight burned with desire to have her. Not considering the agreement he had made or the injury he did in breaking it or the ills that his broken faith might bring, he said: "After you have reserved her for me, and since I am not too late, I should be an ingrate to refuse her." And without delay he solemnized the marriage.

When this action became known, the Amidei and the Uberti, their relatives by marriage, were exceedingly angry. And having met with many of their other relatives, they decided that this injury could not without disgrace be borne, nor revenged with any other revenge than Messer Buondelmonte's death. And though some presented the ills that could result from this, Mosca Lamberti said that he who kept thinking of many things never would finish any of them, utter-ing that common and well-known adage: *What's done is ended.* Therefore they gave the responsibility for this homicide to Mosca, Stiatta Uberti, Lambertuccio Amidei, and Oderigo Fifanti. On Easter morning these men were concealed in the Amidei palace, between the Ponte Vecchio and Santo Stephano. When Messer Buondelmonte crossed the river on a white horse, thinking it as easy to forget an injury as to renounce a marriage, they attacked and killed him at the end of the bridge near a statue of Mars. This homicide divided the whole city; one party adhered to the Buondelmonti, the other to the Uberti. And because these families were strong in houses and towers and men, they fought together many years without one driving the other out. Their hostilities, though they did not end with peace, were calmed by truces, so according to the course of events, they now would lie quiet and now would flame up.

CHAPTER 4

[*Guelfs and Ghibellines; Frederick II. 1220–1250*]

Florence was in these turmoils until the time of Frederick II. Being King of Naples, he decided that he could strengthen his forces against the Church. In order to make his power more solid in Tuscany, he favored the Uberti and their followers; and they with his aid drove out the Buondelmonti. So just as all Italy for a long time was divided into Guelfs and Ghibellines, our city also was divided.

I think it not useless to record the families that belonged to the two parties. Those then who belonged to the Guelf party were the Buondelmonti, Nerli, Rossi, Frescobaldi, Mozzi, Bardi, Pulci, Gherardini, Foraboschi, Bagnesi, Guidalotti, Sacchetti, Manieri, Lucardesi, Chiramontesi, Campiobbesi, Cavalcanti, Giandonati, Gianfigliazzi, Scali, Gualterotti, Importuni, Bostichi, Tornaquinci, Vecchietti, Tosinghi, Arrigucci, Agli, Sizi, Adimari, Visdomini, Donati, Pazzi, Della Bella, Ardinghi, Tedaldi, Cerchi.

Of the Ghibelline party were the Uberti, Mannegli, Ubriachi, Fifanti, Amidei, Infangati, Malespini, Scolari, Guidi, Galli, Cap-piardi, Lamberti, Soldanieri, Cipriani, Toschi, Amieri, Palermini, Migliorelli, Pigli, Barucci, Cattani, Agolanti, Brunelleschi, Cap-onsacchi, Elisei, Abati, Tedaldini, Giuochi, Galigai. In addition, both parties of these noble families were joined by many of the common people, so that by this division almost all the city was tainted.

The Guelfs, then, being driven out, found refuge in the cities of the upper Arno Valley, where they had most of their fortresses; and in that way, they could better defend themselves against the forces of their enemies. But when Frederick died, some in Florence who were neutral and had great influence with the people, thought it would be better to unite the city, rather than by keeping it divided to ruin it. They therefore worked in such a way that the Guelfs, laying aside their injuries, returned, and the Ghibellines, laying aside their fear, received them. And since they were united, they believed it time to form a free state and make arrangements for defending them-selves, before the new Emperor gained power.

CHAPTER 5

[*The government of Florence in the thirteenth century*]

They divided the city, therefore, into sixths, and chose twelve citizens, two for each sixth, to govern them. These were called Anziani, and every year were changed. To take away the reasons for enmity produced by legal decisions, they provided for two foreign judges, one called the Captain of the People and the other the Podestà, to decide cases both civil and criminal that came up among the people. And because no government is stable without providing itself with a protector, they set up in the city twenty standards, and seventy-six in the country, under which they enrolled all the youth, and they ordered each one to be ready and armed under his standard at whatever time either the Captain or the Anziani should summon him. And the devices on these standards varied according to the arms the men carried, for the crossbowmen had one ensign and the pavisers another. And each year, on the day of Pentecost, with great pomp they gave the ensigns to new men and assigned new heads to all the organization. And to give majesty to their armies, and a place where anyone driven back in battle could take refuge and having taken refuge could again resist the enemy, they provided a great car drawn by two oxen covered with red and on it a white and red ensign. And when they decided to lead out their army, they drew this car into the New Marketplace, and with pomp and ceremony the leaders of the people took it in charge. They also had, for splen-dor in their expeditions, a bell called Martinella, which kept ringing steadily for a month before they took their armies out of the city, so that the enemy would have time for defense. So much vigor there was then in those men and with such great nobility of mind they conducted themselves that, whereas today to attack the enemy unex-pectedly is considered a noble action and prudent, then it was considered disgraceful and treacherous. This bell they also took out with their armies, and by means of it the guards were placed and other military actions directed.

CHAPTER 6

[King Manfred assists the Ghibellines; battle of Montaperti. 1250–1260]

With these institutions, military and civil, the Florentines laid a foundation for their liberty. It is not possible to imagine how much authority and power Florence in a short time gained. Not merely did she become head of Tuscany but took her place among the first cities of Italy, and she would have risen to almost any greatness if frequent and new internal dissensions had not tormented her. The Florentines lived under this government for ten years, and in that time they compelled the Pistolese, the Aretines, and the Sienese to make alliances with them; and returning from Siena with their army, they took Volterra; they also destroyed some towns and brought the inhabitants to Florence. These expeditions were all made on the advice of the Guelfs, who were much stronger than the Ghibellines, both because the latter were hated by the people on account of their proud conduct when they ruled in Frederick's time and because the Church party was better loved than the imperial party. With the aid of the Church they hoped to keep their liberty, and under the Emperor they feared to lose it.

The Ghibellines, meanwhile, seeing that they were losing their influence, could not be content, and were waiting only for a good opportunity to regain control. They believed this had come when they saw that Manfred, Frederick's son, had become ruler of the Kingdom of Naples and had greatly lessened the Church's power. Secretly, then, they negotiated with him about getting back their influence, but they did not conduct themselves in such a way that the negotiations they carried on were not revealed to the Anziani. Hence the latter cited the Uberti, who not merely did not obey but, taking arms, fortified themselves in their houses. Angered by this, the people armed themselves, and with the aid of the Guelfs com-pelled the Uberti to abandon Florence and, with all the Ghibelline party, to go to Siena. From there they asked aid from Manfred, King of Naples. And through the effort of Messer Farinata degli Uberti, at the River Arbia the Guelfs were defeated with such great slaughter by the soldiers of the King that those who escaped from the defeat fled for refuge not to Florence, since they believed their city was lost, but to Lucca.

CHAPTER 7

[Farinata degli Uberti protests against the destruction of Florence. 1260]

Manfred had sent to the Ghibellines, as head of his soldiers, Count Giordano, who in those days had a high reputation in war. This man, after the victory, went with the Ghibellines to Florence, and brought that city entirely under Manfred's control, abolishing the magistrates and every custom that showed any image of her liberty. This injury, imprudently inflicted, the populace in general received with much hatred; already hostile to the Ghibellines, it now became exceedingly hostile. In time this caused their utter ruin. When on account of the needs of the Kingdom, Count Giordano had to return to Naples, he left in Florence as the King's vicar Count Guido Novello, lord of the Casentino. This man held a council of Ghibellines at Empoli, where everybody decided that if they were to keep up the Ghibelline party in Tuscany, they must destroy Florence, which alone—since her people were Guelf—was in a position to reinvigorate the party supporting the Church. To so cruel a decision as this, given against so noble a city, no citizen or friend except Messer Farinata degli Uberti made opposition. He openly and without any hesitation defended her, saying that he had not with such hardship undergone so many dangers for any reason except his desire to live in his native city, and that he was not then ready to stop striving for what he always had sought or to refuse what Fortune had given him. On the contrary, he would not be less hostile to those who intended otherwise than he had been to the Guelfs; and anyone among them who was afraid of his native city would try in vain to ruin her,[1] because he himself, with vigor such as he had shown in driving out the Guelfs expected to defend her. This Messer Farinata was a man of great courage, excellent in war, head of the Ghibellines, and highly esteemed by Manfred. His prestige put an end to that debate, and they considered other methods for maintaining their party.

1. *This is perhaps the meaning of the clause. Leonardo Bruni (Aretino) makes Farinata say: "I do not now make this complaint because I fear the ruin of my native city, for in whatever way things go, while I live she will not be destroyed .... Nothing could be more cowardly than to destroy your city for fear that she will be a refuge for your enemies .... I say that if of the number of the Florentines I only were left, I would not allow my native city to be destroyed; if I needed to die for this a thousand times, a thousand times I am prepared for death." (*ISTORIA FIORENTINA, Bk. 2, year 1261).*

CHAPTER 8

[Manfred defeated by Charles of Anjou; Florence divided into gilds. 1260–1266]

The Guelfs who took refuge in Lucca, being dismissed by the Lucchese after threats by the Count, went on to Bologna. Soon the Guelfs of Parma summoned them against the Ghibellines. To reward the valor with which they conquered, they received as a gift all their opponents' property. Being thus increased in riches and honor, when they knew that Pope Clement had summoned Charles of Anjou to take the Kingdom away from Manfred, they sent ambassadors to the Pontiff to offer him their forces. The Pope not merely received them as allies but gave them his ensign, which ever after was carried in war by the Guelfs and still is used in Florence. Charles then deprived Manfred of the Kingdom and killed him. Since the Florentine Guelfs assisted Charles, their party grew stronger and that of the Ghibellines weaker. Hence the Ghibellines who with Count Guido Novello were ruling Florence judged it wise by means of favors to win the support of the people, whom before they had oppressed with every sort of injury; so those remedies which if applied before necessity arose would have been effective, when applied late and ungraciously not merely were not effective but hastened their ruin.

The Ghibellines thought, however, that they would get the friendship and partisan support of the people if they gave back to them part of the offices and influence they had taken away; so they chose thirty-six citizens from among the people, who, together with two aristocrats brought from Bologna, were to reform the government of the city. As soon as they met, these divided all the city into gilds, and over each gild they set a magistrate who would administer justice to those included in it. Besides this, they bestowed on each one a banner, in order that under it every man should present himself armed when the city had need of him. In the beginning these gilds numbered twelve, seven major and five minor; then the minor were increased to fourteen, so that in all there were twenty-one, as now. And the thirty-six reformers also adopted other measures for the common good.

CHAPTER 9
[*Count Guido and the Ghibellines abandon Florence. 1267*]

Count Guido, to support the soldiers, ordered a tax to be levied on the citizens, but met so many difficulties in this that he dared not use force to collect it. Seeing that he had lost control of the city, he consulted with the leaders of the Ghibellines; they determined to take from the populace by force what they had imprudently granted. When they decided that their arms were ready, at a time when the thirty-six were assembled, they raised their war-cry; thereupon the thirty-six in terror withdrew to their houses, and at once the banners of the gilds were out of doors with many armed men behind them.

Since they had learned that Count Guido and his party were at San Giovanni, they assembled at Santa Trinita and chose as their commander Giovanni Soldanieri. The Count, on the other hand, learning where the populace was, started to attack it. The populace also did not avoid conflict. As it moved against its enemy, it met him at the place where today the Tornaquinci Loggia stands. There the Count was forced back, with the loss and death of many of his men. Hence, being unnerved, he feared that his enemies would attack him in the night and, finding his men defeated and without courage, would kill him. So strong was this fancy of his that, without thinking of any other remedy, he determined to save himself by flight rather than by combat; so, against the advice of the rectors and of the Party, with all his men he went off to Prato. But on finding himself in a place of safety, he at once got over his fear, realized his mistake, and decided to correct it. So in the morning at daybreak he returned with his men to Florence, in order to re-enter by force the city he abandoned in cowardice. But his plan did not succeed, because that populace which could hardly have driven him out could easily keep him out. So in grief and shame he went off to the Casentino, and the Ghibellines retired to their country places.

Thereupon the victorious populace, to encourage those who loved the well-being of the republic, determined to reunite the city and to call back all the citizens, both Ghibellines and Guelfs, who were outside. Thus the Guelfs returned, six years after they had been driven out, and the Ghibellines as well had pardon for their recent injury and were put back in their native city. Nevertheless, by the populace and by the Guelfs they were greatly hated, because the latter could not blot their exile from their memories, and the populace remembered too clearly the Ghibellines' tyranny while it had lived under their government. As a result, neither party felt peace of mind.

While Florence was in this condition, a report was spread that Conradin, Manfred's grandson, was coming with soldiers from Germany to conquer Naples, so that the Ghibellines were filled with the hope that they could get back their authority, and the Guelfs were considering how they could make themselves secure against their enemies. Hence they asked aid from King Charles so that, if Conradin entered the land, they could defend themselves. When, as a result, the soldiers of Charles approached, the Guelfs became so haughty and the Ghibellines were so frightened that, two days before the soldiers arrived, without being driven out, they took to flight.

CHAPTER 10

[*The Guelfs again rule Florence; Gregory X; Nicholas III. 1267–1278*]

When the Ghibellines had gone, the Florentines, in reorganizing the city government, elected twelve leaders, who were to occupy the magistracy two months; these were called not Anziani but Good Men. In addition to these there was a council of eighty citizens, called the Credenza. Next there were a hundred and eighty from the populace, thirty for each ward, who, with the Credenza and the twelve Good Men, were called the General Council. They organ-ized also another council of a hundred and twenty citizens, common people and nobles, through which they executed all the things deter-mined in the other councils; and by means of it they distributed the offices of the state. Having established this government, they made the Guelf party strong with magistracies and other arrangements, so that with greater power they could defend themselves from the Ghib-ellines. They divided the property of the latter into three parts; of these they turned over one to the public treasury, assigned the second to the magistracy of the Guelf Party, called the captains, and gave the third to the Guelfs, as recompense for the damage they had received.

The Pope also, to keep Tuscany Guelf, made King Charles imperial vicar of Tuscany. When the Florentines, then, by virtue of this new government, were keeping up their reputation inside the city through laws and outside it through arms, the Pope died. After long debate, at the end of two years Pope Gregory X was chosen. Having been a long time in Syria and still being there at the time of his election, far from the hatreds of the parties, he did not regard them as his predecessors had done. Therefore, reaching Florence on his journey to France, he believed it a good shepherd's function to reunite the city. He achieved so much that the Florentines were willing to receive the Ghibelline syndics into Florence to discuss the manner of their return, but though an agreement was reached, the Ghibellines were so afraid that they were not willing to return. The

Pope blamed the city for this and in anger excommunicated her. Under that ban she remained during the Pontiff's lifetime but after his death she was reblessed by Pope Innocent V.

The papacy had come to Nicholas III, one of the Orsini family. Because the pontiffs always feared any man whose power in Italy had become great, even though it had grown up as a result of the Church's support, and because they tried to reduce it, their policy caused the frequent disturbances and the frequent changes that took place in the country. The pontiffs' fear of a powerful man caused a weak one to grow, and when he had grown strong, made them fear him, and since they feared him, made them try to bring him low. This policy led them to take the Kingdom from Manfred's hands and give it to Charles; this in turn made them dread the latter and attempt his ruin. Nicholas III, then, moved by these causes, accomplished so much that by means of the Emperor he wrested from Charles the control of Tuscany, and in the name of the Emperor sent into that province as his legate Messer Latino.

CHAPTER 11

*[Priors set up in Florence; battle of Campaldino; new city walls.
1279–1289]*

Florence was then in a very bad condition, because the Guelt nobility had become arrogant and did not fear the magistrates. Hence every day there were many homicides and other violent acts, without any punishment of those who committed them, since some noble or other aided them. It was decided, therefore, by the leaders of the people that, in order to restrain this arrogance, it would be well to bring back the exiles. This gave the Legate a chance to reunite the city, and the Ghibellines returned. Instead of the twelve governors the popular leaders set up fourteen, seven from each party, who were to govern a year and would be chosen by the Pope. Florence continued this government two years, until there came to the papal throne Pope Martin, of French birth, who restored to King Charles all the power Nicholas had taken from him. As a result, new life at once was given to the parties in Tuscany, because the Florentines took arms against the Emperor's governor and, to wrest the government from the Ghibellines and to hold the powerful in check, arranged a new form of administration.

It was the year 1282, and the gilds, since they had received the magistrates and the banners, had a high reputation. Hence they decreed on their own authority that instead of the fourteen, three citizens should be chosen, to be called Priors, who should remain two months in the government of the republic; they could be of the middle classes or of the nobles, so long as they were merchants or carried on professions. They changed them, after the first magistracy, to six, in order that from each ward there might be one. This number was kept until 1342, when they changed the city into quarters and the Priors to eight, though in the course of that period they sometimes, for some special case, appointed twelve.

This magistracy, as in time appeared, caused the ruin of the nobles, who for various reasons were excluded from it by the people, and later without any consideration were crushed. In the beginning the nobles, not being united, consented to this exclusion, because they desired too much to take the government from one another; hence as a body they lost it. To this magistracy was assigned a palace where it could have permanent quarters, for the earlier custom was that the magistrates and the councils met in the churches; and they also honored it with beadles and other necessary officers. And though in the beginning they were called only Priors, nonetheless later, for more grandeur, they received the name of Signors.

The Florentines were quiet within the city for some time, during which they carried on a war with the Aretines, because the latter had driven out the Guelfs; at Campaldino the Florentines totally defeated them.

And since the city grew in men and in wealth, they decided also to expand her walls; so they enlarged their circuit in the manner now to be seen, since earlier their diameter was only the distance between the Ponte Vecchio and San Lorenzo.

CHAPTER 12

[*Strife between the nobles and the people. 1290–1295*]

The wars without and the peace within had almost destroyed in Florence the Guelf and the Ghibelline parties. There remained active only those disagreements that naturally exist in all cities between the powerful and the people, because, since the people wish to live according to the laws and the powerful to control the laws, it is not possible for them to agree. Such disagreement was not re-vealed as long as both feared the Ghibellines, but as soon as they were conquered, it showed its power; every day someone of the people was injured, and the laws and the magistrates were not strong enough to avenge him, because relatives and friends protected every noble against the power of the Priors and the Captain. The heads of the gilds, therefore, eager to remedy this abuse, provided that every Signoria, at the beginning of its term, should choose a Gonfalonier of Justice, one of the people, to whom they gave a thousand men, enrolled under twenty standards. He with his standard and his armed men, was to be ready to aid justice whenever he was sum-moned by the Signors or by the Captain. The first chosen was Ubaldo Ruffoli. He brought out his standard and destroyed the Galletti mansion because in France one of that family had killed a man of the people.

It was easy for the gilds to make this law, since serious enmities were rife among the nobles, who paid no attention to the provision made against them until they saw the harshness of that act of enforce-ment. This at first excited in them great terror; nevertheless they soon after returned to their arrogance, because, since there were always some of them among the Signors, they had means for keeping the Gonfalonier from carrying out his duties. Besides this, since the accuser needed a witness when he suffered any offense, nobody was willing to act as witness against the nobles, so that in a short time Florence returned to the same lawlessness, and the people received from the rich the same injuries, because the judges were slow and the sentences failed of execution.

CHAPTER 13

[Giano della Bella attempts to enforce justice. 1293–1295]

And when the people did not know what measures to take, Giano della Bella, of the noblest descent, but a lover of the city's freedom, gave to the heads of the gilds courage for reorganizing the city; on his advice it was decreed that the Gonfalonier should live with the Priors and should have four thousand men under his orders. In addition, all the nobles were deprived of the power to sit as

Signors; the accomplices of a criminal were subjected to the same penalties as the criminal himself; public report was made a basis for legal judgment. Through these laws, which were called the Ordinances of Justice, the people gained much reputation and Giano della Bella much hate, because he was very badly regarded by the powerful as the destroyer of their power, and the rich among the people envied him because they thought his influence too great. This, as soon as opportunity permitted, became evident.

It chanced that a man of the people was killed in a fight in which several nobles took part, among whom was Messer Corso Donati. On him, as bolder than the others, the blame was laid, and therefore the Captain of the People arrested him. And however the thing should have gone, whether Messer Corso was not at fault or whether the Captain feared to condemn him, he was acquitted. This acquittal so offended the people that they took arms and ran to Giano della Bella's house to ask him to work for the observance of those laws which he had originated. Giano, who wished Messer Corso to be punished, did not make them lay down their arms, as many thought he should have done, but encouraged them to go to the Signors to complain of the happening and ask them to attend to it. The people, therefore, very angry, because they believed they had been wronged by the Captain and abandoned by Giano, went not to the Signors but to the Captain's palace, which they seized and sacked. This action offended all the citizens, and those who wanted the ruin of Giano accused him, attributing to him all the blame. Hence, since some of the Signors then serving were his enemies, they accused him to the Captain as one who had stirred up the people. While they were debating his case, the people took arms and ran to his mansion, offering him their protection against the Signors and his enemies. Giano was unwilling to test this popular aid or to commit his life to the magistrates, because he feared the malice of the second and the instability of the first. Hence, to take from his enemies any chance for injuring him, and from his friends any chance for doing harm to his native city, he determined to go away, to yield to envy, to free the citizens from their fear of him, and to leave that city which with toil and danger to himself he had freed from servitude to the powerful. So he chose for himself voluntary exile.

CHAPTER 14
[Revolt by the nobles; compromise. 1295]

After his departure, the nobles had higher hopes of regaining influence; and concluding that their trouble came from their divisions, they united and sent two men to the Signoria, which they thought favorable to them, to beg it to consent to moderate in some measure the sharpness of the laws against them. This request, when it was made known, disturbed the spirits of the people because they feared that the Signors would grant it. And so, between the wish of the nobles and the suspicion of the people, they took up arms. The nobles assembled in three places: at San Giovanni, in the New Marketplace, and on the Piazza de' Mozzi; and under three leaders: Messer Forese Adimari, Messer Vanni de' Mozzi, and Messer Geri Spini. The people in very great numbers assembled under their banners at the palace of the Signors, who then lived near San Procolo. And because the people were suspicious of that Signoria, they deputed six citizens to govern with them.

While both parties prepared for a fight, some, both of the people and of the nobles, and with them certain clergy of good reputation, became go-betweens to pacify them, reminding the nobles that their deprivation of the right to hold office, and the laws made against them, had been caused by their arrogance and their wicked conduct; and that now to take arms and try to get back by force what, through their disunion and their bad methods, they had allowed to be taken from them, was nothing other than to try to ruin their city and make their own condition worse. They should remember that the people greatly surpassed them in numbers, wealth, and hatred, and that high birth, which they thought made themselves superior to the others, would not fight, but when they came to cold steel would turn out an empty word, not strong enough to defend them against so many. On the other hand, they reminded the people that it was not prudent always to strive for complete victory and that it was never wise to make men despair, because he who does not hope for good does not fear ill. They ought also to keep in mind that in the city's wars the nobles had done her honor. Therefore it was not good or just to persecute them with so much hate, for the nobles could easily endure not to take part in the supreme magistracy, but they could by no means endure that anybody should have power through the laws to drive them out of their native city. Therefore it would be well to soften those laws, and through that benefit to get them to lay down their arms. The people should not so trust in their numbers as to wish to tempt the fortune of combat, because often it has happened that by the few the many have been defeated.

The people held varying opinions. Many wished for combat. Since it must come some day, they had better have it then than wait until the enemy was stronger. If it were likely that the nobles would be satisfied with a softening of the laws, the laws should be softened, but the nobles' pride was such that they would never give up, unless they were forced to. Many others, wiser and of calmer spirit, believed that moderating the laws would not mean much and that coming to combat would mean a great deal. Their opinion at last prevailed, and they provided that for charges against nobles it would be necessary to find witnesses.

CHAPTER 15

[*The prosperity of Florence about 1298*]

Though they had put aside their arms, both parties remained very suspicious, so that each strengthened itself with towers and weapons. The people, influenced by the support those Signors had given to the nobility, reorganized the government, limiting it to a smaller number. The chief in authority were the Mancini, Magalotti, Altoviti, Peruzzi, and Cerretani. When the government had been settled, for the Signors' greater magnificence and greater security, in the year 1298 they laid the foundations of their Palace, making a piazza for it where the houses of the Uberti once stood. Almost at the same time they began the public prisons, which were completed in a few years. Nor was our city ever in a higher and more prosperous state than at that time, for she abounded in men, in riches, and in reputation. The citizens fit for arms amounted to thirty thousand, and the inhabitants fit for arms in the surrounding district to seventy thousand.[1] All Tuscany, partly as subject, partly as ally, obeyed her. And though among the nobles and the people there were some ill feeling and suspicion, they did not produce any bad effect, but everybody was passing his life in harmony and peace.

1. *Villani,* History *8. 38.*

If this peace was not disturbed by new enemies inside, it did not need to fear those outside, because the city was in such a condition that she no longer dreaded either the Empire or her own exiles. With her own forces she could resist all the Italian states. That harm, then, which forces from without could not do to her, those within brought upon her.

CHAPTER 16

[Cerchi and Donati; Blacks and Whites in Pistoia. 1300]

There were in Florence two families, the Cerchi and the Donati, very powerful in riches, position and men. Between them, since they were neighbors in Florence and in the country, there had been some disagreements, but not so serious that they had come to arms; perhaps they would not have produced serious results if a new cause had not increased these evil tendencies.

Among the chief families of Pistoia was that of the Cancellieri. It happened that when Lore son of Messer Guglielmo and Geri son of Messer Bertacca, both of that family, were playing cards, they came to words and Geri was slightly wounded by Lore. The affair troubled Messer Guglielmo, and thinking by kindness to get rid of the quarrel, he made it worse, for he ordered his son to go to the house of the father of the wounded man and ask for pardon. Lore obeyed his father; nevertheless this gracious action did not in any way soften Messer Bertacca's harsh spirit, for having Lore seized by his servants, as a greater insult he had them cut off his hand on a manger, saying to him: "Go back to your father and tell him that with steel, and not with words, wounds are cured." The cruelty of this act so enraged Messer Guglielmo that he had his men take arms to avenge it, and Messer Bertacca also armed to defend himself; so not merely that family but all the city of Pistoia was divided. The Cancellieri were descended from Messer Cancelliere, who had had two wives, one of whom was named Bianca; one of the parties, after her descendants, was called Bianca [*White*]; the other, in order to take a name op-posite to that, was called Nera [*Black*]. There were between them, as time went on, many fights, in which numbers of men were killed and houses destroyed. Unable to unite among themselves, worn out by the evil, and wishing either to put an end to their discords or by spreading dissension among others to increase them, they came to

Florence. The Blacks, because they were related to the Donati, were assisted by Messer Corso, the head of that family. As a result, the Whites, in order to have a powerful support that would hold them up against the Donati, had recourse to Messer Veri de' Cerchi, a man in every way not at all Messer Corso's inferior.

CHAPTER 17

[*Whites and Blacks in Florence; the Pope interferes. 1300*]

This party strife coming from Pistoia increased the ancient hatred between the Cerchi and the Donati, which was already so evident that the Priors and the other good citizens feared every hour that the two families would take arms, and that afterward all the city would be divided. Therefore they resorted to the Pontiff, asking that, against these contentions which had been started, he with his authority would apply such measures as they could not apply. The Pope sent for Messer Veri and required him to make peace with the Donati. Messer Veri acted astonished, saying that he had no quarrel with them. And because peace presupposes war, he did not know, since there was no war between them, why peace should be needed. Since Messer Veri, then, returned from Rome without any settlement, there was such an increase in hostile feelings that the slightest accident, however it happened, would be enough to make them burst out.

It was the month of May, a time, especially on holidays, when there are public festivities in Florence. So some Donati youths with their friends, on horseback, halted near Santa Trinita to watch some women dancing. In the same place next arrived some of the Cerchi, also accompanied by many nobles; not recognizing the Donati, who were ahead, and desirous also to see, they urged their horses among them and pushed them. Then the Donati, thinking themselves in-sulted, seized their weapons; the Cerchi valiantly opposed them; after many wounds given and received by each side, they separated. This tumult was the beginning of much evil, for all the city was divided, the men of the people as well as the rich. The parties took the names of the Whites and Blacks.

The leaders of the White party were the Cerchi, and with them sided the Adimari, the Abati, part of the Tosinghi, the Bardi, the Rossi, the Frescobaldi, the Nerli, and the Mannelli, all of the Mozzi, the Scali, the Gherardini, the Cavalcanti, Malespini, Bostichi, Giandonati, Vecchietti, and Arrigucci. These were joined by many families from the people, together with all the Ghibellines then in Florence. Hence, because of the great number that followed them, they had almost entire control of the city. The Donati, on the other hand, were heads of the Black party, and with them were all those portions of the families named above that did not side with the Whites, and in addition all the Pazzi, the Bisdomini, the Manieri, Bagnesi, Tornaquinci, Spini, Buondelmonti, Gianfigliazzi, and Brunelleschi. This partisan spirit not merely infected the city but divided also the whole surrounding district.

Hence the Party Captains and all who loved the Guelfs and the republic, greatly feared that—to the ruin of the city—this new dissension would revive the Ghibelline forces. So they again informed Pope Boniface that he would have to devise a remedy if he did not want that city, which had always been the shield of the Church, either to be destroyed or to become Ghibelline. So the Pope sent to Florence his legate, Matteo d'Acquasparta, a Portuguese cardinal. And since he had trouble with the White party which, because it thought itself more powerful, was less afraid, he left Florence in anger and pronounced an interdict; thus she remained in greater confusion than before his coming.

CHAPTER 18

[Further quarrels; both parties banished. 1300]

When the minds of all men were thus disturbed, it happened that at a funeral attended by many of the Cerchi and the Donati, they came to words and then to blows, from which at the time nothing other than uproar resulted. But after both parties had returned to their houses, the Cerchi determined to attack the Donati, and with a great number of men assailed them. But through Messer Corso's vigor the Cerchi were repulsed and many of them wounded. The whole city was under arms; the Signors and the laws were overcome by the vehemence of these powerful men. The wisest and the best citizens lived in continual fear. The Donati and their party were more afraid because they were less strong. Hence, to provide for their affairs, Messer Corso met with the other leaders of the Blacks and the Party Captains. They agreed to ask from the Pope a man of royal blood, who would come to reform Florence, thinking that by this means they might overcome the Whites. This assembly and decision were made known to the Priors, and by the opposite party were denounced as a conspiracy against the freedom of the city.

Since both parties were under arms, the Signors, through the advice and prudence of Dante—at that time one of them—took courage and called the people to arms; many from the surrounding district joined them. Then they forced the heads of the parties to lay down their arms, and banished Messer Corso Donati and many of the Black party. Yet to show that they were neutral in this decision, they banished also some of the White party, who soon after, with the excuse of proper reasons, returned.

CHAPTER 19

[Charles of Valois in Florence; the Blacks return and gain power. 1301]

Messer Corso and his partisans, because they thought the Pope favorable to their party, went to Rome, and what they had already written to the Pope, they convinced him of in an interview. At the Pontiff's court was Charles of Valois, brother of the French king, who had been called into Italy by the King of Naples in order to cross into Sicily. So the Pope, since he was excessively urged by the Florentine exiles, decided to send Charles to Florence until the proper season for his voyage. So come he did. And though the Whites, who were ruling, were suspicious of him, nevertheless, since he was head of the Guelfs and sent by the Pope, they did not dare hinder his coming; on the contrary, to make him their friend, they gave him authority to regulate the city according to his judgment. Having received this authority, Charles had all his friends and partisans arm themselves. This caused the people to suspect so strongly that he was going to take away their liberty that every man made ready his weapons and remained in his house, to be prepared if Charles should make any move.

At this time the Cerchi and the heads of the White party, because they had for some time been heads of the state and conducted themselves haughtily, had come to be universally hated. This gave courage to Messer Corso and the other Black exiles to come to

Florence, especially since they knew that Charles and the Party Captains were going to support them. So when the city, for fear of Charles, was in arms, Messer Corso with all the exiles and many others who followed him, without being hindered by anybody, entered Florence. Though Messer Veri de' Cerchi was encouraged to oppose him, he was not willing to do so, saying that he wanted the people of Florence, against whom Messer Corso was coming, to punish him. But what happened was the reverse: he was received, not punished, by the people, and Messer Veri had to flee to save himself, because Messer Corso, when he had forced the Pinti gate, assembled a force at San Piero Maggiore, a place near his mansion. Having gathered many supporters and people eager for change who assembled there, he first took from the prisons all held in them for either public or private reasons; then he forced the Signors to return as private citizens to their houses, and chose new ones from the people and the Black party; for five days he engaged in plundering the leaders of the White party.

The Cerchi and the other heads of their faction had gone out of the city and retired to their fortresses, seeing that Charles was opposed to them, and the greater part of the people hostile. And whereas before they had never been willing to follow the Pope's advice, they were forced to turn to him for help, showing him that Charles had come to disunite, not to unite Florence. So the Pope for the second time sent there his legate, Messer Matteo d'Aquasparta. He had the Cerchi and Donati make peace and strengthened the treaty with marriage contracts and new weddings. And though he wished that the Whites also should share in the offices, the Blacks who held the government would not agree to it. Hence the Legate did not go away with more satisfaction or less anger than he did the other time, but departed leaving the city, as disobedient, under an interdict.

CHAPTER 20

[*The Whites, including Dante, exiled. 1302*]

So in Florence both parties continued, and each was discontented: the Blacks, since the hostile party was on the spot, feared that, to their ruin, it would regain its lost influence; the Whites were without their former influence and honors. Their angry feelings and natural suspicions were increased by new injuries. Messer Niccola de' Cerchi, when going with many of his supporters to his country properties, at the bridge over Affrico was attacked by Simone, Messer Corso Donati's son. The fight was severe, with a sad end for both sides, for Messer Niccola was killed and Simone so badly wounded that he died the next night. This event again upset the whole city. The Black party, though more to blame, was defended by those in power. Then, before any sentence had been pronounced in the case, a conspiracy was discovered between the Whites and Messer Piero Ferrante, one of Charles' barons, with whom they were negotiating about being put back in control. This came to light through letters the Cerchi wrote him, though some believed that the letters were forged and devised by the Donati to conceal the infamy brought on them by Messer Niccola's death.

The result was the banishment of all the Cerchi and their followers of the White party, among whom was Dante the poet. Their goods were confiscated and their houses destroyed. Along with many Ghibellines who had sided with them, they were scattered through many places, seeking new fortunes with new labors. Charles, having done what he visited Florence for, left and returned to the Pope to continue his Sicilian expedition. In this he was not wiser or better than he had been in Florence; in disgrace, with the loss of many of his men, he returned to France.

CHAPTER 21

[Further strife; Niccolao da Prato fails to make peace; the great fire of 1304.]

Affairs in Florence after Charles' departure were very quiet. Only Messer Corso was restless, because he believed he did not hold in the city the rank he deserved; on the contrary, since the government was controlled by the people, he saw the republic administered by many of his inferiors. Moved therefore by these feelings, he planned to give honor to his dishonorable purpose by means of an honorable cause; so he slandered many citizens who had administered public funds, as having used them for their private advantage, and said it would be well to find them out and punish them. This view of his was accepted by many who had the same desire as he did; and it was reinforced by the ignorance of many others, who believed that Messer Corso was acting through love for the city. On the other side, the citizens who were slandered, since they had the support of the people, defended themselves; this dispute went so far that, after legal methods, it came to weapons. On one side were Messer Corso and Messer Lottieri, the bishop of Florence, with many of the nobles and some of the people; on the other were the Signors and the larger part of the people, so that there was fighting in many parts of the city. The Signors, seeing the great danger they were in, sent for aid to the Lucchese; immediately there appeared in Florence all the populace of Lucca. Through their strength things were quieted for the time and the disorders repressed; yet the people retained the government and their own freedom without at all punishing the inciters of the conflict.

Meanwhile the Pope heard of the troubles in Florence; to put them down he sent Messer Niccolao da Prato, his legate. Being a man who by rank, learning, and habits was of high reputation, he gained at once such confidence that authority was given him for establishing a government according to his own ideas. Because he was from a Ghibelline town, he had in mind the repatriation of the exiles, but first he wished to win the people's favor; and for the sake of this he renewed the ancient Companies of the People. This arrangement greatly increased their power and lessened that of the nobles. Since, then, it appeared to the Legate that he had gained the support of the masses, he planned to secure the return of the exiles; but as he tried various ways, not merely did he not succeed in any of them but he came to be so suspected by those who ruled that he was obliged to leave. So in great anger he returned to the Pontiff, and left Florence greatly disturbed, and interdicted. The city indeed was upset not merely by one quarrel but by many, namely, the hostilities between the people and the nobles, the Ghibellines and the Guelfs, the Whites and the Blacks. The whole city, then, was in arms and there was fighting everywhere, because by the departure of the Legate many were disappointed, since they were hoping the exiles would return. The leaders in starting the trouble were the Medici and the Giugni, whose support of the rebels, like that of the Legate, was evident. There was fighting, therefore, in many parts of Florence.

To these ills a fire was added, which broke out first near Orto San Michele in the houses of the Abati; from there it leaped into those of the Caponsacchi, and burned them, with the houses of the Macchi,

Amieri, Toschi, Cipriani, Lamberti, and Cavalcanti, and all the
New Marketplace. From there it went into Porta Santa Maria, and
burned it all; and circling from the Ponte Vecchio, it burned the
houses of the Gherardini, Pulci, Amidei, and Lucardesi, and many
others with them, so that their number reached seventeen hundred or
more. As to this fire, many believed that it was started by chance, in
the ardor of combat. Some others insisted that it was started by Neri
Abati, prior of San Piero Scheraggio, a dissolute man and fond of
evil, who, seeing the citizens busy fighting, decided to do a wicked
deed that the people, because they were busy, could not protect
themselves against; and that he might succeed better, he set fire to the
house of his relatives, where it was easier for him to do it. It was the
year 1304 and the month of July when by fire and by sword Florence
was thrown into confusion. Messer Corso Donati alone, in the
midst of so many disturbances, did not arm himself, because he
judged he would more easily become arbiter between the two parties
when, worn out by the fight, they turned to agreements. They laid
down their arms, however, more through satiety with evil than
through any union between them. The only result was that the
rebels did not return, and the party supporting them continued to
be weaker.

CHAPTER 22

*[Unsuccessful attempt of the Ghibellines to return; Corso Donati.
1304-1307]*

The Legate, returning to Rome and hearing of the new broils
which had broken out in Florence, persuaded the Pope that to
reunite her he needed to make twelve leading citizens of Florence
come before him. Then, having thus taken away what nourished
the disease, he could probably count on wiping it out. This advice
the Pontiff took, and the citizens who were summoned obeyed,
among them Corso Donati. After their departure, the Legate indicated to the exiles that then was the time, when Florence was
without leaders, for them to return. So, getting together a force, they
came to Florence, entered the city through the still unfinished walls,
and pushed on to the Piazza di San Giovanni.

It was noteworthy that citizens who a little before had fought for
the exiles' return when, unarmed, they prayed to be restored to their

native city, on seeing those exiles armed and trying by force to get control of her, took arms against them (so much higher those citizens esteemed the common good than they did private friendship) and, uniting with the people, drove the invaders back with force to the place whence they had come. The exiles failed in this undertaking because they left part of their men at Lastra and did not wait for Messer Tolosetto Uberti, who was to come from Pistoia with three hundred horsemen; for they thought that speed rather than force was going to give them the victory. Often in such undertakings sluggish, ness takes away one's opportunity and speed one's strength.

On the rebels' departure, Florence returned to her old dissensions. And to take away the power of the Cavalcanti family, the people took from them by force le Stinche, a walled town in the valley of the Greve, which had from early times belonged to that family. And because those who were captured there were the first to be put in the prisons just built, those prisons, after the town whence the prisoners came, were then called and still are called le Stinche.

The chief men in the republic restored the Companies of the People, and gave them banners, because earlier they had assembled under those of the gilds. Their heads were called Gonfaloniers of the Companies and Colleagues of the Signors, and it was decreed that in troubles they should aid the Signors with arms, and in peace with advice. They added to the two long-established Rectors an Executor, who was to act with the Gonfaloniers against the lawless, ness of the nobility.

Meanwhile the Pope died and Messer Corso and the other citizens returned from Rome, and things would have been quiet if Messer Corso's restless spirit had not again upset the city. That man, in order to get himself reputation, always held a view contrary to that of the most powerful, and wherever he saw the people inclining, in that direction he turned his influence, to make them better disposed toward himself. Hence he was the leader in all quarrels and revolts, and to him resorted all those who wished to gain something unlaw, ful, so that many respected citizens hated him. This hate increased so continuously that the party of the Blacks came to an open split, because Messer Corso relied on his forces and his private influence, and his adversaries on the government; but so impressive was his bearing that everybody feared him. Nonetheless, in order to take away from him the people's support—which by such means could easily be destroyed—his enemies spread a rumor that he wished to seize absolute power. For this rumor it was easy to get credit, be-cause his way of living exceeded all private bounds. This belief grew much stronger after he took as his wife a daughter of Uguccione della Faggiuola, head of the Ghibelline and White party, and very powerful in Tuscany.

CHAPTER 23

[*The last fight and the death of Corso Donati. 1308*]

This marriage, when it became known, gave his adversaries courage, and they took up arms against him; for the same reasons the people did not defend him; on the contrary, the greater part of them joined with his enemies. The leaders of his adversaries were Messer Rosso della Tosa, Messer Pazzino de' Pazzi, Messer Geri Spini, and Messer Berto Brunelleschi. These, with their followers and the greater part of the people having gathered armed in front of the Palace, by means of the Signors laid before Messer Piero Branca, Captain of the People, the accusation that with Uguccione's aid Messer Corso was planning to make himself tyrant. After this he was cited, and next pronounced a rebel for contempt of the author-ities; between the accusation and the sentence there was no more time than two hours. When the sentence had been pronounced, the Signors, with the Companies of the People under their banners, set out to attack him.

Messer Corso, on the other hand, not frightened by seeing many of his followers abandon him, not by the sentence that had been pronounced, not by the authority of the Signors, and not by the numbers of his enemies, fortified himself in his mansion, hoping to defend himself there until Uguccione, for whom he had sent, came to rescue him. He barred off his mansion and the streets around it and then garrisoned them with his partisans. These so defended them that the people, though in great numbers, could not take them. So the fight was severe, with death and wounds on both sides. Since the people saw that from the open places they could not overcome him, they took possession of the houses next to his and, by breaking their walls, through unexpected places entered into his house. Mes-ser Corso, therefore, seeing himself surrounded by enemies and trusting no further in Uguccione's aid and despairing of victory, resolved to see if he could find a means of safety. So he and Gherardo Bordoni, forming a body with many of their strongest and most trusted friends, made a rush on the enemy, and the latter opened enough to let Corso's party, by dint of fighting, pass through; they went out of the city by Porta alla Croce. They were nevertheless pursued by many, so that near the Affrico, Gherardo was killed by Boccaccio Cavicciuli. Messer Corso also was overtaken and captured at Rovezzano by some Catalan cavalry in the pay of the Signors. But in coming to Florence, in order not to look upon the faces of his victorious enemies and be tortured by them, he let himself fall from his horse; and as he lay on the ground, his throat was cut by one of those who were conducting him. His body was taken up by the monks of San Salvi and without any honor buried. Such was the end of Messer Corso, to whom his city and the Black party should acknowledge obligation for many good things and many bad ones. And if he had had a quieter spirit, he would be more gratefully remembered. Nevertheless, he deserves to be named among our able citizens. True it is that his restlessness kept his city and his party from remembering the debts they owed him, and at last he brought death on himself and many ills on both of the others.

Uguccione, coming to his soninlaw's rescue, when he reached Remoli heard that the people had overcome Messer Corso. Thinking therefore that he could not do him any good, he turned back, in order not to harm himself without benefiting him.

CHAPTER 24

[Quiet after Corso's death; the Emperor Henry VII attacks Florence in vain. 1308–1313]

After Messer Corso's death, in the year 1308, there was a pause in Florentine dissensions; and the citizens lived quietly until they heard that Henry the Emperor with all the Florentine rebels was coming into Italy; he had promised to restore them to their native city. So the heads of the city, in order to have fewer enemies, decided to diminish the number of exiles; therefore they decreed that all of them should be restored except those to whom by name the law forbade return. As a result, there remained outside the larger part of the Ghibellines and a few of the White party, among whom were Dante Alighieri and the sons of Messer Veri de' Cerchi and of Giano della Bella.

In addition, the Florentine rulers sent for aid to Robert King of Naples; and being unable to get help as allies, they gave the city to him for five years, in order that he might defend them as his vassals. The Emperor in his passage followed the Pisan road and went through the Maremma to Rome, where he was crowned in the year 1312. Then, determined to master the Florentines, he came by way of Perugia and Arezzo to Florence. He placed himself with his army at the monastery of San Salvi, a mile from the city, where for fifty days he remained without any advantage. Hence, despairing of his power to overthrow the government of that city, he went off to Pisa, where he agreed with Frederick King of Sicily to make an expedition to the Kingdom. And having set out with his soldiers, when he was hoping for victory and King Robert was in fear of ruin, on reaching Buonconvento he died.

CHAPTER 25

[The Florentines defeated by Uguccione at Montecatini; Lando di Gubbio in Florence. 1314–1316]

A little later it happened that Uguccione della Faggiuola became Lord of Pisa, and soon afterward of Lucca, where he was placed by the Ghibelline party, and with the aid of those cities he did their neighbors very great damage. In order to free themselves from it, the Florentines asked King Robert to send his brother Piero to lead their armies. Uguccione on the other side kept increasing his power, and by force and by trickery took many towns in Val d'Arno and in Val di Nievole. When he then besieged Montecatini, the Florentines decided that it was necessary to relieve the town, if they did not wish that fire to burn all their country. So having gathered a large army, they went into Val di Nievole, where they met Uguccione in battle and after a great struggle were defeated. There died Piero the King's brother, whose body was never found; with him more than two thousand men were slain. Nor on Uguccione's side was the victory happy, for in that battle one of his sons was killed, with many other leaders of his army.

The Florentines, after this defeat, strengthened their towns round about, and King Robert sent as their general the Count of Andria, called Count Novello. Because of his conduct, or even because it is natural to the Florentines that every government displeases them and every happening divides them, the city, in spite of its war with Uguccione, divided itself between the King's friends and his enemies. The leaders of the enemies were Messer Simone della Tosa, the Magalotti, and certain men from the people who were more influential in the government than others of their class. They attempted sending to France and then to Germany for commanders and soldiers, so that when these arrived they could drive out the Count, who was governor for the King; but Fortune prevented them from obtaining any. Nonetheless, they did not abandon their undertaking. And as they sought for someone to revere, and could not find him in France or in Germany, they found him in Gubbio. Having first driven out the Count, they had Lando di Gubbio come as executor or police officer; to him they gave complete power over the citizens. This fellow was grasping and cruel, and going with many armed men through the city, he took the life now of one man, now of another, according to the decision of those who had chosen him. And so overbearing did he become that he coined a false coin with the Florentine stamp, without anybody's daring to oppose him. To such greatness the discords of Florence had brought him! A great, indeed, and a miserable city! for neither the memory of past dissensions nor fear of Uguccione nor a king's influence could hold her firm, so that she was in a most wretched state, being on the outside pillaged by Uguccione, and on the inside plundered by Lando di Gubbio.

The King's friends and those opposed to Lando and his followers were noble families, powerful men of the people and all the Guelfs. Nevertheless, because their adversaries had the government in their hands, they could not make themselves known without serious danger. Yet, determined to free themselves from so dishonorable a tyranny, they wrote secretly to King Robert that he should appoint as his vicar in Florence Count Guido da Battifolle. The King at once decreed this, and though the Signors were opposed to the King, the hostile party, because of the Count's good qualities, dared not oppose him. Nevertheless he did not have much authority, because the Signors and the gonfaloniers of the Companies supported Lando and his party.

While Florence was occupied with these difficulties, she was visited by the daughter of King Albert of Germany, who was going to meet Carl, King Robert's son, her husband. She was much honored by the King's friends, who complained to her about condi tions in the city and about the tyranny of Lando and his partisans. So before she went away, by means of her help and some from the King, the citizens united, and Lando was stripped of his authority and, rich in booty and reeking with blood, sent back to Gubbio. In reforming the government, the King's control had been extended for three years; and because already seven Signors had been chosen from Lando's party, six were chosen from the King's party. After ward there were some magistracies with thirteen Signors, but later, quite in accord with the ancient custom, the seven were resumed.

CHAPTER 26

[*Prato delivered from Castruccio Castracani. 1316–1323*]

In these days the lordship of Lucca and of Pisa was taken from Uguccione; Castruccio Castracani, a citizen of Lucca, then became their ruler. Because he was a young man, fiery and vigorous, and fortunate in his undertakings, in a short time he became chief of the Tuscan Ghibellines. In this matter the Florentines, having quieted their civil discords, for some years thought, first, that Castruccio's forces would not increase, and later, when against their expectation they did increase, considered how they were going to defend them selves against him. And in order that the Signors should make decisions on better advice, and carry them out with greater authority, they chose twelve citizens, whom they named Good Men, without whose advice and agreement the Signors were to do nothing im portant. Meanwhile the end of King Robert's rule had come, and the city, now lord of herself, with the usual Rectors and magistrates resumed her government. The great fear she had of Castruccio kept her united.

After many attacks on the lords of Lunigiana, he attacked Prato. Hence the Florentines, determined to rescue that town, locked their shops and in a popular movement went there; near Prato they as sembled twenty thousand on foot and fifteen hundred on horseback. And to take forces from Castruccio and add them to themselves, the Signors through a proclamation made known that whatever Guelf rebel came to the rescue of Prato would, after the campaign, be restored to his native city; hence more than four thousand rebels gathered there. This army of such size, with such speed brought to Prato, so frightened Castruccio that, without trying the fortune of battle, he retired toward Lucca. As a result, the nobles and the people in the Florentine army held different opinions. The people wished to pursue and attack Castruccio in order to destroy him; the nobles wished to turn back, saying it was enough to have imperiled Florence for the sake of freeing Prato. That had been proper, since they had been forced by necessity, but now that the need had van﹁ ished, and they might gain little and lose much, they should not tempt Fortune. Not being able to agree, the army turned over the decision to the Signors, who found in the councils the same differ﹁ ences of opinion as between the people and the nobility. This condition, when it became known in the city, brought into the public squares many men who spoke very threatening words against the nobility, so that the latter yielded in fear. This decision, made late and by many unwillingly, gave the enemy time to retire in safety to Lucca.

CHAPTER 27
[*The city breaks her promise to the exiles. 1323*]

This miscarriage made the people so angry with the nobles that the Signors resolved not to observe the pledge given, on their order and with their support, to the exiles. With a premonition of this, the exiles determined to anticipate it; so at the head of the army, in order to be the first to enter Florence, they presented themselves before the city gates. This attempt having been foreseen was not successful; those who had remained in Florence drove them back. Yet to see if they could get by agreement what they had not obtained by force, the exiles sent eight men as ambassadors to remind the Signors of the pledge that had been given, and of the dangers they had undergone in reliance on it, hoping for the promised reward. The nobles, be﹁ lieving they were committed to the obligation, since they had promised individually what the Signors had pledged, labored hard in the exiles' behalf. Yet the anger felt by the people generally—who were not in the same temper as if they had been victorious in the campaign against Castruccio—kept the nobles from succeeding. This brought blame and dishonor upon the city.

As a result of the affair, since many of the nobles were angry, they tried to gain by force what, when they requested it, was refused. They made an arrangement with the exiles by which these were to come armed to the city, and the nobles, who were inside the walls, were to take arms in their behalf. Before the appointed day, this plan was revealed. Hence the exiles found the city in arms and so prepared for restraining those outside and frightening those inside that nobody dared take up arms; hence without getting any results the exiles gave up the attempt. After their departure there was a desire to punish those believed most blameworthy for encouraging the exiles. And though everybody knew who the offenders were, yet nobody dared name them, much less give testimony against them. Therefore, to learn the truth without reservation, it was decreed that in the Councils everybody should write down the names of the offenders and secretly give what he had written to the Captain. In this way, accusation was brought against Messer Amigo Donati, Messer Teghiaio Frescobaldi and Messer Lotteringho Gherardini. These, since their judge was more sympathetic than their crimes perhaps deserved, were punished with fines.

CHAPTER 28
[*The method of choosing magistrates in Florence. 1323*]

The disturbances caused in Florence by the appearance of the exiles at the gates showed that for the Companies of the People one head alone was not enough. Therefore it was decreed that for the future each Company should have three or four heads; hence to each gonfalonier they added two or three officers whom they called pen-non-bearers, so that in emergencies in which all the Company did not need to come together, a part of it could act under a head. It happens in all republics that after a striking event some old laws are always annulled and others are renewed. So on this occasion, though earlier the Signoria had been chosen at the time when it was to serve, the Signors and the members of the College then in office, because they had great power, took authority to choose the Signors who were to sit for the next forty months. The names of these they put in a bag and every two months drew them out for the coming term. But before the end of the forty months came, because many citizens suspected that their names had not been put in the bag, there was a new bagging. From this beginning came the method of putting in a bag for a long time the names of all who were to be magistrates, both in the city and outside. Before this the councils elected successors at the end of each term. These baggings were later called *squittini*. Because they occurred every three years, or at the most every five, it was supposed that they would save the city bother and remove the cause of the disturbances that always arose at the choosing of every group of magistrates, since there were many competitors. Since the Florentines did not know how otherwise to get rid of such troubles, they took this way, not realizing the harm concealed under this slight convenience.

CHAPTER 29
[*Castruccio defeats the Florentines at Altopascio. 1325*]

It was the year 1325. Castruccio, having taken Pistoia, had become so powerful that the Florentines, fearing his greatness, determined to attack him and get Pistoia out of his control before he fully mastered her. For that purpose they raised among their citizens and allies twenty thousand infantry and three thousand horsemen. With this army they besieged Altopascio, in order by occupying the town to deprive Castruccio of power to aid Pistoia. Having succeeded in capturing that place, the Florentines then went on toward Lucca, laying the country waste; but by reason of their general's slight prudence and less fidelity, they did not make much progress.

Their general was Messer Ramondo di Cardona. This man, seeing that the Florentines in the past had been liberal with their liberty, and had yielded it now to the King, now to the Legates, now to other men of lower rank, inferred that if he brought them into some necessity, it might easily happen that they would make him prince. He did not fail to mention it often, and asked to have the same authority in the city that they had given him in the armies; he showed that otherwise he could not get the obedience necessary to a general; and because the Florentines did not allow it to him, he kept

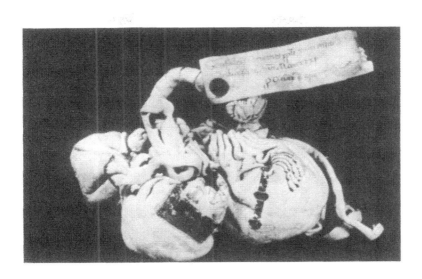

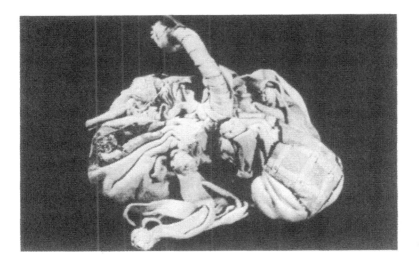

Bags from which the names of Florentines who were to hold public office were drawn, preserved in the Florentine public records office. They would have appeared more capacious when the leather was new and flexible. See bags *in the index.*

on losing time and Castruccio gaining it, for to the latter came the assistance that the Visconti and the other tyrants of Lombardy had promised him. But after Messer Ramondo's army had been strength, ened, just as at first he could not win through his slight fidelity, so afterward through his slight prudence he could not save himself; for moving on slowly with his army, he was attacked by Castruccio near Altopascio and in a great battle was defeated. Many citizens were captured and killed, and with them Messer Ramondo, who for his slight faith and his bad advice received from Fortune such punishment as he deserved from the Florentines.

The damage that Castruccio after his victory did the Florentines in plunder, prisoners, destruction and fire cannot be told; without having any army opposed to him, for months he rode and plundered as he chose. After so great a defeat, the Florentines thought it enough to save their city.

CHAPTER 30

[Charles Duke of Calabria becomes ruler of Florence; Castruccio takes Pistoia. 1326]

The Florentines were not, however, too frightened to provide great supplies of money, hire soldiers and send to their allies for aid. Nevertheless no provision was enough to restrain so powerful an enemy. They were obliged to accept as their ruler Charles Duke of Calabria, King Robert's son, if they wished him to defend them, for since he was accustomed to being lord of Florence he preferred their obedience to their alliance. But because Charles was tied up in the Sicilian wars and therefore unable to come to take the lordship, he sent to Florence as his vicar Walter, a Frenchman by birth and Duke of Athens. Walter took possession of the city for Charles and ar, ranged the magistrates as he wished. Nevertheless his conduct was so modest and so contrary to his nature[1] that everybody loved him.

Charles, after settling the wars in Sicily, came to Florence with a thousand horsemen. He made his entrance there in July in the year 1326. His coming deprived Castruccio of freedom to lay Florentine territory waste without restraint. Nevertheless, such reputation as was gained outside was lost inside: those damages not inflicted by

1. *His nature as later revealed. See chap. 36, below.*

enemies were suffered from friends, because without the Duke's consent the Signors could not do anything, and in the period of one year he got from the city four hundred thousand florins, notwith' standing that according to their agreement with him the sum was not to exceed two hundred thousand—so many were the burdens with which every day he or his father weighed the city down.

To these damages were joined new fears and new enemies, for the Ghibellines of Lombardy, on the appearance of Charles in Tuscany, became so apprehensive that Galeazzo Visconti and the other Lombard tyrants, with money and promises, got Ludwig of Bavaria to cross into Italy, for against the Pope's will he had been chosen Emperor. He came into Lombardy and thence into Tus' cany, and with Castruccio's help made himself master of Pisa; from there, freshly supplied with money, he went on to Rome. This caused Charles to depart from Florence in his fear for the Kingdom; as his vicar he left Messer Filippo da Saggineto. Castruccio, after the departure of the Emperor, made himself master of Pisa, but the Florentines by a conspiracy got Pistoia away from him. Castruccio besieged her, and remained there with such great efficiency and stubbornness that, although the Florentines many times made efforts to relieve her and attacked now Castruccio's army, now his territory, never with either force or ingenuity could they detach him from that enterprise—such desire he had to punish the Pistolese and to over' come the Florentines! Hence the Pistolese were forced to accept him as lord. This affair, though it brought him so much glory, brought upon him also so much toil that on returning to Lucca he died.

And because it is unusual for Fortune not to match a good or an ill with another good or another ill, Charles, Duke of Calabria and lord of Florence, also died in Naples, so that in a short time and contrary to every expectation the Florentines were set free from the rule of the one and the fear of the other. Since they were free, they then reorganized their city and annulled the entire system of the old councils; and they set up two of them, one of three hundred from the people, the other of two hundred and fifty from the nobles and the people. The first of these they called the Council of the People, the second that of the Community.

CHAPTER 31

[*The Florentines refuse to purchase Lucca; Florence quiet from 1328 to 1340; the flood of 1333*]

The Emperor, when he arrived at Rome, set up an antipope and arranged many things opposed to the Church; many others he tried without result, so that at last he departed in disgrace and came to Pisa. There, either because they took offense or because they were not paid, about eight hundred German cavalry rebelled against him and fortified themselves at Montechiaro[1] above the Ceruglio. These, after the Emperor had gone from Pisa into Lombardy, took Lucca and drove out Francesco Castracani, who had been left there by the Emperor. Thinking to get some profit from their spoil, they offered that city to the Florentines for eighty thousand florins; on Messer Simone della Tosa's advice, Florence refused. This decision would have been very useful to our city if the Florentines had always held to that policy; because a little later they changed their minds, their decision was very harmful. If then, for so low a price, they could have had Lucca peacefully and did not want her, later, when they did want her, they did not get her, though they would have paid a much higher price—which was the reason why Florence many times, with great damage to herself, changed her government. Lucca, then, refused by the Florentines, was bought by Messer Gherardino Spinoli, a Genoese, for thirty thousand florins. And because men are slower to take what they can have than they are to want what they cannot get, as soon as they discovered Messer Gherardino's purchase, and the low price for which he had got Lucca, the Florentines burned with an extreme longing to have her, reproaching themselves and him who had discouraged them. In order to get her by force, since they had chosen not to buy her, they sent their soldiers to spoil and plunder the Lucchese.

Meanwhile the Emperor had left Italy; and the Antipope as the result of an arrangement by the Pisans had gone as a prisoner to France. After the death of Castruccio in 1328, the Florentines were quiet within their city until 1340, giving attention only to the external affairs of their state; in Lombardy, on account of the coming of King

1. *Now Montecarlo.*

John of Bohemia, and in Tuscany, for the sake of Lucca, they made many wars.

They also ennobled the city with new buildings, because, with Giotto's advice, a painter very famous in those days, they then con- structed the tower of Santa Reparata. In 1333, as the result of a deluge, the waters of Arno in some places in Florence rose more than twenty-four feet, destroying part of the bridges and many buildings. With great care and expense the Florentines rebuilt what had been destroyed.

CHAPTER 32

[Rebellion of the Bardi and Frescobaldi. 1340–1341]

But on the coming of the year 1340, new causes for change appeared. At that time the powerful citizens had two ways for in- creasing and keeping their power: first, they restricted the baggings of the magistrates to make the offices always come to them or to their friends; second, they were leaders in the choice of the rectors, in order afterward to obtain favorable judgments from them. And on this second method they put so high a value that, since the ordinary rectors were not enough for them, they sometimes set up a third one. So in these times they had in an extralegal manner employed, with the title of Captain of the Guard, Messer Iacopo Gabriegli di Gubbio, and given him full authority over the citizens. This man every day, for the advantage of those who ruled, inflicted many injuries, and among those injured were Messer Piero de' Bardi and Messer Bardo Frescobaldi. They, being noble and naturally proud, could not bear that a foreigner, wrongfully and for the advantage of a few powerful men, should insult them. To get revenge they formed a conspiracy against him and those in power. In this conspiracy were many noble families, with some of the people to whom the tyranny of those in power was hateful.

The arrangement among the conspirators was that each one should assemble many armed men in his house, and the morning after the holiday of All Saints, when everybody was in the churches to pray for his dead relatives, they were to take arms, kill the Captain and the leaders of those in office, and then, with new Signors and a new constitution, reform the government. But because when resolu- tions are dangerous, the more they are considered, the less willingly they are put in practice, conspiracies always are discovered whenever there is an interval of time before their execution. One of the conspirators was Andrea de' Bardi, in whom, as he meditated on the thing, fear of punishment became stronger than hope of revenge; he revealed the whole to Jacopo Alberti, his brother-in-law. Jacopo made it known to the Priors, and the Priors to those managing the government. So because the affair was close to its danger point, All-Saints' Day being near, many citizens held a meeting in the Palace; judging postponement dangerous, they urged the Signors to ring the bell and call the people to arms. Taldo Valori was Gonfalonier and Francesco Salviati one of the Signors. Being relatives of the Bardi, these two did not favor the bell-ringing, asserting that it was unwise to have the people take arms for every trivial thing, because authority given to a multitude not restrained by any bridle never does any good, and that to start strife is easy but to check it is hard. Therefore they believed a better plan would be first to learn the truth of the matter and then to inflict lawful punishment rather than to ruin Florence on the basis of a mere statement by attempting to suppress the conspiracy with an uprising. Nowhere were these words listened to, but with insulting acts and abusive words the Signors were obliged to ring the bell. When it was rung, all the people ran armed to the Piazza.[1]

On the other hand, the Bardi and Frescobaldi, seeing that they were discovered, seized arms in order to conquer with glory or to die without shame, hoping to defend the part of the city on the south side of the river, where they had their houses. They fortified the bridges, trusting in the aid they were expecting from the nobles of the surrounding district and others of their friends. This plan was thwarted by the people inhabiting that part of the city, who took arms to aid the Signors. Hence, finding themselves surrounded, the two families abandoned the bridges and withdrew into the street where the Bardi lived, as stronger than any other; this they defended bravely. Messer Jacopo di Gubbio, knowing that against him all this conspiracy was directed, in fear of death and altogether bewildered and terrified, placed himself near the Palace of the Signors, in the midst of his armed soldiers. But the other rulers, who were less blameworthy, had more courage, especially the Podestà, Messer

1. *The Piazza Signoria, in front of the present Palazzo Vecchio, the palace and fortress of the Signors. See 2. 15, above.*

Maffeo da Carradi. He appeared where the fighting was going on and, without being afraid of anything, passed the Rubaconte bridge, put himself among the swords of the Bardi, and made a sign that he wished to speak with them. Whereupon their respect for the man, his character, and his other great qualities made them at once lay down their arms and quietly listen to him. With modest and serious words, he blamed their conspiracy, showed the peril in which they would be if they did not yield to this popular movement, gave them hope that then they would be heard and judged with mercy, and promised that for their reasonable complaints he would secure consideration. Then returning to the Signors, he persuaded them not to insist on conquering with the blood of their citizens and on judging them unheard. And so much did he achieve that, with the Signors' consent, the Bardi and the Frescobaldi with their friends left the city, and without being impeded retired to their strongholds in the country.

When they had gone and the people had laid down their weapons, the Signors began legal action only against those of the Bardi and Frescobaldi families who had taken arms; to deprive them of power, the Signors bought from the Bardi the walled towns of Mangone and Vernia, and by law provided that no citizen should possess a walled town within twenty miles of Florence. A few months after this, Stiatta Frescobaldi was beheaded and many others of that family proclaimed rebels. It was not enough for those who were governing that they had beaten and mastered the Bardi and Frescobaldi, but—as men almost always do, who, the more authority they have, the worse they use it and the more overbearing they become—whereas earlier they set up a Captain of the Guard who distressed Florence, now they added one for the surrounding district and gave him very great power; hence men they suspected could not live either in Florence or outside her. Thus those who were governing the city so angered all the nobles that they were prepared to sell the city and themselves, in order to get revenge; while the nobles were waiting for their chance, it came well and they used it better.

CHAPTER 33

[Lucca lost to the Pisans; the Duke of Athens. 1341-1342]

As a result of the many troubles in Tuscany and Lombardy, the city of Lucca had come under the rule of Mastino della Scala lord of Verona. This man, though according to agreement he was to hand Lucca over to the Florentines, had not done so, because, being lord of Parma, he thought he could hold her; for the pledge he had given he cared nothing. So the Florentines, to avenge themselves, joined with the Venetians and carried on such a war against him that he was on the point of losing his whole territory. Nevertheless, the Florentines gained no other profit than a little satisfaction of mind in defeating Mastino, because the Venetians, as do all those with whom the less powerful ally themselves, when they had gained Treviso and Vicenza, made peace, without any regard for the Florentines.

But since a little later the Visconti, rulers of Milan, took Parma from Mastino, and he judged that therefore he could no longer hold Lucca, he decided to sell her. The competitors were the Florentines and the Pisans; as the bargaining approached its end, the Pisans saw that the Florentines, as the richer, were going to get her. So they turned to force, and with the aid of the Visconti went to besiege Lucca. The Florentines did not for that back out of the purchase but, concluding their agreement with Mastino, paid part of the money and for another part gave hostages. Then they sent Naddo Rucellai, Giovanni di Bernardino de'Medici, and Rosso di Ricciardo de' Ricci to take possession. These went into Lucca by force, and Mastino's soldiers turned the city over to them. The Pisans nonetheless continued their enterprise and with every effort sought to get her by force, and the Florentines tried to free her from the siege. After a long war, the Florentines, with loss in money and gain in disgrace, were driven away, and the Pisans became masters of Lucca. The loss of this city, as in such instances always happens, made the people of Florence angry with their rulers, and in all places and in all the public squares they openly denounced them, blaming their avarice and their bad policies.

At the beginning of this war, twenty citizens were appointed to manage it; they chose Messer Malatesta da Rimini as general of the expedition. He carried it on with little courage and less prudence.

And because they sent to Robert King of Naples for aid, the King sent them Walter duke of Athens. That man, by will of the Heav﹍ ens, which were preparing conditions for future evils, arrived in Florence exactly at the time when the Lucchese expedition entirely failed. Hence those Twenty, seeing that the people were angry, thought by choosing a new general to fill them with new hope, and by such a choice either to check or to remove the causes for slandering themselves. So in order that the people also should have reason to fear, and that the Duke of Athens could defend them with more power, they put him in office first as Conservator, and then as general of their men﹍at﹍arms.

The nobles, who for the reasons given above were discontented, and many of whom had been acquainted with Walter when at other times, in the name of Charles Duke of Calabria, he had ruled Florence, thought the time had come when by ruining the city they could put out the fire that was burning themselves. In their judg﹍ ment there was no other way to master the populace that had persecuted them than to put themselves under a prince who, realizing the merits of one party and the haughtiness of the other, would re﹍ strain the people and favor the nobles. To this belief they joined the hope of the benefits their deserts would bring them if through their efforts Walter became prince. They were, therefore, many times with him in secret, urging him to take complete control and offering him their aid to the utmost. To their influence and encouragement was joined that of some families from the people: the Peruzzi, Ac﹍ ciaiuoli, Antellesi, and Buonaccorsi. These, burdened by debts they could not pay from their own property, wished to pay them from that of others, and with the slavery of their city to free themselves from slavery to their creditors. All these persuasions fired the Duke's ambitious spirit with greater greed for ruling. In order, then, to give himself a reputation for being severe and just and in that way to increase his favor among the lowest classes, he laid charges against those who had directed the war over Lucca; he took the lives of Messer Giovanni de'Medici, Naddo Rucellai, and Guglielmo Alto﹍ viti, and punished many with exile, many with fines.

CHAPTER 34

[The Duke moves toward tyranny; some of the Signors reason with him. 1342]

These executions greatly frightened the middle-class citizens. They pleased only the nobles and the lower class; the latter because their nature is to take pleasure in evil, the former because they saw themselves revenged for the many injuries they had received from the people. As the Duke passed through the streets, loud voices praised his gallant spirit, and everybody gave him open encouragement to find out the frauds of the citizens and punish them. The function of the Twenty was diminished, the Duke's reputation great, and fear of him very great. Hence everybody, to show that he was his friend, had the Duke's insignia painted on his house; the Duke lacked nothing of being prince except the title. And since he thought he could securely attempt anything, he informed the Signors that he judged it necessary for the good of the city that he be granted authority without limit. He wished, therefore, since all the city agreed to it, that they also should agree. All the Signors, though they had much earlier foreseen their city's ruin, were alarmed by this request. Nevertheless, though they knew their danger, in order not to fail their city, courageously they refused.

Before that, in order to give himself a greater appearance of religion and of kindness, the Duke had chosen for his dwelling the convent of the Minor Friars of Santa Croce; so in his eagerness to put his wicked plan into practice, he had it announced by criers that on the following morning all the people should assemble in the piazza of Santa Croce, in his presence. By this proclamation, the Signors were more frightened than earlier they had been by his words, and they consulted with those citizens whom they judged to be lovers of their country and of liberty. Nor did they imagine, knowing the Duke's power, that they could use any other remedy than to beg him and, in this condition where their force was not enough, to see whether their prayers would suffice to divert him from the undertaking or to make his rule less harsh. Hence part of the Signors went to talk with him, and one of them spoke to this effect:

"We come to you, My Lord, moved by your earlier requests and now by the commands you have given for assembling the people, for it seems to us certain that you intend to get unlawfully what we have not granted you by law. It is not our intention to oppose your designs with force, but only to show you how heavy will be the weight that you are taking upon yourself, and how dangerous the decision you are making, in order that always you may remember our advice and that of men who, not for your profit but to vent their own madness, advise you differently.

"You seek to make a slave of a city that has always lived free, because the lordship we once granted to the royal house of Naples was alliance and not servitude. Have you considered how important and how strong in a city like this is the name of liberty, which no force crushes, no time wears away, and no gain counterbalances? Consider, My Lord, what great forces are needed to hold as a slave so great a city. Those whom—foreigners—you can always get are not enough. Those inside you cannot trust, because they who are now your supporters and who encourage you to make this decision, first through your authority will overcome their enemies, and then will try to find a way for destroying you and making themselves rulers. The common people, in whom you trust, are whirled about by any accident, however slight. Hence, in a short time you must fear that all this city will be hostile. This will give cause for her ruin and yours. Against this evil you cannot find defense; because those rulers only can make their rule secure who have few enemies, such as by death or exile they can easily destroy. But in the midst of universal hatred no security is ever to be found, because you do not know from where the evil is going to come; and he who fears all men cannot secure himself against anybody, and if you do try to do so, you augment your dangers, because those who are left are more fiery in their hate and more prepared for vengeance. That there is not time enough for destroying our desire for liberty is most certain, because in a city one often sees it taken up again by men who never have experienced it, but merely because of the tradition that their fathers have left them they continue to love it; therefore, when it has been regained, with the utmost stubbornness and peril they preserve it. And even if their fathers have not recalled it, the public buildings, the offices of the magistrates, the insignia of the free organizations recall it. Of a certainty the citizens will perceive t he meaning o these things with the utmost longing.

"What actions do you intend yours shall be that can counterpoise the sweetness of free government or can cause men to lack all desire for their present state? Not if you should join to this state all of Tuscany, and if every day you should return into this city triumphant over your enemies; because all that glory would be not hers but yours, and the citizens would gain not subjects but fellow slaves, who would assist in laying on the Florentines a heavier burden of servitude. And though your conduct be holy, your manners benig- nant, your judgments just, they will not be enough to make you loved. If you think they will be enough, you deceive yourself, be- cause to one wonted to living unbound, every chain has weight and every bond pinches. So to find a violent government joined with a good prince is impossible, because of necessity either they become alike or one by the other is quickly destroyed. You must then be- lieve either that you can hold this city with the utmost violence (something for which citadels, garrisons, friends from outside are many times not enough) or must be content with what authority we have given you. To this we encourage you by reminding you that only authority freely given is durable; so do not decide, blinded by a little ambition, to get yourself into a place whence, since you cannot remain there or climb higher, by sheer necessity you will fall, with the greatest injury to yourself and to us."

CHAPTER 35

[*The Duke of Athens seizes supreme power. 1342*]

No effect of any sort did these words have on the Duke's hardened mind. He said it was not his purpose to take away the city's liberty, but to give it back again, because only disunited cities were slaves and united ones free. And if Florence, through his government, was rid of factions, ambitions, and enmities, he would give back— not take away—her liberty, and not his own ambition but the prayers of many citizens led him on to undertake this duty. Therefore the Signors addressing him would do well to be pleased with what pleased the others. As to the dangers into which he might enter as a result of this, he did not regard them, because it is the part of a man who is not good to abandon what is right through fear of ill, and of a cowardly one not to carry on a glorious undertaking, because its outcome is uncertain. He believed his conduct would be such as to make them soon recognize that they had trusted him too little and feared him too much. Thereupon the Signors, seeing they could not do anything useful, agreed that on the next morning the people should meet on their Public Square, and that with popular sanction the Duke should receive the sovereignty for a year, under the same conditions as Charles Duke of Calabria earlier accepted.

It was the eighth day of September in the year 1342 when the Duke, accompanied by Messer Giovanni della Tosa and all his companions and by many other citizens, came to the Public Square. Together with the Signoria he mounted the *ringhiera*, for so the Florentines called the steps in front of the Signors' Palace. There the agreements made between the Signoria and him were read to the people. And when they came, in the course of reading, to that part where for one year he obtained sovereignty, there was a shout among the people: "For life!" On the rising of Messer Francesco Rustichegli, one of the Signors, to speak and calm the disturbance, his words were interrupted with shouts. Hence, with the people's consent, not for one year but for life he was chosen ruler, and taken up and carried among the multitude which was shouting his name throughout the Square. It is the custom that he who is in charge of the Palace guard should, in the Signors' absence, be locked inside; that office Rinieri di Giotto was then holding. Bribed by the Duke's friends, without awaiting any violence, he put the Duke inside, and the Signors, bewildered and dishonored, returned to their houses. By the Duke's retinue the Palace was sacked, the people's banner torn up, and his ensigns placed above the Palace. This took place to the incredible sorrow and affliction of good men, and to the great pleasure of those who through either ignorance or malice agreed to it.

CHAPTER 36

[The bad government of the Duke; a conspiracy against him. 1343]

The Duke, when he had gained dominion, in order to deprive of influence those who were accustomed to act as liberty's defenders, forbade the Signors to hold their meetings in the Palace, and assigned them a private house. He took away the ensigns from the gonfaloniers of the Companies of the People; he abolished the Ordinances of Justice made against the nobles; he freed the prisoners from the jails; he had the Bardi and Frescobaldi return from exile. He forbade everybody to carry arms. And to be better able to defend himself from those inside Florence, he made friends of those outside. He showed great favor, therefore, to the Aretines and all the other Florentine subjects; he made peace with the Pisans, though he had been made prince so that he would carry on that war; he confiscated the treasury bills of merchants who had lent money to the republic for the Lucchese war; he increased the old imposts and established new ones; he deprived the Signors of all authority. His rectors were Messer Baglione of Perugia and Messer Guglielmo of Assisi, with whom, and with Messer Cerrettieri Bisdomini, he took council. The taxes he levied on the citizens were heavy and his judgments unjust; the severity and kindness he had pretended were transformed into pride and cruelty, so that many citizens who were nobles or highly esteemed men of lower rank were fined or put to death or tortured in strange ways. And in order not to conduct himself better outside the city than inside, he established six rectors for the surrounding district, who oppressed and plundered the country people.

He was suspicious of the nobility, though they had benefited him and he had restored many of them to their native city, because he could not believe that lofty spirits, such as are likely to be found among the aristocracy, could under his sway feel contented. Therefore he turned to benefiting the lower class, thinking that with their aid and that of foreign arms his tyranny could be preserved. So on the coming of the month of May, a time in which the people are wont to have festivals, he established for the lower class and the humble people more companies, to which, honoring them with splendid titles, he gave banners and money, so that one part of them went through the city in festive array and the other with great pomp received those who were celebrating. When the report was spread of the new authority of this man, many of the French people came to visit him, and to all of them, as to trusted friends, he gave high position, so that in a short time Florence became subject not merely to the French but to their manners and clothing, because men and women, without any respect for orderly life or any shame, imitated them. But above everything else, that which caused indignation was the violence that he and his followers rashly used upon women.

So the citizens were filled with indignation when they saw the majesty of their state ruined, her customs destroyed, her statutes annulled, all honorable living corrupted, all public modesty ex/ tinguished. Those accustomed not to see any regal splendor could not but feel pain whenever they encountered that ruler, surrounded with armed retainers on foot and on horseback. For thus, seeing their shame near at hand, they were forced to honor him whom they especially hated. To their pain was added fear, since they saw the frequent executions and incessant taxes with which he impoverished and devoured the city. Their anger and fear the Duke knew and dreaded. Nevertheless he determined to show everybody that he believed the citizens loved him. For this reason, when Matteo di Morozzo, either to get favor or to free himself from peril, revealed to the Duke that the Medici family with some others had conspired against him, the Duke not only did not investigate the charge but inflicted on the discloser a disgraceful death. By that decision he deprived of resolution those who would have warned him about his safety and gave it to those seeking his ruin. He also had Bettone Cini's tongue cut out with such great cruelty that he died of it, be/ cause Bettone railed at the taxes laid on the citizens. This incident increased the anger of the citizens and their hatred for the Duke, because a city accustomed to doing and speaking of everything and with the utmost latitude, could not endure to have her hands bound and her mouth tight shut.

This anger and this hatred so increased, then, that not merely the Florentines—who cannot keep their liberty and yet cannot endure servitude—but the most servile of peoples would have flamed up for the regaining of their liberty. Hence many citizens, of every sort, determined to lose their lives or to have their liberty again; and in three parties, by three kinds of citizens, three conspiracies were made: the nobles, the people of some wealth, and the working men. They were moved, in addition to general causes, through realization by the nobles that they were not going to get control of the government again, by the people of the middle class that they had lost it, and by the working men that their earnings were diminishing.

At that time the Archbishop of Florence was Messer Agnolo Acciaiuoli, who in his sermons had earlier praised the Duke's ac/ tions and won him much favor with the people. But when he saw the Duke in power and realized his tyrannical ways, he knew that he had deceived his own city, and to make good the fault he had com/

mitted, he believed he had no other means than that the hand that gave the wound should heal it. So he made himself head of the first and strongest conspiracy; in it were the Bardi, Rossi, Frescobaldi, Scali, Altoviti, Magalotti, Strozzi, and Mancini. Of one of the other two, the heads were Messers Manno and Corso Donati; and with these were the Pazzi, Cavicciuli, Cerchi, and Albizzi. Of the third, the leader was Antonio Adimari; and with him were the Medi- ci,[1] Bordoni, Rucellai, and Aldobrandini. At first these thought of killing him in the Albizzi mansion, where he was going on St. John's day to see the horses race, as they supposed, but since he did not go there, they did not succeed. They thought of attacking him when he was going through the city for pleasure, but saw that this method was difficult because he usually went well accompanied and armed, and always varied his routes, so that they could not await him in any certain place. They talked of killing him in the Council Chamber, but they knew that there, even though he was killed, they would be in the power of his forces.

While among the conspirators these things were being discussed, Antonio Adimari revealed himself to some of his Sienese friends, in order to get soldiers from them, disclosing to them part of the con- spirators and asserting that the whole city was inclined to free herself. One of the Sienese spoke of the matter to Messer Francesco Brunel- leschi, not to expose it, but in the belief that he too was one of the conspirators. Messer Francesco, either in fear for himself or in his hatred for the others, revealed it all to the Duke. Therefore Pagolo del Mazzeca and Simone da Monterappoli were arrested. By reveal- ing the quality and the number of the conspirators, they frightened the Duke, and he was advised rather to summon them than to arrest them because, if they fled, he would without disorder, by means of their exile, make himself secure. So the Duke had Antonio Adi- mari summoned, and he, confiding in his companions, at once appeared. He was imprisoned. Messer Francesco Brunelleschi and Messer Uguccione Buondelmonti advised the Duke to ride armed through the city and to put to death those he arrested. But he did not think it a good thing, since for so many enemies his forces were too small. And therefore he chose another plan, by means of which, if it had succeeded, he would have secured himself against his ene-

---

1. *The Medici here appear with others as leaders of the humble Florentines; otherwise they would be ranked among those engaged in the second conspiracy.*

mies and made provision against their forces. The Duke was in the habit of calling citizens together to give him advice on current mat⁄ters. So, after sending out of the city to obtain soldiers, he made a list of three hundred citizens, and had them summoned by his officers, with the excuse that he wished to consult with them, and when they had come together, he intended to get rid of them, either with death or with imprisonment. The arrest of Antonio Adimari and the sending for the soldiers, which could not be done secretly, had frightened the citizens, especially those who were guilty, so that the more courageous said they were not going to obey. And because everybody had read the list, they learned about each other, and were given courage to take arms and plan to die like men with arms in their hands, rather than like cattle to be led to the slaughterhouse, so that in a short time the three groups of conspirators were all disclosed to each other. Hence they decided on the day following, which was the twenty⁄sixth of July, 1343, to start an uproar in the Old Market⁄place, and after that to arm themselves and call the people to liberty.

CHAPTER 37
[*The Duke is expelled from the city. 1343*]

When the next day came, at the stroke of nones, according to arrangement, the conspirators took arms, and on hearing the word *liberty* all the people armed themselves; each man got ready for fighting in his neighborhood, under banners with the people's in⁄signia which the conspirators had prepared secretly. All the heads of families, both noble and from the people, came together and pledged their own defense and the death of the Duke, except some of the Buondelmonti and the Cavalcanti and those four families from the people that had joined to make him ruler. These, with the butchers and others of the lowest class, gathered in arms on the Public Square in support of the Duke. At this uproar the Duke armed the Palace; his followers, who were lodged in various places, mounted their horses to go to the Public Square. On the way they were in many places attacked and killed; yet about three hundred cavalry got there. The Duke was uncertain whether he should go out and fight his enemies or whether, remaining inside, he should defend the Palace.

On the other hand, the Medici, Cavicciuli, Rucellai, and other families whom he had most injured feared that if he should come out many who had taken arms against him would show themselves his friends; so, to give him no chance for coming out and increasing his force, they united and attacked the Public Square. At their ap' proach, those families from the people who had openly declared for the Duke, seeing that they were boldly attacked, changed their opin' ion, since the Duke's fortune had changed, and all sided with their fellow citizens except Uguccione Buondelmonti, who went into the Palace, and Messer Gianozzo Cavalcanti, who, retreating with part of his associates into the New Marketplace, got on a bench and begged the people who were going armed to the Public Square to go on the Duke's behalf; to terrify them, he exaggerated his forces and threatened that they would all be killed if they stubbornly continued their attempt against the ruler. Not finding a man who would fol' low him or one who would punish him for his arrogance, and seeing that he worked in vain, in order to tempt Fortune no longer, he retired to his house.

Meanwhile, the combat in the Public Square between the popu' lace and the soldiers of the Duke was severe; though the Palace gave aid, the soldiers were overcome, and part surrendered to their enemies, part, leaving their horses, fled into the Palace. While in the Square the fighting was going on, Corso and Messer Amerigo Donati, with part of the people, broke open the Stinche, burned the writings of the Podestà and of the Public Chamber, sacked the Rectors' houses, and killed such officers of the Duke as they could take. The Duke, on the other hand, seeing that he had lost the Square, that all the city was hostile, and that he was without hope of any aid, attempted to gain the people over by various kind acts; having the prisoners come before him, with loving and gracious words he freed them; Antonio Adimari, though to that man's displeasure, he made a knight. He had his ensigns removed from over the palace and those of the people put there—things which, done late and at the wrong time, because they were forced and without generosity, helped him little. Meanwhile he was anxious, besieged in the Palace, for he saw that by wanting too much he had lost everything, and feared that either by hunger or by steel he would in a few days have to die.

The citizens, to give form to the government, went to Santa Reparata and put in authority fourteen citizens, half nobles and half from the people, who with the Bishop had complete power to re' organize the government of Florence. They also chose six who would have the Podestà's power until the arrival of him who was chosen.

Many had come to Florence to assist the people, among whom were some Sienese with six ambassadors, men in their native city much respected. These tried to arrange terms between the Duke and the people, but the people refused to discuss any agreement until Messer Guglielmo of Assisi and his son were given into their power, together with Messer Cerrettieri Bisdomini. By no means did the Duke wish to agree, but, threatened by the people who were shut up with him, he let himself be compelled. It is evident beyond doubt that hatreds are greater and wounds more serious when liberty is got back than when it is defended. So then Messer Guglielmo and his son were put among thousands of their enemies—his son was not yet eighteen years old; nevertheless not his age, not his beauty, not his innocence could save him from the fury of the multitude—and they who could not wound them when alive wounded them when dead and, not sated by rending them with steel, tore them with their hands and teeth. And that all their senses might be satisfied with revenge, after having first heard their laments, seen their wounds, touched their torn bodies, they let taste also take pleasure in them, so that, since all the outside parts had been sated, those within might also gain satiety. This insane fury, in proportion as it injured Messer Guglielmo and his son, was useful to Messer Cerrettieri, because when the multitude was exhausted with its cruelty to these two, it did not remember him; not being further asked for, he remained in the Palace, from which, the night after, certain of his relatives and friends safely brought him out.

The multitude's rage having vented itself on the blood of these two, an agreement was made: the Duke with his men and property was permitted to go out in safety; he must renounce all the rights he had to Florence; then, outside the Dominion, in the Casentino, he must ratify his renunciation. After this agreement, on the sixth day of August, he departed from Florence accompanied by many citizens, and when he had arrived in the Casentino, he ratified his renunciation, though unwillingly; he would not have kept his pledge if Count Simon[1] had not threatened to take him back to Florence.

This Duke, as his conduct showed, was avaricious and cruel; in interviews unpleasant, in replies arrogant; he desired the servitude,

1. *Count of Poppi, in the Casentino.*

not the good will of men; therefore he wished to be feared rather than to be loved. Nor was his appearance less hateful in its nature than were his manners, for he was little and dark, his beard was long and thin, so that in every way he deserved to be hated. Hence in the space of ten months his wicked conduct took from him the lordship which the wicked advice of others had given him.

CHAPTER 38
[*Revolt of various Tuscan cities. 1343*]

These events in the city gave courage to all the towns subject to the Florentines to return to their liberty, so that Arezzo, Castiglione, Pistoia, Volterra, Colle, and San Gimignano rebelled. Hence Florence, in an instant, was deprived of her tyrant and of her empire, and in regaining her own liberty, she taught her subjects how to regain theirs. After the expulsion of the Duke and the loss of their empire, the fourteen citizens and the Bishop decided it was better to please their subjects with peace than to make them enemies with war, and to show that they were as well pleased with the liberty of others as with their own. Therefore they sent ambassadors to Arezzo to renounce the control they had over that city and to establish an agreement with the Aretines so that though Florence could not have their support as subjects, she could still get assistance from them as allies. With the other towns also Florence made such agreements as she could, asking only that the towns would continue as her allies, so that their free citizens could help Florence keep her liberty.

This policy, prudently adopted, had a most happy result, because Arezzo not many years later came back under Florentine sovereignty, and the other cities in a few months were brought back to their earlier subjection. Thus many times things are gained more quickly and with fewer dangers and expense by running away from them than by striving with all one's force and determination to overtake them.

CHAPTER 39
[*The new government of Florence; quarrels between rich and middle class. 1343*]

Having quieted things outside, the Florentines turned to those inside. And after some dispute between the nobility and the people, they decided that the nobility should have a third part in the Signoria, and half in the other offices. As we showed above, the city was divided into sixths, so that always six Signors were chosen, one from each sixth, except that, because of something unusual, sometimes twelve or thirteen were elected, but soon after they were put back to six. It appeared good, therefore, to reorganize her in this matter, both because the sixths were badly distributed and because, if part were to be given to the nobles, the number of the Signors had to be increased. So they divided the city into quarters, and from each one chose three Signors. They omitted the Gonfalonier of Justice and those of the Companies of the People, and in exchange for the twelve Good Men, eight Councillors, four of each sort, were set up.

On the confirming of a government with this organization, the city would have been quiet if the nobles had been content to live with the modesty demanded by life as citizens, but they did the opposite, because in private life they tolerated no equals, and in the magistracies they were determined to be lords, and every day there was some instance of their arrogance and pride. This offended the people, who lamented that for one tyrant who had been removed a thousand had sprung up. There was such an increase, then, in one party's arrogance and the other's anger that the heads of the people showed the Bishop the nobles' lack of integrity and their poor co-operation with the people, and persuaded him to try to arrange to satisfy the nobility with their part in the other offices, entirely aban-doning to the people the magistracy of the Signors. Now the Bishop naturally was good, but it was easy to turn him now in this, now in that direction. As a result, at the urging of his companions he had first favored the Duke of Athens, and later, on the advice of other citizens, had conspired against him. He had, in the reorganization of the government, favored the nobles, and so it now seemed to him right to favor the people, moved by the reasons that those unaristo-cratic citizens presented to him. Believing he would find in others the same instability as in himself, he supposed he could bring the thing about by agreement. So he assembled the Fourteen, who still had not lost their authority and, with the best words he could use, encouraged them to consent to yield the office of the Signoria to the people, promising as a result the quiet of the city, otherwise ruin and undoing for themselves. These words roused to great anger the spirits of the nobles, and Messer Ridolfo de' Bardi in harsh words censured him, calling him a man of little fidelity, and rebuking him as fickle for his friendship with the Duke, and as a traitor for the Duke's expulsion. And he ended by saying that those offices which with danger to themselves they had secured, they were resolved with danger to themselves to defend.

With the others, he left the Bishop's presence in anger, and made it known to his associates and to all the noble families. The leaders of the people also expressed their opinion. And while the nobles with their helpers were getting ready for the defense of their Signors, the people decided not to wait until they were in order, and ran armed to the Palace, shouting that they wanted the nobles to re nounce the magistracy. The noise and disturbance were great. The Signors saw that they were abandoned, because the nobles, seeing all the people armed, did not dare to take arms, and each man remained in his mansion. Hence the non aristocratic Signors first made an effort to quiet the people by insisting that their companions were modest and good, but did not succeed. Then, as the least bad choice, they sent the aristocratic Signors each man to his own house, where with difficulty they were safely brought. When the nobles had left the Palace, the four noble Councillors were also deprived of their offices, which were given to twelve men of the people. The eight Signors who were left chose a Gonfalonier of Justice and sixteen gonfaloniers for the Companies of the People, and reorganized the councils in such a way that the entire government was in the control of the people.

CHAPTER 40

[The rebellion of Andrea Strozzi; the nobility and the people prepare for civil war. 1343]

While these things were going on, there was a serious shortage of food in the city, so that the nobles and humbler people were both discontented, the latter through hunger, the former because they had lost their offices. This situation gave Messer Andrea Strozzi the belief that he could seize the liberty of the city. He sold his grain at a lower price than the others, and so at his house many people gathered. Hence one morning he took courage to mount his horse, with some supporters following him, and to call the people to arms; in a short time he brought together more than four thousand men, with whom he went to the Square of the Signors and asked that the Palace should be opened to them. But the Signors with threats and arms got them away from the Square. Then they so frightened the rioters with proclamations that little by little they all returned to their houses; hence Messer Andrea, finding himself alone, with difficulty saved himself from the hands of the magistrates by flight.

This attempt, though it was foolhardy and had such an end as similar risings are wont to have, gave the nobles hope that they could overcome the people, since the lowest class was at variance with the more prosperous. In order not to lose this opportunity, the nobles decided to furnish themselves with all sorts of assistance, in order to get again by force, reasonably, what unjustly by force had been taken from them. And they grew into such confidence of success that they openly provided themselves with arms, fortified their houses, and sent to their friends, as far as Lombardy, for help. The people also, together with the Signors, made their preparations, arming themselves and calling on the Perugians and the Sienese for aid. Already some help for both sides had appeared; the whole city was under arms.

By this time the nobles had assembled on the north side of Arno in three places: at the houses of the Cavicciuli near San Giovanni, at the houses of the Pazzi and the Donati near San Piero Maggiore, at those of the Cavalcanti in the New Marketplace. Those on the south side of Arno were fortified at the bridges and in the streets passing their houses: the Nerli at the Ponte alla Carraia, the Frescobaldi and Mannegli at Santa Trínita, the Rossi and Bardi at the Ponte Vecchio and Rubaconte were ready for defense. The people on the other hand, under the Gonfalon of Justice and the banners of the Companies of the People, had united their forces.

CHAPTER 41
[*The rich are defeated. 1343*]

In these conditions, the people decided that they should no longer defer the combat. The first that moved were the Medici and the Rondinegli, who attacked the Cavicciuli on that side where the Piazza of San Giovanni gives entrance to their houses. There the combat was serious, because from the towers they were struck with stones and from below they were wounded with cross-bows. This battle lasted three hours; and all the time the people were increasing, so that the Cavicciuli, seeing themselves outnumbered by the multitude and lacking help, were frightened and gave themselves into the hands of the people. These protected for them their houses and their property; they merely took away their arms and commanded that, without weapons, they should scatter among the houses of such of the people as were their relatives and friends. After the success of this first attack, the Donati and Pazzi were also easily defeated, because they were less powerful than the others. There remained on the north side of Arno only the Cavalcanti, who in men and in physical situation were strong. Nonetheless, seeing all the companies against them and the others overcome by three companies only, without making much resistance they surrendered.

Already three parts of the city were in the hands of the people; there remained one in the hands of the nobles, but it was the most difficult, both because of the strength of those who defended it and because of its site, since it was protected by the Arno River, so that it was necessary to win the bridges, which were defended in the ways described above. The Ponte Vecchio was the first attacked; it was vigorously maintained, because the towers were armed, the streets were barricaded, and the barricades were defended by very spirited men, so that the people were driven back with serious loss. Realizing, as a result, that there they were laboring in vain, they tried to cross on the Ponte Rubaconte, and finding there the same difficulties, they left as a guard for those two bridges four companies, and with the others attacked the Ponte alla Carraia. Though the Nerli vigorously defended themselves, they could not sustain the fury of the people, both because the bridge (not having towers that defended it) was weaker, and because the Capponi and other popular families who were their neighbors attacked them. So, being assailed on all sides, they abandoned the barricades and gave passage to the people, who after this overcame the Rossi and the Frescobaldi, so that all the people on the other side of the Arno joined with the winners. There remained, then, only the Bardi, whom neither the overthrow of the others, nor the union of the people against them, nor their slight hope of aid could terrify; they preferred either to die in combat or to see their houses burned and sacked than of their own will to submit to the power of their enemies. They defended themselves, therefore, so well that the people tried many times in vain, both at the Ponte

Vecchio and at the Ponte Rubaconte, to defeat them. And always with death and wounds for many they were driven back. It happened that in times past a street had been made leading from the Via Romana and passing among the houses of the Pitti to the walls built on the hill of San Giorgio. By this street the people sent six companies, with the arrangement that from the rear they should attack the houses of the Bardi. This attack made the Bardi lose courage and made the people succeed in their attempt, because, when those guarding the barricades in the streets learned that their houses were attacked, they abandoned the combat and ran to their defense. This enabled the people to take the barricade of the Ponte Vecchio, and the Bardi were everywhere put to flight; they were sheltered by the Quaratesi, the Panzanesi, and the Mozzi. The people (the most worthless part of them) thirsty for booty, in the meantime spoiled and sacked all the Bardi houses, and destroyed and burned their palaces and towers with such fury that of such great ruin the cruelest enemy of the Florentine name would have been ashamed.

CHAPTER 42

[*The Florentine nobility ruined; pestilence. 1343–1353*]

When the nobility were conquered, the people reorganized the government, and because there were three sorts of people, the powerful, the average and the lowly, they arranged that the powerful should have two Signors, the average three, and the lowly three; the Gonfalonier was to be now of one, now of the other class. Besides this, all the Ordinances of Justice were re-enacted against the nobles and (further weakening them) many nobles were mingled with the general multitude. This ruin of the nobles was so great and so humbled their party that never afterwards did they have courage to take arms against the people; on the contrary they steadily became more courteous and abject. Thus Florence was stripped not merely of arms but of all magnanimity.

After this ruin, the city continued quiet until the year 1353. That was the time of that memorable plague made famous with such eloquence by Messer Giovanni Boccaccio; in Florence it destroyed more than ninety-six thousand souls. Also the Florentines carried on their first war with the Visconti, caused by the ambition of the Archbishop, then prince of Milan. No sooner was this war ended than party strife within the city began, for though the nobility was destroyed, nonetheless Fortune did not lack ways for making new dissensions cause new woes.

BOOK THREE

[FLORENCE FROM 1353 TO 1414]

CHAPTER 1

[Enmity between nobles and people in Rome and in Florence]

The serious and natural enmities between the people and the nobles, caused by the latter's wish to rule and the former's not to be enthralled, bring about all the evils that spring up in cities; by this opposition of parties all the other things that disturb republics are nourished. This kept Rome disunited. This, if small things with great may be compared, has kept Florence divided, though in the two cities diverse effects were produced, because the enmities that at the outset existed in Rome between the people and the nobles were ended by debating, those in Florence by fighting; those in Rome were terminated by law, those in Florence by the exile and death of many citizens; those in Rome always increased military power, those in Florence wholly destroyed it; those in Rome brought that city from an equality of citizens to a very great inequality; those in Florence brought her from inequality to a striking equality.

It must be that this difference of effects was caused by the different purposes of these two peoples, for the people of Rome wished to enjoy supreme honors along with the nobles; the people of Florence fought to be alone in the government, without any participation in it by the nobles. Because the Roman people's desire was more reasonable, their injuries to the nobles were more endurable, so that the nobility yielded easily and without coming to arms; hence, after some debates, they agreed in making a law with which the people would be satisfied and by which the nobles would remain in their public offices. On the other hand, the Florentine people's desire was harmful and unjust, so that the nobility with greater forces prepared to defend themselves, and therefore the result was blood and the exile of citizens, and the laws then made were planned not for the common profit but altogether in favor of the conqueror. From this it also resulted that through the people's victories the city of Rome became more excellent, because, along with nobles, men from the people could be appointed to administer the magistracies, the armies, and the high offices; thus the latter acquired the same ability the former had, and that city, as she increased in excellence, increased in power. But in Florence, since the people won, the nobles continued to be deprived of high offices, and if they wished to get them again, they were forced in their conduct, their spirit, and their way of living not merely to be like the men of the people, but to seem so. From this came the changes in ensigns, the alterations in the titles of families that the nobles carried out in order to seem like the people. Hence the ability in arms and the boldness of spirit possessed by the nobility were destroyed, and these qualities could not be rekindled in the people, where they did not exist, so that Florence grew always weaker and more despicable. Whereas Rome, when that excellence of her citizens was turned into pride, was brought to such a pass that she could not keep going without a prince, Florence has come to such a condition that easily a wise lawgiver could reorganize her with al-most any form of government.[1]

These things can in part be clearly recognized on reading the preceding book, which has shown the birth of Florence and the beginning of her liberty, with the reasons for her divisions, and how the parties of the nobles and of the people ended in tyranny by the Duke of Athens and the ruin of the nobility. It now remains to narrate the enmities between the people of the higher classes and those of the lowest class, and the various events they generated.

1. *Cf. the* DISCOURSE ON REMODELING THE GOVERNMENT OF FLORENCE, *on the greater ease of establishing a republic, p. 101, above.*

CHAPTER 2

[The mercenaries of Monreale enter Tuscany, 1353; the quarrels of the Ricci and Albizzi]

When the power of the nobles had been overthrown and the war with the Archbishop of Milan was finished, it seemed that in Flor-ence no reason for division would be left. But our city's ill fortune and her not-good laws made enmity arise between the Albizzi family and the Ricci family. This enmity divided Florence, as earlier that between the Buondelmonti and Uberti, and later that between the Donati and Cerchi had divided her.

The pontiffs, who were then living in France, and the emperors, who were in Germany, in order to maintain their reputations in

Italy, at various times sent soldiers of various nationalities in great numbers, so that in those times there were English, Germans, and Bretons in the country. These, when at the end of the wars they were left without pay, served under the banner of some adventurer, and made requisitions upon this prince and that one. In the year 1353, then, one of these companies came into Tuscany, led by Monreale, a Provençal. His coming terrified all the cities of the province, and the Florentines not merely provided soldiers by government action, but also many citizens, among them the Albizzi and the Ricci, took arms for their own safety.

These families were full of hatred against one another, and each was considering how to put the other down, in order to gain first place in the state. They had not yet, however, come to blows, but opposed one another merely in the magistracies and the councils. When the whole city was armed, then, there chanced to be a quarrel in the Old Marketplace, where many people gathered, as is usual when such things happen. As the news spread, a report came to the Ricci that the Albizzi were attacking them, and to the Albizzi that the Ricci were coming to assail them. The city was all upset by this, and the magistrates with difficulty managed to restrain both families, so that the combat, which by chance and without the fault of either, had been rumored, would not actually occur. This event, though slight, made their spirits still more fiery, and with greater effort each one sought to gain partisans. Yet because already, through the ruin of the nobility, the citizens had attained such equality that the magistrates were respected more than had been usual in the past, the two families planned to gain superiority in a lawful way and without private violence.

CHAPTER 3

[Guelfs and Ghibellines again; admonition. 1357-1366]

We have already related that, after the victory of Charles I, the magistracy of the Guelf party was set up and received great authority over the Ghibellines. This authority through time, through various happenings, and through new divisions had so nearly fallen into oblivion that many descended from Ghibellines held the chief magistracies. Uguccione de' Ricci, therefore, head of his family, strove for renewal of the law against the Ghibellines, among whom, as many thought, were the Albizzi, who, having originated many years before in Arezzo, had come to live in Florence. So Uguccione by re^ newing this law intended to exclude the Albizzi from public offices, since it laid down that any descendant from a Ghibelline would be penalized if he carried on any duties as a magistrate. Uguccione's plan was discovered by Piero di Filippo degli Albizzi; and he decided to favor it, thinking that if he opposed it he would himself be declared a Ghibelline. This law, then, renewed by the ambition of the other man, did not take away reputation from Piero degli Albizzi but gave it to him, and was the beginning of many evils. No law more damaging for a republic can be made than one that looks back a long time.

Since, then, Piero favored the law, what his enemies had devised to impede him became his road to greatness, because having made himself the chief of this new party, he continually got new authority, since this new sect of Guelfs favored him more than any other. Because no magistrate would try to find out who the Ghibellines were, and the law that had been made was not of much force, he provided that authority should be given to the Captains to learn who were Ghibellines, and when that had been learned, to notify them and admonish them not to take any magistracy. If they did not obey this admonition, they were to be penalized. This is the reason why all those in Florence who are deprived of power to act as magistrates are called *admonished*. The Captains, then, as with time their boldness increased, admonished without any hesitation not merely those who deserved it but whomsoever they pleased, when moved by any sort of avaricious or ambitious reason. And from 1357, when this plan was begun, to 1366, more than two hundred citizens had already been admonished. Through this the Captains and the faction of the Guelfs became powerful, because everybody, through fear of being admonished, showed respect to them and especially to their heads, who were Piero degli Albizzi, Messer Lapo da Castiglionchio, and Carlo Strozzi. Though this high^handed mode of proceeding ex^ asperated many, the Ricci were more vexed than any others, since they knew they had caused this abuse, by which they saw that the republic was ruined and that contrary to their plan their enemies the Albizzi had become very powerful.

CHAPTER 4

[Further enmity between the Ricci and the Albizzi, 1366–1371]

Uguccione de' Ricci, then, being himself one of the Signors, determined to end the evil that he and his associates had caused, and with a new law he provided that to the six Captains of the Party three should be added, two of which should come from the minor gildsmen; and he provided that the Ghibellines who had been discovered must be so declared by twenty-four Guelf citizens, chosen for that purpose. This provision for the time moderated to a great extent the power of the Captains, so that the admonishing for the most part disappeared; though some were admonished, they were but few. Nevertheless, the factions of the Albizzi and the Ricci were active; and they opposed laws, actions, and decisions because of their hate for each other. So things went on with such troubles from 1366 to 1371, the time when the Guelf faction regained power.

In the Buondelmonti family there was a knight named Messer Benchi, who by reason of meritorious deeds in a war against the Pisans had been made one of the people; therefore he was qualified to be one of the Signors. Yet when he expected to sit in that magistracy, a law was made that no noble who had been made one of the people should occupy it. This action greatly offended Messer Benchi, who joined forces with Piero degli Albizzi; they determined with admonition to crush the people of the lower class and to remain alone in the government. Through the favor that Messer Benchi had with the ancient nobility, and through that which Piero had with the greater part of the influential men among the people, they caused the Guelf faction to regain its power, and by means of new reorganizations in the party, they so arranged things that they managed the Captains and the Twenty-four Citizens as they pleased. Then they went back to admonishing with more boldness than before, and the Albizzi house, as head of that faction, always grew more powerful. On the other side, the Ricci and their friends did not fail to impede their designs as much as they could. Hence life was full of fear, and everybody dreaded complete ruin for himself.

CHAPTER 5

[*An oration on factions and disregard for the common good in Flor- ence. 1372*]

Hence many citizens, moved by love for their country, met in San Piero Scheraggio, and after much debate among themselves over these abuses, they went to the Signors, to whom the one of most standing spoke as follows:

"Many of us, reverend Signors, were afraid to meet together by private arrangement, even for a public reason, judging that we would be marked as presumptuous or condemned as ambitious. But having observed that every day, and without any precaution, many citizens assemble in the loggias or in houses, not for any public profit but for their own ambition, we judged that since these who come together for the ruin of the republic have no fear, they too should have no fear who come together for its good and profit, and that we ought not to care what opinion others have about us, since the others do not regard what opinion we have about them. The love we bear, reverend Signors, to our native city has first made us assemble, and now makes us come to you to talk of that evil which is already great and which all the time is increasing in our republic, and to offer ourselves as ready to assist you in getting rid of it. You can succeed in this, though the undertaking seems difficult, if you will disregard private concerns and use your authority over the public forces.

"The general depravity of all Italian cities, reverend Signors, has depraved and continues to deprave our city, because, from the time when this region withdrew itself from under the power of the Empire, its cities, not having a strong rein to guide them, have organized their states and governments not as free but as divided into factions. From this has come all the other ills, all the other enormities that appear in them. First, there is among the citizens neither union nor friendship, except among those who are sharers in some wickedness, undertaken either against their city or against individuals. And because religion and the fear of God have been extinguished in all men, an oath and a pledge are valuable as far as they are profitable, for men employ them not with the purpose of observing them, but to use them as means for deceiving more easily. And the more easily and securely the deception succeeds, the more glory and honor it gains. Hence pernicious men are praised for their ingenuity, and good men blamed as foolish. Truly in the cities of Italy all is collected that can be depraved and that can deprave any man: the young are lazy, the old licentious, and both sexes and every age abound in vile habits. Good laws, because they are ruined by bad customs, do not remedy this condition.

"The result is the avarice which the citizens display, and their thirst not for true glory but for despicable honors depending on hates, enmities, disputes, factions. From these result deaths, exiles, persecutions of the good, honors for the wicked. The good, trusting in their innocence, do not seek, like the wicked, for those who will unlawfully defend and honor them; hence they fall undefended and unhonored. This situation produces love of parties and their power, the wicked adhere to factions through avarice and ambition, the good through necessity. Still more harmful it is that the movers and originators of these parties with a pious word make their plan and purpose seem honorable; because always, since they are all enemies to liberty, they crush her under the pretense of defending a state of aristocrats or a popular government because the reward they desire from victory is not the glory of having freed the city, but the satisfaction of having conquered the others and usurped their dominion. Once having succeeded, there is not a thing so unjust, so cruel, so avaricious that they do not dare to do it. Hence they make laws and statutes not for the public benefit but for their own; hence wars, truces, alliances are decided not for the common glory but for the pleasure of a few.

"If other cities are filled with these abuses, ours is more soiled with them than any other, for the laws, the statutes, the methods of government here always have been managed and now are managed not as required by free government but as required by the ambition of the party on top. The result is that when one party has been defeated and one division has been got rid of, another appears, because if a city tries to sustain herself by means of factions rather than of laws, when one of her factions is left without opposition, of necessity that city becomes divided, because those private methods that she earlier adopted for her security cannot defend her. That this is true, our city's ancient and recent divisions show. Everybody believed, when the Ghibellines were destroyed, that the Guelfs would then long live in happiness and honor; nevertheless, after a short time they were divided into Whites and Blacks. After the Whites were overcome, the city was never without parties; we were always fighting, now to aid the exiles, now because of the hostilities between the people and the nobles. In order to give to someone else what we would not or could not keep by agreement among our-selves, we subjected our liberty now to King Robert, now to his brother, now to his son, and finally to the Duke of Athens.

"Yet we never were quiet in any condition, since we never have agreed on living in freedom, and yet are not willing to be slaves. We did not hesitate, so greatly are our ways inclined to divisions, when we were living under the authority of the King, to subordinate his majesty to an utterly vile man born in Gubbio. The Duke of Athens should not be mentioned, for the honor of this city; his harsh and tyrannical spirit should have made us wise and taught us how to live. Nonetheless, as soon as he was driven out, we had our weapons in our hands and, with more hatred and greater fury than ever at any other time we fought with each other, we fought until our ancient nobility was overcome and surrendered itself to the decision of the people. And many believed that never again would any cause for division or for parties appear in Florence, since a bridle had been put upon those who through their pride and unbearable ambition seemed to have caused the trouble.

"But now it can be seen from experience how deceptive the opin-ion of men is and how false their judgment, for the pride and ambition of our nobles were not destroyed but were taken away from them by our people, who now, according to the habit of ambitious men, strive to gain first rank in the republic. Since they have no other way to gain it than through dissensions, they have divided the city once more, and the names of Guelf and Ghibelline, which had been destroyed—and it would have been well if they had never existed in this republic—they are now reviving. It is given from on high, in order that in human things there may be nothing either lasting or at rest, that in all republics there are fated families, born for their ruin. Our republic, more than any other, has abounded in these, for not one but many have stirred up and distressed her, as the Buondelmonti and Uberti did first, then the Donati and Cerchi, and now, oh thing shameful and ridiculous! the Ricci and the Albizzi stir her up and divide her.

"We have not reminded you of our corrupt habits and our ancient and continual divisions in order to frighten you, but to remind you of their causes and to show you that, just as you can remember them, we remember them, and to tell you that the example of those ought not to make you despair of restraining the present ones. Because in those ancient families power was so great, and so great the favors that they had from princes, that legal methods and ways were not enough to restrain them. But now that the Empire has no power over us, the Pope is not feared, and all Italy and this city are brought to such equality that by herself she can govern herself, the difficulty is not great.

"This republic of ours, indeed, notwithstanding the ancient instances on the other side, is especially adapted not merely to union but to reformation by means of good procedures and lawful methods, if only Your Lordships decide to act. Moved by love of our city, not by any private passion, we encourage you to this. Though her depravity is great, destroy at once the disease of which she is sick, the fury that wastes her, the poison that kills her; charge the ancient abuses not to the nature of the people but to the times. Since they have changed, you can hope for better Fortune for our city as a result of better laws. Fortune's malice can be overcome with prudence, if you check the ambition of the men I have mentioned, annul the laws that breed factions, and adopt those suitable for a truly free and law-abiding government. We trust that you will decide to do it now with the help of the laws rather than, by deferring it, to force men to do it by using weapons."

CHAPTER 6

[An unsuccessful attempt at reform. 1372]

The Signors, moved first by what they already knew for themselves, and then by the influence and encouragement of the speakers, gave power to fifty-six citizens to provide for the safety of the republic. It is very true that most men are better suited to keeping a good system than to understanding how, by themselves, to devise one. These citizens thought more about getting rid of the existing factions than about taking away the causes for future ones. Hence they did not succeed in doing either, since they did not remove the causes for new factions, and of those which existed they made one more power-ful than the other, with increased danger to the republic.

They excluded, then, for three years, from all magistracies, except those of the Guelf party, three of the Albizzi family, and three of the Ricci family, among whom were Piero degli Albizzi and Uguccione de' Ricci. They prohibited all citizens from entering the Palace, except when the magistrates were sitting. They provided that any-body who was assaulted, or interfered with in the possession of his goods, could with one complaint accuse the guilty man to the Councils and have him declared one of the nobility, and as so declared have him subjected to its disabilities. This provision took away the zeal of the Ricci faction and increased that of the Albizzi, because, though they were equally designated as guilty, yet the Ricci suffered more from it. The Palace of the Signors was indeed closed to Piero degli Albizzi, but that of the Guelfs, where he had very great power, remained open to him, and though earlier he and his followers were hot to admonish, after this injury they became very hot. To this ill will, further new causes were added.

CHAPTER 7
[*War with Pope Gregory XI. 1375*]

Since Pope Gregory XI, who was seated on the papal throne, lived at Avignon, he governed Italy through legates, as his prede-cessors had done. These legates, being very avaricious and proud, had oppressed many cities. One of them, who in those days was at Bologna, taking advantage of the famine in Florence that year, planned to make himself master of Tuscany; hence not merely did he not supply the Florentines with food, but in order to take from them the hope of future harvests, he assailed them, as soon as spring came, with a large army, since when they were unarmed and hungry, he hoped to conquer them easily. Perhaps he would have succeeded if the troops with which he attacked had not been faithless and subject to purchase, because the Florentines, having no better remedy, gave his soldiers a hundred and thirty thousand florins and caused them to abandon the campaign. Wars are begun at will but not ended at will. This war, begun by the legate's ambition, was con-tinued by the Florentines' anger. They made an alliance with Messer

Bernabò Visconti of Milan and with all the cities hostile to the Church, and appointed eight citizens to take charge of the war, with authority to act without appeal and to spend without giving any account.

This war undertaken against the Pope, though Uguccione de' Ricci was dead, roused to activity the partisans of the Ricci faction. Being opposed to the Albizzi, they had always supported Messer Bernabò and acted against the Church, and so much the more because the Eight were all enemies to the Guelf faction. This caused Piero degli Albizzi, Messer Lapo da Castiglionchio, Carlo Strozzi, and others to draw more closely together for the injury of their adversaries, so while the Eight carried on the war, the Guelfs admonished. The war lasted three years, ending only with the Pope's death. The Eight managed it with such effectiveness and satisfaction to the citizens generally that every year their term of office was extended. They were called saints, even though they had little regard for the Censures, stripped the churches of their property, and forced the clergy to celebrate the offices. So much higher did those citizens then value their city than their souls! They proved to the Church that just as earlier, being her friends, they had defended her, so, being her enemies, they could distress her, for they caused all the Romagna, the March, and Perugia to rebel against her.

CHAPTER 8

[The Guelfs plan to seize the government. 1378]

Nevertheless, while against the Pope they carried on such an important war, they could not defend themselves from the Captains of the Party and their faction, because the envy of the Guelfs against the Eight made them bolder, and they did not hold back from injuring not merely other noble citizens but the Eight themselves. And to such arrogance the Captains of the Party climbed that they were more feared than the Signors, and men went to the latter with less respect than to the former, and the palace of the Party was more respected than theirs, so that no ambassador came to Florence without a message for the Captains. Hence, though Pope Gregory was dead and the city had no foreign war, life inside her was in great confusion, for on one hand the Guelfs were unbearably bold, and on the other no one saw any way for quelling them. Yet it was believed that necessarily the Florentines would come to blows, to see which of the two seats of power would win.

To the Guelf party belonged all the ancient nobles, with the greater part of the more influential of the people; among them, as we said, Messers Lapo, Piero, and Carlo were leaders. Of the other party were all the less important people, whose heads were the Eight of War, Messer Giorgio Scali, and Tommaso Strozzi; with them the Ricci, Alberti, and Medici joined. The rest of the multitude, as almost always happens, sided with the discontented party.

The heads of the Guelf faction saw the power of their adversaries and their own great danger, whenever a Signoria hostile to them decided to suppress them. Hence, in order to be beforehand, they met and examined the conditions of the city and of their power. They then decided that the admonished, having increased to such a large number, had brought them such great blame that all the city had become hostile to them. They saw no way to deal with this except that, since they had taken from their opponents all their offices they should take from them the city too, occupying by force the Palace of the Signors and bringing the entire government under the control of their faction, in imitation of the ancient Guelfs, who lived in security in the city for no other reason than that they had driven out all their adversaries. All the Guelfs agreed to this, but they disagreed about the time.

CHAPTER 9
[*Plot of the Guelfs; Salvestro de'Medici Gonfalonier. 1378*]

It was the year 1378 and the month of April; Messer Lapo thought their seizure of the government could not be delayed, declaring that nothing so much harms the right time as does time—[1] and for them especially, since the gonfalonier in the next Signoria could easily be Salvestro de'Medici, whom they knew to be opposed to their faction. Piero degli Albizzi, on the other hand, favored delay, because he judged that they needed forces and could not gather them without publicity; if they were revealed they would run into obvious danger. He judged, therefore, that they must wait

---

1. *When the right time for action comes, delay is injurious.*

until the next St. John's day. At that time, since it was the chief
holiday of the city, a great crowd gathered, among whom they could
then hide as many men as they wished, and in order to provide
against what they feared from Salvestro, he could be admonished.
If they thought admonishing him unwise, they could admonish one
of the College from his quarter of the city, and because the bags were
empty, when the substitute was drawn, the lot could easily cause
Salvestro or some relative of his to be drawn, which would prevent
him from acting as Gonfalonier. The Guelfs decided, then, on this
course. Yet Messer Lapo agreed unwillingly, judging that delay is
injurious, and that never is there a time in every way fit for doing a
thing, so that he who waits for complete fitness either never tries
anything, or if he tries, usually does so to his own loss. They did
admonish one of the College, but did not succeed in impeding
Salvestro, because, since the Eight discovered the reasons, they managed to keep the substitute from being drawn. Salvestro son of
Messer Alamanno de'Medici was therefore drawn as Gonfalonier.

He, being born of a very noble family of popular origin, could
not endure that the people should be oppressed by a few who were
powerful. And having decided to put an end to this arrogance, since
the people supported him and he had many noble companions
among the middle class, he imparted his plans to Benedetto Alberti,
Tommaso Strozzi, and Messer Giorgio Scali, who promised to
secure him every aid. They secretly, therefore, determined on a law
that renewed the Ordinances of Justice against the nobles, lessened
the authority of the party Captains, and gave the admonished a way
of being called back to their offices.

And that it might be almost at the same time proposed and
enacted, since it must be decided first by the members of the College
and then in the Councils, and since Salvestro was provost (a position that made one almost prince of the city during the time it lasted),
he had the College and the Council assemble on the same morning,
and first to the members of the College, apart from the Council he
submitted the law that had been drawn up. This, as something
new, found in this small group such lack of support that it did not
pass. Hence Salvestro, seeing that he was cut off from the first means
for passing it, pretended to leave the place because of bodily needs,
and without anybody's knowing it, went to the Council. And
having taken a high place, where everybody could see and hear him,

he said that he believed he had been made gonfalonier not that he might be a judge in private cases, which have their prescribed judges, but in order to guard the state, to restrain the arrogance of the power-ful, and to modify those laws by the enforcement of which the republic would be ruined; that he had attended with care to both these things and provided for them as well as he could, but that the malice of men so opposed his just efforts that it took from him all power for doing anything good, and it took from them the power not merely to discuss such a thing but even to hear of it. Hence, seeing that in nothing could he be of further use to the republic or to the general good, he did not know for what reason he should longer retain that office, which either he did not deserve or others believed that he did not deserve. Therefore he intended to go home,[2] in order that the Florentine people could put in his place another who would have either greater ability or better fortune then he. And having spoken these words, he left the council chamber to go home.

2. To resign.

CHAPTER 10
[*The people take arms; the Guelfs flee. 1378*]

Those in the Council who understood the affair and the others who wished for revolution raised an outcry, to which the Signors and the members of the College ran, and seeing their Gonfalonier leaving, with requests and commands they held him back, and made him return to the council chamber, where the confusion was great. There, with insulting words, many noble citizens were threatened. Among them Carlo Strozzi was seized by the breast by a gildsman who intended to kill him; with difficulty he was protected by the bystanders. But he who stirred up greatest confusion and put the city under arms was Benedetto degli Alberti; from the windows of the Palace he called the people to arms with a loud voice; and im-mediately the Piazza was full of armed men. As a result the members of the College, when threatened and in fear, did what earlier they had not been willing to do when requested. The Party Captains at the same time gathered many citizens in their palace to confer on how to defend themselves against the law of the Signors. But when they heard the alarm raised and understood what the councillors had decided, each man fled to his house.

Nobody should start a revolution in a city in the belief that later he can stop it at will or regulate it as he likes. It was the purpose of Salvestro to make that law and quiet the city; but the affair went otherwise, because the dissensions then begun had so angered everybody that the shops were not opened, the citizens fortified themselves in their houses, many concealed their goods in the monasteries and churches, and it seemed that every man feared some immediate evil. The societies of the gilds met and each chose a syndic. Then the Priors sent for their Colleges and those syndics. These consulted all day on how, to everybody's satisfaction, the city could be quieted, but because opinions were diverse they reached no agreement.

The day following, the gilds brought out their banners. The Signors, learning this and fearing what might happen, summoned the Council to find some way to avoid trouble. The Council had hardly assembled when the alarm was raised, and at once the banners of the gilds, with a great number of armed men behind them, were in the Piazza. As a result the Council, in order to give the gilds and the people hope of satisfaction, and to take away from them any opportunity for evil, gave general authority, which in Florence is called *balía*, to the Signors, the members of the College, the Eight, the Party Captains and the syndics of the gilds to reorganize the city government for the common benefit. Yet while this was being arranged, some standards of the Arts and of people from the lower orders, influenced by those who wished to revenge themselves for recent injuries received from the Guelfs, detached themselves from the others, and sacked and burned the house of Messer Lapo da Castiglionchio. He himself, when he learned that the Signoria had made an effort opposed to the arrangements of the Guelfs, and saw the people in arms, having no other recourse than to hide or to run away, first hid in Santa Croce and then fled to the Casentino dressed as a friar. There he was many times heard lamenting over himself for yielding to Piero degli Albizzi, and over Piero for wanting to wait for St. John's day to make sure of the government. But Piero and Carlo Strozzi hid at the beginning of the rioting, in the belief that when it was over, since they had many relatives and friends, they could safely remain in Florence.

After the house of Messer Lapo was burned, because troubles are hard to start and easily grow greater, many other houses were plundered and burned, because of either general hatred or private enmity. And in order to have company that with a thirst greater than theirs would join them in stealing other men's goods, the mob broke open the public prisons; then they sacked the monastery of the Agnoli and the convent of Santo Spirito, where many citizens had hidden their property. Nor would the public treasury have escaped the hands of these plunderers if it had not been protected by their respect for one of the Signors, who, on horseback, with many armed men behind him, withstood to his utmost the fury of that multitude.

This popular excitement having in part abated, both through the authority of the Signors and because night had come on, the next day the *balìa* extended grace to the admonished, with the condition that for three years they should not act as magistrates. It annulled the laws made to the damage of the citizens by the Guelfs; it declared that Messer Lapo da Castiglionchio and his companions were rebels, and along with him many others who were generally hated. After these decisions, the new Signors were announced. Luigi Guicciardini was Gonfalonier. Many hoped that these officials, believed to be peaceful men and lovers of the common tranquillity, would stop the riots.

CHAPTER 11

[The Guelfs lose power; Luigi Guicciardini makes a speech against disunion. 1378]

Nevertheless the shops were not opened, the citizens did not lay down their arms, and strong guards were placed throughout the city. For this reason the Signors did not assume the magistracy outside the Palace with the usual pomp, but inside, without observing any ceremony. These Signors judged that at the outset of their term of office they could do nothing more useful than to bring peace to the city. Therefore they had the people lay down their arms and open their shops, and expelled from Florence many whom citizens had called in for aid from the surrounding district; they set guards in many places in the city. Hence, if the admonished could have been kept quiet, the city would have been quiet. But they were not willing to wait three years to get their positions again. Hoping to satisfy them, the gilds again assembled and asked the Signors that, for the good and quiet of the city, they should decree that no citizen at any time should be admonished as a Ghibelline by the Signors, the

College, a party Captain, or a consul of any Art; and also that new bags [*containing the names of those eligible for office*] should be made in the Guelf party and the present ones burned. These demands were accepted not merely by the Signors but by all the councillors; it seemed that this concession would stop the disturbances, which already had begun again.

Yet because it is not enough for men to get back their own, but they wish to seize that of others and to revenge themselves, those who put their hopes in the disturbances showed the gildsmen that they never would be secure if many of their enemies were not driven out and destroyed. The Signors, realizing these things, had the magis, trates of the gilds come before them together with their syndics. To them Luigi Guicciardini, the Gonfalonier, spoke in this manner:

"If these Signors, and I with them, had not for a long time known the Fortune of this city, who brings it about that when wars outside are finished, those inside begin, we should have been more astonished at the disturbances that have gone on and should have felt more displeasure at them. But because things one is used to cause less distress, we have endured with patience the late disturbances, espe, cially since they were begun without any fault of ours, and have hoped that, after the pattern of those in the past, they would some time have their end, since to you so many and such heavy demands have been conceded. But since we learn that you are not quiet, but on the contrary want new injuries done to your fellow citizens and more of them punished by exile, our vexation grows with your dishonor. And truly, if we had believed that in the times of our magistracy our city, either through opposing you or through yielding to you, was going to fall, we should have avoided these honors by flight or by exile. But since we expected to be associated with men who had in them some humanity and some love for their native city, we took the magistracy willingly, believing that with our humanity we could in all respects overcome your ambition. But now we see through experience that the more humbly we bear ourselves and the more we yield to you, the prouder you are and the more dishonorable things you ask. If we speak thus, we do not do it to anger you but to make you repent, because we intend that some other man shall say what pleases you, but we intend to say what will be of use to you.

"Tell us, on your faith, what is it that you can honorably ask from us? You have demanded that authority be taken from the Party

Captains; it has been taken away. You have asked that their bags should be burned and that new reorganizations should be carried out; we have agreed. You have asked that the admonished should return to their offices; it has been allowed. On your request, we have pardoned those who burned the houses and plundered the churches, and to satisfy you, many honored and powerful citizens have gone into exile. The nobles, in your behalf, have been restrained with new laws. What end will these demands of yours have or how long will you make a bad use of our liberality? Do you not see that we bear defeat with more patience than you bear victory? To what will these disunions of yours bring this city of yours? Do you not recall that, when the state was disunited, Castruccio, a humble citizen of Lucca, defeated you, and a Duke of Athens, your hired soldier, subjugated you? But when the state was united, an archbishop of Milan and a Pope could not overcome her, but after many years of war they suffered disgrace.

"Why then do you wish that your dissensions, in peace, should make a slave of this city that so many powerful enemies have, in war, left free? What will you get from your disunions, except slavery? or from the goods that you have stolen from us or will steal, except poverty? For they are the things that, joined with our efforts, feed all the city, and if we are deprived of them we cannot feed her; and those who have seized them will not know how to keep them, as property wickedly gained; so the result will be hunger and poverty in the city. I and these Signors command you and, if honor permits, once for all we pray you to settle your minds and be willing to remain in repose with the measures we have adopted; and when you do wish something new, be so good as to ask it lawfully and not with uprisings and arms. Because if your desires are honorable, they will always be granted, and you will not with blame and injury to yourselves give wicked men an opportunity to ruin your native city with your support."

These words, because they were true, greatly moved the spirits of those citizens, and they graciously thanked the Gonfalonier for performing to them the duty of a good Signor and to the city that of a good citizen, and offered themselves as ready to obey anything that might be commanded them. To give them reason for obedience, the Signors deputed two citizens for each of the more important offices, who, together with the syndics of the gilds, were to consider whether anything needed reform for the sake of the common tranquillity, and report it to the Signors.

CHAPTER 12
[Labor troubles in Florence. 1378]

While these things were thus going on, another disturbance arose, which troubled the republic much more than the first one. The greater part of the arsons and robberies that had taken place in the preceding days had been committed by the poorest people in the city, and those among them who had shown themselves boldest feared that, when the greater differences were quieted and settled, they would be punished for the offenses they had committed and, as it always happens, would be abandoned by those who had incited them to do evil. To this was added a grievance of the lowest class against the wealthy citizens and the chiefs of the gilds, for they were not paid for their labor according to what they believed their just deserts. This was the reason: when in the time of Charles I the city was divided into gilds, a head and form of government was given to each one, and it was provided that the subjects of each gild should be judged by their heads in municipal affairs. These gilds, as we said before, were at first twelve; then with time they increased so much that they reached twenty-one. They were of such power that in a few years they took over the entire government of the city, and because some of them were more and some were less honored, they were divided into the greater and the lesser; seven of them were called Greater and fourteen Lesser. From this division and from the other reasons given above, came the arrogance of the Party Captains, for citizens from families that for many years had been Guelfs, under whose control the office of Captain had always been exercised, favored the people in the Greater Gilds but maltreated those in the Lesser Gilds and their supporters. For that reason there were as many rebellions as we have described.

Moreover, in organizing the corporations or the gilds, many of those trades in which the lower class and the very poorest people engage did not have corporations or gilds of their own, but were subject to various gilds according to the nature of their trades. Hence when they were dissatisfied with their labors or in any way oppressed by their masters, they had nowhere to go for refuge except to the magistrate of the gild that ruled them; yet they believed he did not furnish them proper justice. Of all the gilds, the one that had and still has most of these dependents was the Wool Gild. This, because it was very powerful, and through its strength the chief of them all, by its business has long given employment and still gives employment to the greater part of the poor and the lower classes.

CHAPTER 13

[A speech on the wrongs of the lower class. 1378]

The poorest of the people, then, both those subject to the Wool Gild and the others, were, for the reasons given, very indignant; since to this was added fear as a result of the arson and robbery they had committed, they met together at night many times, discussing the events that had taken place and showing one another the dangers they were in. There one of the most fiery and of greatest experience, in order to arouse the others, spoke to this effect:

"If now we could decide whether arms were to be taken up, the houses of the citizens robbed and burned, and the churches plundered, I should be one of those who would think it a matter to be deliberated over, and perhaps I should approve the view that a quiet poverty is to be preferred to a dangerous gain. But because arms have been taken up and many evils done, we must consider how to avoid laying them down, and how we can make ourselves safe from the ills that have been committed. I certainly believe that when nothing else teaches us, necessity teaches us. You see all this city full of complaints and of hatred against us. The citizens meet together; the Signoria is always with the magistrates. You must agree that traps are being designed for us and new forces prepared against our lives. We ought, therefore, to seek for two things and to have two ends in our discussions: one, not to be punished for the things we have done in the past days; the other, to live with more liberty and more satisfaction to ourselves than in the past. We must, therefore, as it seems to me, if we expect to be pardoned for our old transgressions, commit new ones, doubling our offenses and multiplying our arson and robbery, and must strive to have many companions in this, because where many err, nobody is punished; little faults are punished, great and serious ones are rewarded. When many suffer, few seek to avenge themselves, because universal injuries are borne with more patience than individual ones. To multiply offenses, then, will cause us to find pardon more easily and will open to us the way for getting those things that, for our liberty, we wish to get.

"For my part, I hold that we shall go to sure gain, because those who might hinder us are disunited and rich. Their disunion, therefore, will give us the victory, and their riches, when they become ours, will support us. And do not be frightened by their antiquity of blood which they shame us with, for all men, since they had one and the same beginning, are equally ancient; by nature they are all made in one way. Strip us all naked; you will see us all alike; dress us then in their clothes and they in ours; without doubt we shall seem noble and they ignoble, for only poverty and riches make us unequal. I am very sorry to hear that many of you, for reasons of conscience, repent of the things you have done and wish to refrain from anything more; if it is true, you certainly are not the men I believed you were. Neither conscience nor ill fame ought to frighten you, for those who conquer, in whatever way they conquer, never because of it come to disgrace. Of conscience we need take no account, for when people fear hunger and prison, as we do, they cannot and should not have any fear of Hell.

"If you will observe the way in which men act, you will see that all those who attain great riches and great power have attained them by means of either fraud or force; those things, then, that they have snatched with trickery or with violence, in order to conceal the ugliness of their acquisition, under the false title of profit they make honorable. But those who, through either lack of prudence or great folly, avoid these ways, always are smothered in servitude and poverty, for faithful servants are always servants, and good men are always poor; none come out of servitude except the unfaithful and the bold, and out of poverty except the rapacious and fraudulent. God and Nature have put all men's fortunes in their midst,[1] and these fortunes are more open to stealing than to labor, and to bad rather than good arts. From this it comes that men devour one another; and they who are weakest always come off worst. We ought, then, to use force when we get a chance. None greater can be offered to us by Fortune, since now the citizens are disunited, the Signoria hesitating, the mag-

1. *Wealth is accessible to all.*

istrates frightened. Hence, before they unite and confirm their cour/
age, they can easily be defeated, and as a result we shall either be com/
pletely rulers of the city, or shall have such a share of her that not
merely our past errors will be forgiven us, but we shall have so much
power that with new damage we can threaten her.

"I admit that this plan is daring and dangerous, but when neces/
sity pushes, rashness is judged prudence; in great things spirited men
never take account of danger; undertakings that begin with danger
end with reward, and from any danger one never escapes without
danger. So I believe, when we see prisons, tortures, and death pre/
pared, that we should fear standing still more than seeking to make
ourselves safe, for in the first the ills are sure, in the second doubtful.
How many times I have heard you complain of the avarice of your
superiors and of the injustice of your magistrates! Now is the time
not merely to free yourselves from them but to become so much
superior to them that they will have to complain of and fear you
more than you will them. The opportunity that Occasion brings
you is fleeting; when she has escaped, one seeks in vain to catch her
again. You see the preparations of our adversaries; let us get ahead of
their plans; for whichever of us first takes arms will without doubt be
the winner, with the ruin of his enemy and his own exaltation.
Thus many of us will gain honor and all will gain security."

These arguments so greatly inflamed their spirits, which were of
themselves already hot for evil, that they determined to take arms as
soon as they had brought more companions to their way of thinking;
so with an oath they bound themselves to help each other, if any of
them were tyrannized over by the magistrates.

CHAPTER 14
[*The revolt of the* Ciompi *succeeds. 1378*]

While these men of the lower classes were preparing to seize
control of the republic, their design came to the knowledge of the
Signors, since the latter had in their power a man named Simone
dalla Piazza, from whom they learned the whole conspiracy and that
the next day the plotters intended to raise the alarm. Hence, seeing
the danger, they brought together the members of the College and
those citizens who with the syndics of the gilds were considering the

union of the city. Before they were all assembled evening came. These men advised the Signors to have the consuls of the gilds come. The consuls all recommended that all the men-at-arms in Florence should be ordered to the Public Square and that in the morning the Gonfaloniers of the people with their armed companies should also be there. A man named Niccolò da San Friano was regulating the Palace clock at the time when Simone was being tortured and the citizens were assembling. Having learned what was happening, he returned home and roused his whole neighborhood. At once, more than a thousand armed men gathered in the square before Santo Spirito. Rumor of this came to the other conspirators, and San Piero Maggiore and San Lorenzo, places they had selected, were filled with armed men.

Day had already come, on the twenty-first of July, and in the Public Square not more than eighty men-at-arms were ready to aid the Signors, and none of the Gonfaloniers had come, because, knowing the whole city to be under arms, they feared to leave their houses unguarded. The first group of men of the lower classes to reach the Public Square were those who had assembled at San Piero Maggiore. On their arrival the men-at-arms did not move. Afterward the rest of the multitude came. Meeting no resistance, they demanded the prisoners from the Signoria with horrible shouts, and in order to get them by force, since they were not handed over on threats, they burned the mansion of Luigi Guicciardini. Then the Signors, for fear of worse, released the prisoners. When the crowd had them, it took the Banner of Justice from the executioner and under that burned the houses of many citizens, seeking vengeance on those who were hated for either public or private reasons. And many citizens, in order to revenge their private injuries, led them to the houses of their enemies, because it was enough that one voice in the midst of the crowd should shout: "To So and So's house!" or that he who had the banner in his hand should go there. All the records of the Wool Gild were also burned. After the rioters had done many bad things, in order to associate with them some praise-worthy acts, they conferred knighthood on Salvestro de'Medici and so many other citizens that the total number reached sixty-four; among these were Benedetto and Antonio degli Alberti, Tommaso Strozzi, and similar men who were in their confidence. Nonetheless many were knighted by force. More striking than anything else in this affair is that the mob burned the houses of men who a little later on the same day (so close was benefit to injury) were knighted. This happened to Luigi Guicciardini, Gonfalonier of Justice.

The Signors, amid such confusion, seeing themselves abandoned by the men-at-arms, by the heads of the gilds and by their Gonfalon-iers, were bewildered because nobody rescued them as directed; of sixteen standards of the gilds, only the ensign of the Lion of Gold and that of the Squirrel, under Giovenco della Stufa and Giovanni Cambi, appeared. These remained but a short time in the Square, for not seeing any others follow them, they soon departed. On the other hand, when the citizens saw the fury of this unrestrained mob and knew that the Palace was abandoned, some remained in their houses, others went along in the mob of armed men, in order by being among them better to defend their own houses and those of their friends. So the mob's power kept growing and that of the Signors decreasing.

This riot lasted all day, and when night came they halted at the palace of Messer Stefano, behind the Church of San Barnaba. They numbered more than six thousand. Before day appeared, the gilds were compelled by threats to send their banners. When morning came, the rioters went to the palace of the Podestà with the Gonfalon of Justice and the banners of the gilds before them; and since the Podestà refused them possession of his palace, they attacked and took it.

CHAPTER 15

[The Signors abandon their palace to the Ciompi. *1378]*

The Signors, deciding to attempt negotiation, since they saw no means for checking them by force, summoned four men belonging to their College and sent them to the palace of the Podestà to learn the mob's purpose. These found that the heads of the lower class and the syndics of the gilds and some citizens had settled what to ask from the Signoria. Hence the four returned to the Signoria with four men selected by the lower class, with these demands, namely: the Wool Gild should no longer have a foreigner as judge;[1] three new gilds should be formed, one for the carders and dyers, a second for the barbers, doublet-makers, tailors, and like mechanic occupa-

1. *Not a Florentine though presumably an Italian.*

tions, a third for people of the lower class; from these three new gilds there were always to be two Signors, and from the fourteen lesser gilds three; the Signoria should provide houses where these new gilds could meet; no one subject to these gilds should within two years be forced to pay a debt for a sum smaller than fifty ducats; the *Monte* should keep its interest and pay back the capital only;[2] that the banished and condemned should be cleared; all the admonished should be restored to their positions. In addition to these they asked many other things for the benefit of their own supporters. And on the opposite side they wanted many of their enemies banished and admonished.

These demands, though they were dishonorable and hard for the republic, were, for fear of worse, at once granted by the Signors, the members of the College and the Council of the People. But if they were going to be fully ratified, it was necessary that they also be passed by the Council of the Commonwealth. Since on one day two councils could not be brought together, it was agreed to put this off until the next day. Nevertheless it seemed that for the time being the gilds were pleased and the lower class satisfied, and they promised that when the law was ratified, all disorder would be quieted.

When morning came, while discussion was going on in the Council of the Commonwealth, the crowd, impatient and restless, came to the Square under their usual banners, with such loud and terrible shouts that all the Council and the Signors were terrified. Because of this, Guerriante Marignolli, one of the Signors, moved more by fear than by any other private feeling, went downstairs, with the excuse of guarding the lower door, and fled to his house. When he went out, he could not disguise himself well enough not to be recognized by the crowd. No injury was done him, though the throng shouted when it saw him that all the Signors should abandon the Palace, and if they did not, the people would kill their children and burn their houses. Meanwhile the law was decided on and the Signors had gone to their chambers, and the Council, having gone downstairs, without going outside, was standing in the loggia and in the court, despairing of the safety of the city, seeing so much dishonor in a mob, and so much malice or fear in those who might have checked or quelled it.

2. *The* Monte *(literally, Mountain) was the organization for administering the city debt.*

The Signors also were confused and fearful for the safety of the city, seeing that they had been abandoned by one of themselves, and were not assisted by a single citizen with arms or even with advice. Being then uncertain of what they could or ought to do, Messer Tommaso Strozzi and Messer Benedetto Alberti, moved either by their own ambition, since they wished to remain lords of the Palace, or perhaps because they actually thought their advice good, urged the Signors to yield to this popular pressure and return as private persons to their houses. This advice, given by those who had been leaders of the uprising, angered Alamanno Acciaiuoli and Niccolò del Bene, two of the Signors, though the others yielded, so that these two, when a little of their vigor had returned, said that if the others wished to leave, they could do nothing about it, but that they themselves did not intend to lay down their power, if they did not lose their lives with it, before they were released on the proper date. These disputes redoubled the fear of the Signors and the anger of the people. Meanwhile the Gonfalonier, choosing to end his term with shame rather than with danger, asked help from Messer Tommaso Strozzi, who took him from the Palace and led him to his mansion. The other Signors in like fashion departed one after the other; then Alamanno and Niccolò, in order not to be thought more brave than wise, seeing that they were alone, went away too. So the Palace remained in the hands of the lower class and of the Eight of War, who had not yet laid down their office.

CHAPTER 16

[Michele di Lando, a woolcomber, made lord of the city. 1378]

When the men of the lower class entered the Palace, Michele di Lando, a woolcomber, had the standard of the Gonfalonier of Justice in his hand. This man, barefoot and wearing little clothing, with all the crowd behind him, went up the stairs,[1] and when he was in the audience chamber of the Signors he stopped and, turning to the crowd, said: "Look; this Palace is yours and this city is in your hands. What do you think we should do now?" They all answered that they wanted him to be Gonfalonier and Signor, and to rule them and the city as he wished. Michele accepted the lord-

1. *The stairs leading to the official rooms of the Palazzo Vecchio.*

ship, and because he was a sagacious and prudent man, more indebted to Nature than to Fortune, he determined to quiet the city and stop the tumults. To keep the people busy and give himself time for arranging matters, he ordered a search for one Ser Nuto, who had been appointed chief of police by Messer Lapo da Castiglionchio. On this search the greater part of those who were around him went away. Then, in order to begin with justice the dominion he had received by favor, he had it publicly proclaimed that nobody should burn or rob anything; and to frighten everyone he set up a gallows in the Public Square. To make a beginning of reform in the city, he dismissed the syndics of the gilds and appointed new ones; he deprived the Signors and the members of the College of their positions; he burned the bags of the offices.

Meanwhile Ser Nuto was carried to the Square by the mob and hanged on the gallows by one foot; and since everybody around cut off a piece of him, in a short time only that foot remained.

On the other hand, the Eight of War, believing that the departure of the Signors left them rulers of the city, had already designated the new Signors. Foreseeing this, Michele sent them orders to leave the Palace at once, because he wished to show everybody that he could rule Florence without their advice. He then had the syndics of the gilds meet and choose the Signoria: four from the lowest classes, two from the Greater Gilds, and two from the Lesser Gilds. Besides this, he made a new list of those eligible for office and divided the state into three parts, decreeing that one part should belong to the new gilds, a second to the Minor Gilds, a third to the Greater. He gave Messer Salvestro de'Medici the revenues from the shops on the Ponte Vecchio; to himself he gave the podesterate of Empoli; and he did many other favors to many other citizens who were friends to the people of low station, not so much to reward them for their actions as in order that at all times he might protect himself against envy.

CHAPTER 17

[*The Ciompi revolt against Michele's government. 1378*]

The lower classes believed that in reforming the government Michele had been too much a partisan of the highest classes among the people; they also believed that they did not have a share in the administration sufficient to maintain themselves in it and to defend themselves. Hence, urged on by their usual arrogance, they took arms again and came with uproar into the Square under their banners, and asked that the Signors should come down to the platform,[1] to decide further matters relating to their security and well-being. Michele, seeing their presumption, in order not to let them show further contempt, without at all attending to what they wanted, denounced their manner in asking, advised them to lay down their arms, and said they then would receive concessions which the Signoria could not with dignity yield to force. For this reason the mob, angry with the Palace, went to Santa Maria Novella. There they set up among themselves eight heads, with attendants and with various laws that gave them standing and respect. Hence the city had two seats of government and was ruled by two different authorities.

These heads of the mob determined that eight, selected from the membership of their gilds, should always live with the Signors in the Palace, and that everything determined by the Signoria must have their approval. They took from Messer Salvestro de'Medici and Michele di Lando all that their earlier decrees had granted; they assigned to many of their own group offices and subsidies, so that they could maintain their rank with dignity. Having settled these measures, in order to make them valid, they sent two of their number to the Signoria to ask for approval by the councillors, with suggestions that they would have their new laws by force if they did not receive them by agreement. These two, with great boldness and greater arrogance, delivered to the Signors the message committed to them; and they rebuked the Gonfalonier because of the office they had given him, the honor they had done him, and the great ingratitude and slight consideration which he had shown them. Then, when at the end of their speech they came to threats, Michele, unable to bear such arrogance and remembering rather the office he held than his humble birth, determined in an unusual way to check unusual insolence: drawing the sword with which he was girded, he first wounded them severely and then had them bound and imprisoned. This act, when it was known, kindled all the crowd to wrath, and believing that when armed they could obtain what, when unarmed, they had not gained, they took up arms and with rage and confusion set out to use violence against the Signors.

1. *In front of the Palace, from which the assembly in the Square could be addressed.*

Michele, on the other hand, suspecting what was going on, determined to act beforehand, thinking that it would be more glorious for him to make an attack than to wait for his enemy within walls and, like his predecessors, to have to run away with dishonor to the Palace and shame to himself. So gathering a large number of citizens who had already begun to realize their mistake, he mounted a horse and, followed by many armed men, went to Santa Maria Novella prepared to fight. The lower class had, as we said above, made a similar decision, so almost at the time when Michele started they set out for the Public Square. Chance caused the parties to take different streets, so that they did not meet on the way. Hence Michele on his return found that his enemies had occupied the Public Square and were attacking the Palace. Joining battle, he defeated these enemies, drove part of them from the city and forced the rest to lay down their arms and go into hiding. Since he was successful in his attempt, the riots were quieted solely through the Gonfalonier's ability.

In courage, in prudence and in goodness he surpassed every citizen of his time. He deserves to be numbered among the few who have benefited their native city, because if his spirit had been either wicked or ambitious, the republic would have entirely lost her liberty and would have come under a tyranny more severe than that of the Duke of Athens, but Michele's goodness never let come into his mind a thought opposed to the general good. His prudence enabled him to manage affairs in such a way that many of his party yielded to him; the others he overcame with arms. His actions made the lower class lose courage, and made the better gildsmen recognize their mistakes and think what a shame it was for those who had overcome the pride of the nobility to endure the stench of the lower class.

CHAPTER 18

[Popular tendencies in government; the Popular Party and the Plebeian Party. 1378]

When Michele gained his victory over the lower class, the new Signoria had already been drawn; in it were two of such a vile and disreputable sort that men felt an increasing desire to free themselves from such shame. On the first day of September, then, when the new Signors took office and the Public Square was full of armed men, as soon as the old Signors were outside the Palace, the armed men raised a tumultuous shout that they did not want any Signors from the lowest class. Hence the Signoria, to satisfy them, took their offices from those two, one of whom was called Il Tria and the other Baroccio. In their places Messer Giorgio Scali and Francesco di Michele were chosen. They also did away with the gild consisting of people of the lowest rank, and deprived its members of their offices, except Michele di Lando and Lorenzo di Puccio and some others of good quality. They divided the dignities into two parts, one of which they assigned to the Greater, the other to the Lesser Gilds. However, for the Signors they decreed that there should always be five for the Lesser gildsmen and four for the Greater, and the Gonfalonier should be in the choice now of one, now of the other body.

This government so arranged made the city, for the time being, remain quiet. Though the administration had been taken from the hands of the lowest class, the gildsmen of lower station continued more powerful than the people of highest standing. The latter were obliged to concede this to the gilds in order, by satisfying them, to deprive the lowest class of their support. This arrangement was also favored by those wishing the continued suppression of all who, under the name of the Guelf Party, had with such great violence done injury to so many citizens. Because among the supporters of this type of goverment were Messer Giorgio Scali, Messer Benedetto Alberti, Messer Salvestro de'Medici and Messer Tommaso Strozzi, they continued to be almost princes in the city.

These proceedings, so continued and managed, fixed between the men of the people who had now become aristocrats and the lesser gildsmen the division already begun by the ambition of the Ricci and the Albizzi. Because at various times this division produced the most serious effects and must often be mentioned, we shall call one party Popular and the other Plebeian. This government lasted three years and caused numerous exiles and deaths, since those in power were very suspicious of the many malcontents within and without the city. The malcontents within the city every day either attempted or were believed to attempt something subversive. Those outside, not subject to any restraining influence, sowed various dis⁄ sensions now here now there.

CHAPTER 19

[Guelf exiles plot with Charles of Durazzo; Piero degli Albizzi and others executed; Sir John Hawkwood. 1378–1380]

In these times Giannozzo of Salerno, a general under Charles of Durazzo, was at Bologna. Charles, a descendant of the royal family of Naples, intending to make an expedition into the Kingdom against Queen Joanna, kept this general of his in Bologna because of the favors done him by Pope Urban, an enemy to the Queen. There were also there many Florentine exiles, who were often in close consultation with that general and with Charles. For that reason the rulers of Florence were all the time in the greatest fear and easily credited slanders against such citizens as they suspected. While the magistrates, then, were in such uncertainty of mind, they were informed that Giannozzo of Salerno was going to appear at Florence with the exiles and that many within the walls were going to take up arms and deliver the city to him. Because of this story many were accused. Their leaders were named as Piero degli Albizzi and Carlo Strozzi, and after them Cipriano Mangioni, Messer Jacopo Sac-chetti, Messer Donato Barbadoro, Filippo Strozzi and Giovanni Anselmi. All these except Carlo Strozzi, who escaped, were ar-rested. The Signors, that nobody should dare to take up arms to aid the prisoners, deputed Messer Tommaso Strozzi and Messer Bene-detto Alberti, with many armed men, as a guard for the city. The citizens arrested were examined, and according to the accusation and the examinations, no fault was found in them. Since the Captain therefore did not intend to condemn them, their enemies so stirred up the populace and with such fury excited it against them that by force they were condemned to death.

Piero degli Albizzi received no aid from the greatness of his house or from his long-standing reputation: for years he had been honored and feared above every other citizen. Once when he was giving a banquet to many citizens, somebody—either one of his friends, to make him more courteous in such greatness, or one of his enemies, to threaten him with the uncertainty of Fortune—sent him a silver cup full of sweetmeats with a nail hidden among them. When the nail was found and seen by all the guests they interpreted it as a suggestion that he nail Fortune's wheel in its present place;

since she had brought him to the top of it, it could do nothing else, if it kept turning, than carry him to the bottom. This interpretation was verified first by his ruin, then by his death.

After his execution, the city was greatly confused because the conquered and the conquerors were in fear; but the more injurious effects resulted from the fear of those who governed, because even the slightest happening made them do the Party[1] more harm, either condemning or admonishing or exiling their fellow citizens. To this were added numbers of new laws and new regulations made to strengthen the government. All these things went on to the injury of those who were suspected by the ruling faction. In its fear it chose forty-six men, who, together with the Signors, were to purge the city of all who were suspected by the government. These admonished thirty-nine citizens and classified many of the people as nobles and many of the nobles as people.

And to repel forces from outside, they hired Sir John Hawkwood, an Englishman with a very high reputation in arms, who had for a long time served the Pope and others in Italy. Their fear of events outside the city came from learning that many companies of men-at-arms were being formed by Charles of Durazzo to carry on his expedition to the Kingdom; with him, according to report, were many Florentine exiles. Against these dangers, besides the forces arranged for, they provided themselves with a sum of money, so that when Charles arrived in Arezzo he received from the Florentines forty thousand ducats and promised not to molest them. He then continued his expedition, easily conquered the Kingdom of Naples, and sent Queen Joanna as a prisoner into Hungary. This victory again increased the terror of those controlling the government of Florence, because they could not believe that their money would be stronger in the King's mind than the ancient friendship of his house with the Guelfs, whom with such great injustice they were persecuting.

1. *The Guelf Party.*

CHAPTER 20

[*Messer Giorgio Scali, of the Plebeian Party, executed. 1382*]

This terror as it grew made outrages grow more numerous; and these did not extinguish the terror but made it grow greater, so that the majority of men lived a most unhappy life. To this unhappiness was added the insolence of Messer Giorgio Scali and Messer Tom-maso Strozzi, whose power surpassed that of the magistrates, since every man feared that the two, with the aid of the Plebeian Party, would persecute him. Not merely to the good but to the seditious that government seemed tyrannical and violent. But because the haughtiness of Messer Giorgio had some time to end, one of his confidants accused Giovanni di Cambio of making secret plans against the government. He was found innocent by the Captain. Hence the judge was about to punish the accuser with the penalty with which the accused, if found guilty, would have been punished. When Messer Giorgio could not rescue him with requests or with any exercise of his influence, he and Messer Tommaso Strozzi with a crowd of armed men freed him by force, sacked the Captain's palace and obliged the Captain to hide to save himself. This action roused in the city such hatred against Messer Giorgio that his ene-mies imagined they could get rid of him and take the city not merely from his hands but from those of the Plebeian Party, which by its presumption had kept her under subjection for three years.

The Captain also gave a good opportunity for this, since, when the confusion had ceased, he went to the Signors and said he had entered willingly upon that office to which the Signors had chosen him, because he thought that he was going to serve just men who would take arms to aid and not to obstruct justice. But since he had seen and tested the manners of the city and her way of living, the office which he had gladly taken in order to gain profit and honor, he would gladly return to them in order to escape danger and harm. The Captain was consoled and encouraged by the Signors, who promised him recompense for past damages and security in the future. Then part of them consulted with some citizens, chosen from those whom they thought lovers of the common good and less to be feared by the government; they concluded that a great oppor-tunity had arrived for getting the city out of the power of Messer Giorgio and the Plebeian Party, since the citizens generally were estranged from him by this last high-handed action.

Therefore they decided to use this opportunity before offended spirits could become reconciled, because they knew that by the slightest accident the favor of the multitude is lost and gained. They judged, if they were going to put the thing through, that they needed to bring to their way of thinking Messer Benedetto Alberti, without whose approval they considered the undertaking dangerous. Messer Benedetto was a very rich man, merciful, stern, a lover of the liberty of his city, and much opposed to tyrannical measures. Hence the Signors easily convinced him and got him to approve Messer Giorgio's ruin. Messer Benedetto had earlier been an enemy to those of the people who had become aristocrats and to the Guelf faction; he had been a friend to the Plebeian Party because of the haughtiness and tyrannical ways of the Guelfs. But when he saw that the heads of the Plebeian Party had become like the others, he detached himself from them, long before Messer Giorgio's violence against the Captain. Hence the injuries done to many citizens had been entirely without his approval. Thus the causes that made him earlier take the side of the Plebeian Party were the same as made him then leave it.

When the Signors, then, had brought Messer Benedetto and the leaders of the gilds to their opinion, and had provided soldiers, Messer Giorgio was arrested, though Messer Tommaso escaped. The following day Messer Giorgio was beheaded—with such dismay to his party that nobody stirred; on the contrary, all competed in bringing about his ruin. Hence since he saw he was about to die in the presence of that people which a little before had worshipped him, he bewailed his evil fate and the wickedness of the citizens, who, by harming him unjustly, had forced him to aid and honor a multitude in which there was neither any faith nor any gratitude. Recognizing Messer Benedetto Alberti among the armed men, he said to him: "And do you, Messer Benedetto, agree that an injury should be done such as, if I were in your place, I would never allow to be done to you? But I warn you that this day is the end of my unhappiness and the beginning of yours." Then he censured himself because he had trusted too much in a people which every word, every act, every suspicion influences and misleads. And with these laments he died in the midst of his enemies, who were armed and, as a result of his death, happy. After him some of his closest friends were put to death and torn to pieces by the people.

CHAPTER 21

[Reaction against the Plebeian Party. 1381]

The death of this citizen moved the whole city, because, in carrying it out, many took arms to aid the Signoria and the Captain of
the People; many others also took them up either on account of their
ambition or on account of their own terrors. And because the city
was full of diverse partisan views, every man had a different purpose,
and all, before arms were laid down, wished to carry them out. The
ancient nobles, called the *Grandi*, since they could not endure being
deprived of the public offices, labored with all their zeal to get them
back; to this end they would have loved to have power given back
to the Captains of the Party. The men of the people who had become aristocrats and the Greater Gilds did not like sharing the
government with the Lesser Gilds and the lowest class. On the
other hand, the Lesser Gilds wished to increase rather than to lessen
their importance. And the lowest class feared they would lose the
members of the College chosen from their gilds. For the space of a
year these differences many times caused rioting in Florence, and
now the ancient nobles took arms, now the Greater Gilds, now the
Lesser, and the lowest class with them, and many times of a sudden
in different parts of the city they all were armed. From this resulted
many combats, both among themselves and with the soldiers of the
Palace, because the Signoria, now yielding, now fighting, dealt with
so many troubles as well as it could.

So at the end, after two parliaments and many *balie*, set up to
reform the city, after many injuries, struggles, and very serious dangers, a government was established, by which all who had been
banished when Messer Salvestro de'Medici was Gonfalonier were
reinstated; it took away special advantages and privileges from all
those who had been allowed them by the *balia* of 1378; offices were
restored to the Guelf Party; the two new gilds were forced to give up
their organization and rulers, and each of the members was put back
under his old gild; the Lesser Gilds had to give up the Gonfalonier
of Justice, and their share of the offices was reduced from half to
one-third; all the offices of high rank were taken away from them.
Thus the popular and Guelf Party took back the government and

the Plebeian Party lost it, after having been first in it from 1378 to 1381, when these changes took place.

CHAPTER 22

[Ingratitude to Michele di Lando; Benedetto Alberti; Louis of Anjou in Italy. 1382–1384]

This government was not less harmful to the Florentine citizens nor less severe at its beginning than that of the Plebeians had been, for many of the people who had become aristocrats and who were known as defenders of the Plebeian Party were banished, together with a great number of Plebeian leaders, among whom was Michele di Lando. The many good things of which his authority had been the cause when the unchecked mob was lawlessly ruining the city, did not save him from the fury of the parties. His native city, indeed, was not grateful to him for his good deeds. Into this transgression princes and republics many times fall; its result is that, frightened by such instances, men attack their rulers early, before any experience of princely or public ingratitude is possible for them.

The exiles and executions I have mentioned, as they had always been offensive to Messer Benedetto Alberti, were still offensive to him, and publicly and privately he censured them. Therefore the chiefs of the government feared him, because they thought him one of the leading friends of the lower classes, and believed that he had approved the death of Messer Giorgio Scali not because he objected to Messer Giorgio's conduct but in order to remain alone in the government. His words and his ways increased their suspicion. This made the entire party in control keep their eyes on him, in order to grasp an opportunity for crushing him.

When they were living in such conditions, things outside the city were not very dangerous, so that whatever resulted from them was more terrifying than harmful. For at that time Louis of Anjou came into Italy to give back the Kingdom of Naples to Queen Joanna and drive out Charles of Durazzo. His passage greatly frightened the Florentines, for Charles, as is usual with old friends, asked them for help, and Louis, like anyone seeking for new friend-ships, asked them to remain neutral. Hence the Florentines, to make it appear that they were satisfying Louis, and to help Charles, re-

moved Sir John Hawkwood from their payroll and had him serve
Pope Urban, who was Charles's friend. Since Louis easily recognized this deception, he believed himself much injured by the Florentines. While the war was being waged between Charles and Louis
in Apulia, new soldiers came from France to aid Louis, and when
they reached Tuscany, they were taken into Arezzo by the Aretine
exiles, and the party that was ruling for Charles was expelled. But
when they planned to change the government of Florence, as they
had changed that of Arezzo, Louis died. Thus affairs in Apulia
and in Tuscany varied their position with Fortune, because Charles
became secure possessor of the kingdom that he had almost lost, and
the Florentines, who doubted whether they could defend Florence,
gained Arezzo, because they bought her from the soldiers who held
her for Louis. Charles, then, feeling sure of Apulia, went to occupy the kingdom of Hungary, which came to him by inheritance,
and left his wife in Apulia with Ladislas and Joanna his children,
who were still small, as we showed in its place. Charles gained
Hungary, but a little later he was killed there.

CHAPTER 23

[Benedetto Alberti banished; his speech on his love for the city. 1387]

Over gaining Arezzo, Florence indulged in celebrations as splendid as ever did any city for a real victory. Both public and private
magnificence were to be seen there, since many families competed
with the public in their celebrations. But the one that surpassed the
others in splendor and magnificence was the Alberti family; the
devices and the spectacles at arms that it prepared were those not of a
private house, but worthy of any prince. These things greatly increased the envy against that family. This envy, joined with the
suspicion the government had of Messer Benedetto, caused his downfall, for those in power could not feel secure about him, since they
thought that at any hour, with the aid of the Party, he might regain
his influence and drive them from the city. While they were in this
uncertainty, it happened that, when he was Gonfalonier of the Companies, his son-in-law, Messer Filippo Magalotti, was drawn as
Gonfalonier of Justice. This redoubled the fear of the leaders in the
government, because they thought the power of Messer Benedetto

and the danger to the government too much increased. Since they desired to remedy the danger without strife, they encouraged Bese Magalotti, his relative and enemy, to indicate to the Signors that Messer Filippo, since he had not reached the age required for holding that office, could not and ought not to hold it. The case was examined among the Signors, and part of them for hate, part to avoid strife, judged that Messer Filippo was not eligible for that office. In his place Bardo Mancini was drawn, a man altogether opposed to the Plebeian faction, and very hostile to Messer Benedetto. So when he had assumed office, he set up a *balìa* which, in taking over and reorganizing the government, banished Messer Benedetto Alberti and admonished the rest of the family, except Messer Antonio.

Before his departure, Messer Benedetto summoned all his relatives, and seeing that they were sad and were shedding many tears, said to them:

"You see, fathers and my elders, that Fortune has ruined me and threatened you. I do not wonder at it, and you ought not to wonder, because it always happens so to those who among many that are wicked try to be good and try to hold up what the majority try to pull down. Love for my native city made me side with Messer Salvestro de'Medici and then side against Messer Giorgio Scali. This same thing made me hate the methods of those now ruling, who, just as they have not had anbody to punish them, also do not want anybody who will censure them. I am glad, by means of my exile, to free them from the fear that they feel not of me alone but of everybody who they know understands their tyrannical and wicked ways; and therefore with my suppression they have threatened others. I do not feel sorry for myself, because the offices my native city has given me when she was free, she cannot take away when she is a slave; and the memory of my past life will always give me happiness greater than the unhappiness the affliction of my exile will bring upon me. I do indeed grieve that my city is left as a spoil for a few, and is subject to their pride and avarice. I am sorry for you, because I fear that the ills today ending for me and beginning for you may afflict you with greater injuries than have afflicted me. I exhort you, then, to brace your spirits against every misfortune and so conduct yourselves that if anything adverse comes upon you—and many such may come upon you—everybody will know that they have come when you are innocent and without any fault."

Then, in order not to give a lower opinion of himself abroad than he had given in Florence, he went to the Sepulchre of Christ. On his return he died at Rhodes; his bones were taken to Florence and he was buried with the greatest respect by those who when he was alive had persecuted him with all sorts of slander and calumny.

CHAPTER 24

[Further anti-plebeian measures. 1387]

During these troubles in the city, injury was done not to the Alberti family alone, for along with it many other citizens were admonished and banished. Among them were Piero Benini, Matteo Alderotti, Giovanni and Francesco del Bene, Giovanni Benci, Andrea Adimari, and along with them a great number of lesser gildsmen. Among the admonished were the Covini, the Benini, the Rinucci, the Formiconi, the Corbizzi, the Mannegli, and the Alderotti. It was the custom to set up a *balìa* for a fixed time, but citizens selected, when they had done what they were chosen for, would resign, as decency required, even though the fixed date had not come. Since it seemed to the men acting in this *balìa* that they had done their duty by the government, they therefore intended to resign according to custom.

Learning of this, many ran to the Palace in arms, asking that before they resigned they would banish and admonish many others. This much annoyed the Signors, and with fair promises they kept these disturbers occupied until they themselves had gathered forces; then the Signors so acted that fear made the malcontents lay down those arms that fury had made them take up. Nevertheless, in order to satisfy in part such a furious partisanship and to deprive the working men of the lowest class of more power, they arranged that whereas such men had had a third part of the offices, they should have a quarter of them; and in order that two of those most trusted by the government should always be among the Signors, they gave power to the Gonfalonier of Justice and to four other citizens to prepare a bag of selected persons, two of whom should be drawn for every Signoria.

CHAPTER 25

[*War with Giovan Galeazzo Visconti; temperate and unambitious behavior of Veri de'Medici. 1387–1393*]

When the government that had been organized in 1381 had thus, after six years, come to its end, the city lived until 1393 in great internal quiet. During that time Giovan Galeazzo Visconti, called the Count of Virtù, captured Messer Bernabò his uncle and thus became ruler of all Lombardy. Believing he could become King of Italy by force, as he had become Duke of Milan by trickery, in 1390 he started a great war against the Florentines. As it went on, this war varied in its course in such a way that many times the Duke was in greater danger of losing it than were the Florentines, who, if he had not died, would have lost. Nevertheless their defense was spir‑ ited and wonderful for a republic, and the end was much less evil than the war had been terrifying, for when the Duke had taken Bologna, Pisa, Perugia, and Siena, and prepared the crown with which he was to be crowned King of Italy in Florence, he died. His death did not allow him to enjoy his past victories and did not allow the Florentines to realize their present losses.

While this war with the Duke was going on, Messer Maso degli Albizzi was made Gonfalonier of Justice. Since the death of Piero had made him an enemy of the Alberti, and the struggles of the parties all the time continued, Messer Maso determined, even though Messer Benedetto had died in exile, that before he ended his term he would revenge himself on the remainder of that family. He got his chance from one who was examined because of certain dealings he had had with the exiles and who named Alberto and Andrea degli Alberti. They were immediately arrested, to the indignation of the whole city. Thereupon the Signors, furnishing themselves with troops, called the people to a parliament and chose men for a *balìa*, by virtue of which they banished many citizens and made new baggings for the offices. Among the banished were almost all the Alberti. Many working men were also admonished and executed. Hence, after so many injuries, the gilds and the lowest class rose in arms, since they saw that their honor and their life were taken from them. One part of them came to the Public Square; another part went to the house of Messer Veri de'Medici, who, after the death of

Messer Salvestro, had become the head of that family. To lull the suspicions of those who came to the Public Square, the Signors appointed as their heads Messer Rinaldo Gianfigliazzi and Messer Donato Acciaiuoli, as the men from the people more acceptable to the lowest class than any others; in their hands were put the banners of the Guelf Party and of the people.

Those who ran to Messer Veri's house begged him to consent to take over the government and to free them from the tyranny of those citizens who were destroyers of worthy men and of the common good. All who have left any record of those times agree that if Messer Veri had been more ambitious than he was good, he could without any hindrance have made himself prince of the city, because the serious damage that, rightly or wrongly, had been done to the gilds and to their friends had so fired their spirits to revenge that, to satisfy their appetites, they needed only a head to lead them. A man was not lacking to remind Messer Veri of what he could do, because Antonio de'Medici, who had cherished for a long time special enmity against him, urged him to seize the rule of the republic. To this Messer Veri answered: "Your threats when you were my enemy never caused me fear, and now that you are my friend your advice will not harm me." Turning to the crowd, Messer Veri exhorted them to be of good courage, because he was willing to be their defender, if only they would take his advice. Having gone in the midst of the crowd to the Public Square, and from there climbed the stairs up into the Palace, he said in the presence of the Signors that he could not at all lament that he had lived in such a way that the people of Florence loved him, but he did lament that they had formed an opinion of him not justified by his past life; since he had never made himself an example of faction and ambition, he did not know how it was that he was believed a supporter of factions, as a restless man, or a usurper of the government, as an ambitious one. He begged their Lordships, therefore, that the ignorance of the crowd should not be attributed to any sin of his because, so far as he was concerned, as soon as he could he had put himself in their power. He urged them indeed to use their fortune humbly and to be satisfied to enjoy a half victory with the safety of the city rather than, by attempting a complete triumph, to ruin her.

The Signors praised Messer Veri and encouraged him to have arms laid down, saying that they would not fail to do what he and

the other citizens had advised. After these words Messer Veri returned to the Square and united his followers with those of Messer
Rinaldo and Messer Donato. Then he said to all that he had found
the Signors excellently disposed toward them and that many things
had been spoken of, but that because the time was short and some
officials were absent, they had not been settled. However, he begged
them to lay down their arms and obey the Signors, assuring them
that courtesy more than pride, petitions more than threats were likely
to move them, and the people would not lack their rank and security
if they let him direct them. So under his pledge everybody returned
to his house.

CHAPTER 26

*[Treachery of the Signors; they crush the opposition of Messer Donato
di Jacopo Acciaiuoli. 1395]*

After arms had been laid down, the Signors first fortified the
Square.[1] Then they enrolled two thousand citizens trusted by the
government, divided equally into companies, which they ordered to
be ready to rescue them whenever they were called, and they prohibited those not enrolled from carrying arms. Having made these
preparations, they banished and executed many working men who
had shown themselves more vigorous than the others in the disorders; and so that the Gonfalonier of Justice would have more
dignity and reputation, they decreed that in order to hold that office
it would be necessary to be forty-five years of age. To strengthen the
government, they also made many rules that could not be endured
by those against whom they were made and were hateful to the good
citizens of their own party, who did not think a government good
and secure that needed to protect itself with such violence. Not
merely those of the Alberti who remained in the city and the Medici,
who felt that the Signors had deceived the people, but many others
felt so much violence to be obnoxious.

The first who tried to oppose them was Messer Donato di Jacopo
Acciaiuoli. Though he was an important man in the city and rather
superior than equal to Messer Maso degli Albizzi, who because of
the things he did when he was Gonfalonier was like the head of the
republic, Messer Donato could not live content among so many

1. *The Piazza Signoria, in front of the Palace of the Signors, now the Palazzo Vecchio.*

malcontents nor, as many do, could he get private profit from public loss. Therefore he decided to find out whether he could restore their city to the banished or at least restore their offices to the admonished. He kept sowing his opinion in the ears of this and that citizen, showing that it was not possible in any other way to quiet the people and put a stop to the quarrels of the parties, and that he was only waiting until he was one of the Signors to put this desire of his into effect.

Because in men's actions delay brings anxiety and haste brings danger, in order to avoid anxiety, he decided to try danger. Among the Signors were Michele Acciaiuoli his relative and Niccolò Ricoveri his friend; hence Messer Donato, believing he had a chance not to be lost, asked them to propose to the councillors a law that would include restoration of the citizens. These two men, persuaded by him, spoke of it with their colleagues, who replied that they were not for trying anything new, in which gain is doubtful and danger sure. So Messer Donato, having first in vain tried all methods, in anger gave them to understand that since they would not allow the city to be organized according to the plans that were ready, she would be organized by force of arms. These words were so obnoxious, when the affair was made known to the heads of the government, that Messer Donato was cited. When he appeared, the man by whom he had sent the message testified against him; hence he was banished to Barletta. Alamanno and Antonio de'Medici were also banished, along with all those of that family who were descended from Messer Alamanno, together with many non-aristocratic gildsmen who were esteemed by the lowest class of people. These events happened two years after Messer Maso reorganized the government.

CHAPTER 27

[*Exiles attempt a revolution. 1397*]

When the city thus had many malcontents within her walls and many exiles outside them, among the exiles at Bologna were Picchio Cavicciuli, Tommaso de'Ricci, Antonio de'Medici, Benedetto degli Spini, Antonio Girolami, Cristofano di Carlone and two others of humble station. These were all young, eager, and willing to tempt any Fortune in order to return to their native city. In secret ways Piggiello and Baroccio Cavicciuli, who after admonition[1] were living in Florence, informed the exiles that if they came secretly into the city, the two would then receive them into their houses, from which they could then go out and kill Messer Maso degli Albizzi and call the people to arms. The latter, being discontented, could easily be roused, especially because the liberators would be followed by the Ricci, Adimari, Medici, Mannegli, and many other families.

Moved, therefore, by these hopes, on the fourth of August 1397, they came to Florence, and having secretly entered where it had been arranged, they sent someone to watch Messer Maso, intending to start the uprising with his death. Messer Maso went out of his house and stopped at a drugstore near San Piero Maggiore. The man who was watching him ran to tell the conspirators; taking arms and coming to the place indicated, they found he had gone. So, not troubled because their first plan had not succeeded, they turned toward the Old Marketplace, where they killed one of the opposite party. Raising the alarm and shouting "People, arms, liberty," and "Death to the tyrants," they turned toward the New Marketplace, and at the end of Calimala killed another. Continuing their course with the same shouts, though nobody took arms, they came to the loggia of the Nighittosa. There they got on a high place, having a great multitude around, which had run more to see them than to aid them, and with loud voices they exhorted the men to take arms and escape from the servitude they so much hated. They asserted that the lamentations of dwellers in the city who were ready to rebel had moved them more than their own injuries to try to set her free, and that they had learned of many citizens who prayed God to give them a chance for avenging themselves; they would do so whenever they had a leader who would provide them a beginning. Yet now that the occasion had come and they had leaders who had made a beginning, they looked at each other and, as though senseless, waited for those who had begun their liberation to be killed and they themselves again weighed down with slavery. The speakers declared themselves astonished that those who on the smallest injury were wont to take arms, for such great ones did not stir, but were willing to endure having so many citizens banished and so many admonished. Now it was in their choice to restore the city to the banished and the government to the admonished.

1. *For admonition, see bk. 3, chap. 3, above.*

These words, though true, did not stir the crowd in any way, either through fear or because the deaths of those two had made the killers hateful. Those who had begun the rebellion saw that neither their words nor their deeds had power to move anybody, finding out too late the great danger of attempting to set free a people that in every way prefers to be in slavery. Despairing of their undertaking, they retreated to the church of Santa Reparata, where, not to save their lives but to put off their deaths, they shut themselves up. The Signors, frightened when the riot began, took arms and locked up the Palace, but when they learned about the matter, and knew who they were who had begun the rebellion and where they were shut up, they were reassured; they ordered the Captain to go with many armed men to arrest the rioters. Without much trouble the doors of the church were forced, and part of the men were killed when de-fending themselves and part captured. When the prisoners were examined, none in addition to them was found guilty except Baroccio and Piggiello Cavicciuli, who were executed with them.

CHAPTER 28

[A conspiracy against Florence supported by the Duke of Milan. 1400]

After this event, another of greater importance took place. As we said above,[1] the city was then at war with the Duke of Milan. He, seeing that open forces were not enough to overcome her, turned to secret ones. By means of Florentine exiles, of whom Lombardy was full, he arranged a conspiracy of which many within the city were aware. The plan was that on a certain day a great number of exiles skilful in arms were to leave places near Florence and enter the city by the Arno River. Together with their friends inside, they were to run to the houses of the heads of the government, and when they had killed these leaders, they would as they wished reorganize the republic.

Among the conspirators inside the city was one of the Ricci named Saminiato; as often happens in conspiracies—where the few are not enough and the many reveal them—through seeking to gain allies, he found an accuser. Saminiato talked about the matter to Salvestro Cavicciuli, whom injuries to his relatives and himself

1. See 3. 25, above.

should have made faithful. Nonetheless, he gave more weight to immediate fear than to future hope, and at once divulged the entire plot to the Signors. Having Saminiato arrested, they forced him to disclose the complete organization of the conspiracy. Yet of the confederates nobody except Tommaso Davizi was caught; he, coming from Bologna and not knowing what had happened in Florence, was seized before he got there. All the others, after Saminiato's arrest, fled in terror.

After Saminiato and Tommaso had been punished according to their crimes, a *balìa* was given to a number of citizens, who with their authority were to seek for the guilty ones and make the government safe. They proclaimed as rebels six of the family of the Ricci, six of that of the Alberti, two of the Medici, three of the Scali, two of the Strozzi, Bindo Altoviti, Bernardo Adimari, and many humble men. They also admonished all the family of the Alberti, Ricci, and Medici, except a few of them, for ten years.

Among the Alberti not admonished was Messer Antonio, since he was thought a quiet and peaceful man. It happened, when fear of the conspiracy had not yet subsided, that a monk was seized, who, in the days when the conspirators were plotting, had many times been seen going from Bologna to Florence. He confessed that he had many times carried letters to Messer Antonio. Hence the latter was at once seized, and though at the outset he denied everything, he was proved guilty by the monk, and therefore fined and banished three hundred miles from the city. And so that the Alberti would not every day put the government in danger, all those of the family older than fifteen were banished.

CHAPTER 29

[Florence relieved from war by the deaths of Giovan Galeazzo Visconti and Ladislas of Naples. 1400–1414]

These events took place in 1400. Two years later, Giovan Galeazzo Duke of Milan died. His death, as we said above,[1] put an end to a war that had lasted twelve years. Since the government had in that time gained more power, being without enemies inside and outside, it undertook the affair of Pisa and carried it through with glory.

1. *See 3. 25, above.*

And life in the city was quiet from 1400 to 1433. Only in 1412, because the Alberti had broken their exile, a new *balìa* was set up against them, which reinforced the government with new laws and crushed the Alberti with taxes.

In that time the Florentines also made war with Ladislas King of Naples, which, because of the death of the King, ended in 1414. And in the course of this, the King, seeing himself weaker, granted the Florentines the city of Cortona, of which he was lord. But a little later he regained his power and undertook against Florence a further war, much more dangerous than the first; if it had not ended with his death, as that with the Duke of Milan had ended earlier, he, like that duke, would have brought Florence into danger of losing her freedom. Nor did this war end with less good fortune than the other, because after he had taken Rome, Siena, all the March, and Romagna and needed nothing else than Florence before going with his army into Lombardy, he died. So death was always more friendly to the Florentines than any other friend, and stronger to save them than any ability of their own.

After the death of this king the city was quiet, outside and inside, for eight years. At the end of that time, along with the wars with Filippo Duke of Milan, the parties were renewed. And they were quiet only with the fall of that government which had been in power from 1381 to 1434, and had carried on with such glory so many wars and had added to the Florentine dominion Arezzo, Pisa, Cortona, Livorno, and Monte Pulciano. And it would have done greater things if the city had kept united and the ancient party quarrels had not been stirred up, as will be shown in detail in the next book.

BOOK FOUR

[FLORENTINE AFFAIRS FROM 1414 TO 1434]

CHAPTER 1

[Liberty and license in cities]

Those cities, especially such as are not well organized, that are administered under the semblance of republican government, often vary their rulers and their constitutions not between liberty and slavery, as many believe, but between slavery and license. The promoters of license, who are the people, and the promoters of slavery, who are the nobles, praise the mere name of liberty, for neither of these classes is willing to be subject either to the laws or to men. I allow that when it comes about (and it seldom does come about) that by a city's good fortune a wise, good and powerful citizen gains power, who establishes laws that repress strife between the nobles and the people or so restrain these parties that they cannot do evil, at such a time a city can be called free and her government can be considered firm and solid; being founded on good laws and good institutions, it does not need, as do other governments, the strength and wisdom of one man to maintain it.

With such laws and institutions many ancient republics, whose governments had long lives, were gifted. Such customs and laws have been wanting to all those which have often varied their governments and are at present varying them from the tyrannical form to the licentious, and from that back to the other; on account of the powerful enemies both have, they are not and cannot be stable. The tyrannical form does not satisfy good men; the licentious dissatisfies the wise. The first can do evil with ease; the second can do good with difficulty. In one, too much power is given to arrogant men; in the other, too much to stupid men. Either one has to be maintained by the ability and the good fortune of a single man, who may be removed by death or become incompetent through disease.

CHAPTER 2
[Suppression of the Popular Party. 1414–1422]

I say, then, that the administration beginning with the death of Messer Giorgio Scali in 1381 was supported by the capacity of Messer Maso degli Albizzi, then by that of Niccolò da Uzzano. The city was quiet from 1414 to 1422, since King Ladislas was dead and the state of Lombardy divided into many parts, so that outside Florence or inside her there was nothing to cause fear. Less important than Niccolò da Uzzano, yet powerful, were Bartolommeo Valori, Nerone di Nigi, Messer Rinaldo degli Albizzi, Neri di Gino, and Lapo Niccolino. The parties that resulted from the strife of the Albizzi and the Ricci and that Messer Salvestro de'Medici then revived to cause so much discord, were never wiped out. And though the party most favored by the mass of the inhabitants had only three years of control and in 1381 was defeated, yet since its party principles were those of the greater portion of the city, it could not be wholly got rid of. True it is that the frequent parliaments and the continual persecutions of its leaders from 1381 to 1400 reduced it almost to nothing. The chief families harassed as its leaders were the Alberti, the Ricci, and the Medici, who many times were stripped of men and of wealth. If any of them were left in the city, their offices were taken from them. These oppressions made that party humble and almost destroyed it. Nevertheless many men continued to recollect the injuries they had received and hoped to revenge them. This hope, finding no support anywhere, lay hidden in their breasts. The aristocrats of popular origin who peacefully ruled the city made two mistakes that were the overthrow of their administration: first, as a result of their steady power, they grew haughty; second, as the result of their envy for each other and of their long tenure in office, they were not so careful about who had power to injure them as they should have been.

CHAPTER 3
[The rise of Giovanni de'Medici, in spite of the warnings of Niccolò da Uzzano; a treaty with Filippo Visconti. 1421]

Renewing every day the multitude's hatred by their obnoxious ways, and not watching things that might injure their party because they did not fear injuries, and even encouraging them through their envy of one another, these aristocrats who were ruling Florence caused the Medici family to regain power. Giovanni di Bicci de' Medici began this recovery of prominence. Having grown very rich and being by nature kind and courteous, he was by a concession of those in control chosen to the chief magistracy. At this choice the masses of the city showed great satisfaction, since the crowd believed it had gained a defender, but properly this was to the wiser a cause of foreboding, because they saw that all the old partisan quarrels were gaining vigor once more. Niccolò da Uzzano did not fail to warn the other citizens, showing how dangerous it was to cherish one who had so high a reputation with the masses and that it was easy to counteract subversive movements in their early stages, but if they were allowed to grow, they were hard to cure; he discerned in Gio-vanni many qualities surpassing those of Messer Salvestro. Niccolò's associates did not listen to him, because they envied his reputation and wished to have partners in suppressing him.

While in Florence such partisanship was secretly boiling again, Filippo Visconti, the second son of Giovanni Galeazzo, by the death of his brother became ruler of all Lombardy. Believing he could project any undertaking whatever, he longed exceedingly to make himself also lord of Genoa, which under the dogeship of Messer Tommaso da Campo Fregoso was then living in freedom. But he doubted whether he could carry through that or any other undertaking if he did not first make public a new agreement with the Florentines, the fame of which he judged would be enough to let him carry out his wishes. He therefore sent ambassadors to Florence to ask such an agreement. Many citizens advised against it, but thought that without granting it they should continue the treaty that for many years had been kept with him, because they knew how much help their consent to a new agreement would give him and how little profit the city would get. Many others favored making the agreement and by virtue of it imposing terms upon him; if he ex-ceeded them, everybody would realize his wicked purpose, and if he broke the treaty, Florence could more justifiably make war on him. So after the business had been much debated, the treaty was made. In it Filippo promised not to concern himself with affairs on this side of the Rivers Magra and Panaro.[1]

1. *That is, would not expand in the direction of Florence.*

CHAPTER 4

[Filippo goes beyond the limits set in the treaty; Florence prepares for war. 1422]

When this agreement had been made, Filippo took Brescia, and a little later Genoa, against the expectation of those who in Florence had advised the treaty, because they believed that Brescia would be defended by the Venetians and Genoa would defend herself. And because in the agreement Filippo made with the doge of Genoa the latter left to him Sarzana and other towns on this side of the Magra, with the condition that if he wished to give them up he should be bound to give them to the Genoese, the conclusion was that Filippo had violated the treaty. He had, besides this, made an agreement with the Legate of Bologna. These things disturbed the minds of our citizens and forced them, since they feared new ills, to think about new safeguards. When this excitement in Florence came to the attention of Filippo, either to justify himself or to test the purposes of the Florentines or to lull them to sleep, he sent ambassadors pretending astonishment at the suspicions formed in Florence and offering to draw back from anything he had done that could excite any suspicion.

These ambassadors produced no other effect than to divide the city, for one party, made up of those who had most influence in the government, judged it wise to take arms and prepare to spoil the plans of the enemy; then if preparations were made and Filippo remained quiet, war would not be begun and there would be reason for peace. Many others, either in envy of those who ruled or in fear of war, judged that a friend should not be lightly suspected and that what the Duke had done did not justify such great suspicion of him, and moreover they asserted that their opponents knew well that to choose the Ten[1] and to hire troops amounted to beginning war. War against so great a prince would bring the city sure ruin, without the possibility of hoping for any benefit: we could not become masters of any conquests we might make, with Romagna between us and them, and the neighborhood of the Church forbade any dreams about the affairs of Romagna. Nevertheless the influence of those wishing to prepare for war was stronger than that of those wishing to

1. *The Florentine board or committee in charge of warfare.*

arrange for peace. Hence they chose the Ten, hired soldiers, and imposed new taxes. These, because they weighed more heavily on the lesser than on the greater citizens, filled the city with laments; everybody condemned the ambition and avarice of the powerful and charged them (for the sake of sating their appetites and crushing the people, so as to rule them) of bringing about an unnecessary war.

CHAPTER 5

[Filippo seizes Forlì; debate over aggressive and defensive war. 1423]

Florence had not yet come to an open break with the Duke, but everything looked suspicious because, at the request of the Legate of Bologna—who feared Messer Antonio Bentivoglio, in exile at Castel Bolognese—Filippo had sent soldiers to that city. Being near Florentine territory, they kept her government in anxiety. But what made everybody tremble still more, and gave an important reason for beginning the war, was the Duke's expedition against Forlì. The lord of Forlì was Giorgio Ordelaffi, who on his death left his son Tibaldo under Filippo's guardianship. Tibaldo's mother, suspicious of the guardian, sent her son to Lodovico Alidosi her father, lord of Imola. Nevertheless, in order to carry out the will of his father, the people of Forlì forced her to put the boy into the Duke's hands. Then Filippo, to rouse less suspicion of himself and better to conceal his intention, ordered the Marquis of Ferrara to send as his deputy Guido Torello, with soldiers, to take over the government of Forlì. Thus the town came into Filippo's power.

This situation, when known in Florence, together with the news of the soldiers who had come to Bologna, made easier the decision for war, though it met much opposition, and Giovanni de'Medici publicly advised against it. He showed that even if the Duke's ill will was certain, it was better to wait for him to attack you than to move your forces against him.[1] In the latter situation the rulers of Italy would see in the war as much justice on the Duke's side as on our side, and it would not be possible to ask assistance with confidence, though we could do so if he had revealed his ambition. With different courage and different forces the rulers would defend

1. *In his interest in the general principle, Machiavelli turns from historical narrative to address his reader directly, as in* THE PRINCE.

their own property than they would that of some other man.² Other Florentines said it was good not to wait for the enemy at home but to attack him, that Fortune is more friendly to him who attacks than to him who defends, and with less damage, even though with more expense, war is made in another's territory than in one's own. In the end, the last opinion prevailed, and it was determined that the Ten should use every means for taking the city of Forlì from the Duke's hands.

2. *The minor princes of Italy would, if the Duke attacked, feel that they were defending themselves from aggression.*

CHAPTER 6
[War with Filippo begins; the battle of Zagonara. 1424]

Filippo, seeing that the Florentines intended to seize the things he had undertaken to protect, laying all scruples aside, sent Agnolo della Pergola with a large force against Imola, so that her ruler, occupied in protecting his own property, could not attend to the defense of his grandson. Agnolo, then, came to Imola—the forces of the Florentines being still at Modigliana. Since the cold was so great that ice covered the city moat, one night by surprise he captured her. Lodovico Alidosi he sent to Milan as a prisoner. The Florentines, seeing that Imola was lost and war openly begun, sent their soldiers to Forlì; they laid siege to that city and blockaded it on all sides. To keep the Duke's soldiers from uniting to relieve the place, they hired Count Alberigo, who from his city of Zagonara raided every day as far as the gates of Imola. Agnolo della Pergola saw that he could not with safety relieve Forlì because of the strong position our soldiers had taken up. He therefore decided to attempt the capture of Zagonara, judging that the Florentines would not permit the loss of that town; yet if they attempted to relieve it, they would have to give up the affair at Forlì and come with disadvantage to battle. Pressure by the Duke's soldiers forced Alberigo to ask terms. They were granted on his promise to surrender his city if within fifteen days the Florentines did not relieve him.

When news of this difficulty came to the Florentine army and to the city, all were eager that their enemies should not gain such a victory. But thus the Florentines caused them to gain a greater one, for the army, leaving Forlì to relieve Zagonara, on meeting the enemy was vanquished. This defeat resulted not so much from their adversaries' valor as from the severe weather, because after our men had marched several hours in very deep mud and with rain falling, they encountered the unwearied enemy, who easily overcame them. Nevertheless in so great a defeat, reported everywhere in Italy, nobody died except Lodovico degli Obizzi with two of his followers; these three, falling from their horses, were drowned in the mud.

CHAPTER 7

[Florence dismayed by the defeat at Zagonara; a courageous speech by Rinaldo degli Albizzi. 1524]

The whole city of Florence by the news of this defeat was made melancholy, especially the noble citizens who had advised the war, because they saw the enemy strong, but themselves unarmed, without friends, and opposed by the people, who, in all the piazzas, with insulting words censured them, complaining of the heavy taxes and of the war begun without cause, saying: "See how these fellows set up the Ten to frighten the enemy! See how they relieved Forlì and took her from the Duke's hands! See how their plans are revealed, and the end they are going toward—not to protect liberty, which is their enemy, but to increase their own power, which God has justly decreased. Nor with this undertaking alone have they burdened the city but with many, because like this one was that against King Ladislas. To whom will they now go running for aid? To Pope Martin, whom in the Braccio affair they have made ridiculous? To Queen Joanna, whom, by abandoning her, they have obliged to throw herself into the King of Aragon's arms?" And besides these, they said all the other things that an angry people always says.

Therefore the Signors decided to bring together a number of citizens who with good words could quiet the party feelings stirred up by the crowd. Hence Messer Rinaldo degli Albizzi, who had been left as the oldest son of Messer Maso, and who aspired, through his own ability and the memory of his father, to the chief rank in the city, spoke for a long time, showing that to judge things from their results is not wise, because many times the outcome of affairs well advised is not good and of those badly advised is good. When bad advice is praised because of its good outcome, nothing else is done

than to give men courage in error; this results in great harm to republics because not always does bad advice turn out well. So in the
same way to censure a good plan that has an unhappy outcome is
wrong because such censure destroys the citizens' courage to advise
the city and to say what they believe. Then he showed the need for
undertaking that war, because if it had not been begun in Romagna
it would have been fought in Tuscany. But since God had willed
that the soldiers should be defeated, Florentine loss would be the
more serious the more they despaired, but if they showed Fortune a
bold face and applied what counter measures they could, they would
not realize their loss or the Duke his victory. They should not be
frightened by expenses and future taxes because in all probability
these would change and be much smaller than those in the past, for
smaller preparations are needed by states trying to defend themselves
than by those who attack. He exhorted them, in short, to follow the
example of their fathers who, through not losing their courage in
any adverse condition, had always, against any prince whatever,
defended themselves.

CHAPTER 8

*[Niccolò Piccino employed as general; the rich object to heavy taxes.
1424-1426]*

Encouraged by his support, the citizens hired Count Oddo,
Braccio's son, and gave him as supervisor Niccolò Piccino, pupil of
Braccio and of higher reputation than any other who had served
under his standards; in addition they hired other generals, and some
of the soldiers who had been plundered they again put on horseback.
They chose twenty citizens to levy new taxes; these, taking courage
because they saw the powerful citizens crushed by past defeat, without any consideration for them, laid heavy taxes on them. This
taxation greatly offended the aristocratic citizens, who at first, in
order to appear more honorable, did not complain of their own
burden, but censured the taxes as generally unjust, and advised that
there should be a lightening. Their plan, becoming known to many,
was obstructed in the councils. Hence, in order to make people
actually feel the harshness of those taxes, and to make them hated by
many, the objectors managed to have the taxgatherers collect them
with the utmost severity, giving authority to kill anybody who de-

fended himself against the public officers. From this resulted many unhappy incidents, with death and wounds for citizens, through which it seemed that the parties would come to blood, and every prudent man feared some future ill, since the nobles who were used to being respected, could not endure to have hands laid on them, and the rest wished that all should be equally taxed.

Many of the leading citizens therefore gathered together and decided that it was necessary to take the government up again,[1] because their inactivity had made men bold in censuring public actions and had given new courage to those accustomed to lead the crowd. Having debated these things among themselves many times, they decided that they should at once assemble in their full number. So in the Church of Santo Stefano more than seventy citizens assembled, with the permission of Messer Lorenzo Ridolfi and of Francesco Gianfigliazzi, who were then acting as Signors. Their meeting was not attended by Giovanni de'Medici, either because he was not invited, as a suspect, or because, being opposed to their view, he was unwilling to take part.

1. *To take the government into their own hands, usually by means of a balìa, or committee with power to make changes.*

CHAPTER 9

[Rinaldo degli Albizzi advises action against the masses; Niccolò da Uzzano declares Giovanni de'Medici's support essential. 1423-1426]

To all of them Messer Rinaldo degli Albizzi spoke. He showed the condition of the city and how through their neglect she was again under the control of the masses, from whom their fathers had taken her away in 1381. He reminded them of the wickedness of the government that ruled from 1378 to 1381 and that among the men present it had killed one's father and another's grandfather. Yet they were going back into the same dangers, and the city was falling into the same abuses, because already the crowd had levied a tax to suit itself, and soon, if not held back by greater force or better policy, it would elect the magistrates as it wished. When that happened, the masses would occupy the places of the present rulers and destroy the government that for forty-two years had been in control—with such great glory for the city. Then Florence would be governed either by chance, according to the will of the crowd, so that one party would live without restraint and the other in danger, or the city would be under the domination of one man who would make himself prince. Moreover, he declared that every man who loved his country and his own honor needed to rouse himself and remember the vigor of Bardo Mancini, who by ruining the Alberti got the city out of the dangers she was then in, and that the present boldness of the crowd resulted from the free choice of candidates that had come about through the inattention of his listeners. Thus the Palace was full of new men of humble family. He then concluded that he saw but this one way to remedy affairs: to give the government to the nobles and to take away the power of the lesser gilds, bringing them down from fourteen to seven. This would give the lowest class less power in the councils, since its numbers would be diminished and more power would be given to the nobles, who on account of their old hostility would not support the masses. He declared that prudence makes use of men according to the times; hence, if their fathers made use of the masses to destroy the haughtiness of the nobles, now that the nobility had become humble and the masses haughty, the haughtiness of the lowest classes could well be checked with the aid of the nobles. To accomplish these things either trickery or force was available; the latter they could employ easily, since some of them belonged to the magistracy of the Ten and could secretly bring soldiers into the city.

Messer Rinaldo was praised and his advice was approved by everybody. Niccolò da Uzzano, among the others, said that everything Messer Rinaldo had said was true and his remedies good and sure, if they could be used without coming to an open split in the city, which would result in any circumstances if Giovanni de'Medici did not come over to their belief. If he agreed with them, the crowd, deprived of its leader and of power, could do no harm. If he did not agree, without using weapons they could not carry out their plan. With weapons, he judged there was danger either that they could not win or could not enjoy their victory. Then he modestly brought to their memories his past advice and their failure to provide against these troubles in times past when easily they might have done so; now they were not in time to do it without fearing greater damage. No resource was left except to gain Giovanni de'Medici to their side. So to Messer Rinaldo was given the duty of going to Giovanni to attempt to bring him to their opinion.

CHAPTER 10

[Giovanni de' Medici opposes action. 1426]

The knight carried out his duty, and with all the best arguments he knew encouraged Giovanni to undertake this action with them and not to decide to make the crowd bold by supporting it, with consequent ruin to the government and the city. Giovanni answered that the duty of a wise and good citizen, as he believed, was not to change the familiar methods of the city, since there is nothing that offends men so much as to vary these; by such variation many are offended, and when many are discontented, every day one must fear some dangerous incident. He also believed that this policy of theirs would have two very harmful results. First, it would give the city offices to those who, never having held them, value them lower and have less cause, not holding them, to complain. Second, if the offices were taken from those who had been accustomed to holding them, such men would never be quiet until their positions were given back to them. Thus the result would be much greater injury to one party than benefit to the other, so that he who caused it would get himself few friends and numerous enemies; and the enemies would be more violent in injuring him than the friends in defending him, since men are naturally quicker in their revenge for an injury than in their gratitude for a benefit; they feel that gratitude causes them loss but revenge brings them profit and pleasure.

Giovanni then addressed Messer Rinaldo personally, saying: "You, if you remember what has happened and with what deceptions we proceed in this city, will be less hot in this decision, because those who advise it will with your forces first take power from the people, and then will take it from you with the people's aid, since this injury will make the people your enemies. It will happen to you as to Messer Benedetto Alberti, who was persuaded by men who did not love him to consent to the ruin of Messer Giorgio Scali and Messer Tommaso Strozzi, and a little later, by the very persons who had persuaded him, he was sent into exile." Giovanni also exhorted him to reflect more adequately on the matter and to try to imitate his father, who, in order to get general good will, decreased the price of salt, provided that anyone with a tax of less than half a florin should be allowed to pay or not as he liked, and decreed that on the day when the councils met everybody should be secure from his creditors. And finally Giovanni concluded that, as far as he was concerned, he was for letting the city's organization stand.

CHAPTER 11

[Giovanni de' Medici stands for union in the city; Florence loses her towns in the Romagna. 1424–1427]

These matters, so discussed, became generally known and brought Giovanni higher reputation and the other citizens hatred. This reputation he tried to avoid, in order to give less confidence to those who, pretending his support, might be planning revolution. In all that he said, he gave everybody to understand that he was not in favor of encouraging factions but of getting rid of them, and so far as he was concerned, he sought for nothing else than the union of the city. For this reason, many who adhered to his party were discontented, because they would have liked him to show himself more active in affairs. Among these was Alamanno de'Medici, who, being by nature violent, did not cease to incite him to persecute his enemies and to aid his friends, condemning his coldness and his method of proceeding slowly, which he said was the reason why Giovanni's enemies without hesitation plotted against him—plots that one day would result in the ruin of his house and his friends. His son Cosimo also urged him in the same way. Nevertheless nothing that was presented or predicted to Giovanni moved him to shift his determination. Yet for all that, the scheme had already been revealed and the city was evidently divided.

In the Palace, in the service of the Signors, there were two chancellors, Ser Martino and Ser Pagolo; the latter adhered to Uzzano's party, the first to the Medicean party. Messer Rinaldo, since Giovanni had not consented to unite with them, thought it would be a good thing to deprive Ser Martino of office, judging that then he would always have the Palace more on his side. Since Messer Rinaldo's attempt was foreseen by his opponents, not merely was Ser Martino defended but Ser Pagolo was deprived—to his party's disgust and damage.

This affair would at once have produced bad effects if war had not been hanging over the city, which was terrified by the defeat suffered at Zagonara. After that reverse, and during the troubles I have mentioned in Florence, Agnolo della Pergola, with the Duke's soldiers, had taken all the cities of Romagna owned by the Florentines except Castrocaro and Modigliana, partly through the weakness of the places, partly through the failure of those who guarded them. In the capture of these cities two things happened which reveal how much courage is admired even by enemies, and how cowardice and wickedness are scorned.

CHAPTER 12

[The heroism of Biagio del Melano; the cowardice of Zanobi del Pino. 1424–1425]

The castellan of the fortress of Monte Petroso was Biagio del Melano. When fire had been kindled around him by his enemies and he saw no resource for the safety of the fortress, he threw cloths and straw down on the side that as yet was not burning, and on the heap threw down his two young children, saying to the enemy: "Take for yourselves these goods that Fortune has given me and that you can take from me; those of the spirit, where my fame and honor lie, I shall not give to you nor will you take them from me." In haste the enemy came to rescue the children, and to him they extended ropes and ladders with which he could save himself, but he did not accept them; he preferred to die in the flames rather than to live in safety furnished by enemies to his native city. A deed truly worthy of that antiquity so much praised! And it is more admirable than ancient deeds in so far as it is more unusual. To his children his enemies restored such things as they could save, and with the greatest care sent them to their relatives. Toward them the republic was not less loving, for as long as they lived they were supported at public expense.

The opposite to this happened in Galeata, where the podestà was Zanobi del Pino: without making any defense, he gave up the castle to the enemy, and besides he encouraged Agnolo to leave the mountains of Romagna and come to the hills of Tuscany, where he could make war with less danger and greater profit. In no way could Agnolo endure the cowardice and base spirit of that fellow, so he turned him over to his servants as their booty. After much mockery, they gave him nothing to eat but pieces of paper painted like snakes, saying that thus they intended to change him from a Guelf to a Ghibelline. And so starving, in a few days he died.

CHAPTER 13

[Niccolò Piccino deserts Florence; alliance with Venice; Carmignuola. 1425–1426]

Count Oddo, in the meanwhile, together with Niccolò Piccino had entered the Valley of Lamona to try to bring the Lord of Faenza back to alliance with the Florentines, or at least to keep Agnolo della Pergola from more easily conquering Romagna. But because that valley is very strong and its inhabitants warlike, Count Oddo was killed and Niccolò Piccino sent as a prisoner to Faenza. But Fortune caused the Florentines to gain through losing what perhaps by winning they would not have gained, for Niccolò so worked on the Lord of Faenza and his mother that he made them friends of the Florentines. On this agreement, Niccolò Piccino was set free, but he did not apply to himself the advice he had given to others: when dealing with the city about his position as general, either because he thought their terms bad or he got better ones elsewhere, almost without warning he left Arezzo, where he was quartered, and went to Lombardy to take employment with the Duke of Milan. The Florentines, frightened by this event and shaken by their frequent losses, judged that by themselves they could no longer keep up this war; hence they sent ambassadors to the Venetians begging them to oppose, while it was easy, the greatness of one who, if they let him grow, was going to be just as harmful to them as to the Florentines.

The Venetians were exhorted to this same undertaking by Francesco Carmignuola, a man in those days thought very excellent in war, who had once been employed by the Duke of Milan but had then broken away from him. The Venetians were in doubt because they did not know how far they could trust Carmignuola, fearing that the hostility between the Duke and himself had been pretended. But while they were thus uncertain, it happened that the Duke, by means of a servant of Carmignuola's, had him poisoned. This poison was not strong enough to kill him though it brought him to the point of death. Finding out the cause of his sickness, the Venetians gave up their suspicion and made a league with the Florentines, who had continued to urge them. Each of the parties pledged himself to carry on the war at the common expense; acquisitions in Lombardy were to belong to the Venetians, those in Romagna and Tuscany to the Florentines; Carmignuola was captain general of the league. The war, then, on this agreement was carried into Lombardy, where it was efficiently managed by Carmignuola: in a few months he took many towns from the Duke, together with the city of Brescia—a capture that in those times, and for those wars, was thought wonderful.

CHAPTER 14

[Heavier taxes for the rich; Giovanni de'Medici tries to calm party feeling. 1422–1427]

Since this war had lasted from 1422 to 1427, the citizens of Florence were worn out by the taxes imposed up to that time, so that they agreed to revise them. And in order that the taxes should be proportionate to men's wealth, it was provided that they should be laid on property, and that he who had a hundred florins in value should pay a tax of half a florin. So, since the law and not men would assign the taxes, they would burden the wealthy citizens heavily; hence before the law passed, the rich did not favor it. Only Giovanni de'Medici openly praised it, so that it passed. Because in determining the tax all the property of every man was recorded, which the Florentines call *accatastare*, this tax was called the *catasto*. This method partly restrained the tyranny of the powerful, because they could not oppress the humbler citizens and by threats make them keep silent in meetings of the council, as they could before. This tax, then, was accepted by the generality, but received by the powerful with great vexation.

Yet since it is true that men are never contented but, having got one thing, they are not satisfied with it and want a second, so the people were not satisfied with the equality of taxation resulting from the law, but asked that there be a review of times past, in order to learn how far, according to the *catasto*, the powerful had fallen short in payment; they intended that the rich should be made to pay enough to equalize them with those who, in order to pay more than was right, had sold their possessions. This demand, much more than the *catasto*, terrified the rich. So, to defend themselves, they did not cease to condemn the tax, declaring that it was very unjust, because it was levied also on movable property, which today men have and tomorrow lose; and that, besides, there are many persons who have money hidden, which the *catasto* cannot find. To this they added that those who, in order to govern the state, leave their businesses ought to be less burdened by taxation, since it is enough that they labor in person, and it is not just that the city should enjoy both their effects and their labor, but only the money of others. Those who approved the *catasto*, answered that if movable property varied, the taxes could also vary, and their frequent variation would remedy that inconvenience. Of those who had money hidden no reckoning was needed, because such money as does not bear fruit does not reasonably pay, and if it bore fruit it would necessarily be discovered. Moreover, if they were unwilling to labor for the republic, they could give it up and not toil at it, because she would find well-disposed citizens who would not think it burdensome to aid her with money and with counsel; and so great are the benefits and the honors that rule brings with it that those ought to be enough for them, without trying not to share in the burdens. But the trouble consisted in something they did not speak of, because it pained them that they could not start a war without damaging themselves, having to share in its expenses like the others; if this method of taxation had been devised before, there never would have been war with King Ladislas, nor would there now be war with Duke Filippo, for these wars were undertaken to enrich the citizens, and not from necessity.

These quarrels that had started were calmed by Giovanni de' Medici, who showed that it was not well to go back over past things, but very much so to provide for future ones. And if the exactions in the past had been unjust, Florentines should thank God that they had found a way for making them just, and should hope that this plan for taxation would serve to reunite, not to divide the city, as would investigation of past taxes and an attempt to equalize them with the present ones. For he who is content with half a victory will always come out better for it, because those who try to do more than win often lose. With such words he calmed these disputes and prevented further discussion of equalized taxes.

CHAPTER 15

[Peace with Duke Filippo; further complaint about taxes. 1428]

To continue, then, with the war against the Duke of Milan, a treaty was made at Ferrara by means of the Pope's Legate. The Duke at the beginning did not observe its conditions, so that the League again took up arms; and coming to a battle with his soldiers, they defeated him at Maclodio. After that defeat, the Duke started new discussions about a settlement. The Florentines agreed to these, having come to lack trust in the Venetians, since they thought they were spending a great deal to give power to another state; the Vene/ tians agreed because they observed that Carmignuola, after defeating the Duke, went slowly, so that they decided they could no longer trust him. Hence a treaty was made in 1428: the Florentines got back the cities they had lost in Romagna; Brescia was left to the Venetians, and in addition the Duke gave them Bergamo and her territory. The Florentine outlay on this war was three million, five hundred thousand ducats, by means of which they increased Vene/ tian territory and might, and their own poverty and disunion.

With the coming of peace outside the walls, war inside began again. Since the noble citizens could not endure the *catasto* and did not see any way for getting rid of it, they thought out methods for making it more enemies in order to have more companions in as/ sailing it. So they showed the officials selected to impose it that the law forced them to register also the property of the people in Floren/ tine territory to see if they had any goods belonging to Florentines. Hence all the subjects were called upon to present within a certain time the lists of their property. As a result the Volterrani complained to the Signoria; whereupon the officials, in anger, sent eighteen of them to prison. This action caused great indignation among the Volterrani, yet, out of regard for the prisoners, they did not rebel.

CHAPTER 16

[The dying words of Giovanni de'Medici; his character. 1429]

At this time Giovanni de'Medici fell sick. Knowing his illness to be mortal, he called Cosimo and Lorenzo, his sons, and said to them: "I believe that I have lived out the time assigned to me by God and by Nature at my birth. I die happy, since I leave you rich, healthy, and in such condition that, if you follow my footsteps, you can live in Florence honored and liked by everybody. Nothing does so much to make me die happy as to remember that I have never injured anyone, but on the contrary, I have, so far as possible, benefited everyone. So I encourage you to do. In the government, if you wish to live in security, take as much part as is given you by the laws and by men. This will not bring on you either envy or danger, because what a man takes for himself, not what is given to him, makes him hated. And you will always have much more authority than those who, wishing the share of others, lose their own, and before they lose it live in continual trouble. With these methods, among so many enemies, among so many dissensions, I have not merely kept but increased my reputation in this city. So, if you follow my footsteps, you will keep and increase yours. But if you do otherwise, believe that your end cannot be more fortunate than that of Florentines who within your memory have ruined themselves and destroyed their houses."

He died soon after, and throughout the city was very much regretted, as for his admirable qualities he deserved to be. Giovanni was charitable, and not merely was in the habit of giving alms to those who asked them, but many times without being asked he supplied the needs of the poor. He loved everybody; the good he praised, and the wicked he pitied. Never did he ask for offices, and he held them all. He never went to the Palace if he was not sent for. He loved peace, avoided war. In times of adversity, he gave men support; in times of prosperity, he gave them aid. He was far from plundering the treasury, and to the common good he made additions. In city offices he appeared well: not of much eloquence but of very great wisdom. He presented the appearance of melancholy, but later in conversation he was pleasant and witty. He died very rich in money, and still richer in good reputation and good will. His legacy, both of the goods of Fortune and of those of the spirit, Cosimo not merely preserved but increased.

CHAPTER 17

[*Giusto's unsuccessful rebellion in Volterra. 1429*]

The Volterrani were tired of being in prison, and in order to get their freedom promised to do what was ordered. After they had been freed, then, and had returned to Volterra, the time came when their new priors took up office. Among them a certain Giusto was chosen, a man of the lower class but of standing with the lower class, who was one of those imprisoned in Florence. This man, fired on his own part with hatred against the Florentines, as the result of both the public and the private injury, was also urged on by Giovanni di . . . ,[1] an aristocrat who was sitting with him in the magistracy, to try to rouse the people with the authority of the priors and with his own influence, and to take the city from the hands of the Floren-tines and make himself her prince. On the advice of this man, Giusto took arms, mastered the city, seized the captain who was there for the Florentines, and with the consent of the people made himself ruler.

This rebellion in Volterra greatly disturbed the Florentines; yet, since they had made peace with the Duke and their agreements were recent, they judged they had time to regain her. And in order not to lose their opportunity, they appointed as commissioners in this busi-ness Messer Rinaldo degli Albizzi and Messer Palla Strozzi. Giusto meanwhile, since he thought the Florentines would attack him, asked the Sienese and the Lucchese for help. The Sienese refused, saying that they were in league with the Florentines; Pagolo Guinigi, who was ruler of Lucca, in order to regain favor with the people of Florence, which in the war with the Duke he lost by showing him-self a friend to Filippo, not merely refused aid to Giusto but sent to Florence as a prisoner the man who had come to ask it. The Floren-tine commissioners, meanwhile, in order to come upon the Volterrani unprepared, got together all their men-at-arms, levied in Valdarno below the city and in the country about Pisa many infantry, and went to Volterra. But Giusto did not lose courage either because he was abandoned by his neighbors or on account of the attack to be made by the Florentines, but trusting in the city's strong site and her wealth, provided for defense.

1. *Left blank by Machiavelli. The name is Contugi.*

There was in Volterra a certain Messer Arcolano, a brother of that Giovanni who had persuaded Giusto to seize the lordship, a man of standing among the nobility. He brought together certain of his confidants and showed them that God, through this event that had taken place, had brought aid to their city in her necessity, because, if they would take arms and deprive Giusto of the lordship and turn the city over to the Florentines, it would follow that they would be the leaders in that city, and she would maintain her ancient privileges. So having agreed on this, they went to the ruler's palace, and while part of them remained below, Messer Arcolano with three of them went up to the hall. Finding Giusto with some citizens, they drew him aside as if they wished to talk about something important. And from one discussion to another, they got him into a private room, where Arcolano and his companions attacked him with their swords. They were not, however, quick enough not to give Giusto a chance to grasp his weapon. Before they killed him, he seriously wounded two of them, but at last unable to resist so many, he was killed and thrown down to the ground from the Palace. Then taking arms, Messer Arcolano's party gave the city to the Florentine commissioners, who with their soldiers were nearby. Without making any agreements, they marched in. The outcome was that Volterra made her condition worse, because among other things the Florentines cut off from her the larger part of the surrounding territory and made it into a vicarate.

CHAPTER 18

[Niccolò Fortebraccio invades Lucchese territory; Florence divided over war against Lucca. 1429]

After the loss and the regaining of Volterra, as though in a moment, there was no cause for a new war, if men's ambition had not started another. In the wars with the Duke, Niccolò Fortebraccio, the son of Braccio of Perugia's sister, had long borne arms for the city of Florence. When peace came, this man was dismissed by the Florentines, but when the matter of Volterra came up he was still quartered at Fucecchio; hence the commissioners for that affair availed themselves of him and his soldiers. It was supposed that while Messer Rinaldo worked with him in that war, he persuaded

him, with the excuse of some made-up injury, to try attacking the
Lucchese, by showing him that if he did it, Messer Rinaldo himself
would work in such a way at Florence that the city would undertake
a campaign against Lucca, with Niccolò in command. So when
Volterra had been captured and he had returned to his quarters at
Fucecchio, either because of the persuasions of Messer Rinaldo, or
through his own will, in November 1429, with three hundred horsemen and three hundred infantry he captured Ruoti and Compito,
walled towns of the Lucchese. Then, going down into the plains,
he took very great booty. When news of this attack was spread in
Florence, throughout the city there were gatherings of men of every
sort, and the greater part held that they should undertake a campaign
against Lucca. Among the aristocratic citizens who favored it were
those of the Medici party; with them sided Messer Rinaldo, moved
either by the opinion that it was an undertaking profitable for the
state or by his own ambition, believing that he would be the leader
in that victory. Those who opposed it were Niccolò da Uzzano
and his party.

And it seems beyond belief that there should be such diverse
judgments about beginning war in just one city. Many Florentines
after ten years of peace had condemned the war undertaken against
Duke Filippo to defend their liberty, yet now, after so many expenses
had been incurred and there was such distress in the city, the same
citizens and the same populace with great urgency were asking that
war be started against Lucca to take away that city's liberty. But on
the other hand, those who wished the first war condemned this one.
Such variation does time bring in opinions, and so much more ready
the crowd is to take the property of others than to protect its own, and
so much more are men moved by the hope of gain than by the fear
of loss. Loss, except when it is close to them, they do not imagine;
gain, even though distant, they hope for.

The people of Florence were filled with hope by the gains that
Niccolò Fortebraccio had made and was making and by the letters
from the rectors' near Lucca; for the Florentine vicars of Vico and of
Pescia wrote asking permission to receive the towns that were coming
to surrender, so that soon the whole region surrounding Lucca
would be gained. The Florentines were further encouraged by the
ambassador sent by Pagolo Guinigi, the ruler of Lucca, to complain

1. *Florentine rulers of cities subject to Florence.*

of the attacks made by Niccolò and to beg the Signoria not to decide on waging war against a neighbor and a city that had always been friendly to her. The name of the ambassador was Messer Jacopo Viviani. A little earlier Pagolo had this man in prison for plotting against him, and though he found him guilty, he granted him his life; then, because he believed that Messer Jacopo had forgiven the injury, Pagolo trusted him. But Messer Jacopo, remembering the danger better than the benefit, when he reached Florence secretly urged the citizens on to the business. These urgings, added to other hopes, caused the Signoria to summon the Council, for which there was an assembly of four hundred and ninety-eight citizens, before whom the chief men of the city debated the matter.

CHAPTER 19

[Rinaldo degli Albizzi favors war on Lucca; Niccolò da Uzzano advises against it. 1429]

As we said above, Messer Rinaldo took the lead in favoring the expedition against Lucca. He set forth the profit that would come from her conquest; he set forth the opportunity for the expedition: Lucca was left as Florentine booty by the Venetians and the Duke; the Pope, who was mixed up in the affairs of the Kingdom, could not hinder them. To this he added the ease of taking her, since she was in servitude to a citizen and had lost her natural vigor and her ancient zeal for defending her liberty. Hence, either by the people in order to drive out the tyrant, or by the tyrant in fear of the people, she would be surrendered. He related the injuries done by the ruler to our republic and his malicious spirit toward it, and how dangerous he would be if the Pope or the Duke should again wage war on Florence. He concluded that the Florentine people never had under-taken an enterprise that was easier, more profitable, or more just.

Against this opinion, Niccolò da Uzzano said that the city of Florence never undertook an enterprise more unjust, more dangerous or from which greater damage was likely to result. First, we should be striking at a Guelf city which had always been friendly to the Florentine people and, to her peril, had many times received into her bosom Guelfs who could not remain in their native city. In the records of our affairs it cannot be found that free Lucca ever injured

Florence. But if someone (such as Castruccio long ago and now this man) who had enslaved her had injured Florence, the blame was to be laid not on her but on the tyrant. If they could make war on the tyrant without making it on the citizens, he would be less vexed, but because such a war was impossible, he could not agree that the goods of a friendly body of citizens should be plundered.

But since we were living today in such a manner that not much account was taken of just and unjust, he would let that matter go and deal only with Florence's advantage. He believed, as to this, that things can be called advantageous which cannot easily bring harm. He did not know, then, how anybody could call an undertaking advantageous in which the losses were sure and the advantages uncertain. The sure losses were the expenses it would require, which evidently were large enough to frighten a city brought back into good condition, not merely one exhausted by a long and serious war, as Florence was. The advantages to be got from it were those of the conquest of Lucca. These he admitted would be great, but he was for considering the uncertainties of the attempt, which appeared to him so many that he judged the conquest impossible. Moreover, they should not believe that the Venetians and Filippo would approve this conquest, for the Venetians would pretend to agree only in order not to seem ungrateful, since a short time before, by means of Florentine money, they had gained such great power. Filippo would be glad that the Florentines were involved in a new war and new expenses, in order to attack them a second time when they were exhausted and worn out in every way. In the midst of their campaign and in their highest hopes for victory, he would not lack a method for rescuing the Lucchese, either secretly with money or by dismissing some of his troops and sending them to the city as soldiers of fortune.

He therefore advised that they avoid the undertaking and deal with the tyrant in such a way that inside his own city he would make himself as many enemies as possible, because Lucca could not be subdued in any easier way than that of letting her live under the tyrant and be harassed and weakened by him. The tyrant could not hold her and she would not know how to rule herself or be able to do so. Hence Lucca would be brought to such a condition that of necessity she would fall into the lap of Florence. But Niccolò da Uzzano saw that partisan feelings were so excited that his words were not listened to. Yet all the same he was going to foretell these things: they would enter a war in which they would spend much and run into many dangers; instead of conquering Lucca, they would free her from her tyrant; out of a city that was friendly, in subjection and weak, they would make one that was free and hostile and in time would be an obstacle to the greatness of Florence.

CHAPTER 20

[War against Lucca; the cruelty of Astorre Gianni in Seravezza. 1430]

So after there had been speeches for the expedition and against the expedition, they secretly ascertained the verdict of the men, according to custom, and of the entire number only ninety-eight voted against it. Having made their decision, then, and chosen the Ten to carry on the war, they hired infantry and cavalry. They appointed as commissioners Astorre Gianni and Messer Rinaldo degli Albizzi, and they made an agreement with Niccolò Fortebraccio to receive from him the towns he had taken and to have him continue the campaign as in our employ. The commissioners, when they arrived in Lucchese territory, divided their army; Astorre spread out through the plain toward Camaiore and Pietrasanta, and Messer Rinaldo went toward the mountains, thinking that when the city had been deprived of her surrounding district she could easily be taken.

Yet the attempts of these men turned out badly, not because they did not gain many towns, but because of the censures on their management of the war that were directed against both of them. It is true that for the censures against himself Astorre Gianni gave good cause. There is a valley near Pietrasanta called Seravezza, rich and full of inhabitants. Knowing of the commissioner's coming, the men of Seravezza met him and begged him to accept them as faithful servants of the Florentine people. In appearance, Astorre accepted their offer. But he had his soldiers seize all the passes and the strong places in the valley, and had the men come together in their largest church; then he made them all prisoners and let his soldiers lay waste and destroy all the country in a cruel and avaricious fashion, not sparing holy places or women, either virgins or wives. These events, as soon as they happened, were known in Florence and angered not only the magistrates but the whole city.

CHAPTER 21

[The Seravezzese complain in Florence; Astorre is punished. 1430]

Some of the Seravezzese who escaped from the hands of the commissioner hastened to Florence and in every street and to every man related their miseries. As a result, being encouraged by many who were eager that the commissioner be punished, either as a wicked man or as opposed to their faction, they went to the Ten and asked to be heard. When they were brought in, one of them spoke to this effect:

"We are sure, magnificent Signors, that our words will find credit and pity with your Lordships when you know how our country was seized by your commissioner and in what way he then treated us. Our valley, as the records of your earlier affairs abundantly show, has always been Guelf and has many times been a sure harbor for your citizens who, when harassed by the Ghibellines, have taken refuge there. And always our ancestors and ourselves have adored the name of this famous republic, because of her being chief and leader of that party; and as long as the Lucchese were Guelfs, we gladly were subject to their authority, but when they came under the tyrant who has left his old friends and followed the Ghibelline party, rather through force than of our free will we have obeyed him; and God knows how many times we have prayed that occasion would be given us to show our inclination toward the old party. How blind men are in their wishes! What we longed for as our security has been our ruin. When we first knew that your banners were coming toward us, we approached your commissioner as though to meet not enemies but our ancient rulers, and we put our valley, our fortunes, and ourselves in his hands, and relied upon his faith, believing that he possessed the spirit, if not of a Florentine, at least of a man.

"Your Lordships will pardon us, because not being able to endure worse than we have endured gives us courage to speak. This commissioner of yours has nothing of man except his appearance, nothing of a Florentine except the name—a death-bringing plague, a cruel wild beast, a repulsive monster, such as never has been described by any writer. Because, having brought us into our church, with the excuse of wishing to speak to us, he made us prisoners and destroyed and burned our whole valley, and her inhabitants and her property he spoiled, sacked, struck down, killed; he defiled the women, deflowered the virgins and, dragging them from the arms of their mothers, made them the prey of his soldiers. If through any harm done to the Florentine people or to him, we had deserved such a great evil, or if he had taken us armed and defending ourselves, we would complain less, indeed we should blame ourselves as having deserved it because of our offenses or our arrogance. But since when we were unarmed and had surrendered freely to him, he then robbed us and with such injury and insult plundered us, we are forced to complain.

"And though we could have filled Lombardy with complaints, and with blame for this city could have scattered through all Italy the report of our wrongs, we have not done so in order not to befoul so honorable and merciful a republic with the dishonor and cruelty of one wicked citizen. As to him, if before our ruin we had known his avarice, we should have attempted to find some satisfaction for his gluttonous spirit, even though it has neither measure nor bottom, and in that way with part of our property would have saved the rest. But since we are now too late, we have determined to have recourse to you and to beg you to relieve your subjects' distress, so that other men will not be afraid, because of our example, to come under your power. If you are not moved by our countless ills, may you be moved by fear of God's wrath, since he has seen his churches sacked and burned and our people betrayed in his bosom."

Having said this, they threw themselves on the ground, shrieking and praying that their property and their country be given back to them, and that (though honor could not be restored) Florence should at least restore wives to husbands, and to fathers their daughters. The savagery of the affair, first learned by report, and then heard from the living voices of those who had undergone it, excited the magistracy; without delay they recalled Astorre, and then he was condemned and deprived of the right to hold office. They sought for the property of the Seravezzese, and what could be found they restored; for the rest, the city in the course of time and in various ways made compensation.

CHAPTER 22

[Rinaldo degli Albizzi accused of peculation; his defense; new commissioners appointed. 1430]

Messer Rinaldo degli Albizzi, on the other hand, was reviled as having carried on the war not for the profit of the Florentine people but for his own. It was said that when he became commissioner he forgot his eagerness to take Lucca, because it was enough for him to sack the country regions and fill his pastures with cattle and his houses with spoil, and that he was not content with the booty his dependents took for his personal profit but that he bought that of the soldiers, so that from a commissioner he turned into a merchant. These slanders, when they came to his ears, disturbed his honest and noble spirit more than was fitting for so dignified a man; they so troubled him that, in anger against the magistracy and the citizens, without waiting for or asking permission, he returned to Florence.

Presenting himself before the Ten, he said that he well knew how much difficulty and danger there is in serving an undisciplined people and a divided city: the first accepts every rumor; the second is hard on evil deeds, does not reward good ones, and blames doubtful ones. Hence, if you are victorious, nobody praises you; if you make a mistake, everybody censures you; if you lose, everybody slanders you; the friendly party strives to injure you through envy, the hostile party through hatred. Nevertheless he had never, through fear of empty censure, refrained from carrying on any work that would bring certain benefit to his city. True it was that the vileness of the present slanders had overcome his patience, and made him change his nature. Therefore he begged the magistracy that in the future they would try to be quicker in protecting their citizens in order that they too might be more eager to do good work for the city. And since in Florence it was not customary to offer them a triumph, at least it should be customary to protect them from false revilings. The Ten should remember that they too were citizens of that city, and at any time charges might be brought against them, which would force them to understand how indignant honest men are made by false censures.

The Ten, so far as time allowed, tried to calm him, and asked Neri di Gino and Alamanno Salviati to take charge of the cam paign. Giving up raids on the territory of Lucca, these two moved their army close to the city. But because the season was still cold, the soldiers stationed themselves at Capannori, where the commissioners believed that they were losing time. Yet when they wished to go closer to the city, the soldiers, because of the unfavorable weather, did not consent, even though the Ten urged the siege and accepted no excuse.

CHAPTER 23

[An attempt to flood Lucca damages the Florentine army. 1430]

In those days there was in Florence an excellent architect named Filippo di Ser Brunellesco, of whose works our city is full; such were his merits that after his death his marble statue was put in the chief church of Florence, with an inscription on its pedestal that to all who read still bears witness to his ability. He showed that Lucca could be flooded because of the position of the city and the bed of the River Serchio; and he argued it so well that the Ten arranged to have it tried. From it came nothing else than trouble for our army and security for the enemy; for with a dyke the Lucchese raised the level of the land on that side to which our army was making the Serchio come, and then one night broke the dykes of that ditch by which the army was conveying the waters, so that these, finding the high barrier in the direction of Lucca and the dykes of the canal open, covered the entire plain; hence the army, far from being able to come near the city, had to draw off.

CHAPTER 24

[The Duke of Milan sends Count Francesco Sforza to aid Lucca; Sforza's intrigues. 1430]

Since this attempt did not succeed, the Ten, who were newly taking up office, sent as commissioner Messer Giovanni Guicciardini. As soon as he could, he besieged Lucca. So the ruler, Pagolo Guinigi, seeing himself in straits, on the advice of a certain Messer Antonio del Rosso, a Sienese, who in the name of the common-wealth of Siena was with him, sent Salvestro Trenta and Lionardo Buonvisi to the Duke of Milan. In Pagolo's behalf they asked him for help. When they found him cold, they secretly begged that he would give soldiers to them personally; for this they promised him, in behalf of the people, to give him their ruler as a prisoner, and afterward to put the Duke in possession of the city. They warned him that if he did not make this decision soon, Pagolo would give up his city to the Florentines, who with many promises were urging him. Then the Duke's fear of this really did make him lay scruples aside, and he arranged that Count Francesco Sforza, his hired general, should publicly ask him for permission to go to the Kingdom.

Having received it, he came with his forces to Lucca, notwithstanding that the Florentines, knowing this arrangement and fearing what would come of it, sent to the Count his friend Boccaccino Alamanni to upset it. When the Count came to Lucca, then, the Florentines with their army retired to Librafatta, and the Count at once besieged Pescia, where the vicar was Pagolo da Diacceto. Advised more by fear than by anything more creditable, Pagolo fled to Pistoia; and if Pescia had not been defended by Giovanni Malavolti, who was in garrison there, it would have been lost. The Count, then, not having been able to take it in his first attack, went on to Borgo a Buggiano, which he took. Stigliano, a walled town nearby, he burned. The Florentines, seeing this destruction, turned to schemes that many times had saved them, since they knew that with mercenary soldiers, whenever force is not enough, one can make use of bribery. And therefore they offered the Count money, for which he was not merely to go away but to give them Lucca. The Count, seeing he could get no more money from Lucca, readily turned to get it from those who had it; thus he made an agreement with the Florentines not to give them Lucca—for the sake of his honor he would not grant that—but to abandon her, if they would give him fifty thousand ducats. When this agreement was made, in order that the people of Lucca might excuse him to the Duke, he arranged with them that they should drive out Pagolo Guinigi their ruler.

CHAPTER 25

[Pagolo Guinigi driven from Lucca; the Duke of Milan defeats the Florentines; peace without profit. 1430–1433]

As I said above, Messer Antonio del Rosso, the Sienese ambassador, was in Lucca. With Count Francesco's authorization, he plotted with the citizens Pagolo Guinigi's ruin. The heads of the conspiracy were Piero Cennami and Giovanni da Chivizzano. The Count was encamped outside the city, on the Serchio, having with him Lanzilao, Pagolo's son. The conspirators, forty in number, at night and armed visited Pagolo. At the noise they made, he met them in astonishment and asked the reason for their coming. Piero Cennami answered that Pagolo had ruled them a long time and had brought them to die by sword and famine, surrounded with enemies. Therefore they had determined that in the future they would rule themselves; and they asked for the keys of the city and her treasure. Pagolo answered that the treasure was spent; the keys and himself were in their power. This only he begged, that they would agree that just as his rule had begun and continued without blood, so without blood it might end. Count Francesco took Pagolo and his son to the Duke of Milan; finally they died in prison.

Count Francesco's departure left Lucca free from her tyrant and the Florentines free from fear of Sforza's soldiers, so the citizens prepared for defense and the Florentines returned to the attack. The Florentine general was the Count of Urbino who, pressing the city hard, forced the Lucchese once more to turn to the Duke. Using the same pretense as in sending the Count, he sent to their assistance Niccolò Piccino. When he attempted to enter Lucca, our soldiers opposed him on the Serchio, and in crossing the river they got into combat and were defeated. The commissioner with a few of our soldiers took refuge in Pisa.

This defeat discouraged our whole city, and because the undertaking had been generally supported, the citizens, not knowing against whom to turn, slandered those who had administered it, since they could not slander those who had decided on it; they brought up again the charges against Messer Rinaldo. But more than any other, Messer Giovanni Guicciardini was torn to shreds with charges that after Count Francesco's departure he could have ended the war but that he was bribed with money and had sent home a large sum; they named those who had taken the money to him and those who received it. These rumors and these accusations went so far that the Captain of the People, moved by these public reports and urged on by the supporters of the opposite party, cited Messer Giovanni. He appeared, full of wrath. Whereupon his relatives, for the sake of their honor, made such efforts that the Captain gave up the attempt.

The Lucchese after this victory not merely got their own towns again but took all those of the Pisan district except Bientina, Calcinaia, Livorno and Librafatta, and but for the discovery of a conspiracy made in Pisa, we should have lost even that city. The Florentines reorganized their soldiers and employed as their general Michelotto, Sforza's pupil. On the other hand, Duke Filippo followed up his victory, and in order with larger forces to harass the Florentines, he had the Genoese, the Sienese and the ruler of Piombino join for the defense of Lucca and employ Niccolò Piccino as their general. This action completely revealed Duke Filippo's policy. So the Venetians and the Florentines renewed their league, and war was then made openly in Lombardy and in Tuscany. And in both provinces there were various battles with varying fortunes, so that, since everybody was worn out, an agreement between the parties was made in May 1433; by this the Florentines, the Lucchese, and the Sienese, who in the war had taken many towns from each other, gave them all up, and each one returned to the possession of his own.

CHAPTER 26

[Cosimo de' Medici; the tactics of Averardo de' Medici and Puccio Pucci, his followers. 1429–1430]

While this war was going on, all the dangerous disputes of the parties in Florence boiled up again. Cosimo de'Medici, after the death of Giovanni his father, conducted himself with greater spirit in public matters and with greater zeal and more liberality toward his friends than his father had done. Hence, those who at Giovanni's death had rejoiced, on seeing what Cosimo was, were sad. Cosimo was a very prudent man, of serious and pleasing appearance, very liberal, very humane. Never did he attempt anything against the Guelf Party or against the government, but gave his attention to doing good to everybody and, with his liberality, to making many citizens his partisans. Hence his example brought about further censure of those who ruled; yet he thought in this way either to live in Florence as powerful and secure as anybody or, if through the ambition of his adversaries he came up against something beyond the laws, to be in both arms and support their superior.

Cosimo's great instruments for managing his power were Averardo de'Medici and Puccio Pucci. Averardo with his boldness and Puccio with his prudence and sagacity added to his influence and greatness. And so highly esteemed were the advice and the judgment of Puccio and so well recognized by everybody that the party of Cosimo got its name not from himself but from Puccio. This city thus divided carried on the campaign against Lucca, in which the differences of the parties flamed up rather than were put out. And though Cosimo's party had brought it on, nevertheless for its man-agement many of the other party were sent, as men of high reputation in the state. Since for this action Averardo de'Medici and the others could find no remedy, they employed all manner of skill and effort in slandering such commissioners, and if there was any loss—and there were many—not Fortune or the power of the enemy but the imprudence of the commissioner was blamed. This made them add weight to the sins of Astorre Gianni; this caused the anger of Messer Rinaldo degli Albizzi and his departure from his place without permission; this caused the summoning by the Captain of the People of Messer Giovanni Guicciardini. In this party, hatred originated all the complaints brought against magistrates and commissioners: the genuine, Cosimo's party made greater; those not true they made up; and the genuine and the not-true were believed by the people, who generally hated Cosimo's opponents.

CHAPTER 27

[Niccolò da Uzzano speaks on Cosimo's strength and inevitable triumph. 1429–1430]

Such conditions and unlawful methods were perfectly under-stood by Niccolò da Uzzano and the other heads of the Guelf Party, and many times they discussed together measures against them and found none; they saw that to let evils grow was dangerous and to oppose them difficult. Niccolò da Uzzano was the chief man objecting to unlawful ways. Hence, when there was war outside the city and these disturbances inside, Niccolò Barbadoro, wishing to influence Niccolò da Uzzano to consent to Cosimo's ruin, visited him at home, where in deep thought he was sitting in his study; with the best arguments he could use, the visitor urged him to unite with Messer Rinaldo in driving out Cosimo. Niccolò da Uzzano replied with this discourse:

"It would be well for you, for your house, and for our republic, if you and the others who follow you in this belief had beards of silver rather than of gold,[1] such as your name indicates, because counsels coming from white heads full of experience would be wiser and more useful to everybody. Those who plan to drive Cosimo from Florence should, I think, first of all measure their forces and his. This party of ours you have baptized as the party of the Nobles, and the opposite that of the Plebeians. If the truth corresponded with the names, the victory would be doubtful in every event and we would need rather to fear than to hope, moved by the example of the ancient noble families of this city, which the Plebeians destroyed. But we need to feel greater fear, since our party is divided and that of our adversaries is a unit. First of all, Neri di Gino and Nerone di Nigi, two of our chief citizens, have never declared themselves in such a way that one can say they are more our friends than theirs. Many families, indeed many houses, are divided, for many through envy of their brothers and their relatives do not support us but support them. I shall remind you of some of the more important; the others you will think of for yourself. Of the sons of Messer Maso degli Albizzi, Luca, through envy of Messer Rinaldo, has thrown his lot with their party; in the house of the Guicciardini, of the sons of Messer Luigi, Piero is an enemy to Messer Giovanni and supports our opponents; Tommaso and Niccolò Soderini, through their hatred for Francesco, their uncle, are openly against us. Hence if you consider well of what sort they are and of what sort we are, I do not know why ours more deserves to be called the Noble Party than theirs. If it is because they are supported by all the lower classes, we are thereby in a worse condition and they in a better one; and indeed if it comes to arms or to divisions, we are not in such a state that we

1. Barbadoro *means* beard of gold.

can resist them. If we yet keep our power, it comes from the old reputation of this government, which has been retained for fifty years; but if it should come to the test and to a revelation of our weakness, we would lose it.

"If you say that the just cause that moves us should add to our credit and take theirs away, I answer you that this justice must be understood and believed by others than ourselves, but the opposite is true. The cause that moves us is based on our fear that a prince will be set up in this city. If we have this fear, others do not have it; on the contrary—what is worse—they accuse us as we accuse Cosimo. The doings that make us suspect him are these: with his money he helps everybody, not merely individuals but the public, not merely the Florentines but their generals; he helps this and that citizen who has need of the magistrates; through his favor with the masses, he brings this and that friend of his to the higher ranks of office. So then it will be necessary to urge as the reasons for driving him out that he is compassionate, helpful, liberal, and loved by everybody. Tell me now, what law is it that forbids or that blames and condemns in men, pity, liberality, love? And though they are all methods that bring men flying to the principate,[2] nevertheless, they are not thought so, nor are we such that we can make it understood, because our ways have destroyed confidence in us; the city, which naturally is partisan and—since always divided into parties—corrupt, does not lend her ears to such accusations.

"But let us suppose that you succeed in driving Cosimo out— something that, since you have the Signoria in your favor, can easily happen—how, among so many friends of his as will remain here and will burn with eagerness for his return, can you ever keep him from returning? This will be impossible, because they are so many and they have such general good will that you never can be sure about them; the more of his early and obvious friends you drive out, the more enemies you make for yourself. Hence in a short time he will return, and you gain this, namely, that you drive him out a good man and he returns a wicked one; because his nature will be corrupted by those who call him back, for he cannot oppose them, being under obligation to them. And if you plan to put him to death, never by way of the magistrates will you succeed, because his money

2. *In an early draft,* tyranny. *Various passages in this part of the* HISTORY *are similarly softer than in the early draft.*

and your venal minds will always save him. But let us suppose that he does die or, being driven out, does not return, I do not see that we have made any gain here in our republic, because, if she is freed from Cosimo, she makes herself a slave to Messer Rinaldo. And I, for my part, am one of those who wish that in power and influence no citizen shall exceed the others. But if either of these two is to surpass the other, I do not know what reason should make me love Messer Rinaldo more than Cosimo.

"I do not wish to say more except: God guard this city from having any citizen become her prince. And even if our sins deserve it, may he keep her from having to obey such a one! Do not, then, advise a course that in every way will be injurious, and do not believe that when assisted by a few you can oppose the will of many; for all these citizens, part through ignorance, part through malice, are now ready to sell this republic; and so much is Fortune their friend that they have found their buyer. So be governed by my advice. Try to live modestly, and, as to liberty, you will have as much reason to fear those of our party as those of the opposite one. When any trouble arises, by living neutral you will be in favor with both, and so you will benefit yourselves and will not injure your native city."

CHAPTER 28
[The evils of party strife; Cosimo arrested. 1430–1433]

These words so restrained Barbadoro's purpose that things were quiet as long as the war over Lucca lasted; but when peace came, and with it the death of Niccolò da Uzzano, the city was left without war and without check. As a result, dangerous factions increased without restraint; and Messer Rinaldo, since he alone was now head of the party, did not cease to beg and importune all the citizens that he thought might be gonfaloniers to arm themselves to free the city from that man who necessarily, through the malice of the few and the ignorance of the many, would bring them to slavery. These methods pursued by Messer Rinaldo and those followed by men who favored the opposite party kept the city full of suspicion; and whenever a magistracy was chosen, men would reckon publicly how many of one and of the other party sat in it, and at the choice of the Signoria all the city was stirred up. Every case that came before the magistrates, no matter how small, became a struggle between the parties; secrets were made public; both good and bad were favored and opposed; good men as much as bad were in the same way torn to shreds; no magistrate did his duty.

When Florence was in this confusion, Messer Rinaldo, determined to diminish Cosimo's power and learning that Bernardo Guadagni was likely to be gonfalonier, paid his taxes for him, in order that a debt to the state should not keep Bernardo out of that office. When it came to the drawing of the Signors, then, Fortune, the friend of our dissensions, caused Bernardo to be drawn as gonfalonier to serve for September and October. Messer Rinaldo at once went to see him, and told him that the party of the aristocrats and all hoping to be ruled well were happy that he had reached that dignity and that it was his duty to act in such a way that they would not rejoice in vain. He then showed him the risks of disunion and that there was no way to avoid disunion except to destroy Cosimo, who alone, through the influence resulting from his enormous riches, kept them weak, and that he had been brought so high that, unless something were done about it, he would become their prince, and that it was the part of a good citizen to apply a remedy, to call the people to the Public Square, and to take the government over,[1] in order to give back to his native city her liberty. Messer Rinaldo reminded Bernardo that without justice Messer Salvestro de'Medici checked the greatness of the Guelfs, to whom, because of the blood their ancestors had shed, the government belonged; and what Messer Salvestro against so many had been able to do without justice, Bernardo with justice surely could now do against one alone. He exhorted him not to fear, because his friends were ready to aid him with their weapons, and to take no account of the lower classes who worshiped Cosimo, because they would not give him other aid than once they gave to Messer Giorgio Scali. Bernardo should not fear Cosimo's wealth because when he was in the power of the Signors that wealth would be theirs. Messer Rinaldo ended by asserting that this deed would make the republic safe and united, and Bernardo famous. To these words Bernardo briefly answered that he thought it necessary to do all Messer Rinaldo said, and since the time had come

---

1. *He would call a parliament or assembly of the people, which, being suitably packed, would choose a* balìa *or committee having power to reorganize the government and to exercise authority generally.*

to get rid of Cosimo in very deed, he would busy himself in providing forces, so as to be ready when he had won over his companions.

When Bernardo had taken office, gained the support of his associates and made an agreement with Messer Rinaldo, he cited Cosimo,
who, though many of his friends advised against it, appeared, trusting
more in his innocence than in the mercy of the Signors. When
Cosimo was in the Palace and in prison, Messer Rinaldo with many
armed men left his house, and along with him the entire aristocratic
party came to the piazza. There the Signors had the people summoned and chose two hundred men as a *balìa* to reform the government of the city. In that *balìa*, as soon as possible, they dealt with
reform and with the life and the death of Cosimo. Many held that
he should be sent into exile; many that he should be put to death;
many others were silent either in pity for him or in fear of his enemies.
These disagreements precluded any decision.

CHAPTER 29

[Cosimo fears poison; he is banished. 1433]

In the Palace tower there is a room as large as the size of the tower
permits, called the Alberghettino; there Cosimo was shut up, under
the charge of Federigo Malavolti. When from that place Cosimo
heard the parliament going on, the noise of arms in the piazza, and
the frequent ringing of bells for the *balìa*, he feared for his life; but he
was still more afraid that without legal measures his individual
enemies would kill him. On this account he abstained from eating,
so that in four days he ate nothing except a little bread. When
Federigo observed this, he said to him: "You fear, Cosimo, that you
will be poisoned; and you are killing yourself with hunger and doing
me little honor, if you think I am willing to put my hands to such a
piece of rascality. I do not believe that you are going to lose your
life—you have so many friends in the Palace and outside. But if you
are going to lose it, you can be sure that they will employ other means
than me as a minister to take it from you, because I do not intend to
foul my hands in the blood of anybody, and especially of you who
never have injured me. Be therefore of good courage, take your food
and keep yourself alive for your friends and your country. And that
with greater confidence you may do it, I am going to eat with you

the same things as you do." These words greatly encouraged Cosimo; and with tears in his eyes he embraced and kissed Federigo and with vigorous and lively words thanked him for so compassionate and loving an action, promising to show himself very grateful for it if ever Fortune gave him opportunity.

Cosimo, then, being somewhat encouraged, and his case under discussion among the citizens, that Federigo, to entertain him, brought to supper with him a friend of the Gonfalonier called Farganaccio, an amusing and witty man. And when they had almost finished supper, Cosimo, who thought he would make use of that man's visit, for he knew him very well, made a sign to Federigo to go out. Knowing the reason, the keeper pretended to go for something that was needed in serving the supper. When the two were left alone, Cosimo, after having used some kindly words to Farganaccio, gave him a countersign and instructed him to go to the superintendent of Santa Maria Nuova for a thousand and one hun-dred ducats. A hundred of them he was to take for himself; a thousand he was to take to the Gonfalonier, and when he found a suitable opportunity was to come to speak with him. The man accepted the commission; the money was paid; so Bernardo became milder, and the result was that Cosimo was banished to Padua against the will of Messer Rinaldo, who wished to get rid of him. Banishment was also inflicted on Averardo and many others of the Medici family, and with them Puccio and Giovanni Pucci.

And to frighten those who were opposed to Cosimo's exile, they gave a *balìa* to the Eight of Guard and to the Captain of the People. After these decisions, Cosimo, on the third of October 1433, came before the Signors, by whom his sentence of banishment was pro-nounced; he was exhorted to obey if he did not wish them to act more harshly against his goods and himself. Cosimo accepted the banishment with a cheerful face, declaring that wherever that Signo-ria might send him he would remain with pleasure. He begged, however, that since they had preserved his life they would protect it for him, because he had learned that in the Public Square were many who wished his blood. Then to the city, to the people, to their Signors, in whatever place he might be, he offered himself and his property. The Gonfalonier encouraged him and kept him in the Palace until night came. Then he took Cosimo home with him, and after giving him supper, had him escorted to the border by many armed men. Wherever he went, Cosimo was honorably received; the Venetians visited him publicly and, not as a banished man but as one who had been put in the highest position, treated him with honor.

CHAPTER 30

[Rinaldo degli Albizzi declares that Cosimo should have been executed; he advises a balía. *1433]*

When Florence was left widowed by a citizen so great and so universally loved, everybody was bewildered; those who had won and those who had lost were equally afraid. Hence Messer Rinaldo, dreading future ill for himself, in order not to fail himself and his party, called together many citizens who were his friends and said to them that he saw their ruin prepared for them, through their having allowed themselves to be overcome by the prayers, by the tears and by the money of their enemies; and they had not understood that a little later they would have to beg and weep themselves, and that their prayers would not be listened to, and for their tears they would find nobody who would feel pity; and as to the money taken, they would restore the capital and pay the interest with tortures, death, and exile; and they might much better have done nothing than to have left Cosimo alive, with his friends still in Florence; for great men must either not be touched or, if they are touched, must be destroyed. He saw no other resource for them than to make themselves strong in the city, so that when their enemies woke up—and they would wake up soon—he and his friends could drive them out with arms, since they could not by lawful methods send them away. His party's resource was that which long before he had presented to them: namely to regain the support of the nobles by turning over and conceding all the offices of the city, and to make themselves strong with that party, since their adversaries had made themselves strong with the lower class. In this way, their party would be more powerful, since it would have more life, more vigor, more courage, and more reputa-tion. But he asserted that if this last true resource was not employed, he did not see with what means they could preserve a government among so many enemies; he discerned the approaching ruin of their party and of the city. To this Mariotto Baldovinetti, one of those assembled, offered opposition, demonstrating the pride of the nobles and their unbearable natures, and declaring that it would not be a good thing to put themselves under certain tyranny in order to escape dubious perils from the lower class. As a result, Messer Rinaldo, seeing that his advice was not listened to, lamented his misfortune and that of his party, blaming everything rather on the Heavens that willed thus than on the ignorance and blindness of men.

When the affair, then, was in this condition, and no necessary preparation was made, someone found a letter written by Messer Agnolo Acciaiuoli to Cosimo, which showed the disposition of the city toward him and encouraged him to attempt stirring up wars, and to make a friend of Neri di Gino, because Messer Agnolo judged that the city would have need for money and would find nobody to provide it; thus the citizens would be reminded of Cosimo and wish him to return. If Neri separated himself from Messer Rinaldo, Messer Rinaldo's party would be so much weakened that it would not be strong enough to defend itself. This letter, having come into the hands of the magistrates, caused Messer Agnolo to be arrested, tortured with the strappado, and sent into exile. But no such example gave any check to the party that favored Cosimo.

When almost a year had already rolled around from the day when Cosimo was driven out, at the end of August 1434, the man drawn as gonfalonier for the following two months was Niccolò di Cocco, and with him eight Signors, all partisans of Cosimo. Hence such a Signoria frightened Messer Rinaldo and all his party. And because, before the Signors took over their office, they were for three days private citizens, Messer Rinaldo was again with the heads of his party. He showed them their certain and imminent danger, and that their resource was to take arms and have Donato Velluti, who then was in the office of gonfalonier, bring the people together in the Public Square, make a new *balía*, deprive the new Signors of their office and choose new ones, such as the government wanted, burn the bags and, making a new selection of eligible persons, refill the bags with friends to their party. Many thought this plan safe and necessary; many others thought it too violent and likely to cause too much condemnation. Among those who opposed it was Messer Palla Strozzi, a quiet man, cultured and courteous, and fitted rather for the study of letters than for controlling a party and opposing civil dissensions. And therefore he said that plans that are either clever or bold seem good at the beginning, but in practice are difficult, and at the end are injurious, and that he believed that the fear of new wars outside, since the soldiers of the Duke of Milan were in Romagna near our borders, would make the Signors think more about that than about discords inside. And if they did intend to make changes (which they could not do without its being known), his party would always have time enough to take arms and do whatever seemed necessary for the general safety; and if they did this from necessity, it would be less astonishing to the people and bring less blame on themselves. Therefore it was decided that the new Signors should be allowed to take office and that their movements should be watched; and if Messer Rinaldo's party learned of any action against it, everybody should take arms and meet on the Piazza San Pulinari, a place near the Palace, from which they then could go where it was necessary.

CHAPTER 31

[Rinaldo degli Albizzi takes arms; his party does not support him. 1434]

Since they separated with this decision, the new Signors took up their offices. The Gonfalonier, in order to give himself a reputation and to frighten those who intended to oppose him, condemned to prison his predecessor, Donato Velluti, as a man who had made use of the public money. After this, he tested his companions about bringing back Cosimo; finding them inclined toward it, he spoke with those whom he considered the heads of the Medici party. Being further encouraged by them, he cited Messer Rinaldo, Ridolfo Peruzzi, and Niccolò Barbadoro, as the leaders of the party opposed.

After this citation, Messer Rinaldo thought it unwise to wait any longer, and came out with a large number of armed men; he was at once joined by Ridolfo Peruzzi and Niccolò Barbadoro. Among them were many other citizens and numerous soldiers who were in Florence without employment. They all gathered according to agreement in the Piazza San Pulinari. Messer Palla Strozzi, though he had assembled many men, did not come out; neither did Messer Giovanni Guicciardini. Hence Messer Rinaldo sent to urge them, and to reproach them for their sluggishness. Messer Giovanni replied that he made war enough on the hostile party if, by remaining in his house, he kept Piero his brother from coming out to rescue the

Palace. Messer Palla, after many messages were sent to him, came to San Pulinari on horseback, with two men on foot and without arms. Messer Rinaldo met him and strongly reproached him for his indifference, and said that his failure to join the others came from either little fidelity or little courage, and that both of these reproaches ought to be avoided by a man who wished the sort of reputation he had; and if he believed, because of not doing his duty to his party, that his enemies when they had won would excuse him from death or exile, he was deceived. Messer Rinaldo added that for his part if anything bad happened, he would have the satisfaction that before the danger he was not lacking with advice, and in the danger, with force. But Messer Palla and the others would redouble their regrets, meditating on having betrayed their city three times: once when they preserved Cosimo, again when they did not take Rinaldo's advice, and the third time when they did not save Florence with their weapons. To these words Messer Palla did not answer a thing that the bystanders heard; muttering, he turned his horse and went back to his house.

The Signors, learning that Messer Rinaldo and his party had taken up arms and seeing themselves abandoned, had the Palace locked, but then being without a plan, they did not know what to do. Yet Messer Rinaldo by delaying to come to the Public Square, through expecting those forces that did not come, deprived himself of opportunity for winning, gave the Signors courage for making preparations, and gave many citizens courage to go to them and exhort them to try measures for laying down arms. Consequently some who were less fearful went on behalf of the Signors to Messer Rinaldo and said that the Signoria did not know any reason for his movements and that it never had dreamed of injuring him. Though they had talked somewhat about Cosimo, they had not thought of bringing him back; if for that reason Rinaldo and his friends were fearful, they might feel secure. If they would be good enough to come to the Palace, they would be well received and satisfied in all their requests. These words did not make Messer Rinaldo change his resolution; he said he wished to make himself safe by turning the Signors into private citizens; then for everybody's benefit the city could be reorganized. But it always is true that where powers are equal and opinions different, anything of value can seldom be decided upon. Ridolfo Peruzzi, moved by the words of the citizens who spoke for the Signoria, said that for his part he sought nothing except that Cosimo should not come back; if that was agreed, he thought it victory enough; for the sake of a more complete victory he did not wish to fill his city with blood; therefore he intended to obey the Signoria. Then with his followers he went into the Palace, where he was pleasantly received. So the delay of Messer Rinaldo at San Pulinari, the small courage of Messer Palla, and the departure of Ridolfo deprived Messer Rinaldo of victory in his enterprise; moreover, the spirits of the citizens who followed him were losing their first warmth. To this was added the Pope's influence.

CHAPTER 32
[*Pope Eugene acts as mediator. 1434*]

Pope Eugene was in Florence, having been driven from Rome by the people. Seeing these tumults and thinking it his duty to calm them, he sent Messer Giovanni Vitelleschi the Patriarch, a good friend to Messer Rinaldo, to beg him to come to the Pope, who did not lack influence and credit with the Signoria sufficient to make Messer Rinaldo satisfied and secure, without blood and harm to the citizens. Persuaded therefore by his friend, Messer Rinaldo with all his armed followers went to Santa Maria Novella, where the Pope was living. Eugene set forth the pledge the Signors had given him, saying they had turned over to him every difference; if Messer Rinaldo would lay down his arms, everything would be settled as the Pope thought best. Messer Rinaldo, having seen Messer Palla's coldness and Ridolfo Peruzzi's instability, and lacking any better plan, put himself in the Pope's hands, thinking that surely his influence could preserve him. So the Pope sent instructions to Niccolò Barbadoro and to the others outside, who were waiting for him, to lay down their arms, because Messer Rinaldo was remaining with the Pontiff to arrange the agreement with the Signors. At that announcement they all separated and disarmed.

CHAPTER 33

[Rinaldo degli Albizzi defeated; Cosimo de' Medici returns in triumph. 1434]

The Signors, seeing their adversaries disarmed, were slow in negotiating the agreement with the Pope's mediation; but on the other hand they secretly sent into the mountains of Pistoia for infantry and, with all their men-at-arms, had them come into Florence at night. When they had seized the city's fortresses, they summoned the people to the Public Square and set up a new *balìa*. As soon as it met, this *balìa* restored Cosimo to the city, along with the others who had been banished with him. Of the hostile party it banished Messer Rinaldo degli Albizzi, Ridolfo Peruzzi, Niccolò Barbadoro and Messer Palla Strozzi, with many other citizens in such numbers that few cities were left in Italy to which they were not sent in exile, and many outside Italy were full of them. Thus through this event Florence was deprived not only of able men but of riches and industry.

The Pope, seeing what ruin had come on those who on his request had laid down their arms, was very angry. He lamented the injury done Messer Rinaldo under cover of his pledge and encouraged him to patience and to be hopeful because of Fortune's variability. Messer Rinaldo replied: "The little faith which men who ought to have believed me have put in me and the too great faith which I have put in you have ruined me and my party. But I censure myself more than I do anybody else for believing that you, who have been driven from your own city, could keep me in mine. With Fortune's fickleness I have had a great plenty of experience; and as I have put little trust in prosperous times, so adverse times less disturb me. I know that Fortune when she pleases will show herself more favorable to me, yet if she pleases never to do so, I shall not set high value on living in a city where the laws are less powerful than men. Indeed that city is desirable as a man's home in which his property and his friends can be safely enjoyed, not a city in which your property can easily be taken from you and where your friends, for fear of their own possessions, in your greatest necessity desert you. Always wise men and good have been less distressed on hearing of the ills of their native city than on seeing them, and have thought it more glorious to be an honorable exile than a slave citizen." Then in great indignation leaving the Pope and often in his own mind condemning his own plans and the coldness of his friends, he went into exile.

Cosimo on the other hand, getting notice of his restoration, returned to Florence. Seldom has a citizen returning in triumph after a victory been received by his own city with a concourse of people and with a manifestation of good will as great as those marking his reception when he returned from exile. And everybody eagerly addressed him as benefactor of his people and father of his native city.

BOOK FIVE

[THE GOVERNMENT OF COSIMO UNTIL THE BATTLE OF ANGHIARI. *1434-1440*]

CHAPTER 1

[The cycle of human affairs; the weak rulers, soldiers, and peoples of Italy.]

In their normal variations, countries generally go from order to disorder and then from disorder move back to order, because—since Nature does not allow worldy things to remain fixed—when they come to their utmost perfection and have no further possibility for rising, they must go down. Likewise, when they have gone down and through their defects have reached the lowest depths, they necessarily rise, since they cannot go lower. So always from good they go down to bad, and from bad rise up to good. Because ability brings forth quiet; quiet, laziness; laziness, disorder; disorder, ruin; and likewise from ruin comes order; from order, ability; from the last, glory and good fortune. Therefore the discerning have noted that letters come after arms, and that in countries and cities generals are born earlier than philosophers. Because, after good and well-disciplined armies have brought forth victory, and their victories quiet, the virtue of military courage cannot be corrupted with a more honorable laziness than that of letters; nor with a greater and more dangerous deception can this laziness enter into well-regulated cities. When the philosophers, Diogenes and Carneades, came to Rome, sent by the Athenians as ambassadors to the Senate, Cato thoroughly realized this; hence, seeing that the Roman youth began to follow them with admiration, and knowing the evil that such honorable laziness might bring upon his country, he made a law that no philosopher should be received in Rome. By such means, then, countries come to ruin; and when they have suffered it, and their people through afflictions have grown wise, they return to good order, as I have said, unless indeed an unusual force keeps them stifled.

These causes, first through the ancient Tuscans, then through the Romans, brought Italy sometimes happiness, sometimes misery. Upon the Roman ruins nothing has afterwards been built to redeem her from those ruins so that under the government of a strong ruler she could proceed gloriously; nonetheless some of the new cities and new states born among the Roman ruins showed such great ability that, though one of them did not master the others, they nevertheless were so united and so well organized that they freed Italy and de‐ fended her from the barbarians. Among these states the Florentines, though they had a smaller territory than others, were not smaller in power and influence; on the contrary, being placed in the midst of Italy, rich and ready for attack, they either successfully carried on any war begun against them or secured victory for any one they joined.

If then from the vigor of those new princedoms times quiet through long peace did not result, yet they were not dangerous through the harshness of war; for peace it cannot be called in which princedoms are continually attacking one another with armies. Wars, however, they cannot be called in which men are not killed, cities are not sacked, princedoms are not destroyed, because those wars became so feeble that they were begun without fear, carried on with‐ out danger, and ended without damage. So the vigor that in other countries is usually destroyed by long peace was in Italy destroyed by the cowardice of those wars, as is made clear by what we shall relate from 1434 to 1494. The reader will see there that at last a new road was opened to the barbarians, and Italy put herself back into slavery to them. So if the things done by our princes, abroad and at home, cannot, like those of the ancients, be read of with wonder because of their ability and greatness, perhaps for their other qualities they will be viewed with no less wonder; for one can see how such weak and badly handled armies held in check so many splendid peoples. And if in describing the things that happened in this corrupt world, I do not tell of the bravery of soldiers or the efficiency of generals or the love of citizens for their country, I do show with what deceptions, with what tricks and schemes, the princes, the soldiers, the heads of the republics, in order to keep that reputation which they did not deserve, carried on their affairs. It is perhaps as useful to observe these things as to learn ancient history, because if the latter kindles free spirits to imitation, the former will kindle such spirits to avoid and get rid of present abuses.

CHAPTER 2

[The followers of Sforza and of Braccio. Pope Eugenius. 1434]

Italy was brought by her rulers to such a condition that when peace followed an agreement among the princes, after a short time those who had the armies in their control disturbed it. Thus they did not gain glory through war, or quiet through peace. When in 1433 peace was made between the Duke of Milan and the League, the soldiers, in order to live through war, turned against the Church. In those days there were two military factions in Italy, that of Braccio and that of Sforza. Of the second, the head was Count Francesco, the son of Sforza; of the first, the leaders were Niccolò Piccino and Niccolò Fortebraccio. With these factions almost all the Italian armies were connected. Sforza's had the higher reputation of the two, because of the Count's ability and because the Duke of Milan had promised him Madonna Bianca, his natural daughter. The expectation of this marriage brought the Count very great reputation.

These factions of armed men, as soon as truce was made in Lombardy, for different reasons attacked Pope Eugenius. Niccolò Fortebraccio was moved by Braccio's ancient unceasing enmity against the Church. The Count was moved by ambition. Hence Niccolò attacked Rome and the Count made himself master of the Marches. As a result the Romans, who did not want war, drove Eugenius from Rome. Escaping with difficulty and danger, he came to Florence. Considering his danger, since the princes, unwilling to take up again for his sake the weapons they had so gladly laid down, abandoned him, the Pope came to terms with the Count. To him Eugenius granted the sovereignty of the Marches, even though to the injury of seizing them the Count added insult, for when according to the Italian custom he gave in Latin the place where he wrote letters to his agents, he said: "From our Gerfalcon at Fermo,[1] in spite of Peter and Paul." Nor was he satisfied with the grant of the cities, for he insisted on being made Gonfalonier of the Church. Yet everything was yielded to him—so much more did Eugenius fear a dangerous war than a disgraceful peace! Having therefore become a friend to the Pope, the Count strove to harm Niccolò Fortebraccio; hence in the cities of the Church for many months there were various

1. *His castle was named Gerfalcon.*

incidents between them, all of which resulted in injury to the Pope and his subjects rather than to those who were carrying on the war. Finally, through the mediation of the Duke of Milan, an agreement by way of a truce was made by which both Count Francesco and Niccolò were left as princes in the cities of the Church.

CHAPTER 3

[Further wars by the condottieri, the Duke of Milan, and the League; Batista da Canneto, tyrant of Bologna. 1434]

This war, when finished at Rome, was stirred up again by Batista da Canneto in Romagna. He killed in Bologna some of the Grifoni family and drove out of the city the Pope's governor and other enemies of his. In order to hold that state by force, he applied for aid to Duke Filippo; the Pope, in order to avenge the injury, asked for it from the Venetians and the Florentines. Both of them received this aid, so that immediately there were in Romagna two large armies. Filippo's general was Niccolò Piccino; the Venetian and Florentine soldiers were commanded by Gattamelata and by Niccolò da Tolentino. Near Imola they fought a battle, in which the Venetians and the Florentines were defeated and Niccolò da Tolentino was sent as a prisoner to the Duke of Milan. Whether through treachery by the Duke or in sorrow over the defeat, in a few days he died. The Duke, after this victory, either because he was weak on account of the past wars or because he thought that after this defeat the League would lapse, did not follow his Fortune further but gave the Pope and the allies time to reorganize. They chose as their general the Count Francesco, and made an expedition to drive Niccolò Fortebraccio from the towns of the Church, in order to see if they could end this war that they had begun to aid the Pope. The Romans, when they saw the Pope strong in the field, sought to make a truce with him, and they obtained it and received his commissioner.

Niccolò Fortebraccio was holding, among other towns, Tivoli, Montefiasconi, Città di Castello, and Assisi. To the last city Niccolò, not being able to remain in the open country, had fled, and there Count Francesco besieged him; since the siege was long drawn out, because Niccolò manfully defended himself, the Duke saw that he must either deprive the League of that victory or if it came about arrange to defend his own property. Wishing, therefore, to divert the Count from the siege, he ordered Niccolò Piccino to go into Tuscany by way of Romagna. Hence the League, thinking it more necessary to defend Tuscany than to take Assisi, ordered the Count to keep Niccolò from going. The latter already was with his army at Forlì. The Count on the other hand came with his soldiers to Cesena, having left to Lione his brother the war in the March and the care of his states. And while Piccinino[1] tried to go and the Count to hinder him, Niccolò Fortebraccio attacked Lione and, with great glory to himself, captured him and plundered his soldiers; following up his victory, he took with the same speed many towns of the March. This action greatly distressed Count Francesco, since he thought he had lost all his states. And leaving part of his army to oppose Piccinino, with the rest he went against Fortebraccio and attacked and beat him. In that defeat Fortebraccio was taken prisoner and mortally wounded.

This victory restored to the Pontiff all the towns that Niccolò Fortebraccio had taken from him and forced the Duke of Milan to ask peace; a treaty was concluded by means of Niccolò d' Esti the Marquis of Ferrara. By this treaty the cities taken by the Duke in Romagna were returned to the Church, and the Duke's soldiers went back into Lombardy. Then—as happens to all those who are supported in a high position by the forces and ability of others—when the Duke's soldiers had gone from Romagna, Batista da Canneto fled, since his own forces and ability could not keep him in Bologna. Messer Antonio Bentivoglio, head of the opposing party, returned.

1. *When the Christian name of Niccolò Piccino is not given, he is referred to as Piccinino.*

CHAPTER 4
[Cosimo's party uses severe measures in Florence. 1434]

All these things happened during the time of the exile of Cosimo. After his return, those who had brought him back and a large number of injured citizens set out, without any scruples, to secure themselves in power. Moreover the Signoria that held office in November and December, not content with what its predecessors had done in favor of their party, prolonged and changed the banish-

ments of many, and banished many others for the first time. Moreover not party feeling alone brought suffering upon various citizens,
but also wealth, relatives and private grudges harmed them. If this
proscription had been accompanied with blood, it would have
shown likeness to those of Octavian and Sulla. Yet to some extent
it was dyed with blood, because Antonio di Bernardo Guadagni
was beheaded, and four other citizens were dishonorably put to
death. Among them were Zanobi de' Belfrategli and Cosimo Barbadoro, whom, since they went outside the bounds set for their exile
and were in Venice, the Venetians—valuing Cosimo's friendship
higher than their own honor—sent to him as prisoners. This gave
great reputation to the party and caused very great terror to its enemies, when they observed that so powerful a republic would sell its
liberty to the Florentines.[1] She is believed to have done this not so
much to aid Cosimo as further to stir up the parties in Florence and
by means of blood to make the division in our city more dangerous,
because the Venetians did not see other opposition to their greatness
than her union.

Since, then, the city was cleared of enemies and of those feared by
the government, they turned to benefiting new people in order to
make their party stronger; and the family of the Alberti and any
others listed as rebels they restored to their native city; all the great
nobles except a very few they reduced to the rank of the people; the
property of the rebels they divided among themselves at a low price.
Besides this, they strengthened themselves by means of laws and new
regulations, and made new lists of those eligible for office, taking
their enemies from the bags and filling them with their friends.[2] In
addition, warned by the ruin of their adversaries, since they judged
that the selected lists of eligible names would not be enough to keep
their government firm, they determined that the magistrates having
authority to shed blood should always be chosen from the leaders of
their faction. Hence they saw to it that the couplers in charge of
putting in the bags the new lists of eligibles, together with the old
Signoria, should have power to choose the new one. They gave to

1. *The Venetians sold their honor by giving up the exiles to win Cosimo's favor.*
2. *Slips bearing the names of those eligible for office were kept in bags, from which they were
drawn out when the offices were to be filled. As appears in a later sentence, those in charge of
the bags were called couplers, a name applied to those who negotiated marriages. According to the
state of affairs, the couplers were more or less able to put in the bags and to draw out names acceptable to the ruling party.*

the Eight of Guard authority for shedding blood. They provided that the banished, even when their time was up, could not return unless first the Signors and the members of the College, who are thirty-seven in number, agreed by a vote of thirty-four to their restitution. They forbade the exiles to write and others to receive their letters; every word, every gesture, every habit that in any way displeased those who ruled was very heavily punished. And if any suspected man who had not been reached by these inflictions was left in Florence, he was distressed by the taxes that they newly imposed. So in a short time, having driven out and impoverished all the hostile party, they felt secure in their position. Yet in order not to be without help from outside, and to remove it from those who planned to attack them, they allied themselves with the Pope, the Venetians, and the Duke of Milan, in defense of their states.

CHAPTER 5

[War between René of Anjou and Alfonso of Aragon over the throne of Naples; the Duke of Milan aids first one, then the other. 1435]

When the affairs of Florence were in this shape, Joanna the Queen of Naples died, and by her will left René of Anjou heir to the Kingdom. Alfonso King of Aragon, then in Sicily, by means of the friendship he had with many of the barons, was preparing to seize that Kingdom. The Neapolitans and many barons supported René. The Pope, on the other hand, did not want either René or Alfonso to take it, but wished it to be administered by his own governor. Meanwhile Alfonso came into the Kingdom and was received by the Duke of Sessa. There he took into his pay some princes, with the intention (since he held Capua, which the prince of Taranto was occupying in his name) of forcing the Neapolitans to do his will. He sent his fleet to attack Gaeta, which was held for the Neapolitans. Hence the Neapolitans asked help from Filippo.

He persuaded the Genoese to undertake this expedition. They, not merely to please the Duke their prince but in order to save the merchandise they had in Naples and in Gaeta, equipped a powerful fleet. Alfonso on the other hand, learning this, strengthened his own fleet and in person went to meet the Genoese. When they came to battle near the island of Ponza, the Aragonese fleet was defeated and

Alfonso and many princes were captured and given by the Genoese into Filippo's hands. This victory frightened all the princes in Italy who feared Filippo's power, because they judged that he had an excellent opportunity to make himself master of the whole. But he (so different are the opinions of men) made a decision entirely contrary to their expectation.

Alfonso was a prudent man; he explained to Filippo, as soon as he talked with him, how much the Duke was deceived in favoring René and disfavoring Alfonso himself. René, if he became King of Naples, would make every effort to have Milan become the property of the French king, so that his helpers would be near and in case of need he would not have to try to open the road for his rescuers; he could not assure himself of this by any other method than Filippo's overthrow, thus making Milan French. But the contrary would happen if Alfonso became prince, because, not fearing any other enemy than the French, he was obliged to love and favor and even to obey any ruler who could open the road to his enemies; and for this reason the title of the Kingdom would become Alfonso's, but the authority and power would be Filippo's. So it would be much more important for the Duke than for himself to consider the dangers of the first plan and the benefits of the second, unless indeed Filippo preferred to satisfy a whim rather than to make himself sure of his state. In the second case he would be prince and free; in the first, being between two very powerful princes, he would either lose his state or live always in fear and like a slave have to obey them.

So effective were these words on Duke Filippo's mind that, changing his plan, he freed Alfonso and sent him honorably back to Genoa and thence to the Kingdom. The King betook himself to Gaeta, which, as soon as his liberation was known, had been seized by some lords who were his partisans.

CHAPTER 6

[The parties in Genoa; Francesco Spinola. 1435]

The Genoese, seeing that the Duke, without any regard for them, had set the King free and had gained himself honor from their dangers and expense, and that he had the gratitude for the King's liberation, and they were subject to resentment for his imprisonment and defeat, were all angry with the Duke.

In the city of Genoa, when it is at liberty, they select by free vote a head whom they call Doge, not to be absolute prince, not to decide things alone, but as head to propose what their magistrates and councils are going to consider. This city has many noble families, which are so powerful that they have little regard for the authority of the magistrates. Among these, the Fregoso family and the Adorno family are the most powerful. They cause dissensions in that city and overthrow the laws of the community because when they fight against each other for the ruling position, not according to law but generally with arms, it follows that one party is always defeated and the other rules. And sometimes those who are deprived of their offices turn to foreign arms, and that city of theirs, which they cannot rule, they subject to the dominion of a foreigner. From this it has resulted and still results that those who rule in Lombardy are usually masters in Genoa, as happened at the time when Alfonso of Aragon was captured.

Among the leading Genoese who had been the cause of sub-jecting the city to Filippo was Francesco Spinola, who, not long after he had made his native city a slave, as often happens in such cases, came to be suspected by the Duke. Because of this, he, in anger, had chosen for himself an almost voluntary exile to Gaeta. He had been there at the time of the naval battle with Alfonso, and had shown skill and courage in the enterprise; so he believed that again he had deserved so much of the Duke that at least, as a reward for his merits, he could live safely in Genoa. But when he saw that the Duke continued to be suspicious, since Filippo could not believe that a man who had not loved the liberty of his native city would love him, Francesco determined to tempt Fortune again, and at once to give his native city liberty and himself fame and security, judging that in dealing with his fellow citizens he had no other possibility than to act in such a way that from whence the wound had come, thence should come medicine and healing. And seeing the general indignation that had risen against the Duke as a result of his liber-ating the King, he concluded that the time was suitable for carrying out his designs. Hence he shared his plan with some whom he knew to be of the same opinion, and encouraged them and induced them to follow him.

CHAPTER 7

[Genoa frees herself from Duke Filippo. 1435]

The festival day of Saint John the Baptist had come, when Arismino, the new governor sent by the Duke, was to enter Genoa. When he had actually entered, accompanied by Opicino the old governor and by many Genoese, Francesco Spinola decided not to wait; he came out of his house armed, together with those who shared his determination, and when he was in the square in front of his mansion, he shouted the name of Liberty. It was a wonderful thing to see with what promptness that people and those citizens ran together at that name, so that anybody who favored the Duke, for his own profit or for any other reason, not merely did not have time to take arms but scarcely had a chance to think of flight. Arismino, with some Genoese who were with him, fled into the castle that was garrisoned for the Duke. Opicino, thinking that if he fled to his palace, where he had two thousand armed men at his command, he could save himself or give his friends courage to defend him, turning in that direction, was killed before he came to the palace square; his body, cut into many pieces, was scattered throughout Genoa. After the Genoese had put the city under free magistrates, in a few days they took the castle and the other strongholds belonging to Duke Filippo, and from his yoke they wholly freed themselves.

CHAPTER 8

[The Florentines join a league against Duke Filippo; Rinaldo degli Albizzi tries to get his aid against Cosimo's government. 1435]

These things thus managed—whereas in the beginning they had frightened the rulers of Italy, who feared that the Duke would be‑ come too powerful—gave those rulers, when they saw the outcome, hope that they could hold him in check. And notwithstanding the treaty newly made, the Florentines and the Venetians came to an agreement with the Genoese. Because of this, Messer Rinaldo degli Albizzi and the other leaders of the Florentine exiles, seeing affairs disturbed and the face of the world changed, took hope that they could bring the Duke to open war against Florence; going to Milan, Messer Rinaldo addressed the Duke to this effect:

"If we, once your enemies, now come with confidence to beg your aid so that we may return to our native city, neither you nor anybody who considers how human affairs go and how Fortune varies should wonder at it. All the same, for our past and present actions, both our earlier deeds in relation to you and our present ones in relation to our native city, we can give obvious and reasonable excuses. No good man will ever censure any citizen who strives to defend his native city, in whatever way he defends her. Never did we purpose to harm you but we did purpose to guard our city from harm. Of this you can take as proof that in the course of the greatest victories of our league, when we knew that you were disposed to a true peace, we were more desirous to make one than you yourself were. Indeed we do not fear that we have ever done anything to make us doubt getting some allowance from you.

"Not even our native city can complain that now we exhort you to take up against her those arms from which so obstinately we defended her. By all her people that city deserves to be loved which loves all her people equally, not that city which, neglecting all the others, bows down before a very few of them. No man should condemn in all conditions weapons that citizens turn against their native place. He should not do so because cities, though they are mixed bodies, bear likeness to simple bodies. Just as in simple bodies diseases often appear which cannot be healed without fire and steel, so in cities many times there are such disorders that a merciful and good citizen, when steel is the necessary remedy, would sin much more in leaving them untreated than in treating them. In the body of a republic what illness can be more serious than servitude? What medicine is more necessary than that which relieves it from this disease? Only those wars are just that are necessary; and arms are holy when there is no hope apart from them. I do not know what necessity can be greater than ours, or what holiness can surpass that which takes any man's native city from slavery. It is therefore most certain that our cause is holy and just—something that ought to be considered both by us and by you.

"Nor on your side is this justice lacking, because the Florentines have not been ashamed, after a peace proclaimed with such solemnity, to league themselves with the Genoese in rebellion against you. So if our cause does not move you, let anger move you. And so much the more when you see the undertaking easy, because you should not be alarmed by past instances in which you have seen the power of that people and their stubbornness in defense. These are two things that you could reasonably fear if they were still of the same vigor as then. But now you will find them entirely the opposite; for what power do you think a city can have that recently has driven away from herself the greater part of her riches and of her industry? What stubbornness do you think there can be in a people disunited through such varied and new enmities? This disunion is the reason why even such wealth as remains there cannot be spent in the way then possible; for men willingly use up their family property when they use it up for glory, for their own honor and power, hoping to gain back in peace that wealth which war takes from them; but they are not willing to exhaust their property when they see that in war and in peace they are equally oppressed, having in war to endure the injuries of their enemies, in peace the haughtiness of their rulers. Moreover, the people are much more injured by the avarice of their fellow citizens than by the rapacity of the enemy; of such enemy's rapacity men expect some day to see an end; of domestic oppression, never.

"You sent your armies, then, in earlier wars, against an entire city; now against the smallest part of her you send them. You came to take dominion from citizens many and good; now you come to take it from few and bad. You came to take liberty from a city; now you come to give it back. According to reason, in such an inequality of causes, equal effects cannot result; on the contrary, you may look forward to certain victory. What a support that will be for your power you can easily judge, since Tuscany will be your ally—and bound by a bond of such sort and so great. Of her you can make more use in your undertakings than you can of Milan. And whereas in other times this conquest would have been thought ambitious and violent, at present it will be thought just and holy. Do not, therefore, let this opportunity pass; and remember that if your other expeditions against that city with difficulty yielded you expense and shame, with ease this one will yield you the greatest profit and the most honorable reputation."

CHAPTER 9

[The Duke of Milan moves against Genoa and Lucca. 1436]

Not many words were needed to persuade the Duke of Milan that he should begin war against the Florentines, because he was moved by hereditary hate and blind ambition that thus directed him, and so much the more since he was pushed on by new causes for anger resulting from the Florentine agreement with the Genoese. Nevertheless his past expenses, the risks he had run, the remembrance of his recent losses, and the vain hopes of the exiles frightened him.

Already this Duke, as soon as he heard of the rebellion of Genoa, had sent Niccolò Piccino, with all his men-at-arms and such infantry as he could get together from the country districts, against that city, to make an effort to regain her before the citizens had settled their purpose and organized their new government, putting great faith in the castle within the walls of Genoa that was held for him. Niccolò drove the Genoese from the mountain tops and took from them the valley of Pozeveri, where they had fortified themselves, and pushed them back within the walls of the city; nevertheless he found so much difficulty in going farther because of the stubborn spirits of the citizens in defending themselves, that he was forced to draw back. So the Duke, on the persuasions of the Florentine exiles, ordered him to attack the Eastern Riviera, and near the boundaries of Pisa to carry on war as vigorously as he could in Genoese territory; he imagined that this campaign would from time to time show him what decisions he should make. So Niccolò attacked Sarzana and took it. Then, after doing great damage, in order to make the Florentines more fearful he came to Lucca, announcing that he wished to pass through on his way to the Kingdom to assist the King of Aragon.

Pope Eugenius, on these new events, left Florence and went to Bologna, where he negotiated about a new truce between the Duke of Milan and the League, demonstrating that if the Duke did not agree to the truce, the Pope would be forced to surrender to the League his claim on Count Francesco, who at that time, as the Pope's ally, was in his pay. And though the Pontiff labored hard at this, all his labors were nevertheless without result, for the Duke did not wish to make a treaty without Genoa, and the League wished

Genoa to remain free. And so everybody, feeling no assurance of peace, prepared for war.

CHAPTER 10

[Piccinino defeated near Barga; the Florentines decide to attack Lucca. 1436]

Since meanwhile Niccolò Piccino came to Lucca, the Floren-tines were afraid of new activities. Hence with their own soldiers they had Neri di Gino ravage the territory of Pisa, and from the Pontiff they gained permission for Count Francesco to join them; they halted their army at Santa Gonda. Piccinino, who was at Lucca, asked passage in order to go to the Kingdom, and when it was refused threatened to take it by force. The armies were equal in strength and in generals; therefore, since neither was willing to tempt Fortune and they also were delayed by the cold season, for it was December, they did not attack for many days.

The first to move was Niccolò Piccino, who had been told that if he attacked Vico Pisano at night, he would easily take it. Niccolò made the attempt, but not succeeding in taking Vico, he sacked the country round about, and the hamlet of San Giovanni alla Vena he plundered and burned. This undertaking, though it turned out for the most part useless, still gave Niccolò courage to proceed further, especially since he saw that the Count and Neri had not moved; so he attacked Santa Maria in Castello and Filetto and took them. Not even for this did the Florentine soldiers move, not because the Count was afraid, but because in Florence the magistrates had not yet determined on war, by reason of the respect they had for the Pope, who was negotiating for peace. And what the Florentines did through prudence, since their enemies believed they did it through fear, gave those enemies more courage for new undertakings. Hence they determined to besiege Barga and went there with all their forces. This new attack made the Florentines, laying aside hesitation, deter-mine not merely to relieve Barga but to invade Lucchese territory. So moving against Niccolò and joining battle near Barga, the Count defeated him and made him almost as though routed give up that siege. The Venetians, meanwhile, since they saw that the Duke of Milan had broken the peace, sent their general, Giovan Francesco

Gonzaga, into Ghiaradadda; by greatly damaging the country, he compelled Duke Filippo to call Niccolò Piccino back from Tuscany.

This recall, together with the victory won against Niccolò, gave the Florentines courage to carry on the campaign against Lucca with hope of capturing her. In this they had no fear or hesitation, since the Duke, whom alone they feared, was assailed by the Venetians, and since the Lucchese, having received enemies of Florence into their country and allowed them to attack her, could not in any way complain.

CHAPTER 11

[Florentine campaign against Lucca; the Lucchese determine to resist. 1437]

So in April 1437, the Count moved his army. Before the Florentines attacked others, they wished to recover their own possessions, so they retook Santa Maria in Castello and every other place taken by Piccinino. Then, going into the territory of Lucca, they assailed Camaiore. Though the men of that town were faithful to their lords, the fear of an enemy close at hand was more powerful with them than fidelity to a distant friend; hence they surrendered. By means of the same prestige, the Florentines took Massa and Sarzana. When these things were done, about the end of May the army turned toward Lucca and destroyed all the grain and other crops, burned the country houses, cut down the vines and the trees, and carried off the cattle; nothing that is usually done or can be done against enemies did they omit. The Lucchese on the other hand, abandoned by the Duke and in despair of defending their open country, abandoned it, and with embankments and every other suitable device strengthened their city; for her they did not fear, since she was full of defenders, and they could defend her for a time; so in that they put their hope, moved by the example of the other attempts the Florentines had made on them. Solely they feared the changeable spirits of the lower class, who, tired out by the siege, might be more concerned with their own dangers than with the liberty of others, and force them to some shameful and injurious agreement. So in order to stir them up to defense, they brought them together in the Public Square, and one of the older and wiser spoke to this effect:

"You must always have heard that when things are done through necessity, neither praise nor blame is or can be deserved. Therefore if you accuse us in the belief that this war now waged on us by the Florentines is one we brought upon ourselves by receiving into our city the soldiers of the Duke and allowing them to attack Florentine towns, you greatly deceive yourselves. You know also the ancient enmity of the Florentine people against you, which has been caused not by your injuries to them, not by fear of you, but merely by your weakness and their ambition, for your impotence gives them hope of overcoming you, their greed drives them on to do it. Do not believe that any desert of yours can turn them from such a desire or that any offense of yours can incite them to harm you more. They, therefore, must think of taking your liberty from you, you of defending it; and as to the things that they and we do for that purpose, each can lament over them and not wonder. Let us lament, then, that they attack us, that they assault our towns, that they burn our houses, and lay waste our country. But who of us is so foolish as to wonder at it? For if we could, we would do the same or worse to them.

"And if they have started this war as a result of Niccolò's coming, nevertheless, if he had not come, they would have started it for some other reason, and if this ill had been put off, it would perhaps have been greater. So his coming is not to be blamed, but rather our bad luck and their ambitious nature; besides, we could not refuse to receive the Duke's soldiers, and when they came, we could not restrain them from making war. You know that without the aid of a great power we cannot protect ourselves; and there is no power that can defend us with more fidelity and more strength than the Duke of Milan; he has given us liberty; it is reasonable that he will preserve it for us; to our perennial enemies he has always been very hostile. If then, in order not to injure the Florentines, we had made the Duke angry, we should have lost our friend, and made our enemy more powerful and more speedy in injuring us. So it is much better to have this war with the Duke's love than, with his hatred, to have peace. We can hope that he is going to get us out of these dangers in which he has put us, if only we do not grow faint-hearted.

"You know with what fury the Florentines have many times attacked us, and with what glory we have defended ourselves from them; many times we have had no other hope than in God and in time; and these two have saved us. And if then we defended ourselves, for what reason should we not now defend ourselves? Then all Italy had abandoned us to them as their booty; now we have the Duke for us, and we can believe that the Venetians will be slow to attack us, since they are vexed when the Florentines grow stronger. At the other times the Florentines were less entangled, had more hope for assistance, and by themselves were stronger, while we were in every respect weaker. Then we were defending a tyrant, now we are defending ourselves; then the glory of the defense went to another, now it is our own; then they attacked us when they were united, now when disunited they attack us, since their exiles are everywhere in Italy.

"But even if these hopes did not exist, we should be made stubborn in defense by a last necessity. In reason we should fear all enemies because they all intend their own glory and our ruin. But above all others, the Florentines should terrify us, because they will not be satisfied with our obedience and our tribute, with authority over this city of ours, but they want our persons and our goods, so that with our blood they can satisfy their cruelty and with our property their avarice. Hence, every man of every rank should fear them. For that reason you should not be disturbed on seeing your fields laid waste, your farmhouses burned, your towns captured. If we save this city, they will of necessity be saved; if we lose her, they will be saved without any profit to us; because if we continue free, our enemy only with difficulty can hold them; if we lose our freedom, in vain we hold them. Take up your arms, then, and when you fight, think that the reward of your victory is the security not merely of your native land but of your homes and of your children."

The last words of this man the people listened to with the utmost warmth of spirit, and as one man they promised to die rather than surrender or rather than consider any agreement that in any way would taint their liberty. And they arranged among them everything necessary for defending a city.

CHAPTER 12

[*The Lucchese ask aid from the Duke of Milan. 1437*]

The Florentine army, meanwhile, did not lose time, and after doing much damage to the country, took Monte Carlo by capitulation. After gaining this place, it went to besiege Nozzano, so that the Lucchese, hemmed in on every side, could not hope for aid and would be compelled by hunger to give themselves up. The town was very strong and well provided with a garrison, so that its capture was not as easy as that of the other.

The Lucchese, as was to be expected, seeing themselves hemmed in, applied to the Duke and in every way, both sweet and sour, asked him for help. In their speech they showed now their deserts, now the injuries done by the Florentines; they emphasized how much heart he would give to his other friends by protecting them, and how much terror by leaving them undefended, whereas if they with their liberty lost their lives, he would lose, with his friends, his honor and the confidence of all those who for love of him ever had to undergo any danger. To their words they added tears, so that if his duty did not move him, he might be moved by compassion. Hence the Duke, adding to his ancient hatred for the Florentines his new duty to the Lucchese, and above all wishing that the Florentines should not grow by so great a gain, determined to send a large army into Tus-cany, or to attack the Venetians with such fury that the Florentines, to relieve them, would of necessity give up their own enterprise.

CHAPTER 13

[Florence asks aid from Venice; both states wish Count Francesco Sforza as general; Florence tries to deceive Venice. 1437]

When he had made this decision, Florence quickly learned that the Duke of Milan was getting ready to send soldiers into Tuscany. This made the Florentines lose confidence for their enterprise; and in order that the Duke might be kept busy in Lombardy, they urged the Venetians to press him with all their forces. But the latter also were fearful, because the Marquis of Mantua had deserted them and gone into the pay of the Duke, and for that reason, since they were almost unarmed, they replied that they could not even keep up that war, much less expand it, unless Florence sent them Count Francesco to lead their army, with the compact that he should be obliged to cross the Po in person. They were not willing to continue in the old agreements by which he was not obliged to cross it, because without a general they were not willing to make war, and they could not trust anybody else than the Count, yet the Count they could not employ if he was not bound to carry on war in any place whatever. The Florentines believed it necessary that the war in Lombardy should be carried on with vigor; on the other hand, without the Count, they saw that their enterprise at Lucca would be ruined. And they very well knew that this requirement had been made by the Venetians not so much through any need they had for the Count as in order to upset that conquest of theirs. On the other hand, the Count was ready to go into Lombardy entirely at the disposal of the League, but he was not willing to dishonor his pledge not to cross the Po, since he did not wish to deprive himself of his hope of the marriage alliance promised by the Duke. The Florentines, then, were distracted between two different emotions: the wish to get Lucca, and the fear of war with the Duke. The stronger of the two, however, as always happens, was fear; and they were glad, on the fall of Nozzano, to allow Count Francesco to go into Lombardy.

But there was another difficulty which, since the Florentines had no power to dispel it, gave them more distress and made them hesitate more than did the first one: the Count was unwilling to cross the Po, and the Venetians would not accept him otherwise. Since there was no way of bringing either one to yield freely to the other, the Florentines persuaded the Count to bind himself, in a letter written to the Signoria of Florence, to cross that river, convincing him that this private promise would not break his public agreements and that then he could get on without crossing. And this advantage would result: namely, that the Venetians, when the war had begun, would of necessity continue it, and the effect would be the diversion of the Ducal hostility feared by the Florentines. To the Venetians, on the other hand, the Florentines made it appear that this private letter was enough to bind Count Francesco; and therefore they should be satisfied; if they could protect the Count in his relations with his father-in-law, it was well to do so; and neither he nor they would be profited by revealing it without evident necessity. In this way the Count's entrance into Lombardy was settled. After capturing Nozzano and building some forts around Lucca to keep the Lucchese hemmed in and turning that war over to commissioners, he crossed the Alps and went to Reggio. There the Venetians, suspicious of his movements, in order before anything else to learn his intention, asked him to cross the Po and join their other soldiers. Count Francesco flatly refused. Hence between Andrea Mauroceno, the Venetian agent, and himself there were offensive words, each accusing the other of great pride and small faith. After they had protested much, the soldier that he was not bound to the service, the agent that he was not bound to payment, the Count returned to Tuscany and the other to Venice.

The Florentines had the Count encamp in Pisan territory, hoping to induce him to renew the war against the Lucchese. But they found him unwilling because the Duke, having learned that the Count for his sake had refused to cross the Po, thought that through him the Lucchese could still be saved. So the Duke begged him to try to negotiate a treaty between the Lucchese and the Florentines in which the Duke would be included. Filippo led the Count to hope that when he wished, his marriage with the Duke's daughter would be celebrated. This promised marriage alliance had a strong effect on the Count, because he hoped by means of it, since the Duke had no male children, to make himself lord of Milan. And therefore he always kept cutting off the prosecution of the war for the Florentines and asserting that he did not want to move unless the Venetians kept their agreement to pay him and their contract with him as general. And payment alone was not enough for him, because if he was going to live in security in his states, he needed other support than that of the Florentines. So, if he was abandoned by the Venetians, he was obliged to think of his own affairs. And he cleverly threatened to come to terms with the Duke.

CHAPTER 14

[Cosimo fails to induce the Venetians to pay Count Francesco; peace made with Lucca. 1438]

These pretexts and these tricks greatly angered the Florentines, because they saw the Lucchese expedition lost, and besides they feared for their own state whenever the Duke and the Count were united. Thereupon, to bring the Venetians back to continuing their contract with the Count, Cosimo de'Medici went to Venice, believing that with his reputation he could move them. There in their senate he argued on this subject at great length, showing in what condition Italian politics stood, how great the forces of the Duke were, and where the reputation and the power of armies resided. He ended by saying that if the Count united with the Duke, the Vene-tians would be going back to the sea and the Florentines would be fighting for their liberty. To this the Venetians answered that they knew their own forces and those of the Italians and believed that in any case they could defend themselves; and they asserted that they were not in the habit of paying soldiers who served others. Therefore the Florentines should expect to pay the Count, because they were served by him; and it was more necessary for the Venetians, if they hoped to enjoy their territory in security, to lower the pride of the Count than to pay him, because men have no limit to their ambition, and if now he were paid without rendering service, soon after he would ask something more dishonorable and more dangerous. So they believed they must at some time put a check to his haughtiness, and not let it grow so great that it would get beyond restraint; but if the Florentines, through fear or some other desire, still wished to keep him as a friend, they could pay him. So Cosimo came back with-out accomplishing anything.

Nonetheless, the Florentines used pressure on the Count to pre-vent his withdrawing from the League, and he too was unwilling to leave it. Yet his hope of completing the marriage alliance with the Duke kept him uncertain, so that, as actually happened, a very slight accident could make him decide. The Count had earlier left as guardian of his cities in the March a certain Friulano, one of his chief officers. This man was so much urged by the Duke that he gave up his employment with the Count and joined the Duke. This event caused the Count, abandoning all hesitation in fear for his own position, to make an agreement with the Duke; among the provisions was that there should be no disturbance in the affairs of Tuscany and Romagna.

After this agreement, the Count persistently urged the Florentines to make peace with the Lucchese; and in such a way he pushed them into this that, having no other resource, they made peace, in the month of April in the year 1438. According to this agreement, the Lucchese retained their liberty and the Florentines kept Monte Carlo and some of their other towns. Then they filled all Italy with letters full of complaints, showing that since God and men had not wished that the Lucchese should come under their authority, they had made peace with them. It seldom happens that anybody feels so much vexation at the loss of his own possessions as the Florentines then felt because they had not taken what belonged to others.

CHAPTER 15

[Trouble over Borgo San Sepolcro; the consecration of Santa Reparata. 1436]

In those days, though the Florentines were occupied in such a great enterprise, yet in taking thought about their neighbors and in adorning their city they were not negligent. Already, as we have said, Niccolò Fortebraccio was dead, who had married one of the daughters of the Count of Poppi. On his death his father-in-law had in his hands Borgo San Sepolcro and the fortresses of that place, having ruled them in Niccolò's name during his life. After his death, the Count said he retained them as his daughter's dower and refused to yield them to the Pope. The latter asked for them as Church property and at last sent the Patriarch with soldiers to seize them. The Count of Poppi, seeing that he could not resist the attack, offered the place to the Florentines, who refused it. But when the Pope returned to Florence they mediated between him and the Count in an attempt to reconcile them. Since they could secure no agreement, the Patriarch attacked the Casentino and took Prato Vecchio and Romena, which likewise he offered to the Florentines. They still refused to accept the towns unless the Pope would allow them to be handed over to the Count of Poppi. After long debate the Pope consented to this, requiring the Florentines to promise to arrange that the Count should return Borgo to the Church. Thus the Pope's mind was set at ease.

In Florence the construction of the cathedral church, Santa Reparata (begun long before), had been carried so far that the holy offices could be celebrated there; hence the Florentines decided to ask the Pope to consecrate it personally. To this the Pope gladly agreed, and for the sake of greater magnificence for the city and the church, and for more respect to the Pontiff, a scaffolding was built all the way from Santa Maria Novella, where the Pope was living, to the church to be consecrated; it was eight feet wide and four feet high, covered all above and all round about with the richest draperies, and over it came only the Pontiff with his court, together with the city magistrates and the citizens appointed to accompany him. All the rest of the citizens and the people were waiting along the way, in the houses and in the church, to see so great a spectacle. After completing all the ceremonies of such a consecration, the Pope, as a sign of the greatest love, honored with knighthood Giuliano Davanzati, then Gonfalonier of Justice and a citizen always of the highest reputation; whereupon the Signoria, in order not to seem less loving than the Pope, granted him for a year the captaincy of Pisa.

CHAPTER 16

[An attempt at union between the Eastern and Western churches. 1439]

In those same times, there were differences between the Roman and the Greek churches, so that in divine worship they did not agree in every respect; and since in the last Council, held at Basle, the prelates of the Western church had spoken much on this matter, it was decided that all diligence should be used to have the Emperor and the Greek prelates take part in the Council at Basle in an attempt to reach an agreement with the Roman Church. Though this de-cision was opposed to the majesty of the Greek Empire, and any concession to the Roman Pontiff would offend the pride of its pre-lates, yet, since the Greeks were hard pressed by the Turks and judged that they could not by themselves make a defense, in order that with more assurance they could ask aid from the others, they decided to yield. And thus the Emperor, together with the Patriarch and other Greek prelates and barons, came to Venice, so that, ac-cording to the decision of the Council, they could be at Basle. But being frightened by the plague, they decided that their differences should be ended in the city of Florence. After the Greek and Roman prelates had met for many days, then, in the Cathedral Church, the Greeks, as the result of many long debates, yielded and made an agreement with the Roman Church and Pontiff.

CHAPTER 17

[*Further disturbances in Italy; Niccolò Piccino by tricking the Pope seizes Ravenna and other cities. 1438*]

When the peace between the Lucchese and the Florentines, and between the Duke and the Count, was concluded, it was believed that the arms of Italy, especially those plaguing Lombardy and Tuscany, could easily be laid down, because those that had been used in the Kingdom of Naples by René of Anjou and Alfonso of Aragon must, on the ruin of one of the two, be laid down. And though the Pope was discontented because he had lost many of his cities, and though everyone knew how great was the ambition of the Duke and the Venetians, yet it was thought that the Pope, through necessity, and the others, through weariness, would be at a standstill. But things went otherwise, because neither the Duke of Milan nor the Venetians remained quiet. The result was that arms were taken up anew, and Lombardy and Tuscany were again given over to war.

The Duke's proud spirit could not endure having the Venetians hold Bergamo and Brescia, and the more so because he saw them under arms and every day in many places raiding and upsetting his country. Moreover he thought that he could not merely keep them in check but could get his cities back whenever the Venetians were abandoned by the Pope, the Florentines, and the Count. Hence he planned to take Romagna from the Pontiff, since he thought that if he held that province the Pope could not attack him, and that the Florentines, seeing the fire near them, either through fear for them-selves would not act, or if they did act, could not easily attack him. Furthermore, the Duke also knew that the Florentines, as a result of the Lucchese affair, were indignant with the Venetians; hence he thought they would be less ready to take arms for Venice. As to Count Francesco, Duke Filippo believed that their new alliance and the Count's hope for the marriage would be enough to keep him faithful. So in order to escape blame and give everybody less reason for acting, and especially since he could not attack Romagna, be-cause of his agreements with the Count, the Duke arranged that Niccolò Piccino, as though acting through his own ambition, should undertake a campaign in Romagna.

Niccolò, when the Count and the Duke made their agreement,

was already in Romagna. By arrangement with Duke Filippo, he pretended to be angered by the Duke's alliance with the Count, Niccolò's permanent enemy. He took his forces to Camurata, a place between Forlì and Ravenna, where he fortified himself as though intending to remain there a long time, until he found new employment. Since the report of his pretended anger was spread everywhere, Niccolò gave the Pope to understand how much he deserved from the Duke and how ungrateful Filippo had been to him. He also declared that the Duke, having in his service almost all the soldiers of Italy, under her two chief generals, expected to conquer her. But if His Holiness wished, Niccolò could bring about that of the two generals the Duke thought he had, one would be hostile to him and the other useless. Niccolò promised, if the Pope furnished him money and maintained him under arms, to attack the states ruled by the Count and withheld by him from the Church. When so attacked, the Count, forced to think about his own affairs, could not assist Filippo's ambition. The Pope put faith in these words, since he thought them reasonable, and sent Niccolò five thousand ducats and made him big promises, offering states to him and to his children. And though many warned the Pope of the deception, he did not believe them and would not listen to anybody who said Niccolò was false.

At that time the city of Ravenna was ruled for the Church by Ostasio da Polenta. Niccolò, since he thought it no time for putting off his undertaking any longer (because Francesco his son had insulted the Pope by sacking Spoleto), decided to attack Ravenna, whether because he thought that undertaking easier or because with Ostasio he had a secret understanding; in a few days after he had attacked it, he took it on terms. After this conquest, he occupied Bologna, Imola, and Forlì. What was more wonderful was that of twenty castles garrisoned for the Pope in those states, there was not one that did not come into Niccolò's power. Nor was it enough for him that he had harmed the Pope with this injury, for he wished also to mock him with words, as he had done with deeds; so he wrote that he had taken the cities from him deservedly, since the Pope had not been ashamed to try to destroy such a friendship as that between the Duke and himself, and to fill Italy with letters saying that he had left the Duke and sided with the Venetians.

CHAPTER 18

[Duke Filippo of Milan attacks the Venetians; Count Francesco Sforza's marriage with Duke Filippo's daughter is delayed. 1438]

Niccolò after conquering the Romagna left it in charge of his son Francesco and with most of his followers went into Lombardy. Joining the rest of the ducal soldiers, he attacked the district surrounding Brescia and in a short time held it all. Then he laid seige to that city. The Duke, wishing the Venetians left as his prey, made excuses to the Pope, the Florentines and the Count, pretending that Niccolò's actions in Romagna were contrary not only to the agreements but also to his wishes. In secret messages he indicated that when time and opportunity permitted, he would give clear proof of this disobedience. The Florentines and the Count did not give him any credence but believed, as was true, that he had employed Niccolò's troops to delay them until he could overcome the Venetians. The latter, full of pride and believing that they could unaided resist the Duke's forces, did not deign to ask help from anybody but with Gattamelata their general carried on the war. Count Francesco wished to go to the rescue of King René with Florentine help but events in Romagna and Lombardy detained him. The Florentines too would gladly have aided the King because of their old and steady alliance with the royal house of France, but the Duke would have turned his aid to Alfonso, as a result of the friendship he had formed with him during his imprisonment. But both of these, occupied with wars near at hand, refrained from distant expeditions.

So then, seeing the Romagna held by the forces of the Duke and the Venetians defeated, the Florentines, from the ruin of others fearing their own, begged the Count to come into Tuscany. Then they should consider what could be done to oppose the forces of the Duke (which were greater than they had ever been before), for they affirmed that if his arrogance was not in some way checked, everybody who held territory in Italy would in a short time suffer from it. The Count realized that the fear of the Florentines was reasonable; all the same, his wish to secure the marriage alliance with the Duke kept him uncertain. And the Duke, who realized this desire of his, gave him very great hopes of it, if the Count did not move troops against him. Further, because the girl was now old enough to be married, several times Duke Filippo brought the matter to such a state that all the usual preparations for the wedding were made; then, under various pretexts, he broke everything off. Yet in order to make the Count believe him, to promises he added deeds; and he sent him thirty thousand florins which, according to the agreements about the marriage, Count Francesco was to receive.

CHAPTER 19

[*The war goes against the Venetians; they ask aid from Florence; the Florentines persuade Count Francesco to join them. 1439*]

Nevertheless the war in Lombardy was growing more serious; the Venetians daily were losing new cities, all the fleets that they had prepared for the rivers had been beaten by the ducal soldiers, the territory of Verona and of Brescia was entirely occupied, and those two cities were so hard pressed that, according to the general opinion, they could hold out but a short time. The Marquis of Mantua, for many years the Venetian republic's general, had deserted them and taken sides with the Duke, contrary to all their expectations. So what in the beginning of the war the Venetians were not permitted to do by pride, they were made to do, in the course of it, by fear. Recognizing that they had no other recourse than the friendship of the Florentines and of the Count, they supplicated it, though abashed and full of foreboding, because they feared that the Florentines would give the same reply they had received from the Venetians about the attempt on Lucca and the Count's affairs.

But they found Florence more yielding than they had hoped and than their conduct deserved—so much more powerful in the Florentines was their hate for their old enemy than their anger over their old and habitual alliance.[1] Having long before realized the necessity into which the Venetians must come, the Florentines had explained to the Count that Venetian ruin was his ruin, that he deceived himself if he believed Duke Filippo when fortunate would favor him more than when unfortunate, and that the Duke promised his daughter to Francesco because fearing him. Since the things which necessity makes a man promise it also makes him do, the Count ought to hold

1. *Florentine hatred for the Duke of Milan overcame anger at the duplicity of their allies, the Venetians.*

the Duke under necessity; he could not do so without Venetian greatness. Therefore Count Francesco should realize that if the Venetians were compelled to give up their territory on land he would lose not merely the benefits he was getting from them but also all the advantages that in fear of them others might offer him. If he would consider well the states of Italy, he would see that some were poor, others his enemies, and that, as he often had said, the Florentines alone were not strong enough to support him. Hence to support the Venetian land power was in every way to his advantage.

These arguments, added to the hatred the Count felt because he believed the Duke of Milan had duped him about the marriage with his daughter, made him accept the agreement, yet he was still unwilling to pledge himself to cross the River Po. The agreement was settled in February 1438–[1439]. The Venetians assumed two-thirds, the Florentines one-third of the expense of the alliance; both pledged that at their own expense they would protect the Count's territories in the Marches. Nor was the League satisfied with these forces but added to them the ruler of Faenza, the sons of Messer Pandolfo Malatesta of Rimini and Pietro Gianpaolo Orsini. Though with big promises the League tempted the Marquis of Mantua, it could not detach him from the Duke's alliance and pay; and the lord of Faenza, after the League had fixed his pay, returned to the Duke of Milan on getting a better contract. These failures ruined the League's hope for a rapid settlement of affairs in the Romagna.

CHAPTER 20

[The difficulties of the League in aiding Venice. 1439]

At this time Lombardy was in difficulties: Brescia was so strictly besieged by the Duke's soldiers that the League feared her surrender through famine any day; Verona also was so hemmed in that for her it feared the same outcome. If one of these two cities was lost, all the preparations for the war must be considered useless and the expenses incurred up to that time would be lost. No surer remedy was seen than to have Count Francesco go into Lombardy. This offered three difficulties. First, they must induce the Count to cross the Po and make war anywhere. Second, the Florentines saw they would be in the Duke's power unless they kept the Count in Tuscany, for the Duke could easily retire into his strongholds and with part of his soldiers keep the Count wasting time in Lombardy; the other part of his army the Duke could send into Tuscany with those Florentine exiles whom the government in power greatly feared. Third, by what road could the Count lead his soldiers safe into Paduan territory, where the other Venetian troops were? Of these three difficulties the second, which affected the Florentines, was most to be feared. Nevertheless, realizing the need and worn down by the Venetians, who with the utmost persistence kept asking for Count Francesco and making it appear that without him they would surrender, the Florentines put Venetian necessity before their own fears. There still remained the difficulty of the route, which they determined should be made secure by the Venetians. Because to settle these arrangements with the Count and to induce him to cross, the Florentine Signoria had sent Neri di Gino Capponi, they decided he should go on to Venice, in order to make the favor they were granting more pleasing to the Venetian government and to arrange a route and a safe journey for the Count.

CHAPTER 21

[Neri Capponi announces to the Venetian Senate that Florence is sending Count Francesco Sforza to their assistance. 1439]

So Neri left Cesena and went to Venice by sea. Never did that government receive any prince with such honor as they showed him, because they believed that on his coming and on what through him they could decide and arrange must depend the salvation of their power. Taken into their Senate, then, Neri spoke to this effect:

"Those Signors of mine, Most Splendid Prince,[1] have always been of the opinion that the Duke's greatness would be the ruin of this state and of their republic; and likewise the security of both these states would be your greatness and ours. If Your Lordships had believed the same thing, we should find ourselves in better condition, and your state would be secure against those dangers that now threaten it. But because in the times when you should have given us aid or been faithful to us, you have not done so, we have been unable to run quickly to get remedies for your ills. Nor have you

1. *The Doge.*

been quick in asking for them, since in your prosperity and your adversity you have little understood us, and do not know that we are such that him whom we once love we always love, and him whom we once hate, we always hate. The love we have borne to your Most Splendid Senate you yourselves know, because many times, for your rescue, you have seen Lombardy filled with our money and our soldiers. The hate we have for Filippo, and which we have always had for his house, all the world knows. An old love or an old hate cannot by new benefits or new injuries easily be canceled.

"We know and are certain that in this war we can stand neutral with great pleasure to the Duke and not much danger to ourselves; because even if by ruining you he became master of Lombardy, so much vigor would be left in Italy that we should not need to despair of our safety, because when power and territory increase, enmity and envy likewise increase; from these things result war and loss. We realize also how much expense we would avoid by avoiding the present war, how many threatening dangers we would escape, for if we enter this war that now is going on in Lombardy, it can be brought into Tuscany. Nevertheless our ancient affection for this state has canceled all these forebodings and we have determined to rescue your state with the same speed with which we would rescue our own if it were attacked.

"For this reason my Florentine Signors—thinking the relief of Verona and Brescia necessary before anything else, and judging that without the Count it cannot be accomplished—first sent me to persuade him to go into Lombardy and to make war anywhere (for you know he is not obligated to cross the Po). This I accomplished, influencing him with those reasons with which we ourselves are influenced. He too, as he holds himself invincible in war, wishes to appear likewise unconquerable in courtesy. Hence he has decided to surpass the liberality he sees us use toward you, though he well knows among how many dangers Tuscany will be left after his departure. Seeing that we have subordinated to your safety our own dangers, he too has decided to subordinate to that safety his own scruples. I come then to offer you the Count with seven thousand cavalry and two thousand infantry, ready to attack the enemy anywhere. I beg you, indeed, and my Signors and the Count beg you, since the number of his soldiers exceeds that with which he has contracted to serve, in your liberality to compensate him, that he may

not regret entering your service and that we may not regret encouraging him to do so."

To Neri's speech that Senate listened with attention no different
from what an oracle would receive. So fired with his words were the
hearers that they could not wait until the Prince, as custom demanded, made answer, but rising to their feet with lifted hands—the
greater part of them weeping—they thanked the Florentines for so
loving a service and thanked Neri because he had with such care and
speed performed it. They pledged moreover that never at any time
either from their hearts or the hearts of their descendants would its
memory be expunged and that their city would always belong in
common to the Florentines and themselves.

CHAPTER 22

[The roads to Padua; Count Francesco Sforza relieves Verona. 1439]

On the calming of these emotions, they discussed the road the
Count ought to take in order to be provided with bridges, level
ground and everything else. There were four roads. One was by
way of Ravenna, along the sea; this route, for the most part hemmed
in by the sea and the swamps, was not approved. The second was
the direct road; this was blocked by a tower called l'Uccellino,
which was garrisoned for the Duke, and anyone expecting to pass
would be obliged to capture it—which would be hard to do in a
time so short as not to take away the opportunity for relieving Brescia
and Verona, which demanded speed and promptness. The third
was through the forest of Lugo; but because the Po had got out of its
dykes, it rendered that way not merely difficult but impossible.
There remained the fourth, through the plain of Bologna, by the
Puledrano bridge, by Cento and by the Pieve, and between Finale
and Bondeno to Ferrara; after that, both by water and by land the
Count could get into Paduan territory and join the Venetian soldiers.
This road, though it offered many difficulties and could in some
places be attacked by the enemy, was chosen as the least bad. When
this was made known to the Count, he set out with very great speed
and on the 20th of June arrived in Paduan territory.

The coming of this general into Lombardy filled Venice and all
her state with hope, and whereas the Venetians at first seemed desper-

ate of their safety, they began to expect new conquests. The Count, before everything else, set about relieving Verona. To thwart this, Niccolò went with his army to Soave, a walled town between the territories of Vicenza and Verona, and fortified it with a ditch that extended from Soave as far as the swamps of the Adige. The Count, seeing the road by the plain blocked, judged that he could go through the mountains and by that way come close to Verona, imagining that Niccolò either would not believe that he would take that road, since it was rough and mountainous, or if he did believe it, would not have time to block it. Hence, providing supplies for eight days, he crossed the mountain with his soldiers and arrived near Soave in the plain. And though Niccolò had made some fortifications to block that road also for the Count, yet they were not enough to hold him. Niccolò, then, seeing that against all his belief, his enemy had crossed, in order that when at a disadvantage he might not come to a battle with the Count, retired to the other side of the Adige; and the Count without any hindrance entered Verona.

CHAPTER 23

[Unsuccessful attempt to relieve Brescia; Piccinino's strange escape. 1439]

So with ease Count Francesco accomplished his first task by freeing Verona from siege. The second remained, that of relieving Brescia. This city is so close to Lake Garda that, though she were blockaded by land, it would always be possible to get supplies to her by way of the lake. This was the reason why the Duke had put strong forces on the lake, and at the beginning of his victories had taken all those towns that by using the lake could send aid to Brescia. The Venetians too had galleys there, but for fighting with the Duke's men they were not adequate. Therefore the Count judged it neces-sary to aid the Venetian fleet with land forces. Thus he hoped to take easily those towns that were starving Brescia. So he placed his army at Bardolino, a town situated on the lake, hoping that, when he gained her, the other towns would surrender. Fortune in this cam-paign was the Count's enemy, because a good part of his soldiers fell sick; thereupon forsaking the campaign, he went to Zevio, a Vero-nese town well-supplied and healthful. Niccolò, seeing that the

Count had retired, in order not to miss his chance for gaining control of the lake, left his army at Vigasio, and with picked soldiers went to the lake, where with great speed and greater vigor he attacked the Venetian fleet and took almost all of it. As a result of this victory, few towns were left on the lake that did not surrender to Niccolò.

The Venetians, terrified by this loss and fearing that because of it the Brescians would give up, with messengers and letters urged the Count to relieve her. And the Count, seeing that hope of relieving her by means of the lake was gone and that relief by the plain was impossible because of the ditches, forts, and other hindrances ar-ranged by Niccolò—so that one who entered among them in the face of a hostile army went to obvious defeat—determined that as the mountain road had let him rescue Verona, so it would let him relieve Brescia. Having made this plan, then, the Count left Zevio and went by way of the Val d'Affi to Lake Santo Andrea[1] and came to Torbole and Castel Penede on Lake Garda. From there he went to Tenno, to which he laid siege, because, if he intended to go on to Brescia, the taking of that town was necessary. Niccolò, learning the Count's plans, led his army to Peschiera; then, with the Marquis of Mantua and some carefully picked soldiers, he went to meet the Count. And when they came to battle, Niccolò was de-feated and his soldiers scattered; part of them were captured, part fled to the army, part to the fleet.

Niccolò got into Tenno, and when night came, he decided that if he waited there for daylight he could not avoid falling into the hands of the enemy; so in order to escape certain danger, he ran a risk. With him Niccolò had only one of his many servants, a man of German birth, very strong in body, who had always been very faithful. This man Niccolò persuaded to put him in a sack, take him on his shoulders and, as though carrying things for his master, bring him to a safe place. The army was around Tenno but after the victory gained that day, without guards and without any order. Hence it was easy for the German to save his master; putting him on his shoulder, the servant, clad as a forager, passed through the whole army without any hindrance; thus in safety he brought Niccolò to his own soldiers.

1. *Now Loppio.*

CHAPTER 24

[Piccinino takes Verona, except for San Felice, by surprise. 1439]

This victory, then, if it had been used with the skill with which it was won, would have brought Brescia greater relief and the Vene﹣ tians more good fortune, but bad use of it made happiness quickly vanish, and Brescia was left in the same difficulties. Because when Niccolò was again with his soldiers, he decided that with some new victory he must cancel that loss and take from the Venetians their means for relieving Brescia. He knew the site of the citadel of Verona, and from prisoners taken in the war had learned that it was badly guarded and that there was an easy way to capture it. Therefore he saw that Fortune had put in his hands a possibility for getting back his honor and for turning the happiness enjoyed by the enemy, through the recent victory, into sorrow through a more recent defeat.

The city of Verona, in Lombardy at the foot of the mountains that divide Italy from Germany, is so situated she includes both mountain and plain. Out of the valley of Trent the River Adige flows, and as it enters the Italian plain it does not at once spread out but, turning to the left along the mountains, it comes to Verona and passes through her midst—not, however, dividing her equally but leaving much more of the city on the side of the plain than on that of the mountains. On the heights are two castles, one named San Piero, the other San Felice; these appear stronger in their sites than in their walls, and from their high places dominate all the city. In the plain on the south side of the Adige and astride the walls of the town are two other fortresses, distant from each other a thousand paces; one is called the Old Citadel, the other the New. From the inner part of one citadel a wall extends to the other citadel, and forms as it were a string for the bow made by the ordinary city walls extending from one citadel to the other. All the space between the two walls is full of inhabitants, and is called the suburb of San Zeno.[1] These citadels and this suburb Niccolò Piccino planned to take, expecting to suc﹣ ceed easily, through the careless watch that was always kept there and his belief that the recent victory would make it more careless, and

---

1. *When on a visit to Verona, Machiavelli wrote an account of her topography (*LEGATION TO MANTOVA, *30. 20, 12 Dec. 1509; most of the letters of this legation were written from Verona).*

through his knowledge that in war no enterprise is so likely to suc⁄
ceed as that which the enemy does not believe you can carry out.

Taking some selected soldiers, with the Marquis of Mantua he
went by night to Verona; without being observed he scaled and took
the New Citadel. Going from there into the town, his soldiers broke
open the gate of Sant' Antonio, through which they let in all the
cavalry. Those who were guarding the Old Citadel for the Vene⁄
tians, having first heard the noise when the guards of the New were
killed and then when the gate was broken open, realizing that the
enemy were there, began to shout and ring the bells to call the people
to arms. After that, when the citizens woke up, entirely bewildered,
those who had most courage took arms and ran to the Piazza of the
Rectors. Meanwhile Niccolò's soldiers had sacked the suburb of
San Zeno. When they advanced, the citizens, realizing that the
ducal soldiers were inside and having no way for defending them⁄
selves, urged the Venetian rectors to flee into the fortresses and save
their own persons and the city. It was better, the citizens explained,
for the rectors to save their lives and keep the city rich for a better
fortune than, by trying to escape their present one, to die and make
the city poor. And so the rectors and all other Venetians fled to the
castle of San Felice. After this, some of the leading citizens came
before Niccolò and the Marquis of Mantua, begging them to take
that city when rich, with honor to themselves, rather than when poor,
to their own reproach, especially since the Veronese had not de⁄
served gratitude from the Venetians or hatred from the invaders by
defending themselves. They were well received by Niccolò and by
the Marquis, who, as much as they could in that military license,
protected the city from sack.

Because the two generals were almost certain that the Count
would come to retake Verona, with all their might they labored to
get the strongholds into their hands; and those that they could not
get, with ditches and barricades they separated from the city, so the
enemy would have trouble getting inside.

CHAPTER 25

[By his rapidity Count Francesco regains Verona. 1439]

Count Francesco, with his soldiers at Tenno, on hearing that
Verona had fallen, at first thought the news baseless; then from more

certain reports assured of its truth, he determined by speed to atone for his earlier negligence. And though all the leaders of his army advised him to abandon his Verona and Brescia campaign and to go to Vicenza so as not to be besieged by the enemy as a result of delaying there, he refused to yield, and determined to tempt Fortune as to regaining that city. In the midst of this uncertainty of mind, he turned to the Venetian supervisors and to Bernadetto de'Medici, the Florentine commissioner with the army, promising her certain recapture, if one of the castles waited for him.

Having then got his soldiers into order, he went toward Verona with the utmost speed. On seeing him, Niccolò believed that, as his officers had advised, he was going to Vicenza, but when he saw the Count turn his soldiers toward Verona and direct them upon the castle of San Felice, he gave orders to prepare for defense. But he was too late, because the barricades cutting off the castle were not made, and in their lust for booty and ransoms the soldiers were scattered, so that he could not bring them together quickly enough to prevent the Count's soldiers from reaching the fortress and thence descending into the city. Thus the Count triumphantly regained Verona, with shame to Niccolò and harm to his soldiers. With the Marquis of Mantua, Niccolò first fled into the citadel and then through the country to Mantua. Afterward, bringing together the remnants of their soldiers who had escaped, the two joined the forces at the siege of Brescia. So within four days the ducal army won and lost Verona.

After this victory, since it was already winter and the cold was severe, the Count went into winter quarters in Verona, as soon as with great difficulty he had sent provisions into Brescia. He ordered that in the winter some galleys should be built at Torbole, so that in the spring he would be so strong on land and water that he could completely free Brescia.

CHAPTER 26

[Duke Filippo considers attacking Tuscany; the Florentine exiles promise easy victory. 1440]

The Duke, seeing the war for the time at a standstill and his hope for taking Verona and Brescia destroyed, realized that the money and the advice of the Florentines had caused it all, and that not even the injuries they had received had been able to alienate them from their friendship for the Venetians and that the promises he had made had not been able to gain them over to his side. Therefore he determined, in order that they might view from a shorter distance the fruit of their seeds, to attack Tuscany.

The Florentine exiles and Niccolò encouraged him to do so. Niccolò was impelled by his wish to conquer Braccio's states and to drive the Count from the Marches; the exiles were urged on by their hope of returning to their native city; both parties had influenced the Duke with timely arguments conforming with his purpose. Niccolò showed that Filippo could send him into Tuscany and yet maintain the siege of Brescia, because the Duke was master of Lake Garda and on land had strong and well-equipped fortresses; he would still have generals and soldiers able to oppose any movement Count Francesco undertook. Moreover the Count could not reasonably undertake anything before liberating Brescia, yet to liberate her was impossible. Hence Filippo could make war in Tuscany without abandoning the campaign in Lombardy. Niccolò also demonstrated that as soon as the Florentines saw him in Tuscany they would recall the Count; otherwise they would be ruined. Whichever they did would bring the Duke victory. The exiles declared that if Niccolò arrived before Florence with his army, the people, worn out by taxes and by the arrogance of the powerful, could not by any possibility fail to take arms against their oppressors. They showed the Duke that it was easy to approach Florence, since they promised that the road through the Casentino would be open because of Messer Rinaldo degli Albizzi's friendship with the Count of Poppi. Hence the Duke, who had first turned to it for himself, so much the more by the persuasions of these men was fixed upon making that expedition.

The Venetians on the other hand, even though the winter was harsh, did not fail to urge the Count with all his army to relieve Brescia—something the Count declared could not be done in such weather; he needed to wait for spring, meanwhile getting the fleet in order, and then he would relieve her by water and by land. As a result the Venetians were discontented and were slow about every supply, so that in their army many men were missing.

CHAPTER 27

[Fear in Florence; their spies; Giovanni Vitelleschi arrested. 1440]

When assured of all these things, the Florentines were terrified, seeing that the war was coming on them and that in Lombardy not much had been gained. Nor were they given less anxiety by their suspicions about the soldiers of the Church, not because the Pope was their enemy, but because they saw those soldiers obeying the Patriarch, who was very hostile to them, rather than the Pope. For Giovanni Vitelleschi of Corneto was first apostolic notary, then bishop of Recanati, next patriarch of Alexandria, and at last becoming cardinal, he was named Florentine cardinal. He was bold and astute, and therefore so conducted himself that the Pope greatly loved him and put him in charge of the armies of the Church; in all the Pope's campaigns in Tuscany, in Romagna, in the Kingdom and at Rome, he was commander; thus he got such power over the soldiers and over the Pope that the latter was afraid to give him orders, and the soldiers obeyed him only and no other. Since, then, this cardinal with his soldiers was in Rome when the report came that Niccolò was going to cross into Tuscany, the Florentines were doubly frightened. Indeed, after Messer Rinaldo degli Albizzi was driven out, the Cardinal had always been an enemy to that government, because the agreements made in Florence between the parties through his intervention had not been observed but on the contrary had been handled with damage to Messer Rinaldo, for they had caused him to lay down his arms and give his enemies opportunity to drive him out. Hence the heads of the Florentine government thought that the time might have come for Messer Rinaldo to recoup his losses by siding with Niccolò when that general came into Tuscany. They feared so much the more when they considered that the departure of Niccolò from Lombardy was strangely timed, since he was leaving an undertaking almost finished to enter upon one altogether uncertain—which they did not believe he would do without some new information or hidden deception. Of this suspicion of theirs they had informed the Pope, who had already realized his mistake in giving another man too much power.

While the Florentines were thus uncertain, Fortune showed them a way for securing themselves against the Patriarch. That republic kept everywhere diligent inspectors of men carrying letters, in order to discover anybody who might be plotting against her government. At Montepulciano Florentine agents took letters written by the Patriarch, without the Pontiff's authorization, to Niccolò Piccino. The magistrates in charge of the war at once laid them before the Pope. Though they were written in unusual characters and their sense was so involved that no clear idea could be got from them, nevertheless such obscurity and dealings with the enemy roused in the Pontiff so much suspicion that he determined to protect himself. He put in charge of the affair Antonio Rido of Padua, officer of the guard at the castle in Rome. When this man had his instructions and was ready to obey, he waited for his opportunity. At last the Patriarch decided to go to Tuscany. Planning on the next day to leave Rome, he asked the castellan to be at the castle bridge in the morning because he wished in passing to talk with him about some thing. Antonio saw that his opportunity had come. He instructed his men what they were to do and at the time set waited for the Patriarch on the bridge—adjacent to the castle—which for security could be raised and lowered as was necessary. When the Patriarch had crossed, Antonio first brought him to a stand with their conver sation and then made a sign to his men to raise the bridge; so the Patriarch in an instant found himself not a commander of armies but a castellan's prisoner. His soldiers at first made a disturbance, but on learning the Pope's will quieted down. Then when the castellan with kind words encouraged the Patriarch and gave him hope that all would be well, he answered that great men are not arrested to be released, and those who deserve to be seized do not deserve to be released. As he expected, he soon died in prison. The Pope put in command of his soldiers Lodovico the Patriarch of Aquileia. Though never before in the past had the Pope wished to involve himself in the wars of the League and the Duke, he was then willing to take part, and promised to be ready to defend Tuscany with four thousand cavalry and two thousand infantry.

CHAPTER 28

[The Venetians urge an attack on Brescia. 1440]

Though the Florentines were freed from fear of the Patriarch, they still dreaded Niccolò and the confusion of affairs in Lombardy because of the differences of opinion between the Venetians and the Count. So, to understand them better, they sent Neri di Gino Capponi and Messer Giuliano Davanzati to Venice. They charged them to settle how the war was to be managed during the next year. They also gave Neri instructions that, after learning the Venetians' opinion, he should visit the Count to learn his view and to persuade him to do whatever the safety of the League required.

These ambassadors had not even reached Ferrara when they learned that Niccolò Piccino with six thousand cavalry had crossed the Po—which made them hasten their journey. When they came to Venice they found the Signoria very eager to have Brescia relieved without further delay, because the city could not wait for relief until spring or until the fleet was built, but if no troops appeared to aid her, she would surrender to the enemy. Thus the Duke would be wholly victorious and the Venetians would lose all their territory on land.

Neri therefore went to Verona to get the Count's opinion and hear what he opposed to the Venetian desire. That general explained with plenty of reasons that to ride toward Brescia in that season would be useless then and damaging to a future effort; on account of the season and the topography it would do Brescia no good but would merely disorganize and tire out his soldiers; on the coming of spring, a time suitable for the business, he would have to bring his army back to Verona to provide the supplies that had been used up in the winter and were needed for the next summer; thus the whole season fit for war would be used up in going and coming. With Count Francesco at Verona, having been sent to arrange these things, were Messer Orsatto Giustiniani and Messer Giovanni Pisani. With these men, after many discussions, it was decided that for the next year the Venetians would give the Count eighty thousand ducats and their other soldiers forty ducats per lance,[1] that the Count should be urged to go out with the whole army, and that the Duke should be attacked. In fear for his own property, he would then make Niccolò come back to Lombardy. After this decision, they went back to Venice. The Venetians, because the sum of money was large, in all affairs provided slowly.

1. *A "lance" consisted of one heavily armed horseman and four or five other men, partly servants, partly light-armed horsemen.*

CHAPTER 29

[Count Francesco wishes to pursue Piccinino; the Venetians dissuade him. 1440]

Niccolo Piccino meanwhile continued his journey and reached Romagna, where he was so successful with the sons of Messer Pan/ dolfo Malatesta that, deserting the Venetians, they sided with the Duke. This affair disturbed Venice, but Florence much more, be/ cause they had believed that by means of them they could make resistance to Niccolò. But when they saw that the Malatesta had revolted, they were alarmed, especially because they feared that Pietro Gianpaolo Orsini, their general, who was in the cities of the Mala/ testa, had not got away, and that they were left unarmed.

This news likewise upset the Count, because he feared to lose the Marches if Niccolò went into Tuscany; being disposed to rescue his own property, he went to Venice, and when brought before the chief official, showed that his going into Tuscany was useful to the League: war must be made where the army and the general of the enemy are, not where the cities and their garrisons are, because, if the army is defeated, the war is won; but if the cities are won and the army left entire, the war often becomes more active. He declared that the Marches and Tuscany would be lost if he did not strongly oppose Niccolò; and if they were lost, Lombardy would have no recourse, but while she had a recourse, he did not expect to abandon his subjects and his friends. He had come into Lombardy as a lord and did not intend to leave as a soldier of fortune.[1]

To this the head of the government answered that it was evident that if the Count not merely left Lombardy but with his army recrossed the Po, all Venetian territory on land would be lost, and they were not going to spend anything more in defending it, because he is not wise who tries to defend a thing that he is going to lose in any case; and, with less disgrace, it is less damage to lose territory alone than territory and money. When the loss of the Venetian territory followed his action, he would see the importance of Vene/ tian prestige in supporting Tuscany and Romagna. Therefore they were wholly opposed to his opinion because they believed that he

1. *Count Francesco did not intend to remain in Lombardy while his enemies conquered the territory he had acquired elsewhere in Italy.*

who won in Lombardy would win in every other place. To win was easy, since the Duke's condition, through Niccolò's departure, was so weak that he could be ruined before he could either recall Niccolò or provide himself with other means. And they were sure that anybody who would consider everything wisely would see that the Duke had not sent Niccolò into Tuscany for anything else than to get the Count away from these enterprises, and to carry on elsewhere the war now in his own country. Hence, if the Count followed Piccinino without first seeing the utmost necessity, his act would harmonize with the Duke's plans and make him succeed in his purpose. But if the soldiers were kept in Lombardy, and in Tuscany all possible provisions were made, the Duke would realize too late his bad decision, at a time when without any redress he would have lost in Lombardy and would not have won in Tuscany.

After each one had given and repeated his opinion, they settled that for a few days they should remain quiet to observe, in order to see what this agreement of the Malatesta with Niccolò would produce, and if the Florentines could make use of Pietro Gianpaolo Orsini, and if the Pope kept in step with the League, as he had promised. After coming to this decision, they were assured a few days later that the Malatesta had made that agreement more through fear than through any malicious reason, that Pietro Gianpaolo had gone to Tuscany with his soldiers, and that the Pope was more disposed than before to aid the League. This information put at rest the Count's mind; he consented to remain in Lombardy and to let Neri Capponi return to Florence with a thousand of his cavalry and five hundred of the other soldiers. Moreover, if things in Tuscany went so badly that the Count's action was necessary there, he was to be written to; then without any hesitation he would leave. So Neri with those soldiers got to Florence in April, and the same day Pietro Gianpaolo arrived.

CHAPTER 30

[Bartolommeo Orlandini's cowardice permits Piccinino to enter Tuscany. 1440]

Niccolò Piccino, since things were quiet in Romagna, then determined to make a descent upon Tuscany. Attempting to cross by the mountains of San Benedetto and through the valley of Montone, he found those places so well guarded through the efficiency of Niccolò da Pisa that he considered all efforts in that region useless. Because the Florentines on this sudden attack were badly provided with both soldiers and leaders, to these mountain passes they had sent as guards several of their citizens with hastily assembled infantry. Among these was Messer Bartolommeo Orlandini, a knight, to whom were entrusted the town of Marradi and the pass through those mountains. After Niccolò Piccino had decided, then, that he could not take the pass of San Benedetto, since an able man guarded it, he judged that he could take that of Marradi, since a coward had the defense of it. Marradi is a town situated at the foot of the mountains that divide Tuscany from Romagna, but on the side that looks toward Romagna and in the upper part of the Val di Lamona; and though it is without a wall, nonetheless the river, the mountains and the inhabitants make it strong; for the men are warlike and faithful, and the river has in such a way gnawed into the earth, and its gorge is so deep, that to come there from the direction of the valley is impos-sible as long as a little bridge over the river is held. In the direction of the mountains the banks are so rough that they make the site very secure. Nonetheless, Messer Bartolommeo's cowardice made those mountaineers cowardly and that site very weak, for he no sooner heard a report about the hostile soldiers than, leaving everything unwatched, with all his men he fled; he did not stop until he came to Borgo San Lorenzo.

Niccolò, having entered the places that had been deserted, full of astonishment that they had not been defended and of joy at having gained them, descended into the Mugello, where he took some towns. At Pulicciano he halted his army, and from there raided all the country as far as the mountains of Fiesole. He was so bold that he crossed Arno and not more than three miles from Florence sacked and destroyed everything.

CHAPTER 31

[Piccinino wastes time in the Casentino and makes a fruitless attempt to take Perugia. 1440]

The Florentines, on the other hand, were not upset, and before everything else gave attention to keeping their government stable; for that they needed to fear little, on account of Cosimo's popularity with the people, and because they had restricted the chief offices to the powerful few, who with their severity were keeping quiet any who might be discontented or eager for changes. They knew also, through the agreements made in Lombardy, with what forces Neri was coming back, and from the Pope they were awaiting soldiers—a hope that, until the return of Neri, kept them alive.

Neri, having found the city in these confusions and fears, decided to take the field in order in part to check Niccolò, so that he would not be scot free in laying waste the country. So collecting many infantry, all from the people, he went out with what cavalry there were and retook Remole, which the enemy were holding. Encamping there, he kept Niccolò from raiding and gave the citizens hope of driving the enemy away. Niccolò, seeing that the Florentines, when they were stripped of soldiers, had made no movement,[1] and learning with how much security they lived in that city, thought to himself that without result he was using up his time, and decided to carry on other enterprises, to give the Florentines reason to send their soldiers against him and thus to furnish him opportunity to come to battle. If he won that, he expected everything else to come out well.

In Niccolò's army was Francesco, Count of Poppi, who, when the enemy were in the Mugello, revolted from the Florentines, with whom he was in league. Though earlier the Florentines had been doubtful about him, they had increased his subsidy, in order through benefits to make him their friend, and had made him commissioner over all their cities neighboring his territory. Nevertheless (so powerful in men is the love of party), no benefit and no fear could make him forget the affection he had for Messer Rinaldo and the others who were important in the late government. Hence, as soon as he heard that Niccolò was near, he joined him, and with all sorts of persuasions exhorted him to move away from Florence and go into the Casentino, showing him the strength of the country and with what certainty he could there keep the enemy hemmed in. Therefore Niccolò followed this advice, and arriving in the Casentino, took Romena and Bibbiena; then he besieged Castel San Niccolò.

This town is situated at the foot of the mountains that divide the

1. *There was no rebellion against the government, such as the exiles had promised. See chap. 26, above.*

Casentino from the Val d'Arno, and because it is in a place well elevated and had a sufficient garrison, its capture was difficult, though with mangonels and similar artillery Niccolò steadily attacked it. This siege lasted more than twenty days, within which time the Florentines had brought their soldiers together; and already they had assembled under several generals three thousand cavalry at Figline, commanded by Pietro Gianpaolo as general and by Neri Capponi and Bernardo de'Medici as commissioners. To these came four men sent by Castel San Niccolò to beg that they would give them aid. The commissioners, having examined the site, saw that they could not aid the town except by passing through the mountains that rise above the Arno valley; the summit of these mountains could be taken by the enemy sooner than by the Florentines because Niccolò's forces would need to make a shorter journey, and the Florentine approach could not be concealed. Hence the Florentines would be attempting a movement unlikely to succeed, from which could come the ruin of their soldiers. As a result, the commissioners praised the fidelity of the suppliants and instructed them that, when they could no longer defend themselves, they should surrender.

Niccolò took Castel San Niccolò, then, thirty-two days after he went there with his army. The loss of so much time for so small a gain was the chief reason for the ruin of his enterprise, because if he had kept his soldiers near Florence, he would have rendered the rulers of the city unable, except with caution, to force the citizens to provide money. With more difficulty they would have assembled their soldiers and made every other provision, if they had had the enemy close by instead of at a distance; and many would have had courage to propose some agreement in order to secure themselves from Niccolò through a treaty, since the war was likely to last. But the Count of Poppi's wish to revenge himself against the people of Castel San Niccolò, who had long been his enemies, made him give that advice; and Niccolò, to satisfy him, took it—which was the ruin of them both. It seldom happens that individual passions do not act against general advantages. Niccolò, following up his victory, took Rassina and Chiusi. The Count of Poppi tried to induce him to remain in those districts, showing him that he could extend his men between Chiusi, Caprese, and the Pieve San Stefano, and he would become master of the highlands and could at his wish go down into the

Casentino, the Arno valley, Valdichiana and the Tiber valley, and be ready for every move that his enemies might make.

But Niccolò, considering the roughness of the places, answered that his horses could not eat stones, and went off to Borgo San Sepolcro, where he had a friendly reception. From that place he tested the disposition of the men of Città di Castello, who, being friends of the Florentines, did not listen to him. Next, since he wished to have the Perugians as supporters, he went with forty horse-men to Perugia, where, being a citizen of the town, he was received with affection. But in a few days he became suspected there; with the Legate and with the Perugians he tried a number of things, and none of them were successful; hence, after receiving from them eight thousand ducats, he returned to his army.

From there he carried on negotiations in Cortona, in order to take it from the Florentines, but because the affair was discovered early, his plans came to nothing. Among the chief citizens of that town was Bartolommeo di Senso. When one evening, on the Cap-tain's orders, he went to act as guard at a gate, he was told by one from the country, his friend, not to go there if he did not want to be killed. At once Bartolommeo tried to learn the basis of the matter, and found out the plan of the conspiracy that was going on with Niccolò. In turn Bartolommeo revealed it to the Captain, who, making sure of the leaders of the conspiracy and doubling the guards at the gates, waited, according to the plan that had been arranged, for Niccolò to come. He came in the night and at the time arranged, but finding that he was discovered, returned to his camp.

CHAPTER 32

[*Count Francesco relieves Brescia; the Duke recalls Piccinino, who then decides to fight a battle. 1440*]

While in Tuscany things were going on in this way—with little gain for the Duke's army—in Lombardy they did not stand still— and with loss and damage for him. Count Francesco, as soon as the season permitted, took the field with his army. Since the Venetians had replaced their fleet on the lake, the Count planned before doing anything else to master the water and drive the Duke from the lake, judging that when this was done, other things would be easy. With the Venetian fleet he therefore attacked that of the Duke and defeated it, and with the soldiers on land he took the fortified towns that were subject to the Duke; hence the other ducal soldiers, who were pressing Brescia by land, when they learned of that disaster, withdrew; and so Brescia, besieged for three years, was now free from siege. After this victory, the Count attacked enemies who had gathered at Soncino, a town on the Oglio River; he dislodged them and made them retire to Cremona, where the Duke made a stand to defend his states on that side. But since the Count pressed him harder every day, and he feared that he would lose all or a great part of his states, the Duke realized how bad a decision he had made in sending Niccolò to Tuscany; so in order to correct his error, he informed Niccolò of his condition and of the state of his undertakings, and ordered him as soon as possible to leave Tuscany and return to Lombardy.

The Florentines, meanwhile, under their commissioners, had united their soldiers with those of the Pope and had halted at Anghi-ari, a town situated at the base of the mountains that divide the Valley of the Tiber from the Valdichiana, four miles distant from Borgo San Sepolcro by a smooth road; the fields were fit for bearing cavalry and for the operation of war. Because the officials in Flor-ence had news of the Count's victories and of Niccolò's recall, they judged that with sword in scabbard and without dust[1] they had won that war. Therefore they wrote to their commissioners to avoid battle, because Niccolò could not remain many days in Tuscany. These instructions came to Niccolò's knowledge. Seeing that he must depart, he decided, in order not to leave anything untried, to fight a battle, thinking he would find the enemy unprovided and with their thoughts far from combat. In this he was encouraged by Messer Rinaldo, by the Count of Poppi, and by the other Florentine exiles, whose ruin was obvious if Niccolò withdrew. But if a battle was fought, they hoped they would either succeed in their enterprise or lose it with honor. Having made this decision, then, he moved his army from between Città di Castello and Borgo San Sepolcro, and coming to Borgo without the enemy's knowledge, he took from that town two thousand men, who, eager for plunder, trusting in the general's ability and in his promises, followed him.

1. *The Latin* sine pulvere *(Horace,* EPISTLES *1. 1. 51), without effort.*

CHAPTER 33

[The Florentines win the bloodless victory of Anghiari. 1440]

So in this way Niccolò, with his soldiers ready for battle, having set out for Anghiari, was already less than two miles away when Micheletto Attendulo saw a great cloud of dust. Realizing that it was the enemy, he shouted: "To arms!" The confusion in the Florentine army was great because, though ordinarily armies such as theirs encamped without any discipline, now negligence was added, since the Florentine soldiers believed their enemy at a distance and more disposed for flight than for combat. Hence all were unarmed, far from their quarters, and in any place where their wish either to escape the heat, which was great, or to amuse themselves had taken them. Yet so great was the effort of the commissioners and the general that before the enemy got there they were mounted and drawn up to resist attack. And as Micheletto was the first to observe the enemy, so he was the first who was armed to meet them; and he ran with his soldiers to the bridge over the stream that crosses the road, not very far from Anghiari. Before the coming of the enemy, Pietro Gianpaolo Orsini had had all the ditches filled up that bounded the road from the bridge to Anghiari. Hence when Micheletto faced the bridge, Simoncino, the general for the Church, with the Legate, could be placed on the right hand, and on the left the Florentine commissioners with Pietro Gianpaolo their general; the infantry were drawn up on each side along the banks of the stream. To the enemy, therefore, no way was open for attacking their adversaries other than the straight road over the bridge, and nowhere except at the bridge would the Florentines have to fight, though they had instructed their infantry that if the enemy infantry left the road in order to be on the flanks of their menatarms, they should engage them with their crossbows, so that the enemy could not strike on the flank Florentine cavalry that crossed the bridge.

Micheletto strongly resisted the first soldiers who appeared, and, more than that, drove them back; but when Astor and Francesco Piccinino came up with picked soldiers, with such power they struck Micheletto that they took the bridge and pushed him back as far as the slope that rises to the village of Anghiari. Then they were driven back and pushed over the bridge by Florentine forces attacking them on their flanks. This combat lasted two hours, while now Niccolò, now the Florentine soldiers were masters of the bridge. And although the combat at the bridge was a drawn one, nevertheless, both beyond the bridge and on the Florentine side of it, the fighting was greatly to Niccolò's disadvantage, for when his soldiers crossed the bridge, they found the enemy strong, since, by reason of the leveling they had done, they were able to maneuver, and tired men could be relieved by fresh ones. But when the Florentine soldiers crossed over, Niccolò could not conveniently relieve his men, because he was cramped by the ditches and banks that extended along the road. Thus it happened that many times Niccolò's soldiers gained the bridge, but were always pushed back by fresh adversaries. But when the bridge was carried by the Florentines, so that their soldiers gained the road beyond, Niccolò did not have time, through the impetus of the Florentine forces and the inconvenience of the site, to relieve his men; hence those in front mingled with those behind in such a way that the one disordered the other, and the whole army was obliged to turn around, and in disorder everybody fled toward Borgo. The Florentine soldiers gave their attention to the spoil, which in prisoners, in armor and in horses, was very great, because with Niccolò not a thousand horsemen escaped. The people of Borgo, who had followed Niccolò for plunder, instead of plunderers became plunder, and they were all taken and ransomed. The banners and the baggage were captured.

And the victory was much more profitable to Tuscany than harmful to the Duke; if the Florentines had lost the day, Tuscany would have been his; but when he lost, he lost only the arms and the horses of his army, which with no great amount of money he could replace. There never were times less dangerous for those who made war in the lands of others. In this great defeat and long fight lasting from two until six o'clock, not more than one man died, and he perished not from wounds or any honorable blow, but by falling from his horse and being trampled on. At that time men fought with such great safety because, all on horseback and covered with armor and safe against death whenever they surrendered, they had no reason for dying, since they were protected during the fight by armor and when they no longer could fight by surrendering.

CHAPTER 34

[Disorder after the battle; Rinaldo degli Albizzi's later career and death. 1440]

This battle, on account of the things that happened while it was being fought and later, is a good example of the ineffectiveness of these wars; because, when the enemy had been beaten and Niccolò had retreated into Borgo, the commissioners wished to follow him and to besiege him there in order to make the victory complete, but not a single officer or soldier would obey; they all said they had to lay up their booty and care for the wounded. And what is even more noteworthy is that the next day, at midday, without permission from commissioner or officer or regard for them, they went off to Arezzo to leave their booty and then came back to Anghiari—a thing so much opposed to every praiseworthy method and to military discipline that the least relic of any organized army could easily and deservedly have taken from them the victory which they had undeservedly gained. Besides this, though to deprive the enemy of a chance to reorganize, the commissioners gave orders for holding the men-at-arms who had been captured, the soldiers in violation of these orders set the captives free. All these things were enough to make one wonder that in such an army there was so much vigor that they could win, and that in the enemy there was so much weakness that they could be beaten by such disorderly soldiers. In the course of the going and coming of the Florentine soldiers from Arezzo, then, Niccolò had time to leave Borgo with his men and go toward Romagna.

With him the Florentine exiles also fled. These men, seeing that they had lost every hope of returning to Florence, dispersed among various places in Italy and outside, as suited them. Messer Rinaldo degli Albizzi took up his residence at Ancona. Then in order to gain himself a celestial country, since he had lost his earthly one, he went to Christ's sepulchre. After his return, while celebrating the wedding of a daughter, as he sat at the table he suddenly died. In this Fortune was favorable to him, that in the least unhappy day of his exile she had him die. A man indeed worthy of honor in every fortune,[1] but he would have been still more so if Nature had had him

---

1. *In good fortune he was not arrogant; in bad fortune he did not lose courage.*

born in a united city, because in a divided city he was damaged by many of his qualities which in a united one would have honored him.

The commissioners, then, after their soldiers had returned from Arezzo, and Niccolò had gone, moved upon Borgo. The men of Borgo wished to surrender to the Florentines, and the latter refused to take them. But in the dealings about this surrender, the Pontiff's Legate suspected the commissioners did not intend that town to be occupied by the Church, so that they exchanged insulting words, and between the Florentine and the ecclesiastical soldiers there would have been trouble if the discussion had gone on very long, but because it ended as the Legate wished, everything quieted down.

CHAPTER 35

[The Count of Poppi expelled; the commissioners honored in Florence. 1440]

While the affairs of Borgo were being settled, Niccolò Piccino was reported going toward Rome; other information said toward the Marches. Hence the Legate and Sforza's soldiers decided to go toward Perugia in order to support either the Marches or Rome, as Niccolò might have gone. With them was to go Bernardo de' Medici; but with the Florentine soldiers Neri should march to con- quer the Casentino.

Having decided this, Neri besieged Rassina and took her, and with the same speed took Bibbiena, Prato Vecchio and Romena. Then he laid siege to Poppi and hemmed her in on two sides, one that of the plain of Certomondo, the other that of the hill on the road to Fronzoli. The Count of Poppi, seeing himself abandoned by God and by men, had shut himself up in Poppi, not because he hoped to get any help but if he could, to make his surrender less damaging. So when Neri pressed him hard, he asked for terms and received such as at that time he could hope for: that he might preserve himself, his children and his portable goods, but must cede his town and his state to Florence. When they made their agreement, he came down to the bridge over Arno, which flows just below the town, and in great sorrow and distress said to Neri: "If I had properly measured my fortune and your power, I should now be coming as a friend to congratulate you on your victory, not as an enemy to beg that my fall may be less great. The present situation, as for you it is splendid and happy, so for me it is sorrowful and wretched. I had horses, arms, subjects, power and riches; is it strange if I am unwilling to leave them? But if you intend to control all Tuscany and are strong enough to do so, we others must needs obey you. If I had not made this mistake, my fortune would not have been known and your liberality could not be known, for if you will preserve me, you will give to the world an eternal example of your clemency. So let your pity overcome my misdeed; leave at least this one house to the descendants of men from whom your fathers received countless benefits."

To this Neri replied that relying too much on men who had little power had made the Count do great injury to the Florentine republic and that the conditions of the times made his fault so much the worse. Therefore necessity compelled him to yield up all his possessions and, as an enemy of the Florentines, to abandon those places that, as their friend, he had not chosen to hold, because he had given such an example of himself that he could not be kept where in any change of Fortune he might harm that republic. Because not the Count himself but his states were feared, for if he were a prince in Germany, that city would regret him and for love of those ancestors that he mentioned would aid him. To this the Count, very angry, replied that he should like to see the Florentines much further off. And so, abandoning all friendly talk, the Count, not seeing any other resource, ceded his city and all his rights to the Florentines, and with all his property, departed in tears with his wife and children, grieving that he had lost a state that for nine hundred years his fathers had possessed.

All these victories, when known in Florence, were by the leaders of the government and the people received with extraordinary joy. And because Bernardetto de'Medici found it false that Niccolò had gone to the Marches or to Rome, he came back with the soldiers where Neri was; and when together they came again to Florence, the greatest honors that according to the law of the city can be decreed for victorious citizens were decreed for them; and by the Signors and the Captains of the Party, and then by the whole city, they were welcomed as victors.

BOOK SIX

[THE POWER OF COSIMO DE'MEDICI; FROM DUKE FILIPPO'S EFFORTS FOR PEACE TO THE ABANDONMENT OF NAPLES BY THE ANGEVINS. 1440–1463]

CHAPTER 1

[Italian wars enrich mercenaries, impoverish princes and people]

It always has been, and it is reasonable that it should be, the object of those who go to war to enrich themselves and to impoverish the enemy, nor is victory sought for any other reason or gains wished for anything else than to make oneself powerful and weaken one's opponent. From this it follows that whenever your victory impoverishes you or your gain weakens you, you must either have passed beyond or not have reached the goal for which wars are made. A prince (and a republic also) is made rich by victories and by wars in which he destroys his enemies and is master of the booty and of the ransom money; a prince is impoverished by victories who, though he conquers his enemies, cannot destroy them, and not he but his soldiers get the booty and the ransom money. In defeats, such a prince is unfortunate and in victories very unfortunate; if defeated, he suffers injuries from his enemies; if victorious, from his friends. Injuries from his friends, as less reasonable, are less easily borne, especially since he is obliged to lay upon his subjects the weight of taxes and fresh vexations. If he has in him any humanity, he cannot altogether rejoice in any victory for which all his subjects lament. Ancient and well-ordered republics, as the result of their victories, usually filled their treasuries with silver and gold, distributed gifts to the people, remitted tribute to their subjects, and with games and splendid shows entertained them. But victories in the times we are describing first emptied the treasury and then impoverished the people, and from your enemies they did not protect you.[1]

All this came from the bad method with which these wars were carried on. Enemies who were defeated were plundered, but not

---

1. *Such a shift to the second person singular often occurs in* THE PRINCE. *Indeed the clause almost seems to come from* THE PRINCE *12.*

held as prisoners or killed. Hence they delayed in attacking the victor again only as long as they waited for their employer to resupply them with arms and horses. So, in these wars, since the ransoms and spoils belonged to the soldiers, victorious princes could not for their new expenses make use of new money, but tore it from the vitals of their subjects; thus victory produced nothing for the benefit of the people; it only made their prince more eager to tax them and less cautious in doing it. To such a condition those soldiers had brought war that the conqueror and the conquered, if they were to control their soldiers, equally needed new money; the loser had to re-equip them, the winner had to reward them. As the defeated could not fight unless they were put on horseback again, so the victors would not fight without new rewards. As a result, one prince got little satisfaction from victory, and the other scarcely felt defeat, because the conquered had time to reorganize, and the conqueror did not have time to follow up his victory.

CHAPTER 2

[The military habits of the time permit Piccinino to recover quickly; the Duke negotiates for peace. 1440]

This irrational and perverted method of carrying on war enabled Niccolò Piccino to get on horseback again before the news of his overthrow was spread throughout Italy; and after his defeat he carried on more dangerous war against his enemy than he had done before. This was the reason why, after his rout at Tenno, he could take Verona; this was the reason why, having lost his soldiers at Verona, he could come into Tuscany with a great army; this was the reason why, after being routed at Anghiari, before he entered the Romagna he was more powerful in the field than before, and could fill the Duke of Milan with hope of defending Lombardy, which because of his absence seemed to be almost lost.

Indeed while Niccolò was filling Tuscany with confusion, the Duke was brought to such a situation that he feared for his state. And judging that his downfall might occur before Niccolò Piccino, whom he had recalled, came to rescue him, in order to check the Count's aggression and to delay with ingenuity a fortune which he could not resist with force, he turned to the remedies which in like situations had many times been of service to him. He sent to the Count at Peschiera, Niccolò d'Este ruler of Ferrara. This man for his part encouraged the Count to peace, and showed him that that war was not to his advantage, because if the Duke grew so weak that he could not keep up his reputation, the Count himself would be the first to suffer, because the Venetians and the Florentines would no longer value him. In guarantee that the Duke wished peace, Niccolò offered Count Francesco the accomplishment of the marriage alliance; the Duke would send his daughter to Ferrara, with the promise that when peace was made he would give her into the Count's hands. The Count answered that if the Duke truly wanted peace, he could easily get it, as something the Florentines and the Venetians longed for. True it was that he would be believed with difficulty, since it was known that he had never made peace except through necessity. Whenever that disappears, his wish for war always comes back. In the marriage alliance the Count could put no faith, because he had so often been fooled. Nevertheless, if peace should be made, he would do about the marriage alliance what his friends advised.

CHAPTER 3

[Thought of peace abandoned; Piccinino makes a winter campaign in Lombardy. 1441]

The Venetians, who even in unreasonable matters were suspicious of their soldiers, as a result of these dealings formed, with reason, a very strong suspicion. In order to counteract this, the Count pursued the war vigorously. Nevertheless, the zeal of both—his because of ambition and that of the Venetians because of their suspicion—was to such an extent cooled that in the rest of the summer they carried on few enterprises. So when Niccolò Piccino returned to Lombardy and the winter had already begun, all the armies went into quarters, the Count in Verona, in Cremona the Duke, the Florentine soldiers in Tuscany, and those of the Pope in Romagna.

The latter, after the victory at Anghiari, assailed Forlì and Bologna in order to get them out of the hands of Francesco Piccinino, who in the name of his father was ruling them; but they did not succeed, because Francesco defended the cities vigorously. Nevertheless, this coming of theirs caused the people of Ravenna so much fear of returning under the rule of the Church that, in agreement with Ostasio di Polenta their lord, they put themselves in the power of the Venetians; the latter, in reward for the city they had received, in order that Ostasio at no time would be able to take from them by force what by imprudence he had given them, sent him and one of his sons to die in Candia. Since for these enterprises, in spite of the victory of Anghiari, the Pope lacked money, he sold the town of Bor-go San Sepolcro, for twenty-five thousand ducats, to the Florentines.

While affairs were in this condition, and each one thought the winter would secure him against war, no one any longer considered peace, especially the Duke, who was reassured by Niccolò Piccino and by the season. Therefore he broke off with the Count all discus-sion of peace, and with great vigor remounted Niccolò and made every other preparation that a future war demanded. Getting a report of this, the Count went to Venice, in order to consult with the Senate on their policy for the coming year.

Niccolò, on the other hand, being in good order and seeing his enemy disorganized, did not wait for spring to come, but in the coldest winter weather crossed the Adda, entered the territory of Brescia and, except for Asola and Orzi, conquered all that country, where he plundered and took prisoner more than two thousand of Sforza's cavalry, who were not expecting his attack. But what more disturbed the Count, and more frightened the Venetians, was that Ciarpellone, one of the Count's chief officers, revolted from him. The Count, getting news of this, left Venice at once, and when he came to Brescia, he found that Niccolò, without doing more damage, had returned to his quarters. Hence the Count decided, since the war had died down, not to stir it up again. Yet he determined since time and the enemy gave him a chance to reorganize, to use it so that in the spring he could revenge his old injuries. He had the Vene-tians, then, recall the soldiers who were in Florentine service in Tuscany, and in the place of Gattamelata, who was dead, he asked that Micheletto Attendulo be general.

CHAPTER 4

[Piccinino gets Count Francesco into a desperate situation, but angers the Duke by his demands; peace between the League and the Duke. 1441]

When spring came, Niccolò Piccino was the first to take the field; he besieged Cignano, a town twelve miles distant from Brescia. To her relief came the Count. Both generals carried the war on in their customary fashion. The Count, fearing for Bergamo, went to besiege Martinengo, a town so situated that when he had captured it he could easily relieve Bergamo, which Niccolò had seriously dis-tressed. And because the latter had foreseen that he could not be impeded by the enemy except by way of Martinengo, he had fur-nished that town with every defense, forcing the Count to carry on the siege with all his forces. Then Niccolò with his whole army put himself in a place where he blocked the supplies of the Count and was so fortified with breastworks and small forts that the Count could not attack, except with obvious danger to himself. The matter was brought to such a state that the besieger was in greater danger than the people in Martinengo who were besieged. So the Count, through lack of food, could no longer carry on the siege nor, by reason of the danger, could he get away; hence it seemed an obvious victory for the Duke, and a distinct reverse for the Venetians and the Count.

But Fortune, who has no lack of ways for aiding her friends and thwarting her enemies, caused Niccolò Piccino, in his hope of vic-tory, to become so ambitious and haughty that, having no considera-tion for the Duke or for himself, he sent to the Duke saying that, having served under his banner for a long time and not yet having gained so much land that he could be buried in it, he wished to know from him with what rewards he was going to be rewarded for his labors; it was in his power to make the Duke lord of Lombardy and to put all his enemies in his power. And since he believed that from a sure victory there must come a sure reward, he asked the Duke to give him the city of Piacenza, in order that, tired by such long military service, he could sometimes rest. Nor was he ashamed in the end to menace the Duke with abandonment of the campaign if to this demand he did not yield.

This insulting and haughty way of asking so offended the Duke and made him so angry that he determined to lose the campaign rather than yield. So that man whom so many dangers and so many threats by his enemies had not caused to bend, the haughty ways of his friends did bend. He decided to make peace with the Count, to whom he sent Antonio Guidobono of Tortona, and through him offered his daughter and conditions of peace, which the Count and all his allies eagerly accepted. Then when the agreements between them had been secretly made, the Duke sent orders to Niccolò to make a truce for a year with the Count, pretending that he was so distressed by the expense that he could not give up a sure peace for a doubtful victory. Niccolò was filled with amazement at such a decision, since he could not understand what reason could move the Duke to abandon so glorious a victory, and could not believe that in order not to reward his friends he would save his enemies. Therefore as well as he could he opposed that decision, so that in order to quiet him the Duke was forced to threaten, if he did not consent, to give him to his soldiers and to his enemies as prey. Niccolò then obeyed him, with the spirit of a man forced to abandon his friends and his native land, lamenting his evil fate, since now Fortune, now the Duke deprived him of triumph over his enemies.

When the truce had been made, the marriage of Madonna Bianca and the Count was celebrated, and for her dowry the Duke assigned the city of Cremona. When this had been done, the peace was ratified, in November 1441. For the Venetians the agreement was made by Francesco Barbarigo and Paulo Tron, and for the Florentines by Messer Agnolo Acciaiuoli. The Venetians gained Peschiera, Asola and Lonato, towns of the Marquis of Mantua.

CHAPTER 5

[Wars in Southern Italy between René and Alfonso; their effect in the North. 1441–1443]

When the war ended in Lombardy, the armies in the Kingdom were still on foot; since they would not suspend hostilities, they became the cause for further fighting in Lombardy. King René, during the war in Lombardy, had been deprived by Alfonso of Aragon of the entire Kingdom except Naples. So Alfonso, while besieging Naples, in the belief that he had victory in his hand, determined to deprive Count Francesco of Benevento and his other states in that region. Alfonso judged he could carry his plan through without danger because the wars in Lombardy were occupying the Count. Success in this undertaking came easily to Alfonso and without trouble he took possession of all those cities. But when news came of the peace in Lombardy, Alfonso feared that the Count for the sake of his towns would come to aid René, and for the same reason René was hoping for him. Indeed René sent to urge the Count, begging that he would come to rescue a friend and get revenge on an enemy. On the other hand Alfonso begged Filippo that in friendship for him he would cause the Count so many troubles that, occupied in bigger matters, he perforce would let Alfonso alone. Filippo granted Alfonso's request, without expecting to interrupt the peace he had recently secured with such great disadvantage.

Hence he suggested to Pope Eugenius that then was the time to regain those cities of the Church that the Count was holding; and to do this he offered him Niccolò Piccino, with pay while the war lasted; the latter, since peace had been made, was quartered with his soldiers in Romagna. Eagerly Eugenius accepted this advice, by reason of his hatred for the Count and his wish to get again what was his. Though once before with this same hope Niccolò had deceived him, the Pope now believed, since the Duke was taking part in the affair, that he did not need to fear deceit; so, uniting his soldiers with those of Niccolò, he attacked the Marches. The Count, astonished by so unexpected an attack, gathered his soldiers and went against the enemy.

Meanwhile King Alfonso took Naples; then all the Kingdom except Castelnuovo came into his power. As a result, René departed, leaving in Castelnuovo a strong garrison. Coming to Florence, he was most honorably received. Pausing there a few days and deciding that he was not able to carry on further war, he went off to Marseilles. Alfonso, meanwhile, had taken Castelnuovo. On the other hand, the Count found himself inferior in the Marches to the Pope and to Niccolò. Hence he applied to the Venetians and the Florentines for aid with men and money, explaining that if at that time they did not take measures for restraining the Pope and the King, while he himself was still strong, in a little while they would have to think of their own safety, because the Pope and the King would unite with Filippo, and among themselves they would divide Italy.

Thereupon the Florentines and the Venetians were for a time uncertain, not having determined whether it was wise to embroil themselves with the Pope and the King, and being occupied with Bolognese affairs. For Annibale Bentivoglio had driven Francesco Piccinino from that city, and in order to be able to defend himself from the Duke, who was aiding Francesco, he had asked help from the Venetians and the Florentines, and they had not denied it to him; hence, being employed in these affairs, they had not come to a decision on aiding the Count. But after Annibale had defeated Francesco Piccinino, and those matters seemed settled, the Floren-tines resolved to support the Count. But before doing so, to make sure of the Duke, they renewed their league with him. The Duke did not refuse, though he had agreed that war should be made on the Count while King René was under arms, but when he saw that the King had been crushed and entirely deprived of the Kingdom, he did not wish the Count to be stripped of his territories; hence the Duke not merely agreed to aid him, but also wrote to Alfonso asking him to return to the Kingdom and make no more war against the Count. Though Alfonso did this most unwillingly, neverthe-less, because of the gratitude he owed the Duke, he determined to oblige him, and retired with his soldiers to the other side of the Tronto.

CHAPTER 6

[*The repute of Neri Capponi; his friend Baldaccio. 1441–1444*]

While in Romagna things were going on in this way, the Floren-tines were not quiet inside the city. At that time in Florence, one of the citizens of high reputation in the government was Neri di Gino Capponi. Cosimo de'Medici was more afraid of his reputation than of any other man's, because to great influence in the city Neri added favor with the soldiers; having been many times head of the Florentine armies, he had gained the men's support through his ability and his merits. Besides this, the memory of the victories attributed to him and to Gino his father (for the latter had captured Pisa, and Neri himself had defeated Niccolò Piccino at Anghiari) made him loved by many and feared by those who wished to have no associates in the government.

Among the many officers of the Florentine army was Baldaccio di Anghiari, a man very excellent in war; indeed in those times nobody in Italy was superior to him in vigor of body and of mind. Among the infantry, because he had always been their leader, he had such a reputation that everyone thought that in any undertaking and on any wish of his the soldiers would unite with him. Now Baldaccio was very friendly with Neri, who loved him for his good qualities, of which he had always been a witness. This friendship caused the other citizens the utmost apprehension. And judging that to let him go would be dangerous and to retain him very dangerous, they determined to destroy him. To their purpose Fortune was in this way favorable: just then the Gonfalonier of Justice was Messer Bartolommeo Orlandini, who, as we said above, being sent to guard Marradi when Niccolò Piccino came into Tuscany, like a coward had run away and deserted that pass which by its very nature almost defended itself. Such great cowardice disgusted Baldaccio, and with damaging words and with letters he made known the man's lack of courage. This caused Messer Bartolommeo shame and great indignation, and he was exceedingly eager to get revenge, thinking that by the death of his accuser the infamy of his transgressions could be canceled.

CHAPTER 7
[*The murder of Baldaccio; a new* balía. *1444*]

Messer Bartolommeo's eagerness for revenge was known to all the citizens, so without much effort they convinced him that he ought to get rid of Baldaccio, at one stroke revenging his own injuries and freeing the city from a man whom they must either cherish with danger or dismiss with harm. So when Bartolommeo had determined to kill him, he concealed in his chamber many well-armed young men. When Baldaccio came to the Public Square, where he came every day to deal with the magistrates about his military duties, the Gonfalonier sent for him. Without any suspicion he obeyed. The Gonfalonier came to meet him and went up and down with him two or three times along the passage by the chambers of the Signors, talking with him about his command. Then, when it seemed to the Gonfalonier the right time, since he had come close to the chamber where the armed men were hidden, he gave them a signal. They leaped out and, finding Baldaccio alone and unarmed, they killed him; and as soon as he was dead, they threw him out of the window of the Palace that looks toward the Customs House, and carrying him to the Square from there and cutting off his head, all that day they made him a spectacle for all the people. This man's one son, whom a few years earlier Annalena his wife had borne, did not live long. And when Annalena was deprived of her son and her husband, she was not willing after that to ally herself with any other man, and making her house into a convent, she shut herself up with many noble women who joined her, and there in holiness she lived and died. Her memory, because of the convent founded and named by her, as it lives at present, so it will live always. This happening lowered to some extent the power of Neri and took from him reputation and friends.

Yet it was not enough for the citizens in the government. Ten years had already passed since the origin of their government, the power of the *balìa* was ended, and many persons were showing more courage in their speech and their actions than was wanted. Hence the leaders judged that if they did not wish to lose control, they would have to take the government into their own hands again, once more giving authority to their friends and crushing their ene⁄ mies. And so in 1444, by means of the councils, they set up a new *balìa*. This reorganized the offices; it gave to a few men power to choose the Signoria; it renewed the Chancellery of the Reformations, depriving Ser Filippo Peruzzi of it, and putting in charge one who would conduct himself according to the will of the powerful; it lengthened the period of banishment for those who were banished; it imprisoned Giovanni di Simone Vespucci; it deprived of their offices the couplers of the hostile party, and with them the sons of Piero Baroncelli, all the Serragli, Bartolommeo Fortini, Messer Francesco Castellani, and many others. And in these ways they restored their own authority and influence and deprived enemies and suspects of enthusiasm.

CHAPTER 8

[Niccolò Piccino deceived by Duke Filippo; his death. 1445]

When they had thus settled the government and got it under their control again, they turned to things outside. Niccolò Piccino, as we said above, had been deserted by King Alfonso, and the Count, through the help he had from the Florentines, had become powerful. Attacking Niccolò near Fermo he so defeated him that Niccolò, deprived of almost all his men, took refuge with a few in Montecchio. There he fortified and defended himself so well that in a short time all his men returned to him, in such great numbers that he could easily defend himself from the Count, especially since winter had already come, obliging both generals to send their men to quarters. Niccolò worked all winter at increasing his army, and was helped by the Pope and by King Alfonso. When the spring came, then, both generals went into the field, where Niccolò was so superior that the Count was brought to the utmost need; he would have been beaten if the Duke had not destroyed Niccolò's plans. For Filippo sent asking Niccolò to come at once because he wanted to speak to him with his own mouth on very important matters. So Niccolò, eager to hear them, gave up for an uncertain good a certain victory. Leaving his son Francesco as head of the army, he went to Milan. When the Count learned this, he did not lose the chance for fighting while Niccolò was gone; in a battle near the town of Monte Loro, he defeated Niccolò's soldiers and captured Francesco. When Niccolò, arriving in Milan, saw that Filippo had tricked him and learned of his son's defeat and capture he died of grief in the year 1445, at the age of sixty-four years, having been an able rather than a fortunate general. He was outlived by his sons Francesco and Jacopo, who had less ability and worse fortune than their father, so that the arms of the party of Braccio almost disappeared and those of the Sforza party, always aided by Fortune, became more glorious.

The Pope, seeing Niccolò's army defeated and its leader dead, and not putting much confidence in the aid of Aragon, sought peace with the Count, and through the Florentines he obtained it. Thereby the Pope, among the cities of the Marches, got back Osimo, Fabriano and Ricanati; all the rest were left under the Count's rule.

CHAPTER 9
[Civil strife in Bologna. 1445]

With the making of peace in the Marches, all Italy would have been peaceful if she had not been disturbed by the Bolognese. There were in Bologna two very powerful families, the Canneschi and the Bentivogli; Annibale was head of the second, Battista of the first.

So that they could better trust each other, they had made marriage alliances; but among men who aspire to the same greatness, it is easy to make marriages, but not friendship. Bologna was in league with the Florentines and the Venetians; this alliance had been made through Annibale Bentivoglio, after Francesco Piccinino had been driven out. Battista, knowing how much the Duke wished to have that city on his side, discussed with him the killing of Annibale and the bringing of that city under his banners. When they had agreed on the method, on the twenty-fourth of June, 1445, Battista and his friends attacked Annibale and killed him; then, shouting the name of the Duke, they rode through the city. The Venetian and Florentine commissioners were still in Bologna. When the rioting began, they retired to their houses; then seeing that the people did not favor the assassins but that on the contrary, assembling armed in great numbers in the Square, they were lamenting the death of Annibale, the commissioners plucked up courage and, with such men as they had, joined the people. Organizing themselves, they attacked the forces of the Canneschi and in a short time overcame them; they killed some of them and drove some out of the city. Since Battista was too late to escape and his enemies too late to kill him, he hid in his own house in a cellar made for storing grain. After his enemies had hunted for him all day, since they knew that he had not gone out of the city, they put such terror into his servants that one of his boys through fear told where he was. Pulled from that place, still clad in armor, he was first killed, then dragged through the city and burned. So the Duke's influence was enough to bring Battista to make that attempt, and his power was too late to rescue him.

CHAPTER 10

[The Bolognese find in Florence an illegitimate son of the Bentivoglio family. 1445]

When these feuds were quieted, then, by Battista's death and the flight of the Canneschi, the Bolognese still remained in the greatest confusion; there was nobody of the Bentivoglio family fit to rule, for Annibale had left only one son, named Giovanni, six years old. Hence those supporting the Bentivogli feared that some division among them would enable the Canneschi to return, with the ruin of their city and of their party.

And while they were in this uncertainty of mind, Francesco, who had been Count of Poppi, being in Bologna, informed the chief men of the city that if they wished to be ruled by a descendant from Annibale's family, he could show them one. And he told them that about twenty years ago, when Ercole, Annibale's cousin, was at Poppi, he knew that he had relations with a girl of that town who bore a son named Santi, whom Ercole many times asserted to be his; and it did not seem that he could deny it, because everybody who knew Ercole and knew the young fellow saw between them very close resemblance. The citizens believed his story, so without delay they sent citizens to Florence to identify the young man, and to deal with Cosimo and Neri in such a way that he would be granted to them. The man supposed to be Santi's father was dead, so that the young man was under the charge of his uncle, named Antonio da Cascese. Antonio was rich and without children and a friend of Neri's. Hence, when he understood the thing, Neri judged that it was neither to be despised nor to be rashly accepted; he advised that Santi, in the presence of Cosimo, should speak with those who had been sent from Bologna. They met together, and the Bolognese not merely honored but almost worshiped Santi—so strong in their minds was love for their parties. Nothing was settled at that time, except that Cosimo called Santi aside and said to him: "No one, in this affair, can advise you better than yourself; you must make the decision to which your mind inclines you. If you are going to be Ercole Bentivoglio's son, you will turn your attention to affairs worthy of that house and of your father; but if you are going to be Agnolo da Cascese's son, you will remain in Florence to spend your life humbly in wool-working." These words stirred the youth; and whereas at first he had almost refused to make such a decision, he said he would rest entirely on what Cosimo and Neri decided about it. So, having come to an agreement with the envoys from Bologna, he was supplied with clothing, horses and servants, and soon after, accompanied by many citizens, he was taken to Bologna and set up as guardian of Annibale's son and of the city. In that position he conducted himself with such great prudence that, whereas his ancestors had all been killed by their enemies, he lived peacefully and died most honorably.

CHAPTER 11

[*Further wars in Lombardy. 1446*]

After the death of Niccolò Piccino and the peace that resulted in the Marches, Duke Filippo, wishing a general to command his armies, carried on secret negotiations with Ciarpellone, one of Count Francesco's chief officers; when the contract had been made, Ciarpellone asked permission from the Count to go to Milan, to enter upon the possession of some towns that in the past wars Filippo had given to him. The Count, fearing what was true, to keep the Duke from employing him against the Count's own plans, first had him put in prison and a little later killed, claiming that he had found him treacherous. Because of this, Duke Filippo was exceedingly vexed and angry. These events delighted the Florentines and the Venetians, who would have been much afraid if the weapons of the Count and the power of the Duke had become allies. This anger, moreover, was the cause for stirring up a new war in the Marches.

At this time the lord of Rimini was Sigismondo Malatesta, who, being the Count's son-in-law, hoped for the lordship of Pesaro; but the Count, when he had taken her, gave her to Alessandro his brother; at this Sigismondo was very angry. It added to his anger that Federigo di Montefeltro, his enemy, with the aid of the Count had conquered the lordship of Urbino. This made Sigismondo take the side of the Duke and urge the Pope and the King to make war on the Count. The latter, to make Sigismondo realize the first fruits of the war he was planning, determined to get in ahead, and quickly attacked him. As a result, at once strife again filled the Romagna and the Marches, because Filippo, the King and the Pope sent much aid to Sigismondo, and the Florentines and the Venetians, with money, though not with soldiers, gave assistance to the Count.

And it was not enough for Filippo to have war in Romagna, for he planned to take Cremona and Pontremoli away from the Count, but Pontremoli was defended by the Florentines, and Cremona by the Venetians. Hence in Lombardy war was begun again; in this, after some troubles in the territory of Cremona, Francesco Piccinino, the general of the Duke, was defeated at Casale by Micheletto and the soldiers of the Venetians. By means of this victory, the Venetians hoped to take that territory from the Duke; they sent a commissioner of theirs to Cremona and attacked the Ghiaradadda and, except Crema, occupied it all. Then, crossing the Adda, they raided as far as Milan. So the Duke had recourse to Alfonso and begged that he would rescue him, showing him the dangers to the Kingdom if Lombardy were in the power of the Venetians. Alfonso promised to send him reinforcements, though without the Count's permission their march would be difficult.

CHAPTER 12

[Count Francesco, treacherously treated, deserts the Venetians for the Duke. 1446]

Filippo then turned to begging the Count not to desert his father-in-law, already old and blind. The Count felt that the Duke had wronged him by starting war against him. On the other hand, the Count disliked Venetian greatness, his money was already getting short, and the League was furnishing it stingily, because the Florentines had lost that fear of the Duke which made them value the Count, and the Venetians were longing for the Count's ruin, since they judged that he only could take from them the control of Lombardy. Nonetheless, while Filippo was trying to draw him into his employ and was offering him the control of all his soldiers, if only he would abandon the Venetians and restore the Marches to the Pope, the Venetians too sent ambassadors to him, promising him Milan if they should take her, and the permanent command of their soldiers, if only he would continue the war in the Marches and keep Alfonso's reinforcements from coming to Lombardy. The Venetians' promises then, were great, and their deserts very great, since they had started that war to preserve Cremona for the Count. And on the other side, the injuries from the Duke were recent and his promises faithless and of little value.

Yet all the same, the Count was in doubt which side he ought to choose. For on one side, his obligations to the League, the pledge he had given, their recent deserts and their promises of future things moved him; on the other were the prayers of his father-in-law, and above all the poison that he suspected the big promises of the Venetians concealed, since he judged that both as to promises and as to territory, whenever they conquered he would be in their power—yet

into another state's power no prudent prince, except through necessity, delivers himself. The Count's difficulties in deciding were
removed by the Venetians' ambition; hoping to take Cremona
because of some understandings they had in that city, with some
excuse or other they had their soldiers come close to her. But the
affair was discovered by the Count's garrison, so their plan turned
out fruitless. Thus they did not gain Cremona and they lost the
Count, who laying aside all scruples, took the Duke's side.

CHAPTER 13

*[The death of Duke Filippo; Count Francesco becomes Milanese
general. 1447]*

By now Pope Eugenius had died, his successor Nicholas V had
been chosen, and the Count had his entire army at Cotignola ready
to move into Lombardy. There news came to him that Filippo was
dead, in the year 1447, on the last of August. This news filled the
Count with anxiety because he knew that his soldiers were not
ready, since they had not had their full pay; he feared the Venetians,
being under arms and his enemies, since he had just left them and
sided with the Duke; he feared Alfonso, his lifelong enemy; he did
not put any hope in the Pope or in the Florentines—in the Florentines since they were allied with the Venetians, in the Pope since
some of the cities of the Church were in his possession. Still he
determined to show his face to Fortune, and according to her shifts
to make his plans; for often when a man is doing something, plans
reveal themselves to him which, if he stood still, would forever hide
themselves. He found hope in believing that if the Milanese wished
to defend themselves from Venetian greed, they could not turn to
other armies than his. Hence, taking courage, he moved into the
territory of Bologna, and then passing Modena and Reggio, he
halted with his soldiers upon the Enza River and sent to Milan to
offer himself.

Part of the Milanese, after the Duke's death, wanted to live in
freedom, part under a prince; of those who loved princes, one party
wanted the Count, the other King Alfonso. However, since those
who loved liberty were more united, they prevailed over the others,
and according to their wishes organized a republic—which many of

the Duke's cities did not obey, since they judged that, like Milan, they also could enjoy their liberty; those that did not aspire to liberty did not want Milanese rule. Lodi, therefore, and Piacenza gave themselves to the Venetians; Pavia and Parma made themselves free. Aware of all this confusion, the Count went to Cremona, where his agents and those of the Milanese met, with the result that he was to be general of the Milanese with those agreements that he had last made with Duke Filippo. To them were added that Brescia should belong to the Count, and if he gained Verona, she should be his, and Brescia should be given back.

CHAPTER 14

[A council at Ferrara plans a peace; on the death of the Duke, the Venetians reject it. 1447]

Before the Duke died, Pope Nicholas, after he assumed the pontificate, attempted to establish peace among the Italian princes; to this end he arranged, with the Florentine ambassadors who were sent to him on his election, that a diet should be held at Ferrara to negotiate either a long truce or a solid peace. So there met in that city the Pope's legate and various envoys, Venetian, Ducal and Florentine; King Alfonso's envoys did not meet with them. He was at Tivoli with plenty of soldiers on foot and on horseback, and from there he aided the Duke; and it was believed that, since the King and the Duke had brought the Count over to their side, they were intending to attack openly the Florentines and the Venetians, and that only as long as the Count's soldiers delayed in getting to Lombardy would they carry on the negotiations for peace at Ferrara; to that city the King sent no envoy, declaring that he would ratify everything the Duke agreed to. The peace was discussed for many days, and after many debates, they decided either for a permanent peace or a truce for five years, whichever of these two might please the Duke; but when the Ducal envoys went to Milan to learn his pleasure, they found him dead.

Notwithstanding his death, the Milanese wished to carry out the agreement, but the Venetians did not. They had formed the highest expectations of conquering Milan, especially since Lodi and Piacenza, immediately after the Duke's death, had surrendered to them;

so they hoped through either force or agreement in a short time to strip Milan of all her territory; then they would so overpower her that she would surrender before anybody could support her. They were the more persuaded of this when they saw that the Florentines had involved themselves in war with King Alfonso.

CHAPTER 15
[*King Alfonso invades Tuscany. 1447–1448*]

That King was at Tivoli and, planning to carry on his campaign in Tuscany as he had decided with Filippo, he thought that the war already begun in Lombardy gave him time and opportunity. Hence, he wished to have a foot in the Florentine state before he made any open movement; therefore he formed a conspiracy in the castle of Cennina in the upper Valdarno, and took it. The Florentines, astonished by this unexpected attack, and seeing that the King had already begun to damage them, hired soldiers, chose the Ten and according to their custom got ready for war. The King had already moved his army close to the Sienese state, and was making every effort to bring that city to his wishes. Nevertheless, the citizens stood firm in their friendship for the Florentines, and did not receive the King into Siena or into any of their cities. They did provide him with supplies, for which they were excused by their weakness and the strength of the enemy. The King decided not to enter by the route of Valdarno, as he had first planned, both because he had lost Cennina again and because already the Florentines were to some extent provided with soldiers; so he turned toward Volterra, and in the Volterrano took many towns. From there he went into the territory of Pisa, and with the aid of Arrigo and Fazio, counts of the Gherardesca family, he captured some towns and by means of them attacked Campiglia, which he could not take because the Floren-tines and the winter defended her. So the King left in the captured towns garrisons to defend them and plunder the country, and with the rest of his army retired to quarters in Sienese territory.

The Florentines, meanwhile, aided by the season, with all dili-gence provided themselves with soldiers; their generals were Federigo the lord of Urbino and Gismondo Malatesta of Rimini; and though there was disagreement between these two, nonetheless through the

prudence of Neri di Gino and of Bernardetto de'Medici, the com
missioners, they were kept united in such a way that they went into
the field while it was still midwinter and regained the towns lost in
the territory of Pisa, and Pomarance in the territory of Volterra. The
soldiers of the King, who before were plundering the Maremma,
were so checked that scarcely were they able to hold the towns given
them to guard.

When spring came, the commissioners halted with all their sol
diers at Spedaletto, to the number of five thousand cavalry and two
thousand infantry. The King came with his, to the number of
fifteen thousand, within three miles of Campiglia. But when they
thought he would turn aside to besiege that town, he threw himself
on Piombino, hoping to take her easily because that town was badly
prepared. He judged her capture very useful for himself and in
jurious for the Florentines; with that place as a base, he could wear
out the Florentines with a long war, since he could supply himself by
sea and could upset the whole territory of Pisa. The Florentines were
therefore disturbed by this attack. Consulting on what they could
do, they thought that if they could remain with their army in the
thickets of Campiglia, the King would be forced to leave, either
defeated or disgraced. Hence they armed four galleasses that they
had at Livorno, and with them put three hundred infantry in Piom
bino. They stationed their army at Caldana, a place hard to attack,
because to camp in the thickets on the plain they thought dangerous.

CHAPTER 16
[King Alfonso retires. 1448]

The Florentine army was getting its food from the towns in the
neighborhood, which, being few and thinly populated, were pro
viding too little. Hence the army was suffering, and was especially
in need of wine; since it could not be bought there and was not to be
had from elsewhere, there was not enough for everybody. But the
King, though tightly hemmed in by the Florentine soldiers, had
plenty of everything except hay, because he was abundantly supplied
by water. Hence the Florentines, to find out whether their soldiers
also could be supplied by sea, loaded their four galleasses with food;
but when they were sent, seven of the King's galleys attacked them,

and two galleasses were taken and two driven off. This loss made the Florentine soldiers abandon hope of fresh supplies. Chiefly on account of the wine shortage, two hundred or more of the foragers fled to the King's army. The other men complained, declaring it was not prudent to stay in very hot places where there was no wine and the water was bad. Hence the commissioners decided to leave that place, and turned to the recapture of some towns that still remained in the King's hands. He, on the other hand, though he was not suffering for supplies and was superior in numbers, saw that he was failing because his army was full of sickness such as at that season marshy seashores cause; it was so severe that many died and almost all his men were sick. Therefore discussions were begun about a treaty of peace, for which the King asked fifty thousand florins and that Piombino should be abandoned to him.

When this was debated at Florence, many, eager for peace, would have accepted it, declaring that they did not know how they could hope to win a war for the support of which such large expenditures were necessary. But Neri Capponi, going to Florence, in such a way with his arguments advised against it that all the citizens with one accord decided not to accept it; and they accepted as their charge the lord of Piombino, and promised to support him in time both of peace and of war, if only he would not lose heart and would continue to defend himself as he had until then. When the King learned of this decision and saw that because of his sick army he could not gain the city, almost as though defeated, he raised the siege; there he left more than two thousand men dead; and with the rest of his sick army he withdrew into the Sienese country and thence into the Kingdom, full of anger against the Florentines, threatening them with war at a later time.

CHAPTER 17

[Count Francesco becomes Lord of Pavia; he captures Piacenza. 1447]

While in Tuscany things were going on in this way, Count Francesco, in Lombardy, having become general of the Milanese, before everything else made a friend of Francesco Piccinino, who was acting as commander for the Milanese, so that he would aid him in his undertakings or be more hesitant in harming him. When the Count led out his army, the people of Pavia judged that they were not able to protect themselves from his forces, and on the other hand, not wishing to be subject to Milan, they offered him their city with the condition that he would not put them under Milanese rule. The Count was very eager to get hold of Pavia, since he thought her possession a splendid beginning for the disguise of his plans, and he was not restrained by the fear or the shame of breaking his word, because great men call it shame to lose, not to gain by trickery. But he feared, if he took her, to make the Milanese so angry that they would give themselves up to the Venetians. Yet if he did not take her, he was afraid of the Duke of Savoy, to whom many citizens wished to give themselves; and in one case and in the other it seemed to him that he was deprived of the rule of Lombardy. Nevertheless, deciding that there was less danger in taking that city than in letting her be taken by someone else, he determined to accept her, convincing himself that he could quiet the Milanese. To them he explained the dangers into which he would get if he did not accept Pavia, because those citizens would give themselves either to the Venetians or to the Duke. In either event Milan would be lost; hence the Milanese ought to be more pleased to have him—a friend of theirs—as a neighbor than to have a formidable power, such as the Duke of Savoy and the Venetians, and an enemy. The Milanese were much troubled by the matter, since they realized that they had found out the Count's ambition and the end toward which he was moving; but they judged that they could not reveal themselves, because they did not see where, on separating from the Count, they could turn except to the Venetians, whose pride and heavy requirements they feared. Therefore they decided not to break off from the Count but for the time to remedy with his aid the evils that hung over them, hoping that when freed from them, they could also free themselves from him; for they were being attacked not merely by the Venetians, but also by the Genoese and the Duke of Savoy, in the name of Charles of Orleans, son of a sister of Filippo. This attack the Count with slight effort repelled. Of their enemies, then, only the Venetians were left, who with a powerful army were trying to take the Milanese state, and held Lodi and Piacenza. To Piacenza the Count laid siege, and after long effort took and plundered her. Then, since winter had come, he put his soldiers into quarters and went off to Cremona, where all that winter he rested with his wife.

CHAPTER 18

[*The Venetians defeated at Caravaggio; the Count defends his reputa-tion. 1448*]

When spring came, both the Venetian and Milanese armies went into the field. The hope of the Milanese was to capture Lodi and then to make peace with the Venetians, because the expenses of the war distressed them, and they suspected the fidelity of their general. Hence they were eager for peace, in order to rest and to secure them-selves against the Count. They decided, however, that their army should attempt to capture Caravaggio, hoping that Lodi would surrender when Caravaggio had been taken from the hands of the Venetians. The Count obeyed the Milanese, though his idea would have been to cross the Adda and attack the territory of Brescia. Having laid seige to Caravaggio, then, he fortified himself with ditches and other works, so that if the Venetians tried to make him abandon the siege, they would have to attack at a disadvantage. The Venetians on the other hand came with their army, under Micheletto their general, as close as two bowshots to the Count's camp, where for many days they remained and fought numerous skirmishes. Nevertheless, the Count continued to hem in the town, and had brought her to such a condition that she was on the point of surren-der. This distressed the Venetians, since they knew that through her loss they lost their campaign. Meanwhile there was much debate among their leaders over means for relieving the town; they saw no other way than to attack the enemy in his fortifications, though in this method their disadvantage was great. But they considered the loss of the town so important that the Venetian Senate, naturally timid and averse to any doubtful and dangerous measure, preferred, in order not to lose the town, rather to put their whole enterprise in danger than through the loss of the town to lose their campaign. So they made a decision that in any possible way they would attack the Count. Getting under arms at an early hour one morning, they attacked him on his least protected side; by the first assault, as happens in unexpected attacks, Sforza's whole army was shaken. But quick-ly the Count in such a way repaired all disorder that his enemy, after making many efforts to pass over the embankments, were not merely thrown back but in such a way put to flight and routed that of the entire army, in which there were more than twelve thousand cavalry, not a thousand saved themselves, and all their property and baggage were captured. Never before that day had the Venetians received a greater and more terrifying overthrow.

Among the spoil and the prisoners was . . . ,[1] a Venetian super-visor who, before the battle and in managing the war, had spoken insultingly of the Count, calling him a bastard and peasant. When after the defeat this supervisor was a prisoner and remembered his transgressions, he feared he would be treated as he deserved. He therefore came before the Count greatly shrinking and terrified, according to the nature of men proud and base, which is to be haughty in prosperity but in adversity abject and meek; throwing himself on his knees, with tears he begged pardon for his insulting words. The Count raised him up and, taking him by the arm, cheered him and encouraged him to hope for the best, adding that he was astonished that a man who wished to be thought prudent and grave, as the supervisor did, should have fallen into the serious error of speaking basely about those who did not deserve it. As to the things he had imputed to him, he did not know what Sforza his father had done with Madam Lucia his mother; he was not there and could not regulate their manner of conjunction, so that for what they had done he believed he should get neither blame nor praise. But he well knew that in what he had done himself, he had so acted that nobody could censure him—something of which the supervisor and his Senate could give recent and true testimony. He exhorted him to be in the future more decent in his speech about others, and more cautious in his undertakings.

1. *The name was left blank by Machiavelli. Two supervisors were captured, Gherardo Dandolo and Almorò Donato.*

CHAPTER 19

[Sforza makes with the Venetians a peace to his own advantage, not to that of the Milanese. 1448]

After this victory the Count led his conquering army into the territory of Brescia and seized all that region. Then he fixed his camp two miles from Brescia. The Venetians, on the other hand, having suffered this defeat and fearing, as happened, that Brescia would be the first town attacked, provided her with a garrison as well and as quickly as they could. Then with all diligence they gathered forces and brought together what remnants of their army they could, and from the Florentines, by virtue of their alliance, asked for troops. The Florentines, then free from the war with King Alfonso, sent to assist them a thousand infantry and two thousand cavalry. The Venetians, with these forces, had time for thinking about peace treaties. It was at one time a matter almost as though decreed by fate that the Venetian republic should lose in war and win in negotiations, for the things they lost in war, peace then many times doubly gave back to them.

The Venetians knew that the Milanese had fears of the Count, and that the Count hoped to be not general but lord of the Milanese; hence the Venetians could choose to make peace with either one of the two, since the Count wished peace through ambition, and the Milanese through fear. They chose to make peace with the Count and to offer him help for the conquest of Milan. They convinced themselves that when the Milanese saw that they were deceived by the Count, they would consent, driven on by their anger, to subject themselves to almost anybody rather than to him, and that having been brought into such a condition that they could not of themselves make any defense nor any longer trust the Count, they would be forced—since they would have no place where they could throw themselves—to drop into the Venetians' lap. After making this plan, the Venetians probed the Count's purpose. They found him much inclined to peace, since he wanted the victory he had won at Cara-vaggio to be his and not Milan's. They made therefore an agreement by which the Venetians were bound to pay the Count, as long as he was making an effort to take Milan, thirteen thousand florins every month and, in addition, during the war to support him with four thousand cavalry and two thousand infantry. The Count for his part bound himself to restore to the Venetians the cities, prisoners and whatever else he had seized in that war, and to be satisfied with only the cities that Duke Filippo possessed at his death.

CHAPTER 20

[The protest of the Milanese against the Count's treachery. 1448]

The compact, when known in Milan, saddened that city much more than the victory of Caravaggio had gladdened it. The leaders lamented, the people complained, the women and children wept and all united in calling the Count a betrayer and faithless. And though they did not believe that with prayers or with promises they could recall him from his ungrateful course, they sent ambassadors to him, to see with what face and with what words he would accompany this wickedness of his. Having come, then, before the Count, one of them spoke to this effect:

"It is usual for those who wish to ask something from somebody else to assail him with prayers, gifts or threats, so that, moved either by compassion or by profit or by fear, all that they wish he may condescend to do. But in dealing with men who are cruel and avaricious, and according to their own opinion powerful, since these three methods have no place, uselessly they labor who believe that with prayers they can humble them or with gifts win them or with threats frighten them. We, then, knowing at present—though too late—your cruelty, ambition and arrogance, come to you, not because we intend to beg for anything nor in the belief that we shall receive it if we ask it of you, but to remind you of the benefits you have received from the Milanese people and to show you with what ingratitude you have rewarded them, so that at least, among so many evils that we feel, we may indulge in the pleasure of rebuking you.

"You must remember very well what your situation was after Duke Filippo's death. You were an enemy to the Pope and the King; you had deserted the Florentines and the Venetians, to whom, both on account of their just and recent anger, and since they had no more need of you, you had become almost an enemy; you were exhausted by your war with the Church; you had few soldiers, were without friends, without money, and bereft of all hope of keeping your territories and your old reputation. Because of these things you would easily have fallen if it had not been for our folly, since we alone received you into our country, impelled by the respect we had for our Duke's happy memory, for since with him you had a marriage alliance and recent amity, we believed that your love would pass over to his heirs, and that if to his favors ours were united, this friendship would be not merely solid but unbreakable; therefore to the old agreements we added Verona or Brescia.

"What more could we have given you or promised you? And you, what could you—I do not say from us but in those times from anybody—I do not say get, but wish? You, then, received from us an unexpected good; as payment, we receive from you an unexpected evil. Nor have you delayed until now to show us your wicked purpose, because no sooner were you leader of our armies than, against all justice, you accepted Pavia—which ought to have warned us what was going to be the end of this friendship of yours. That injury we endured, thinking that such gain would with its greatness satisfy your ambition. Alas; to those who wish the whole, a part cannot give satisfaction! You promised that from then on we should enjoy the gains you made, because you well knew that what you gave us at many times you could in a single moment take away, as it has been after the victory of Caravaggio, which, first prepared for with our blood and our money, was afterward followed by our ruin.

"O unhappy those cities forced to defend their liberty against the ambition of him who wishes to oppress them! But much more unhappy those necessitated to defend themselves with mercenary and faithless weapons such as yours! May at least this example of ours profit posterity! even though that of Thebes and of Philip of Macedon has been of no use to us, for Philip, after a victory against the Thebans' enemies, first became instead of their general their enemy, and then their prince. We cannot, however, be accused of any other fault except trusting much where we should have trusted little; your past life, your enormous aspiration, never content with any rank or position, should have warned us. We should not have rested hope on him who betrayed the lord of Lucca, levied ransom on the Florentines and the Venetians, showed little regard for the Duke, despised a king and above all inflicted on God and his Church so many injuries. We should not have supposed that such great princes would have less influence than the Milanese in the heart of Francesco Sforza, and that he would feel obliged to keep with us the faith he had with the others so many times broken.

"Nonetheless this imprudence of which we accuse ourselves does not excuse your perfidy nor wipe away that disrepute that our just complaints will produce for you throughout the world; nor will they keep the just pricks of your conscience from afflicting you, when those soldiers which we prepared to attack and terrify others come to strike and injure ourselves, for you will judge yourself worthy of the penalty that parricides deserve. If indeed your ambition blinds you, all the world, a witness of your iniquity, will make you open your eyes. God himself will force you to open them, if perjuries, if violated faith, if betrayals offend him and if in the future—as in the past for the sake of some hidden good he has done—he does not decide to befriend the wicked. Do not then think your victory certain, be/cause the just anger of God will impede it. We are determined with death to lose our liberty; if we cannot defend it, we will submit to any other prince rather than to you. If indeed our sins are such that against our every wish we come into your power, you can be assured that the position you gain with deception and infamy will, for you or for your sons, come to an end with scorn and loss."

CHAPTER 21

[The Count justifies himself and attacks Milan; the double treachery of the Venetians. 1448]

The Count felt that by the Milanese he was on every side keenly censured, yet without showing in either his words or his gestures any unusual anger, he replied that he was willing to charge to their enraged spirits the gross insult of their unwise words. He would answer them in detail if he were before a court that could properly judge their differences, because he would appear not as having in/jured the Milanese but as having provided that they could not injure him. They well knew how they had acted after the victory of Caravaggio, because, instead of rewarding him with Verona or Brescia, they sought to make peace with the Venetians, so that his alone might be the blame for hostility, and theirs the fruits of the victory, with the blessing of peace and all the profit that was gained from the war. So they had no right to complain if he had made the agreement which they had first tried to make. Indeed if in making that decision he had somewhat delayed, he would at present have to reproach them for the same ingratitude for which now they were reproaching him. Whether his words were true or not would be revealed, through the outcome of this war, by that God on whom they called as the avenger of their injuries; by means of that outcome, they would see which of them was more His friend, and which had been fighting with greater justice.

When the ambassadors had gone, the Count got ready to attack the Milanese, and they prepared for defense. Francesco and Jacopo Piccinino, because of the ancient hatred cherished by Braccio's fol/

lowers against Sforza's, had been faithful to the Milanese. With their aid, the citizens believed they could protect their liberty until at least they could detach the Venetians from the Count, for they did not believe these allies would be faithful or friendly very long. On the other side the Count, who himself realized this, thought he would act wisely, since he judged an agreement not enough, to keep the Venetians firm with a reward. Therefore, in distributing the campaigns of the war, he agreed that the Venetians should attack Crema, and he with the other soldiers should attack the remainder of the Milanese state. This food placed before the Venetians was the reason why they remained friendly to the Count so long that at last he conquered all the territory of the Milanese and so shut them up in their city that they could not provide themselves with anything neces'sary. Hence, despairing of other help, they sent ambassadors to Venice asking the Venetians to have mercy on their distresses and to decide, as should be the custom of republics, to take the part of Milanese liberty, not that of a tyrant whom, if he succeeded in be'coming ruler of Milan, the Venetians could not at their will restrain. The Venetians should not believe that the Count would be satisfied with the boundaries specified in the treaties; he would expect to restore the ancient boundaries of the Milanese state. The Venetians were not yet in possession of Crema, and since they wished before they showed a different face to occupy her, they replied publicly that they were unable to support the Milanese because of their agreement with the Count. But in private they so dealt with the Milanese ambassadors that those envoys, trusting in this agreement with the Venetians, gave their Signors firm hope of aid.

CHAPTER 22

[The Venetians change sides; the Count outwits both parties. 1449]

Already the Count with his soldiers was so near Milan that he was attacking the suburbs when the Venetians decided, having taken Crema, that they should not put off making an alliance with the Milanese. So they formed an agreement with them, among the first articles promising defense of their liberty to the utmost. When the agreement had been made, the Venetians directed the soldiers whom they had with the Count that, leaving his camps, they should with' draw into Venetian territory. They also informed the Count of the peace they had made with the Milanese, giving him twenty days in which to accept it. The Count was not astonished at the Venetian decision, because for a long time he had been foreseeing it, and every day was fearing it would come about. Nonetheless he could not do anything else, when the thing happened, than lament and feel such vexation as, when he deserted them, the Milanese had felt. He obtained from the ambassadors, who were sent to him from Venice to announce that treaty, two days for his answer; in this time he determined to drag out his dealings with the Venetians and not to abandon his enterprise. Therefore he said publicly that he intended to accept the peace and sent his ambassadors to Venice with full power to ratify it, but he privately instructed them that in no way should they ratify it, but with various devices and objections should put the settlement off. To make the Venetians believe the more that he told the truth, he made a truce with the Milanese for a month, and drew his men away from Milan and scattered them in quarters in places round about that he had captured.

This plan was the cause of his victory and of the ruin of the Milanese, because the Venetians, trusting in the peace, were slower in preparations for the war, and the Milanese, seeing the truce was made, the enemy gone away and the Venetians friendly, fully believed that the Count was going to give up the enterprise. This opinion injured them in two ways: first, they neglected measures for their defense; second, in the country free from the enemy, because it was the time for sowing, they sowed a large amount of grain; hence the Count could more quickly starve them. To the Count, on the other hand, everything was helpful that was injurious to his enemies; and in addition that time gave him an opportunity for resting and getting reinforcements.

CHAPTER 23

[*Debates in Florence over Milan; Cosimo favors the Count. 1449*]

In this war in Lombardy, the Florentines had not declared for either of the parties and had given no aid to the Count, either when he defended the Milanese or later, because the Count, not having need of it, had not with urgency asked them for it. Only after the defeat of Caravaggio, to fulfil the obligations of the League they had sent help to the Venetians. But when Count Francesco was left alone, without anybody to whom he could apply, he was forced urgently to ask aid from the Florentines, both publicly from the government and privately from friends. He applied especially to Cosimo de'Medici, with whom he always kept up a steady friendship and by whom in all his undertakings he had always been faithfully advised and extensively supported. In this great necessity Cosimo did not desert him but as an individual generously supported him and gave him courage to continue his undertaking. Cosimo wished also that Florence should publicly give him aid, but in that he met difficulty.

At this time in Florence, Neri di Gino Capponi was very powerful. He judged it not for the city's advantage that the Count should take Milan; he believed it safer for Italy if he ratified the peace treaty than if he continued the war. First of all, he feared that in anger against the Count, the Milanese would give themselves entirely over to the Venetians—to the ruin of everybody. Second, he thought that if Francesco succeeded in taking Milan, the union of so many soldiers and such a great state would be dangerous, and judged that if he was hard to bear as Count, as Duke he would be wholly unbearable. Hence Neri declared it better, both for the Florentine republic and for Italy, that the Count should continue with only his reputation in arms, and that Lombardy should be divided into two states, which never would be united for an attack on others; neither one alone would have power to do harm. To accomplish this he saw no better way than not to support the Count and to maintain the old league with the Venetians.

These reasons were not accepted by Cosimo's friends, who believed that Neri was urging this policy not from a belief that in it lay the good of the republic, but because he did not wish the Count, Cosimo's friend, to become Duke, believing that thereby Cosimo would be too powerful. But Cosimo nevertheless continued to give reasons why to aid the Count would be very advantageous for the republic and for Italy; in his view it was unwise to believe that the Milanese could keep themselves free; the nature of the body of citizens, their type of government, the old factions in the city were directly opposed to any form of rule by the citizens. Hence either the Count must become their duke or the Venetians must become their masters. In such a choice nobody was so stupid as to be uncertain which was better—to have a powerful friend near one or to have there a very powerful enemy. Cosimo did not believe Florence should fear that the Milanese, in order to carry on war against the Count, would submit to the Venetians; the Count had a party in Milan and the Venetians did not, so whenever they could not defend themselves in freedom, they would always be subject to the Count rather than to the Venetians.

This diversity of opinions kept the Florentines very uncertain; in the end they decided to send ambassadors to the Count to negotiate the terms of the agreement. If they found the Count so strong that they expected him to conquer, they would settle it; if not, they would make difficulties and put it off.

CHAPTER 24

[The Venetians give a little aid to Milan; the Milanese choose Count Francesco as Duke. 1450–1451]

These ambassadors were at Reggio when they learned that the Count had become lord of Milan in the way I shall now relate. The Count, when the period of truce was over, came back to Milan with his soldiers, hoping in a short time to take her in spite of the Venetians, for they could not relieve the city except from the direction of the Adda, a road that he could easily close. He did not fear, since it was winter, that the Venetians would campaign close to him. Before the winter was over, he hoped to gain the victory, especially now that Francesco Piccinino was dead and his brother Jacopo alone was left as head of the Milanese.

The Venetians sent an ambassador to Milan to exhort those citizens to be zealous in defending themselves, promising them great and speedy aid. In the course of the winter, then, there were some slight combats between the Venetians and the Count. When the season was more favorable, the Venetians, under Pandolfo Malatesta, placed their army on the Adda. Yet when they considered whether, to relieve Milan, they ought to attack the Count and try the fortune of battle, Pandolfo their general judged such an attempt unwise since he knew the efficiency of the Count and his army. Moreover, he believed he could, without fighting, be sure of winning, because lack of fodder and grain would drive the Count away. He advised, then, that the Venetian army remain in that encampment in order to give the Milanese hope of relief, so that they would not in despair give themselves up to the Count. This plan the Venetians approved, considering it safe; they also hoped that the Milanese, if kept in straits, would be forced to put themselves under their rule; the Venetians were convinced that the Milanese never would give themselves over to the Count, considering the injuries thay had received from him.

Meanwhile the Milanese were brought almost to the final state of wretchedness: since that city normally had a great many poor, they were dying in the streets of hunger. As a result, there were disturbances and complaints in various parts of the city; the magistrates therefore were in great fear and used every effort to keep people from gathering together. Slow enough are the great masses in turning to evil, but when they do turn to it, any little accident sets them off. Two men, then, of not very high position, talking near the Porta Nuova of the calamities of the city and of their own wretchedness and what means they had for safety, were joined by others until they grew to a fair number. As a result, a rumor spread through Milan that the people of Porta Nuova were opposing the magistrates under arms. As a result, the mass of the people, waiting only to be set going, took arms; and they chose as their leader Gasparre da Vicomercato, and went to the place where the magistrates were assembled. There they made such an attack that they killed all who could not escape; among these they put to death Leonardo Venier the Venetian envoy, as the cause of their hunger and one who rejoiced at their misery. Thus become as it were the rulers of the city, they considered among themselves what had to be done if they were to escape from so many troubles and at some time have repose. Everybody judged, since they could not preserve their liberty, that necessity forced them to take refuge with some prince who would defend them. Some wished King Alfonso, some the Duke of Savoy, some the King of France to be called in to rule them.

Of the Count nobody spoke—so strong as yet was the anger they felt against him. Nonetheless, when the others did not agree, Gasparre da Vicomercato was the first to mention the Count. He showed at length that if they wished to get rid of the war, there was no other way than to ask that man to rule them; the people of Milan needed a sure and immediate peace, not a distant hope of future relief. In his speech he excused the Count's enterprises, accused the Venetians, accused all the other princes of Italy, who had not been willing, one through ambition, another through avarice, that the Milanese should live in freedom. Since then their liberty had to be given away, they ought to give it to one who had wisdom and power enough to defend them, so that at least from servitude might come peace and not greater losses and more dangerous war. Now with extraordinary attention this man was listened to, and everyone, when he had finished his speech, shouted that the Count should be asked to rule them. Gasparre was made envoy to do the asking. On the people's orders, he went to the Count with this news so joyful and satisfying. This the Count received with joy. Entering Milan as prince on the twenty-sixth of February 1450, he was with the greatest and most astonishing gladness received by those who, not long before, had with so much hatred vilified him.

CHAPTER 25

[The alliance of the Venetians and King Alfonso against the Duke of Milan and the Florentines; Cosimo's speech to the Venetian envoys. 1451]

As soon as the news of this conquest came to Florence, orders were sent to the Florentine envoys who were on the road that, instead of going to negotiate an alliance with the Count, they should congratulate the Duke on his victory. These envoys were honorably received and abundantly honored by the Duke, who knew well that, against the might of the Venetians, he could not have in Italy more faithful or stronger friends than the Florentines; for they, having laid aside their fear of the house of Visconti, saw that they would have to fight the forces of the Aragonese and the Venetians. The Aragonese kings of Naples were made their enemies by the friendship which they knew the Florentine people had always had for the house of France; the Venetians realized that the old Florentine fear of the Visconti was a new fear of Venice, and were aware that the very zeal with which the Florentines had striven against the Visconti they would, when fearing like aggressions, turn to the ruin of Venice. These things caused the new Duke readily to draw close to the Florentines, and the Venetians and King Alfonso to make an alliance against their common enemies. The latter two agreed to set their armies in motion at the same time; the King was to attack the Florentines, the Venetians the Duke; he, because he was new in his position, they believed could not keep himself in power either with his own forces or with military assistance from others.

But because the league between the Florentines and the Venetians was still in effect, and the King, after the war of Piombino, had made peace with Florence, the King and the Venetians thought they should not break the peace unless first with some excuse they justified the war. So each one sent an envoy to Florence. On behalf of their superiors these envoys announced that the league was formed not in order to attack anybody but to defend their states. The Venetian envoy then complained that the Florentines had given passage through Lunigiana to Alexander, the Duke's brother, so that with soldiers he had crossed into Lombardy, and besides, that they had been helpers and advisers in the peace made between the Duke and the Marquis of Mantua. All these things the Venetians declared harmful to their state and to the friendship between her and Florence. Therefore they reminded the Florentines in a friendly way that he who injures wrongfully gives cause to the other party to be justly angry, and that he who disturbs peace should expect war.

The Signoria entrusted their reply to Cosimo, who in a long and wise speech went over again all the favors done by his city to the Venetian republic. He showed what a great empire she had gained with the money, the soldiers and the advice of the Florentines; he reminded them that, since from the Florentines had come the cause of the friendship, never would cause for enmity come from them; having always been lovers of peace, the Florentines fully approved the agreement between the King and the Venetians, if it were made for peace and not for war. True it was that at the complaints made against them the Florentines were much astonished, seeing that of so slight and unimportant a thing so great account was made by so great a republic; but if these complaints were indeed worth considering, they gave both envoys to understand that they intended their country to be free and open to everybody, and that the Duke was of such standing that he did not need their help or their advice in making peace with Mantua. Cosimo therefore feared that these complaints concealed some poison not immediately apparent. If that were so, the Florentines could easily let both complainants know that by however much their friendship was profitable, by so much was their enmity damaging.

CHAPTER 26

[Unfriendly acts by the Venetians and the King; Florentine counter-measures. 1451]

Thus for the time being the affair passed off lightly and the envoys seemed to go away satisfied. Nevertheless the league that was formed and the ways of the Venetians and of the King made the Florentines and the Duke fear new war rather than hope for firm peace. So the Florentines allied themselves with the Duke. Meanwhile the ill will of the Venetians was revealed; they made a league with the Sienese, and drove all the Florentines and their subjects from their own cities and territory. A little later Alfonso did the same, without any regard for the peace made the year before, and without giving for his action a just or even a pretended reason.

Efforts were made by the Venetians to gain over the Bolognese. Furnishing aid to exiles from Bologna, they sent them at night through the sewers into the city with many soldiers. Nobody knew of their entrance until they raised an outcry. Thereupon Santi Ben-tivoglio, roused from sleep, heard that all the city was taken by the rebels. Though many advised him to save his life by flight—since by remaining he could not save the government—nonetheless he wished to show Fortune his face. He took arms and gave courage to his followers, and having gathered some of his friends, attacked part of the rebels and defeated them, killing many; the rest he drove out of the city. In this he was judged by everybody to have given the clearest proof that he was of the house of the Bentivogli.

These acts and indications caused in Florence settled belief in future war; and therefore the Florentines turned to their ancient and usual defenses: they chose the magistracy of the Ten, hired new generals, sent envoys to Rome, to Naples, to Venice, to Milan and to Siena to ask aid from their friends, to clear up suspicions, gain over the hesitating and learn the plans of their enemies. From the Pope they brought back nothing further than general words, a favorable inclination and exhortations to peace; from the King, empty excuses for expelling the Florentines, and offering himself as ready to give safe conduct to whoever asked for it. Though he strove to his utmost to conceal his plans for a new war, nonetheless the envoys recognized his unfriendly disposition, and discovered his many preparations for attacking their republic. Once more with various pledges the Floren' tines strengthened their league with the Duke of Milan. Through his mediation they entered into friendly relations with the Genoese, settling their ancient differences about reprisals and many other grievances, even though the Venetians sought by every means to upset such an agreement. The Venetians did not fail to ask the Emperor of Constantinople to drive all Florentines from his country. With such great hatred the Venetians undertook this war and so powerful was their longing to rule that without any hesitation they tried to destroy those who had been the cause of their greatness; but the Emperor did not listen to them. Then the Senate forbade the Florentine envoys to enter the territory of the Venetian republic, with the excuse that, being in alliance with the King, they could not listen to such ambassadors without his participation. The Sienese received the Florentine ambassadors with fair words, fearing that they would be overthrown before the League could defend them; therefore they decided to put to sleep those armies that they could not resist. Yet the Venetians and the King to justify the war, as was conjectured, attempted to send ambassadors to Florence, but the Venetian envoy was not allowed to enter Florentine territory; and since the King's envoy refused to carry out his duty alone, the negotia' tion was left unfinished. From this the Venetians learned that the Florentines estimated them even lower than they, not many months before, had estimated the Florentines.

CHAPTER 27

[The Emperor Frederick III in Florence; war begun in Lom' bardy. 1452]

In the midst of the fear roused by these movements, the Emperor Frederick III crossed into Italy to be crowned. On the thirtieth of January 1451, he entered Florence with fifteen hundred cavalry and was received by the Signoria with the greatest honor; he remained in the city until the sixth of February, when he left for his coronation in Rome. Having been ceremoniously crowned in that city, and having celebrated his marriage with the Empress, who had gone to Rome by sea, he departed for Germany. In May he again passed through Florence, where the same signs of honor were showed him as on his first visit. In the course of his return, he granted to the Marquis of Ferrara, as a reward for his assistance, Modena and Reggio.

Yet at the same time the Florentines did not fail to prepare for the impending war. To gain reputation and cause the enemy terror, they and the Duke made a league with the King of France for the defense of both their states; this they announced throughout Italy with great pomp and joy. By then the month of May 1452 had come. The Venetians decided that they could no longer put off open war against the Duke; in the region of Lodi, with sixteen thousand cavalry and six thousand infantry they attacked him. At the same time the Marquis of Monferrat, whether through his own ambition or driven by the Venetians, also attacked him in the region of Alessandria. The Duke for his part had got together eighteen thou⁄sand cavalry and three thousand infantry. Having provided Ales⁄sandria and Lodi with soldiers and likewise strengthened all the places where the enemy might attack him, he invaded the territory of Brescia, where he did the Venetians very great damage; in every direction he plundered the country and laid waste the weak villages. Then after his soldiers defeated the Marquis of Monferrat at Ales⁄sandria, the Duke was enabled to meet the Venetians with larger forces, and to attack their country.

CHAPTER 28

[Feeble attacks on Tuscany by Alfonso. 1452]

While the war was dragging on in Lombardy with various but slight happenings, little worth recording, in Tuscany also war began between King Alfonso and the Florentines; it was not carried on with greater efficiency or with greater danger than was that in Lom⁄bardy. Into Tuscany came Ferdinand, Alfonso's illegitimate son, with twelve thousand soldiers, led by Frederic the lord of Urbino. Their first enterprise was an attack on Foiano in Valdichiana, be⁄cause, having the Sienese as friends, they entered from that direction into Florentine territory. The town had a weak wall and was little, and therefore not provided with many men but, by the standards of those times, they were accounted vigorous and faithful. There were in the town two hundred soldiers sent by the Signoria to guard it. This town so prepared was besieged by Ferdinand, and such was either the great vigor of those inside, or the little he had, that only after thirty-six days did he become master of it. This time gave Florence opportunity to provide for other places of greater importance, assemble their soldiers and arrange better for defense. After the enemy had taken Foiano, they went into the Chianti, where they could not take two little villages owned by private citizens. Hence, leaving them, they went to besiege Castellina, a town on the borders of the Chianti, ten miles from Siena, weak as to art[1] and very weak as to her site; yet it was not possible for these two weaknesses to surpass the weakness of the army that attacked it; after spending forty-four days in the siege, it went away in disgrace. So much were those armies to be feared and so dangerous were those wars that cities which today are abandoned as impossible to defend, then were defended as impossible to take. While Ferdinand remained with his army in the Chianti, he made many raids and plundering expeditions into the district around Florence and came within six miles of the city, to the terror and considerable damage of the people. At this time the Florentines, bringing eight thousand troops under Astor da Faenza and Gismondo Malatesta toward the town of Colle, kept them at some distance from the enemy, fearing that they would be forced into battle. They judged that if they did not lose a battle they could not lose the war, because the little towns when lost would be regained with peace, and about the large towns they felt secure, knowing that the enemy were unlikely to attack them.

At this time the King still had a fleet of about twenty ships, galleys and foists in Pisan waters. While the siege of Castellina was going on, he directed this fleet against the castle of Vada and through the castellan's heedlessness took it; the enemy then raided all the country round about; but this raiding was easily ended by some soldiers the Florentines sent to Campiglia, who kept the enemy close to the shore.

1. *The art of fortification.*

CHAPTER 29

[The conspiracy of Stefano Porcari at Rome. 1453]

The Pontiff did not concern himself about these wars, except in so far as he believed he could bring about peace between the parties. Yet though he refrained from war abroad, he was going to find one more dangerous at home. There lived in those times a certain Stefano Porcari, a Roman citizen noble by blood and learning, but much more so through the excellence of his mind. He wished, according to the nature of men who long for glory, to do, or to attempt at least, something worth remembering. And he judged he could attempt nothing other than the delivery of his native city from the hands of the prelates, and her restoration to her ancient government. He hoped through such a deed, if he succeeded, to be called the new founder and second father of that city. He was led to hope for a happy end in this undertaking by the evil habits of the prelates and the discontent of the barons and people of Rome, but above all he was given hope by those verses of Petrarch, in the *canzone* beginning *Noble spirit that controls those limbs*, in which the poet says:

On the Tarpeian mount, canzon,[1] you will see
A knight whom all Italy honors,
More thoughtful of others than of himself.

It was known to Messer Stefano that the poets often are directed by a divine and prophetic spirit, so he judged that at all events what Petrarch prophesied in that *canzone* would come to pass, and that he was the one who was to accomplish so glorious an enterprise, since he believed that in eloquence, in learning, in grace and in friends he was superior to every other Roman.

Having taken up this idea, he could not conduct himself in so cautious a fashion that through his words, his conduct and his way of living he did not reveal himself. Thus he became suspected by the Pontiff, who, to deprive him of opportunity for doing harm, banished him to Bologna and instructed the ruler of that city to register him every day. By no means was Messer Stefano upset by this first hindrance; on the contrary, with greater zeal he carried on his undertaking, and in the most cautious ways consulted with his friends;

1. *Petrarch, as often, addresses his own* canzone.

many times he went to Rome and returned with such great speed that he was in time to present himself before the governor within the limits set.[2]

When he believed that he had brought enough men to his way of thinking, he determined not to put off an attempt. He instructed his friends in Rome that at a set time they should arrange a splendid supper, to which all the conspirators should be invited, with the understanding that each should have with him his most trusted friends; and he promised to be with them before the meal was ended. All was done according to his instructions, and Messer Stefano arrived in the house where the supper was going on. When it was over, clad in cloth of gold, with neck chains and other ornaments that gave him majesty and distinction, he appeared before the banqueters, and after embracing them, with a long speech exhorted them to settle their courage and fit themselves for so glorious a deed. He then explained the method, arranging that the next morning one part of them should seize the palace of the Pontiff, and the other part should call the people to arms throughout Rome. But the thing came to the Pontiff's knowledge that night. Some say that it was through the conspirators' lack of fidelity, others that Messer Stefano was known to be in Rome. However it was, the same night that the supper was held, the Pope caused the arrest of Messer Stefano and the greater part of his companions, and then, as their crimes deserved, had them put to death.

Such an end had this project of his. Certainly anyone can praise his intention, but everybody will always blame his judgment, because such undertakings, though when planned they give some appearance of splendor, in their execution offer almost always inevitable ruin.

2. *These limits were evidently more than the single day mentioned above. From Rome to Bologna and return is about 500 miles, by modern roads. A secret journey of that length on horseback, with business in the middle, is not a matter of twenty-four hours.*

CHAPTER 30

[Florentine successes; the treason of Gherardo Gambacorti. 1453]

Already the war in Tuscany had lasted almost a year and the time had come, in the year 1453, for armies to take the field, when to the aid of the Florentines came Signor Alessandro Sforza, the brother of the Duke, with two thousand cavalry; because of this, since the army of the Florentines was increased and that of the King diminished, the Florentines expected to regain what they had lost; and with little effort they did regain some towns. Then they went to the siege of Foiano, which, through the negligence of the commissioners, was sacked, so that the inhabitants were scattered and with great difficulty returned to live there, but with exemptions and various subsidies they were brought back. The castle of Vada was also regained, because the enemy, seeing they could not hold it, withdrew from it and burned it. And while the Florentine army did these things, the Aragonese army, not having courage to approach the enemy, had come near Siena, and many times raided Florentine territory, where it stole a great deal and caused the greatest disturbances and terrors.

Nor did that King fail to attempt in other ways to assail his enemies, divide their forces and by new efforts and assaults weaken them. The lord of Val di Bagno was Gherardo Gambacorti; he and his ancestors, through either friendship or duty, had always been either pensioned or protected by the Florentines. With him King Alfonso plotted that Gherardo should give him that territory, and the King in return would compensate him with other territory in the Kingdom. This plot was revealed in Florence. To learn Gherardo's purpose, they sent to him an envoy, who reminded him of the obligations of his ancestors and himself and exhorted him to continue his fidelity to the republic. Gherardo pretended to be astonished, and with solemn oaths declared that never had so wicked a thought come into his mind, and that he would come in person to Florence to become a pledge for his fidelity; but since he was ill, what he was unable to do he would have done by his son, whom as a hostage he handed over to the envoy so that he might take him along to Florence. These words and this display made the Florentines believe that Gherardo was telling the truth and that his accuser was a liar and worthless; therefore in this opinion they rested. But Gherardo with the more vigor carried on his plot with the King. When it was complete, into the Val di Bagno the King sent Frate Puccio, a Knight of Jerusalem, with plenty of soldiers, to take possession of Gherardo's castles and towns. But the people of Bagno, having a fondness for the Florentine republic, with vexation promised obedience to the commissioners of the King. Already Frate

Puccio had taken possession of almost all that territory; all he lacked was to make himself master of the castle of Corzano.

With Gherardo, when he was making this transfer, among his men who were around him, was Antonio Gualandi, a Pisan, young and fiery, to whom this treachery of Gherardo's was abhorrent. He considered the site of the fortress and the men who were there in the garrison, and saw in their faces and gestures their discontent; so when Gherardo stood at the gate to let the Aragonese soldiers in, Antonio circled around toward the inside of the fortress, pushed Gherardo outside with both hands, and ordered the garrison to lock the fortress in the face of so wicked a man, and to hold it for the Florentine republic. When this event became known in Bagno and in the other places nearby, all those various peoples took arms against the Aragonese and, raising the banner of Florence, drove them away. When this was reported in Florence, the Florentines imprisoned the son of Gherardo who had been given them as a hostage, and sent soldiers to Bagno to defend the region for their republic; that state which had been governed by its sovereign they changed into a vicarate. But Gherardo, traitor to his lord and to his son, scarcely was able to escape, and left his wife and his family, with all his property, in the power of his enemies.

In Florence this event was looked on as of great importance, because if the King had succeeded in making himself master of that region, he could with little expense have raided as he pleased in the Valley of the Tiber and in the Casentino, where he could have given so much trouble to the Republic that the Florentines would not have been able to oppose all their forces to the Aragonese army that was at Siena.

CHAPTER 31

[René of Anjou comes to aid the Duke and the Florentines. 1453-1454]

Meanwhile the Florentines, besides the preparations made in Italy to crush the forces of the hostile league, had sent Messer Agnolo Acciaiuoli as their ambassador to the King of France to arrange with him about furnishing King René of Anjou with means for an expedition into Italy to aid the Duke and themselves; he would come to defend his friends and then, being in Italy, could plan on gaining the Kingdom of Naples; for this purpose they promised him aid in soldiers and in money. So while, as we have related, the war was going on in Lombardy and Tuscany, the ambassador made with King René an agreement that in June he was to come into Italy with twenty-four hundred cavalry; on his arrival in Alessandria the League was to give him thirty thousand florins, and afterward, during the war, ten thousand every month.

When this King attempted, then, by virtue of this agreement, to cross into Italy, he was held back by the Duke of Savoy and the Marquis of Monferrat, for they, being friends of the Venetians, did not allow his passage. So the Florentine ambassador advised the King that in order to give prestige to his friends, he should return into Provence, and with some of his men come into Italy by sea; and on the other hand that he should bring pressure on the King of France to have him work upon that Duke, so that his soldiers would be able to cross through Savoy. As René was advised, so he did, for by sea he got into Italy, and his soldiers, to please the King, were received in Savoy. King René was welcomed by Duke Francesco with the greatest respect. When they had united the Italian and the French soldiers, with such fury they attacked the Venetians that in a short time they retook all the towns the latter had seized in the territory of Cremona. Not satisfied with this, they conquered almost all the territory of Brescia; hence the Venetian army, thinking itself no longer safe in the field, drew close to the walls of Brescia.

When winter came, the Duke decided to put his soldiers into winter quarters; to King René he assigned lodgings at Piacenza. Then, after the winter of 1453 had been spent without military activity, when summer came and the Duke reckoned on taking the field and depriving the Venetians of their territory on land, King René informed him that he was obliged to return to France. Now this decision was to the Duke wholly unexpected; therefore he felt the utmost vexation; but though he at once went to see the King to dissuade him from leaving, by neither prayers nor promises could he change him; René merely promised to leave part of his soldiers and to send his son Jean, who in his place would be at the service of the League. This departure did not displease the Florentines, for, having regained their towns, they no longer feared the King, and on the other side they did not wish the Duke to regain anything besides his cities in Lombardy. So René left and sent his son, as he had promised, into Italy. He did not stop in Lombardy but came on to Florence, where he was received with high honors.

CHAPTER 32
[Peace; the seeds of war. 1454]

The departure of the King made the Duke gladly turn to peace, and the Venetians, Alfonso, and the Florentines, because they all were weary, wished for it. The Pope too had given and was giving every appearance of wishing it, because that same year Mahomet the Grand Turk had taken Constantinople and made himself master of all Greece. That capture frightened all the Christians, and more than any others the Venetians and the Pope, since it already seemed to each of these that they felt his armies in Italy. The Pope, then, besought the Italian powers to send ambassadors to him, with authority to establish a universal peace. All of them obeyed, but after assembling to arrange the matter, they found great difficulty in dealing with it. The King wished the Florentines to reimburse him for his expenses in that war, and the Florentines wanted theirs paid; from the Duke the Venetians asked Cremona; the Duke from them asked Bergamo, Brescia, and Crema. Hence it seemed that to settle these difficulties would be impossible.

Nevertheless, that which at Rome among many seemed impossible to do, at Milan and at Venice between two was very easy because, while at Rome the negotiations over peace were going on, the Duke and the Venetians, on April ninth, 1454, concluded it. By virtue of it, each one returned to the cities he held before the war, and to the Duke was granted the right to recover the cities taken from him by the princes of Monferrat and of Savoy. The other Italian rulers were allowed a month for ratifying it.

The Pope and the Florentines, and with them the Sienese and other lesser powers, within the time limit ratified it. Not content with this, the Florentines, the Duke and the Venetians ratified among themselves a peace for twentyfive years. King Alfonso alone among the Italian powers showed himself discontented with this peace, for he viewed it as made with little credit to himself, since not as a principal but as an accessory he was to be admitted to it; therefore he remained a long time uncertain, without making his views known.

Yet after the Pope and the other princes had sent him many formal embassies, he allowed himself to be persuaded by the others, especially the Pontiff; so he and his son entered this league for thirty years. The Duke of Milan and the King made together a double marriage alliance and a double wedding, each one giving and taking a daughter for the other's son. Nonetheless, in order that the seeds of war might remain in Italy, the King did not consent to make peace unless permission was first granted by his colleagues that he might, without injury to them, make war on the Genoese, on Gismondo Malatesta and on Astor Prince of Faenza. After this peace was made, Ferdinand his son, who was at Siena, returned to the Kingdom, having by his coming into Tuscany made no gain in sovereignty and lost many of his soldiers.

CHAPTER 33

[Jacopo Piccinino causes trouble; abortive plans for a Crusade. 1455]

With the coming, then, of this general peace, there was fear only that King Alfonso, because of the hostility he felt for the Genoese, would interrupt it; but the fact was otherwise, because it was interrupted not openly by the King but, as always had happened before, by the ambition of the mercenary soldiers. The Venetians, according to custom, when peace was made had dismissed from their service Jacopo Piccinino their general. After he had been joined by some other soldiers of fortune who were without employment, they went into Romagna and thence into the territory of Siena; there they stopped, and Jacopo began war against the Sienese and took some towns from them. In the beginning of these disturbances and the opening of the year 1455, Pope Nicholas died, and as his successor Calixtus III was chosen. This Pontiff, to put down this new and neighboring war, at once brought together under Giovanni Ventimiglia his general as many soldiers as he could; these, with soldiers from the Florentines and the Duke, who had also united to put down these disturbances, he sent against Jacopo. When they joined battle near Bolsena, in spite of Ventimiglia's becoming a prisoner, Jacopo was the loser and retreated in defeat to Castiglione della Pescaia; if he had not been supported with money by Alfonso, he would have remained there entirely ruined. This affair made everybody believe that this movement by Jacopo had been arranged by the King. Hence, since Alfonso saw that he had been found out, in order to reconcile with himself through peace those associates that he had almost alienated with this feeble war, he caused Jacopo to restore to the Sienese their towns which he had taken; they were to give him twenty thousand florins. When this agreement had been made, he received Jacopo and his soldiers into the Kingdom.

In these times, although the Pope gave attention to checking Jacopo Piccinino, nonetheless he did not fail to make arrangements to support Christendom, which apparently was going to be attacked by the Turks. And to this end he sent to all Christian countries envoys and preachers to induce princes and peoples to arm in support of their religion, and with their money and their persons to support the enterprise against the common enemy. Hence in Florence many offerings were made; many also marked themselves with a red cross, in order to be ready in person for that war; they also made solemn processions and did not fail, either publicly or privately, to show that with their advice, with their money and with their men, they wished to be among the first Christians in such an undertaking. But this warmth for the crusade was somewhat cooled by news that when the Turk with his army was besieging Belgrade—a town in Hungary on the River Danube—he had been defeated and wounded by the Hungarians. Hence, since the Pontiff and the Christians no longer felt the fear that they conceived on the loss of Constantinople, the preparations for war were more lukewarm; in Hungary itself, after the death of John Hunyadi the Waywode, the leader in that victory, they cooled down.

CHAPTER 34

[A terrible storm in Tuscany. 1456]

But turning to the affairs of Italy, I shall tell how the year 1456 went, after the disturbance roused by Jacopo Piccinino ended. When men's arms were laid down, it seemed that God wished to take up his, so great was a windstorm that then followed, producing in Tuscany effects unheard of in the past, and for those who in the future learn of it, wonderful and noteworthy results. A whirlwind, with a great thick mass of clouds, started on the twenty-fourth of

August, an hour before dawn, in the region of the Upper Sea[1] near Ancona and, crossing Italy, entered the Lower Sea near Pisa. Throughout its course, it covered a space about two miles broad. This mass, driven by superior forces whether natural or supernatural, was broken within itself and carried on a struggle within itself; the shattered clouds, now rising toward the sky, now descending toward the earth, crashed together; and now in circles with the greatest speed they moved on, and before them stirred up a wind furious beyond all measure; flames and the most brilliant flashes appeared thick among them as they fought. From these clouds so broken and confused, from these winds so wild and these thick flashes came a noise such as from no sort or size of earthquake or thunder was ever heard before. From this resulted such terror that everybody who experienced it judged that the end of the world had come, and that the earth, the water and the rest of the sky and the world, confusing themselves together, were going back again to the ancient chaos.

This terrorizing whirlwind, wherever it went, caused incredible and marvelous effects, but more striking than elsewhere were those at the town of San Casciano. This town is eight miles from Florence on the hill separating the valleys of the Pesa and of the Greve. Though between that town, then, and the village of Sant' Andrea, placed on the same hill, this furious storm held its course, it did not reach Sant' Andrea, and it grazed San Casciano in such a way that merely some battlements and chimneys on some of the houses were knocked down; but outside the town, in the space between the two places mentioned, many houses were destroyed down to the ground. The roofs of the churches of San Martino a Bagnuolo and of Santa Maria della Pace, as complete as when they were in position, were carried more than a mile away. A wagoner with his mules was found dead in one of the neighboring valleys more than a mile from the road. All the larger oaks, all the strongest trees, which would not yield to such great fury, were not merely uprooted but were carried to a great distance from where they had had their roots; so when the storm had passed and day came, men were wholly bewildered. They saw the country desolate and laid waste; they saw the ruins of the houses and the churches; they heard the laments of those whose property was destroyed and who under the ruins had left their animals and their relatives dead. This storm, to those who

1. *The Upper Sea is the Adriatic, as the Lower is the Tyrrhenian.*

saw and heard it, brought the utmost pity and terror. The purpose of God without doubt was to threaten rather than to punish Tuscany; for if so great a wind had entered a city, among the houses and the thickly crowded inhabitants, as it came among the oaks and trees and houses that were few and scattered, without doubt it would have made the greatest ruin and destruction that the mind can imagine. But God purposed at that time that this slight example should suffice to refresh among men the memory of his power.

CHAPTER 35

[*King Alfonso attacks Genoa; the Genoese get aid from the French. 1456–1458*]

Now to turn back where I left off, King Alfonso, as I said above, was discontented with the peace. Since the war that he had Jacopo Piccinino start against the Sienese, without any just cause, had produced no important effect, he determined to see what would be produced by one that he could wage in harmony with the agreements of the League. So therefore, in the year 1456, by sea and land he started war against the Genoese, hoping to turn over the government to the Adorni and to take it from the Fregosi, who then were ruling. Moreover in the other direction he had Jacopo Piccinino cross the Tronto against Sigismondo Malatesta. The latter, because he had well fortified his towns, had little regard for Jacopo's attack. So on that side the King's attempt was without effect. But that of Genoa brought him and his kingdom more war than he would have chosen.

At that time the chief man in Genoa was Pietro Fregoso. Fearing that he could not resist the attack of the King, he determined that what he could not hold he would at least give to somebody who would defend him from his enemies and sometime could pay him a proper price for that favor. He sent envoys, therefore, to Charles VII, King of France, and offered him the sovereignty of Genoa. Accepting the offer, Charles sent to take possession of that city Jean of Anjou, King René's son, who a short time before had left Florence and returned to France. Charles had the idea that Jean, because he had adopted many Italian habits, would be better able than another to govern that city; and in part he thought that from there he could plan for an expedition against Naples, a kingdom of which

Alfonso had deprived his father René. Thereupon Jean went to Genoa, where he was accepted as prince, and into his power were given the fortresses of the city and the state.

CHAPTER 36

[Death of Alfonso and succession of Ferdinand; death of Calixtus and succession of Pius II. 1458–1461]

This happening vexed Alfonso, who realized he had brought on himself too important an enemy. Nevertheless, not frightened by it, he continued his enterprise with good courage, and had already brought his fleet to Villa Marina, at Portofino, when, seized by sudden illness, he died. As a result of his death, Jean and the Genoese were left free from war; and Ferdinand, who succeeded to the throne of Alfonso his father, was full of foreboding, having an enemy of such standing in Italy, and distrusting the fidelity of many of his barons, who, hoping for reforms, might join the French. He feared also the Pope, whose ambition he realized, and who, since Ferdinand was new in his kingdom, might plan to deprive him of it. He hoped only in the Duke of Milan, who was not less anxious about the affairs of the Kingdom than was Ferdinand, fearing that, if the French became masters of it, they would plan to take his state also, which he knew they believed they had a right to ask for as belonging to them. So soon after the death of Alfonso, the Duke sent Ferdinand letters and soldiers (the men to give him aid and prestige, the letters to persuade him to have good courage) indicating that in any necessity he was not going to abandon him.

The Pope after Alfonso's death planned to give the Neapolitan kingdom to Pietro Lodovico Borgia his nephew. To make the affair seem honorable and more easily to get the other princes to agree, he announced his intention of bringing that kingdom under the authority of the Roman Church. For this reason he tried to persuade the Duke of Milan not to give Ferdinand any help, offering Duke Francesco the towns in that kingdom which he once had held. In the midst of these projects and new efforts Calixtus died. To the papal throne succeeded Pius II, a Sienese of the Piccolomini family named Aeneas. This pontiff, considering only how he could benefit Christians and strengthen the Church and abandoning all his private feelings, on the Duke of Milan's request gave the crown of the Kingdom to Ferdinand, judging that by supporting a man in possession of the throne he could do more to get arms laid down than either by aiding the French to conquer that kingdom or by trying, like Calixtus, to get it for himself. Nevertheless, to repay this favor Ferdinand made the Pope's nephew Antonio ruler of Amalfi and gave him in marriage his illegitimate daughter. He also restored Benevento and Terracina to the Church.

CHAPTER 37

[War in Genoa and in Naples between Jean of Anjou and Ferdinand. 1459–1460]

Arms appeared to be laid down in Italy, and the Pontiff was preparing to move Christendom against the Turks, carrying on what Calixtus had earlier done, when dissension arose between the Fregosi and Jean the ruler of Genoa which kindled greater and more important wars than those just over. Petrino Fregoso happened to be in a town of his on the Riviera. He believed he had not been rewarded by Jean of Anjou according to his deserts and those of his house, since with their aid Jean had become ruler of Genoa; hence they came to open enmity. This situation suited Ferdinand, as the only means and the sole approach to his own security; so he supported Petrino with men and money, thinking through him to drive Jean from Genoa. Knowing this, Jean sent to France for reinforcements, with which he resisted. Yet Petrino because of the abundant help sent him by Ferdinand was so strong that Jean was reduced to defending the city. Petrino, entering Genoa one night, took some parts of her, but when day came he was attacked and killed by Jean's soldiers, and all his men were either killed or captured.

This victory gave Jean courage to make an expedition to the Kingdom of Naples, so in October 1459 with a powerful fleet he left Genoa for Naples. He stopped at Baia and then at Sessa, where he was received by its duke. To Jean's support came the ruler of Taranto, the people of Aquila, and many other cities and rulers, so that kingdom was almost entirely upset. Seeing this, Ferdinand applied for reinforcements to the Pope and to the Duke; and in order to have fewer enemies, he made an agreement with Sigismondo

Malatesta. This so angered Jacopo Piccinino, who was a natural enemy to Sigismondo, that he left Ferdinand's employ and sided with Jean. Ferdinand also sent money to Federigo of Urbino, and brought together as soon as he could a good army, for those times. On the Sarni River he confronted his enemies. When they came to battle, King Ferdinand was defeated and many of his important officers captured. After this overthrow, the city of Naples with some few princes and cities remained faithful to Ferdinand; the greater part gave themselves up to Jean. It was the opinion of Jacopo Piccinino that Jean upon this victory should go to Naples and make himself master of the chief city of the Kingdom; but he refused, saying that he intended first to get from Ferdinand all his territory and then to attack him, thinking that, if he were deprived of his lands, the capture of Naples would be easier. This decision, taken for an opposite purpose, deprived him of victory in that undertaking, because he did not realize how much more easily the limbs follow the head than the head the limbs.

CHAPTER 38

[Rebellion in Genoa; Jean defeated in the Kingdom; the neutrality of Florence. 1460–1463]

Ferdinand, after his defeat, had taken refuge in Naples. There he received those who had been driven from their states, and with the kindest methods possible he got money together and assembled a small army. For the second time he sent for help to the Pope and to the Duke, and by both of them was supported with greater speed and more generously than before, because they were much afraid he would lose that Kingdom. When therefore King Ferdinand became strong, he went out of Naples; and having partly regained his reputation, he regained some territories he had lost.

While the war went on in the Kingdom, an event occurred that entirely took away Jean of Anjou's reputation and his opportunity for success in that undertaking. The Genoese were disgusted at the avaricious and proud conduct of the French, so that they took arms against the royal governor and compelled him to take refuge in the Little Castle; in this undertaking the Fregosi and the Adorni were in agreement; by the Duke of Milan they were aided with money and with soldiers, both in gaining control of the government as well as in keeping it. Hence King René, who later came with a fleet to aid his son, hoping to regain Genoa by means of the Little Castle, was defeated in such a way while landing his troops that he was compelled to return in disgrace to Provence.

This news, when it was learned in the Kingdom of Naples, greatly frightened Jean of Anjou. Nevertheless he did not give up his effort, but for a long time kept up the war, aided by those barons who, because of their rebellion, did not believe they would find safety with Ferdinand. Yet at the end, after many things had happened, the two royal armies came to battle, and Jean was defeated near Troia, in the year 1463. Yet the defeat did not injure him so much as did the desertion of Jacopo Piccinino, who sided with Ferdinand. Hence Jean, deprived of power, retired into Ischia, from which he later returned to France. This war lasted four years, and through his sluggishness that man lost it who through the excellence of his soldiers had many times won it.

In this war the Florentines did not take part in any open way. It is true that King John of Aragon, newly made king in that king-dom on the death of Alfonso, asked them through an embassy to aid in the affairs of Ferdinand his nephew, as they had promised in the league recently made with Alfonso his father. To this the Floren-tines answered that they had no duty toward him, that they were not going to help the son in a war that the father with his own armies had started; as it was begun without their advice or knowledge, so with-out their aid it could be carried on and finished. Hence those envoys, on the part of their king, affirmed the weight of the Floren-tines' obligation and their share in the damage; and in anger against that city they departed. The Florentines, then, in the time of this war, were at peace as to things outside their city, but they were not at all quiet inside, as in the following book will be set forth in detail.

BOOK SEVEN

[LARGELY BUT NOT WHOLLY ON AFFAIRS IN FLORENTINE TERRITORY DURING THE LATTER YEARS OF COSIMO AND THE EARLY YEARS OF LORENZO. 1427-1478]

CHAPTER 1

[The relation of Florence to Italy; party strife in Florence. 1434-1455]

Perhaps readers of the preceding book will think that as a writer on Florentine affairs I have spent too much time in relating what happened in Lombardy and in the Kingdom.[1] Nevertheless I have not avoided and in the future I am not going to avoid such narratives, because, though I have never promised to write on the affairs of Italy, I do not therefore suppose that I should avoid relating those that are worthy of observation in this land. Indeed if I do not relate them, our history will be less understandable and less pleasing, especially because in the actions of the other Italian peoples and princes the wars in which the Florentines have to take part often originate. For example, in the war between Jean of Anjou and King Ferdinand originated the hatreds and the serious enmities that later existed between Ferdinand and the Florentines, and especially the Medici family; because the King complained that not merely he had no assistance in that war, but aid was given to his enemy. His anger was the cause of very great evils, as will be shown in our narrative. Now, because in writing about affairs outside the city I have reached 1463, if I am to tell of the troubles that occurred inside the city before that time, I must turn back many years.

But first, according to my habit, I wish to some extent to explain in general why those who believe republics can be united are greatly deceived in their belief. It is true that some divisions harm republics and some divisions benefit them. Those do harm that are accompanied with factions and partisans; those bring benefit that are kept up without factions and without partisans. Since, then, the founder of a republic cannot provide that there will be no enmities within it, he needs at least to provide that there will be no factions. Therefore

1. *Actually the two preceding books deal largely with Italy outside Florence.*

he must note that in two ways citizens gain reputation in a city: activity in behalf of the public, and activity for personal ends. Publicly, they gain reputation by winning a battle, capturing a town, carrying on an embassy with diligence and prudence, and advising the state wisely and successfully. In personal ways they gain reputa tion by doing favors to various citizens, defending them from the magistrates, assisting them with money and aiding them in getting undeserved offices, and by pleasing the masses with games and public gifts. From these selfish proceedings come factions and partisans; a reputation so gained injures the state. Yet a reputation gained by unselfish conduct benefits the republic, since it is not mixed with partisanship, being founded on the common good, not on private favor. Even citizens who confer private benefits cannot harm the republic unless they have partisans who follow them for personal profit, though no one can in any way provide against their exciting great hatred. When they have no partisans, even selfishly ambitious men benefit the state, because if they are to succeed, necessarily they attempt to make the republic great, and especially watch each other in order that lawful bounds may not be overpassed.

The enmities in Florence were always those of factions and there fore always dangerous. Not even a victorious faction ever remained united, except so long as the opposing faction was vigorous. But when a beaten faction was destroyed, since the party in power no longer felt any fear that could restrain it and had no law of its own to check it, the victor became divided. In 1434 Cosimo de'Medici's party was superior, but because the defeated party was strong and abounded in powerful men, Cosimo's faction through fear continued for a time to be united and gracious, suffering no discord within itself and not rousing the people's hatred by any wicked conduct. Hence as often as Cosimo's government had need of the people in order to get a new grip on its authority, it found them always in clined to grant its leaders such power and dominion as were asked. Thus from 1434 to 1455, which is twentyone years, Cosimo's party six times, usually through the Councils, took up again the power of the *balìa*.[2]

2. *A committee which had power to reorganize the Florentine government. Though ostensibly chosen by popular acclamation, it was in reality the instrument of those in the city who were strongest, whether the Duke of Athens or the Medici.*

CHAPTER 2

[Cosimo's methods. 1427, 1455, 1466]

In Florence, as we have said many times, there were two very powerful citizens, Cosimo de' Medici and Neri Capponi. Neri had gained his reputation in public ways, so that he had many friends and few partisans. Cosimo, on the other hand, for whom both public and private ways to power were open, had friends and partisans in numbers. Since these two were united while they were both alive, they always got what they wanted from the people without any difficulty, because their power was mingled with kindness. But by the year 1455, when Neri was dead and the hostile party destroyed, the government found difficulty in grasping its authority again. Cosimo's own friends, the most powerful men in the government, were the occasion for it, because they no longer feared the party in opposition, which was destroyed, and were glad to lessen Cosimo's power. This dissension started divisions that appeared later, in 1466, so that the men controlling the government, in the councils where there was public debate on the conduct of public matters, advised that the power of the *balìa* not be taken up again, and that the bags[1] be locked and the magistrates, on account of advantages in the earlier lists of names, be chosen by lot.

Cosimo, to check this dissension, could use either of two methods: he could reorganize the government by force with the partisans who were left to him and oppose all the others; or he could let things go and with time make his friends realize that they were taking power and reputation not from him but from themselves. Of the two methods he chose the second, for he knew well that in such a method of ruling, because the bags were full of his friends, he ran no risk, and that when he chose he could reorganize the government.

The city, having returned, then, to choosing magistrates by lot, seemed to the generality of the citizens to have got back her liberty, and the magistrates judged not according to the will of the powerful but according to their own judgment. Thus now one friend of a

---

1. *These bags contained the names of those eligible for various offices. Thus office was impossible to a man whose name was not "bagged." In this instance no new names were to be put in the bags, so that only Cosimo's supporters, whose names had been put there long before, would hold office.*

powerful man, now one of another was punished; hence some, who were accustomed to seeing their houses full of visitors and of presents, saw that they were empty of things and of men. They saw also that they had become equal to those whom they were accustomed to hold far inferior, and those who were wont to be their equals had become their superiors. They were not respected or honored, rather they were many times mocked and derided, and there was talk about them and about the republic along the streets and in the squares without any caution. So they quickly found out that not Cosimo but they themselves had lost control of the government. Cosimo pretended ignorance of this state of things, and when there came up any decision that would please the people, he was the first to favor it. But that which made the rich fear most, and gave Cosimo the best opportunity to make them take heed, was that the method of the property tax of 1427 was revived, in which not men but laws levied the taxes.

CHAPTER 3

[Cosimo will not consent to violence; Luca Pitti gets a balía *by force. 1458]*

When this law had been enacted, and the magistracy that was to carry it out had been installed, the rich all drew together, went to Cosimo and begged him to be so kind as to take himself and them out of the hands of the masses and give their party a reputation which would make him powerful and them honored. Cosimo answered that he was willing, but that he wished the law to be made by due process and with the consent of the people, and not by force, which he would not discuss with them in any way. A law to set up a new *balía* was attempted in the Councils, and it did not pass. Hence the rich citizens returned to Cosimo and with every sort of humility begged him to give his consent to a parliament. Such consent Cosimo wholly refused, since he wished to bring them to a condition in which they would fully recognize their error. And be-cause Donato Cocchi, who was Gonfalonier of Justice, tried to call a parliament without his consent, Cosimo had him so ridiculed by the Signors who were sitting with him that he became mad and was taken home as insane.

Nonetheless, because it is not well to let things go over the limit so far that they cannot then be brought back to their places, when Luca Pitti, a courageous and reckless man, had become Gonfalonier of Justice, Cosimo thought it the proper time to let Luca control the affair, so that if by that attempt they became liable to some blame, it would be charged to Luca, and not to himself. Luca, then, at the beginning of his magistracy, proposed to the people many times to re-establish the *balía*; when he did not get it, he threatened those who sat in the Councils with insulting words, full of pride. To these a little later he added actions, because in August 1458, on San Lorenzo's eve, after filling the Palace with armed men, he summoned the people to the Public Square, and by force and with weapons made them accept what earlier they had not voluntarily accepted.

So when the government had been taken over and the *balía* and then the chief magistrates selected according to the desire of the few, in order with terror to give a beginning to the government which they had set up by force, they banished Messer Girolamo Machiavelli with some others, and also deprived many of their offices. This Messer Girolamo, who did not keep the rules of his banishment, was declared a rebel; and as he went traveling around Italy, stirring up the princes against his own city, he was arrested in Lunigiana through the treachery of one of those lords; being taken to Florence, he was put to death in prison.

CHAPTER 4

[The bad government of Luca Pitti; his buildings. 1463]

This sort of government, for the eight years that it lasted, was unbearable and violent, because Cosimo, already old and weary and weakened by bad health, was not able to be present at public business in his usual way; hence a few citizens plundered the city. Luca Pitti, as a reward for the work he had done for the benefit of the republic, was made a knight; and he, in order not to be less pleasing to her than she had been to him, decreed that the officials who earlier had been called Priors of the Gilds should thereafter, in order to have the name at least of the possession they had lost, be called Priors of Liberty. He decreed also that whereas in the past the Gonfalonier had been seated above the Priors on their right, in the future he should sit in the midst of them. And that God might seem to be a sharer in this business, public processions and solemn services were arranged to thank him for the regained offices. To Messer Luca, the Signoria and Cosimo made rich presents, and they were imitated by the whole city as though in competition; it was believed that these presents reached the amount of twenty thousand ducats. As a result he rose to such a reputation that not Cosimo but Messer Luca ruled the city.

Because of this he became so confident that he began two build/ ings, one in Florence, the other at Rusciano, a place a mile from the city, both splendid and regal, but the palace in the city was in every way greater than any that had been built by a private citizen up to that day. To bring these to completion he did not spare any method however unusual, for not merely the citizens and individual men gave him presents and assisted him with things necessary to the building, but communities and whole peoples gave him aid. Besides this, all the banished and anybody who had committed murder or theft or anything else for which he feared public punishment, if only he were a person useful in that construction, had a secure refuge in those buildings. The other citizens, if they did not build like Luca, were not less violent or less grasping than he, so that if Florence had not had foreign war to destroy her, she would have been destroyed by her own citizens.

During this time, as we have said, the wars in the Kingdom oc/ curred, and others that the Pontiff carried on in Romagna against the Malatesti because he wished to deprive them of Rimini and Cesena, which they were occupying. So between these attempts and the plans for an expedition against the Turk, Pope Pius spent his reign.

CHAPTER 5

[*The career of Cosimo; his death. 1464*]

But Florence continued in her disunions and difficulties. Dis/ union began in the party of Cosimo in 1455, for the reasons given; through his prudence, as we have related, they were quieted for the time being. But with the coming of the year 1464, Cosimo's illness became so much more serious that he passed from this life. His friends and his enemies sorrowed for his death. Even those who for political reasons did not love him, knowing what the greed of the citizens had been when he was alive—when respect for him made the greedy less unbearable—feared when he was dead to be completely ruined and destroyed. They did not trust much in Piero his son because, even though he was a good man, nonetheless they judged that since he too was sick, and new in the government, he would be obliged to have consideration for the greedy, who therefore, without a bit in their mouths, could be more immoderate. So Cosimo left deep regrets on the part of everybody.

Cosimo was the most talked of and renowned citizen, for an unarmed man, that not merely Florence but any city of which there is record ever had, because not merely did he surpass every other in his time in influence and wealth but also in liberality and prudence, for among the other qualities that made him first in his city, he was above all other men liberal and munificent. His liberality appeared much greater after his death, when Piero his son had his property examined, because there was no citizen of any standing in the city to whom Cosimo had not lent a large sum of money; many times without being asked, when he knew the necessity of a noble man, he aided him.

His munificence appeared in the great number of buildings he erected, because there are in Florence the cloisters and the churches of San Marco and of San Lorenzo and the monastery of Santa Verdiana, and on the Fiesole mountains San Girolamo and the Badia, and in the Mugello a church of the Minor Friars which he not so much restored as built anew from its foundations. Besides this, in Santa Croce, in the Servi, in the Angioli, in San Miniato, he had altars and very magnificent chapels built; and besides building these churches and chapels, he filled them with tapestries and everything needed for the adornment of divine service. To these holy buildings his private houses are to be added. These were: one in the city, of such quality as was suited to so great a citizen; four outside, at Careggi, at Fiesole, at Cafaggiuolo, and at Trebbio—all palaces suited not for private citizens but for kings. And because it was not enough for him to be known in Italy by the splendor of his buildings, he built also in Jerusalem a hospital for poor and sick pilgrims. In these buildings he used up an immense amount of money.

Yet though these dwellings and all his other works and acts were kingly and he alone was leader in Florence, nonetheless he was so controlled by his prudence that he never overstepped the decorum of a citizen, for in his customs, his servants, his horses, in all his way of living, and in his marriage alliances, he was always like any unobtrusive citizen, because he knew that the unusual things that are seen and appear every day make men more envied than those that are done once and for all and are protected by their nobility. So having to give wives to his sons, he did not seek for alliances with princes, but united Giovanni with Cornelia degli Alessandri, and Piero with Lucrezia de' Tornabuoni; and of his grandchildren born to Piero, he married Bianca to Guglielmo de' Pazzi, and Nannina to Bernardo Rucellai.

No other in his time equaled him for his understanding of the conditions of princes and commonwealths. This was the reason why in such great variety of fortune and in a city so variable and among a body of citizens so fickle, he maintained one government for thirty-one years. Since he was very prudent, he recognized ills at a distance, and therefore he was early enough either not to let them grow or to get ready in such a way that after they had grown, they did not harm him. Hence he not merely overcame the internal ambition of the citizens, but he defeated that of many princes with such skill and prudence that whoever allied himself with him and with his country was either equal to his enemies or superior, and whoever opposed him lost either time and money or his position. To this strong witness can be borne by the Venetians, who with his help were always superior against Duke Filippo, and when not united with him always, first by Filippo and then by Francesco, were defeated and humiliated; and when they allied themselves with Alfonso against the republic of Florence, Cosimo with his credit so emptied Naples and Venice of money that they were forced to accept the peace he was willing to grant them.

Of Cosimo's troubles, then, within the city and without, the end was splendid for him and harmful to his enemies; therefore civil strife always increased his influence in Florence, and external wars his power and reputation. Through them he added to the territory of his republic Borgo San Sepolcro, Montedoglio, the Casentino and Val di Bagno. Thus his ability and his fortune destroyed all his enemies and raised up his friends.

CHAPTER 6
[*The character of Cosimo. 1389–1464*]

He was born in 1389, on St. Cosimo and St. Damiano's day. His early life was full of trials, as his exile, his imprisonment, his dangers of death show; and from the Council of Constance, where he had gone with Pope John, he was obliged after the Pope's fall to flee in disguise in order to save his life. But after he was forty years old, he lived very happily, so that not merely those who sided with him in public affairs but also those who had charge of his property in all Europe shared in his prosperity. From this very great riches came to many families in Florence, as the Tornabuoni, the Benci, the Portinari, and the Sassetti; and in addition to these, all who depended on his advice and fortune grew rich. Hence, though he spent continually in building churches and in charity, he lamented many times with his friends that he had never been able to spend for God's honor as much as his books showed was due.

He was of ordinary stature, of olive complexion and of dignified bearing. He was without learning but very eloquent and abounding in natural prudence; by means of the last he was obliging to his friends, merciful to the poor, helpful in consultation, cautious in advice, swift in execution; in his sayings and replies he was keen and weighty.

Messer Rinaldo degli Albizzi, in the first years of his exile, sent to him to say that the hen was brooding, and Cosimo answered that she couldn't brood very well outside her nest; to other rebels, who let him know they were not sleeping, he said he believed it, since he had taken their sleep from them. He said when Pope Pius summoned the princes for the expedition against the Turk, that the Pontiff was an old man and was carrying on an expedition for young ones. To the Venetian envoys who came to Florence with those of King Alfonso to complain of the republic, he showed his uncovered head and asked them what color it was; they replied: "White." He then continued: "No long time will go by before those of your senators will be as white as mine." When his wife asked him a few hours before his death why he kept his eyes shut, he replied: "To get them used to it." When some citizens said to him, after his return from exile, that the city was ruined and that it was an act against God to drive out of it so many important men, he answered that a city ruined was better than one lost, and that five yards of red cloth would make an important man,[1] and that states are not held by carrying rosaries.[2] These sayings gave his enemies a basis for slandering him, as a man who loved himself more than his city and this world more than the other. I could repeat many more of his sayings, which, as not necessary, I omit.

Cosimo was also a lover and patron of learned men; because of this he brought to Florence a Greek named Argyropoulos, very learned for those times, so that from him the Florentine youths might acquire the Greek language and other things he could teach. Cosimo kept in his own mansion Marsilio Ficino, the second father of the Platonic philosophy, whom he greatly loved, in order that Ficino might more conveniently carry on the study of letters; that he himself might more easily make use of him, he gave him property near his own at Careggi.

This prudence of his, then, this wealth of his, his way of living and his fortune made him feared and loved by the citizens of Florence, and very greatly esteemed by the princes not merely of Italy but of all Europe. Hence he left such a structure to his successors that they were able by their ability to equal him and by their fortune greatly to surpass him; such influence as Cosimo had had in Florence they had not merely in that city but in all Christendom. Nonetheless in the last years of his life he suffered very great sorrows because of his two sons Piero and Giovanni; the second, on whom he relied more, died; the other was ailing and, because of the weakness of his body, little fit for public and private affairs. Hence when carried through his house by his servants after Giovanni's death, Cosimo said with a sigh: "This is too big a house for so small a family."

It was a further affliction to the greatness of his spirit that he had not expanded Florentine territory with a conquest worthy of honor. Of this he complained so much the more in that he believed he had been deceived by Francesco Sforza, who, while he was Count, had promised that whenever he became Lord of Milan he would deal

1. *In his portrait by Pontormo (Florence, the Uffizi Gallery) Cosimo himself appears dressed in red.*

2. *In anticipation of the Eighteenth Chapter of* THE PRINCE, *Cosimo realized that statecraft often conflicted with convention and religious teaching. As the next sentence shows, Cosimo did not anticipate Niccolò's advice to keep such sentiments hidden.*

with the business of Lucca for the Florentines. This did not come about, because that Count changed his idea with his fortune, and when he became Duke wished to enjoy in peace the state he had gained with war; therefore he did not try to satisfy Cosimo or any other man in any affair, and when he was Duke made no other wars than those necessary for defending himself. This to Cosimo was the source of very great vexation, since he realized he had endured labor and expense to make a man great who was thankless and deceitful. In addition, he knew that on account of his bodily infirmity he could not give to public and private affairs his earlier attention; hence he saw both of them going to ruin; for the city was damaged by the citizens, and his property by his employees and sons. All these things made the last years of his life pass in disquiet.

Nevertheless he died full of renown and with a very great name in the city and outside. All the citizens and all the Christian princes lamented his death with Piero his son; he was accompanied to his grave by all the citizens with the utmost splendor and buried in the Church of San Lorenzo; by public decree he was described on his monument as Father of his Country. If when writing of the things done by Cosimo, I have imitated those who write the lives of princes, not those who write general histories, nobody should be astonished; since he was a man rare in our city, I have been obliged with an unusual method to praise him.

CHAPTER 7

[The Duke of Milan occupies Genoa; the King of Naples destroys his rebellious barons; the Duke and Jacopo Piccinino. 1464–1465]

In these times, when Florence and Italy were in the condition I have mentioned, Louis the King of France was attacked in a very serious war which his barons carried on against him with the aid of Francis Duke of Brittany and Charles Duke of Burgundy. This was of such importance that he could not consider helping Duke Jean of Anjou in the affair of Genoa and of the Kingdom. Nevertheless, thinking Jean had need of aid from somebody, since the city of Savona remained in the power of the French, he made Francesco Duke of Milan her ruler and gave him to understand that, if he wished, with royal permission he could undertake a movement against Genoa. This offer was accepted by Francesco, who, by means of the reputation he derived from the King's friendship, and with the aid of the Adorni, made himself master of Genoa. To show that he was not ungrateful to the King for the benefits he had received, he sent to aid the King in France fifteen hundred cavalry led by his oldest son Galeazzo.

So here were Ferdinand of Aragon and Francesco Sforza, one Duke of Lombardy and ruler of Genoa, and the other King of all the Kingdom of Naples; having made a marriage alliance together, they considered how they might so establish their states that while they lived they could enjoy them in security and when they died leave them in due course to their heirs. To this end, they judged it necessary that the King should secure himself against those barons who had attacked him in Jean of Anjou's war, and that the Duke should strive to destroy the armies of Braccio's successors, natural enemies to his family. They had risen to a very high reputation under Jacopo Piccinino, now the first general in Italy. Since he had no territory, whoever had territory was forced to fear him, and especially the Duke, who, influenced by his own example, thought that he could not hold his dominion or leave it as a secure inheritance to his sons while Jacopo was alive.

Hence the King with all diligence sought an agreement with his barons, and used every device in securing himself against them; in this he had excellent success, because those princes, if they continued at war with the King, saw their ruin obvious, but if they made an agreement with him and relied on him, they were uncertain about it. Thus because men are always more inclined to try to elude an evil that is sure, the chief powers can therefore easily deceive the lesser ones. Those princes trusted in the peace of the King, since they saw the obvious dangers in war, and after they had put themselves in his hands, they were then destroyed by him in various ways and for various reasons. This frightened Jacopo Piccinino, who with his soldiers was at Sulmona; so in order to deprive the King of any chance to crush him, he negotiated with Duke Francesco, by means of his friends, about a reconcilement. When the Duke had made him the greatest offers he could, Jacopo decided to put himself into his hands; accompanied by a hundred horsemen, he went to visit the Duke in Milan.

CHAPTER 8

[Jacopo Piccinino treacherously slain. 1465]

Jacopo, under his father and with his brother, had carried on war a long time, first for Duke Filippo and then for the people of Milan, so that through long association he had in the city many friends and general good will, increased by present conditions, be, cause the Sforza family's prosperous fortune and present power had excited envy against them, while Jacopo's adversity and long absence had caused the Milanese to pity him and much desire to see him. These things were all revealed on his coming, because there were few of the nobility who did not meet him, and the streets where he passed were full of persons eager to see him; the name of his family was shouted everywhere. These honors hastened his ruin, because the Duke's desire to get rid of him increased along with his suspicion. And to be able to act under cover, he had Jacopo celebrate his wedding with Drusiana the Duke's natural daughter, long before betrothed to him. Then he arranged that Ferdinand should take Jacopo into his pay with the title of General of his soldiers and a hundred thousand florins for remuneration and expenses.

After this was settled, Jacopo, with a ducal ambassador and Drusiana his wife, went to Naples, where he was pleasantly and honorably received and for many days entertained with every sort of festivity. But when he asked permission to go to Sulmona, where his soldiers were, he was banqueted by the King in the Castle, and after the banquet he, with Francesco his son, was imprisoned and in a short time put to death. Likewise most of our Italian princes feared in others that military competence they did not possess, and destroyed it. Thus, since nobody possessed such competence, the princes exposed this land to the affliction which, not much later, wasted and tortured her.

CHAPTER 9

[The failure of the crusade and the death of Pope Pius; Duke Fran, cesco's death. 1465,1466]

Pope Pius in these days had settled the affairs of Romagna. Hence he thought the time suitable, since general peace had come, for rousing the Christians against the Turk, so he resumed those plans his predecessors had made. All the princes promised either money or men; especially Matthias King of Hungary and Charles Duke of Burgundy promised to be with him in person, since the Pope had made them leaders in the crusade. The Pontiff's hopes were so great that he left Rome and went to Ancona, where the army was directed to assemble. The Venetians had promised ships to take it into Slavonia. So many people gathered in that city after the arrival of the Pontiff that in a few days all the food in the city and all that could be brought from neighboring places was used up; hence everybody was suffering from hunger. Besides this, the Pope had no money to supply those who needed it and no arms to equip those who lacked them. Matthias and Charles did not appear, though the Venetians did send there an officer with some galleys, rather to show their splendor and to keep their word than actually to carry the army over the sea. Then the Pope, old and sick, died in the midst of those labors and vexations. After his death everybody returned home.

On the Pope's death, in the year 1465, Paul II, a Venetian by birth, was chosen to the papal throne. And so that almost all the princedoms of Italy should change their rulers, there also died, in the following year, Francesco Sforza Duke of Milan, after he had possessed that Dukedom for sixteen years; his son Galeazzo was declared Duke.

CHAPTER 10

[Dietisalvi Neroni advises Piero de'Medici to collect his debts; this makes Piero unpopular. 1466]

The death of this prince was a reason why the divisions in Florence became deeper and produced their effects more quickly. When Cosimo died, Piero his son, heir to the wealth and the position of his father, sent for Messer Dietisalvi Neroni, a man of high influence and well reputed among the citizens, in whom Cosimo had such faith that when he died he charged Piero that with respect to his property and his position he should conduct himself wholly according to the advice of that man. So Piero made known to Messer Dietisalvi Cosimo's trust in him, and wishing to obey his father after death as he had obeyed in life, Piero asked that man's advice on his inheritance and on the government of the city. To begin with his own property, Piero planned to have all the accounts of his investments brought and put in Messer Dietisalvi's hands, who thus could learn their order and disorder, and when he had learned could advise according to his wisdom. Messer Dietisalvi promised to apply diligence and fidelity in everything. When the accounts came and were well examined, he realized that in every part there was much disorder.

Being more affected by his own ambition than by his love for Piero and the old benefits received from Cosimo, Messer Dietisalvi imagined he could easily take away Piero's reputation and deprive him of the position his father had left him as though it were hereditary. Messer Dietisalvi, therefore, came to Piero with advice that seemed entirely honorable and reasonable, but under it ruin was hidden. He showed the disorder of Piero's affairs and the sum of money necessarily to be provided if he did not wish to lose, with his credit, the reputation of his property and of his position. Then he explained that Piero could not with more honor provide for his difficulties than by trying to collect the money owed to his father by many persons, both Florentines and others, because Cosimo, to gain partisans in Florence and friends outside, had been very liberal in sharing his property with everybody; for these reasons, therefore, the money for which he was creditor rose to a sum not small or of slight importance. To Piero the advice seemed good and honorable, since he wished to provide for his difficulties out of his own property. But as soon as he ordered that money to be collected, the citizens, as if he wished to take away their property, not to ask for his own, became angry and without restraint spoke ill of him and slandered him as ungrateful and avaricious.

CHAPTER 11

[*Feeling against Piero de' Medici. 1466*]

After that, when Messer Dietisalvi saw into what general and popular disfavor Piero had fallen through his advice, he allied himself with Messer Luca Pitti, Messer Agnolo Acciaiuoli and Niccolò Soderini; they determined to take from Piero his reputation and his position. These men were influenced by various reasons. Messer Luca wished to succeed to Cosimo's place, because he had become so great that he disdained having to show regard for Piero. Messer Dietisalvi, who realized that Messer Luca was not fit to be head of the government, thought that if Piero were removed, credit for everything would in a short time necessarily be given to himself. Niccolò Soderini loved to have the city live in freedom, governed according to the decision of the magistrates. Messer Agnolo had a special hatred for the Medici for the following reason. His son Raffaello long before had taken as his wife Lessandra de' Bardi, with a very large dowry. She, either because of her own defects or the shortcomings of others, was badly treated by her father-in-law and her husband, so that, moved by pity for the girl, Lorenzo di Larione, one of her relatives, accompanied by many armed men, one night took her from the house of Messer Agnolo. The Acciaiuoli complained about this wrong done them by the Bardi; the case was referred to Cosimo; he judged that the Acciaiuoli should restore her dowry to Lessandra, and that then any return to her husband should be left to the girl's own decision. To Messer Agnolo it appeared that Cosimo, in this judgment, had not dealt with him as a friend; so since he had been unable to revenge himself upon Cosimo, he determined to revenge himself upon his son.

These conspirators, nonetheless, in such a diversity of inclinations, made public the same cause, declaring that they wanted the city to be governed by the magistrates and not by the decision of a few. In addition to this, hatred against Piero and reasons for speaking ill of him were increased by the failure of many merchants at this time. Piero was publicly blamed for this because, since by trying against all expectation to get his money again, he had made them fail, to the disgrace and injury of the city. Added to this was the discussion about giving Clarice degli Orsini as wife to Lorenzo his eldest son. This gave everybody still more material for slandering him, saying that they plainly saw, since he was going to reject a Florentine marriage for his son, that the city no longer was big enough to hold him as a citizen; therefore he was preparing to seize the principate. He who does not desire his fellow citizens as relatives desires them as slaves, and therefore it is reasonable that he should not have them as friends. These leaders of the revolt believed they had the victory in their hands, because the larger part of the citizens, deceived by the name of liberty that the conspirators had taken for an ensign in order to give their affair an honorable appearance, followed them.

CHAPTER 12

[Festivities in Florence; dispute over an alliance with the Duke of Milan. 1466]

While these disputes were boiling in the city, some of those grieved by the discords between the citizens decided to attempt to quiet them with some new pleasure, because people with nothing to do often are the tool of him who is attempting to cause a revolution. To do away with idleness then, and to give men something to think about that would remove their thoughts from the government—a year already having gone by since Cosimo's death—they found an opportunity for the city to carry on a celebration and planned two festivals very splendid in comparison with those generally held there. One show represented the Three Kings who came from the East following the star that indicated the birth of Christ; this was so elaborate and splendid that the entire city was kept busy for many months in preparing and presenting it. The other was a tournament (for so they called a show representing a combat by mounted men) in which the leading young men of the city and the most renowned knights in Italy took part. Among the young men of Florence the highest reputation was gained by Lorenzo, Piero's eldest son, who not by favor but by worth carried off the first prize. After these shows had been presented, the citizens returned to their earlier thoughts, and each one followed his own opinion with more zeal than ever. From this resulted great differences and troubles, which two events greatly increased. One was that the *balìa's* authority ended; the other was the death of Francesco the Duke of Milan. As a result of the latter, Galeazzo the new Duke sent envoys to Florence to confirm the treaty that Francesco his father had with the city, in which, besides other things, it was laid down that every year there should be paid to that Duke a certain sum of money. The leaders opposed to the Medici, then, made this request their opportunity, and publicly opposed this policy in the councils, arguing that their alliance had been made not with Galeazzo but with Francesco. Therefore when Francesco was dead the obligation was dead; there was no reason for reviving it, because Galeazzo did not have Francesco's ability; hence they should not and could not hope for the same profit from an alliance; if from Francesco they had had little, from this man they would have less; any citizens who wished to employ him be-cause of his power were favoring something opposed to government by the people and to the city's freedom.

Piero, on the other hand, showed that it was not wise to lose through avarice a friendship so necessary; nothing was so likely to bring safety to the republic and to all Italy as an alliance with the Duke. The Venetians, seeing them united, would not hope to crush the Duke either through pretended friendship or open war; but they no sooner would hear that the Florentines were estranged from that Duke than they would have their weapons in their hands against him, and finding him young, new in his position and with-out friends, they could easily gain him over with either trickery or force; either method would cause the ruin of the Florentine republic.

CHAPTER 13
[*Conspiracy against Piero. 1466*]

These reasons were not accepted, and enmities soon showed themselves openly; each of the parties met by night in different companies, for the friends of the Medici met in the Crocetta, and their adversaries in the Pietà. The anti-Mediceans, eager for the ruin of Piero, had written down as favorable to their enterprise many of the citizens. And when, as at various times, they were together one night, they consulted especially on their way of going to work. Everybody hoped to reduce the power of the Medici, but they were divided on the method.

One party, more temperate and moderate, preferred that when the authority of the *balìa* was ended they should take measures to block its being taken up again. When this had been done, every-body intended that the councils and the magistrates should govern the city; thus in a short time Piero's influence would be destroyed. With the loss of his influence over the government, he would lose also his credit as a merchant, because his property was in such a condition that if by strong opposition they kept him from making use of the public funds, he would of necessity be ruined. If that hap-pened, there would be no more danger from him, and their liberty would be regained without exiles and without bloodshed, as every good citizen ought to desire. But if they tried to use force, they might run into very many dangers, because people will let a man fall when he falls of himself, but if he is pushed by somebody they hold him up. Besides this, so long as something contrary to law was not planned against him, he would not have cause to provide weapons and seek allies. If he nevertheless did so, he would be severely blamed and would excite in all men such suspicion that Piero himself would make his own ruin easier and would give his enemies new opportunity for crushing him.

Many others in the assembly did not favor this delay, declaring that time would favor him and not them, for if they decided to be satisfied with lawful measures, Piero would run no risk and they would run many risks; the magistrates, even though they were Piero's enemies, would let him remain in the city, and his friends—to the ruin of the anti-Mediceans, as in 1458—would make him prince. Hence if the advice given earlier was that of good men, this advice was that of wise men. Therefore, while men's spirits were stirred up against him he must be destroyed. The method of Piero's opponents should be to take arms inside the city and from outside to employ the Marquis of Ferrara, in order not to be without soldiers. Then when the lot allowed them a friendly Signoria, they should be prepared to make sure of Piero. At last they made this decision: to wait for the new Signoria and according to its attitude to conduct themselves.

Among these conspirators was Ser Niccolò Fedini, who served them as secretary. Attracted by a more certain hope, he revealed to Piero his enemies' efforts and carried him a list of the conspirators and of those whose names were written down as supporting them. Piero was shocked on seeing the number and stations of the citizens who were against him; after taking counsel with friends, he decided that he too would make a list of his friends. Having given the charge of this to some of those he most trusted, he found such variability and uncertainty in the minds of the citizens that many of those who were written down against him were also written down as his supporters.

CHAPTER 14

[*Niccolò Soderini. 1466*]

While affairs went on in this way, there came the time when the supreme magistracy was renewed, and Niccolò Soderini became

Gonfalonier of Justice. It was wonderful to see with how great a crowd not merely of honored citizens but of all the people he was accompanied to the Palace; and on the way a garland of olive was put on his head, to signify that on him the safety and the liberty of the city depended. This and many other experiences show that it is not a desirable thing to undertake either a magistracy or a princedom with an extraordinary reputation, because, since it is not possible to measure up to it with actions—for men desire more than they can get—at last it brings you dishonor and disgrace.

Messer Tommaso Soderini and Niccolò were brothers. Niccolò was more violent and spirited; Messer Tommaso wiser. The latter, who was very friendly to Piero, realizing the disposition of his brother, knew him to wish merely that the city should be free and that without harm to anybody the government should be established. Hence Tommaso encouraged Niccolò to make a new selection of eligibles, by means of which the bags would be filled with citizens who loved civic freedom; if this were done, it would bring about the establish-ment and security of the government without disturbance and with-out damage to anybody, according to his wish. Niccolò easily believed the advice of his brother and set himself to wasting the time of his magistracy in these vain dreams; the leaders of the conspirators, his friends, allowed him to waste it, since through envy they did not want the government to be renewed by the influence of Niccolò, and always believed that with another gonfalonier they would be in time to effect such a renewal. Finally the end of Niccolò's magistracy came; having begun many things and finished none of them, he left his office with dishonor much greater than the honor with which he had taken it.

CHAPTER 15

[The parties take up arms; Piero's party is superior. 1466]

This evidence made the party of Piero more vigorous, for his friends were confirmed in their hope and those who were neutral joined them. So since the parties were equal, many months were spent without further disturbance. Nonetheless Piero's party was always gaining more power, so that his enemies woke up and met together, and what they had been unable or unwilling to do by means of the magistrates and easily, they imagined they could do through force. They decided to assassinate Piero, who was ill at Careggi. To this end they planned to have the Marquis of Ferrara come with his soldiers to the city, and when Piero was dead, they intended to come armed to the Public Square and cause the Signoria to establish a government according to their will, for though not all of it was friendly to them, they hoped to make the part that was opposed yield through fear. Messer Dietisalvi, in order better to conceal his intention, often visited Piero and talked with him of the unity of the city and advised him. All these plots had been revealed to Piero; and in addition Messer Domenico Martelli informed him that Francesco Neroni, the brother of Messer Dietisalvi, had urged him to join them, demonstrating to him the victory as sure and the undertaking as certain to succeed.

As a result, Piero determined to be the first to take arms and to use the opportunity offered by the dealings of his adversaries with the Marquis of Ferrara. He pretended, therefore, that he had received a letter from Messer Giovanni Bentivoglio, the chief man in Bologna, which informed him that the Marquis of Ferrara was on the River Albo with soldiers and was saying publicly that he was going to Florence. On this notice, Piero took arms and in the midst of a great multitude of armed men came to Florence. Then all those who adhered to his party armed themselves; the opposing party did the same; but that of Piero was in better order, since his followers were prepared but their opponents were not yet in order according to their plan. Messer Dietisalvi, since his mansion was near that of Piero, did not think himself safe there; he kept going to the Palace to encourage the Signoria to make Piero lay down his arms, and kept visiting Messer Luca to keep him firm in their plans.

Among them all, more active than any other was Niccolò Soderini. He took up arms and was followed by almost all the lower classes in the quarter where he lived. Then he went to Messer Luca's mansion and besought him to mount his horse and come to the Public Square in aid of the Signoria, which was on their side; he declared that there was no doubt of victory. Then he begged him not to allow himself, by remaining in his house, to be either basely overcome by the armed enemy or shamefully deceived by the unarmed; in the future—when the time for action had gone by—he would repent not having acted. If he wished Piero's ruin through war, he could easily have it; if he wished peace, he was better off when in a position to give rather than accept conditions. These words did not stir Messer Luca, who had already abandoned his purpose and changed his course as a result of Piero's promises of new alliances and new conditions; indeed a granddaughter of his had already been joined in marriage with Giovanni Tornabuoni. So he exhorted Niccolò to lay down his arms and return to his house, because it should be enough for him that the city was ruled by the magistrates. So she would continue to be ruled. Every man should lay down his arms, for the Signors, most of whom favored them, would be judges of all disputes. Unable, then, to change Messer Luca's opinion, Niccolò went home, but first he said: "I cannot, since I am alone, do my city any good, but I certainly can foretell misery for her. This decision of yours will make our city lose her liberty, and make you lose power and wealth, and me and others lose the privilege of living in our native city."

CHAPTER 16

[Piero justifies his conduct; he wishes only to live in peace. 1466]

The Signoria in this confusion had closed the Palace and shut itself up with its magistrates, not showing favor to either party. The citizens, especially those who had followed the party of Messer Luca, seeing Piero armed and his adversaries unarmed, went to thinking not how they could attack Piero but how they could become his friends. Hence the leading citizens, heads of the factions, gathered in the Palace in the presence of the Signoria, where they discussed many things relating to the government of the city, many about her reunification. Piero, being an invalid, could not be present. Hence all agreed to go to his mansion to visit him except Niccolò Soderini, who entrusted his children and his property to Messer Tommaso and went to his farm to await there the end of the affair, which he expected to be unlucky for himself and damaging for his city.

When the other citizens, then, had arrived at Piero's house, one of them, to whom the speaking had been entrusted, lamented the disorders in the city, making plain that he was most to blame who had first taken arms; yet not knowing what Piero, who had been the first to take them, wanted, they had come to learn his will, and if it was in harmony with the good of the city, they were going to follow it. To these words Piero answered that not he who first takes arms is the cause of strife, but he who first gives cause for them to be taken.[1] If they would think further on what their ways toward him had been, they would wonder less about what he had done to save himself; because they would see that meetings by night, enrollments, plans to take from him the city and his life had forced him to arm. His not having moved those arms from his dwelling gave a clear indication of his purpose, namely, that he had taken them not to attack others but to defend himself. He did not wish anything else, he did not ask anything else than his own security and quiet; he had never given a sign of wishing anything else, because when the authority of the *balìa* expired, he never considered any extralegal method for turning it over to himself; he was quite satisfied that the magistrates should rule the city if that was satisfactory to his audience.

Further, they ought to recall that Cosimo and his sons were able to live in Florence in honor, with the *balìa* and without the *balìa*; for in 1458 not his family but they themselves had once more grasped it; if now they did not want it, he too did not want it; but this was not enough for them, because he had seen that they did not believe they could remain in Florence if he remained there. A situation, truly, that he would never have dreamed of, much less believed: that his friends and those of his father would not believe they could live in Florence with him, since he had never given any indication that he himself was other than a quiet and peaceful man. Then he turned his speech to Messer Dietisalvi and to his brothers, who were present, and rebuked them, with words serious and full of anger, for the benefits they had received from Cosimo, the faith he had had in them, and their great ingratitude. His words were of such power that some of his hearers were so affected that if Piero had not checked them they would have attacked the Neroni with weapons.

At last Piero declared himself ready to approve all that they and the Signoria might decide; he asked nothing else than to live quietly and safely. Besides this many things were spoken of but at the time nothing was decided, except that generally the city must be reformed and new organization given to the government.

1. *These words fit Machiavelli's frequent praise of the foresight that sees an ill in the distance and provides against it. The speech of the Florentine citizen is designed to enable Piero to make this reply.*

CHAPTER 17

[Triumph of Piero; exile and death of his enemies. 1466]

In those days the Gonfalonier of Justice was Bernardo Lotti, a man Piero did not trust. Piero therefore decided that while Bernardo was in office he should not attempt anything; this he did not think of much importance, since the end of the term of office was near. But when there came the choice of Signors who were to sit in September and October, in the year 1466, the choice for the highest office was Roberto Lioni. As soon as he had assumed office, since everything else was ready, he called the people into the Public Square and made a new *balía*, all of the party of Piero, which a little later chose the magistrates according to the will of the new government.

These actions frightened the leaders of the hostile faction. So Messer Agnolo Acciaiuoli fled to Naples, Messer Dietisalvi Neroni and Niccolò Soderini to Venice; Messer Luca Pitti remained in Florence, trusting in the promises made to him by Piero and in the new marriage alliance. Those who had fled were proclaimed exiles, all the family of the Neroni was scattered, and Messer Giovanni di Nerone, then Archbishop of Florence, to escape greater ill chose voluntary exile in Rome. Many other citizens, who speedily de- parted, were banished to various places. Nor was this enough, for Piero's supporters prepared a procession to thank God for the govern- ment's preservation and the city's reunion. During the solemnities of this some citizens were arrested and tortured, and then part of them put to death and part sent into exile.

In this change of things there was no instance so striking as that of Messer Luca Pitti, for he quickly realized the difference there is between victory and loss, between dishonor and honor. His mansion was in complete solitude, though earlier it had been thronged by countless citizens. In the streets his friends and relatives were afraid not merely to accompany him but even to greet him, because some of them had been deprived of their offices, some of their property, and all equally were threatened. The splendid buildings that he had begun were deserted by the builders; the favors that had been done him earlier were changed into injuries, the honors into accusations, so that many of those who had freely given him something of great value asked it back as something loaned; those who were wont to praise him to the skies censured him as a man ungrateful and violent. So he repented, too late, of not believing Niccolò Soderini and seeking rather to die honored, sword in hand, than to live dishonored among his victorious enemies.

CHAPTER 18

[Agnolo Acciaiuoli's letter and Piero de'Medici's reply. 1466]

Those who were driven out of Florence at once considered together various ways for regaining a city which they had been unable to hold. Messer Agnolo Acciaiuoli, however, being at Naples, decided before he planned any rebellion to test Piero's purpose, to see if he could hope for reconciliation. So he wrote a letter to this effect: "I laugh at the sports of Fortune and how at her pleasure she makes friends become enemies, enemies become friends. You can remember that when your father was exiled I was more concerned about the injury to him than about any danger to myself; as a result I lost the privilege of living in my native city and came close to losing my life. While living under Cosimo, never did I fail to honor and favor your house; nor after his death have I had any intention of attacking you. It is true that your bad health and the tender age of your sons so dismayed me that I judged we would be wise in giving such form to the government that after your death our native city would not be ruined. This belief accounts for whatever I have done, not as against you but for the good of my native city. My actions, however mistaken, deserve to be canceled by my good intentions and my past deeds. By no means can I believe that after your house had for so long found in me such great fidelity, I shall not now find in you compassion, and that my many deserts are going to be canceled by a single transgression."

Piero on receiving this letter replied thus: "Your laughing out there is the reason I am not weeping, for if you were laughing in Florence, I should be weeping in Naples. I grant that you wished good to my father, and you will grant that from him you received good, so that your obligation was much more than ours, in so far as deeds are to be valued higher than words. Since in the past you have been rewarded for your good, you ought not now to wonder if you get the proper recompense for your evil. Nor does love of country excuse you, because there never will be anybody who will believe that this city has been less loved and developed by the Medici than by the Acciaiuoli. So live dishonored out there, since to live honored here you have not known how."

CHAPTER 19

[Plots by the exiles; Giovan Francesco Strozzi; aid sought from Venice. 1466]

In despair, then, of being able to get pardon, Messer Agnolo came to Rome and joined the Archbishop and other exiles, and with the strongest efforts they could make they tried to destroy the credit of the Medici business carried on in Rome. Against this Piero provided with difficulty, yet, since he was aided by his friends, their plan failed. Messer Dietisalvi and Niccolò Soderini, on the other hand, with all diligence tried to stir up the Venetian Senate against their native city, judging that if a new war was made on the Florentines, they could not resist, since their government was new and hated.

In Ferrara at that time there lived Giovan Francesco, son of Messer Palla Strozzi, who in the changes of 1434 had been driven from Florence with his father. He had great credit and in comparison with the other merchants was thought very rich. These new rebels showed Giovan Francesco with what ease they could get back into their country if the Venetians would undertake the business; and they believed the Venetians would gladly do so, if something could be contributed to the expense, though otherwise they doubted it. Giovan Francesco, who longed to revenge himself for the injuries he had received, easily put faith in what these men advised and said he was glad to join in their attempt with all his resources.

As a result, they went to the Doge and complained to him of their exile, which they said they were enduring for no other fault than that of wanting their native city to live according to her laws, and wanting the magistrates, and not a few citizens only, to have power; for Piero de'Medici and others, his followers, who were accustomed to live like tyrants, had taken arms with trickery, with trickery had made them lay theirs down, and then with trickery had driven them from their native city. Not content with this, they had used God as a means to wrong many others who had remained in the city because of the pledge that had been given; and in order that God might be a sharer in their treacheries, many citizens had been arrested and put to death in the midst of public and holy ceremonies and solemn prayers—an act very sacrilegious and wicked. In order to avenge this, they did not know where to come with more hope than to that Senate which, because it had always been free, ought to have pity on those who had lost their liberty. They were exhorting free men against tyrants, then, pious men against impious; and they should remember that the Medici family had taken from them their authority over Lombardy when Cosimo, contrary to the will of the other citizens, aided and supported Francesco against that Senate; so that if a just cause did not move them, a just hatred and a just wish to avenge themselves ought to move them.

CHAPTER 20

[*A feeble war between Venice and Florence; the battle of Molinella; peace destroys the hopes of the exiles. 1467*]

These last words affected all that Senate, and they decided that Bartolommeo Colleoni their general should attack Florentine territory. So as soon as possible the army was assembled, and was joined by Ercole da Este, sent by Borso Marquis of Ferrara. At the first attack, since the Florentines were not ready, they burned the village of Dovadola and did some damage in the country round about. But the Florentines, after the party hostile to Piero had been driven out, made a new league with Galeazzo Duke of Milan and with King Ferdinand, and employed Frederick Count of Urbino as their general. Hence, being ready with friends, they put a lower estimate on their enemies; for Ferdinand sent Alfonso his oldest son, and Galeazzo came in person, each with suitable forces. They all assembled at Castrocaro, a town of the Florentines situated at the base of the mountains that slope down from Tuscany into Romagna. The enemy, meanwhile, had retired toward Imola, and so between one army and the other there followed, according to the habits of those times, some slight combats. Neither one or the other attacked or besieged cities nor gave any chance to its enemy to come to battle, but each one remained in its tents and conducted itself with astonˏ ishing cowardice.

The Florentines resented this because they saw themselves afflicted by a war in which much was spent and little could be hoped for; then the magistrates complained about it to the citizens assigned to that campaign as commissioners. The latter replied that the cause of everything was Duke Galeazzo, who, having much authority and little experience, did not know how to make useful plans and had no faith in those who did know; and that it was impossible, so long as he remained in the army, for anything effective or useful to be done. So the Florentines gave that Duke to understand that it was conˏ venient and very useful to them that he had come in person to aid them, because such a report alone was enough to frighten the enemy. Nevertheless they estimated his safety and that of his state much higher than their own advantage, because if his dukedom were safe, they believed everything else would be prosperous, but if it suffered, they feared every sort of adversity. They did not, therefore, judge it very safe for him to be long absent from Milan, since he was new in that government and had neighbors who were powerful and to be suspected, so that whoever wished to plot anything against him could do it easily. Hence they encouraged him to return to his state, leaving part of his soldiers for their defense. This advice pleased Galeazzo, who without further consideration returned to Milan.

When the generals of the Florentines, then, were without this hindrance, in order to show that the reason they had given for their slow movement was the true one, they approached closer to the enemy. Thus they came to a formal combat, which lasted half a day, without either side yielding. Nevertheless, nobody was killed; merely some horses were wounded and some prisoners taken on either side.[1] Winter had already come and the time when the armies were acˏ customed to retire to winter quarters; so Messer Bartolommeo withˏ drew to Ravenna and the Florentine soldiers into Tuscany; those of the King and the Duke each retired into the states of their lords.

But since as a result of this attack no movement had been obˏ served in Florence, such as the Florentine exiles had promised, and since there was no money to pay the soldiers, a truce was discussed

---

1. As usual, Machiavelli makes the battles of the condottieri *absurd by reducing their small losses to nothing. Cf.* HISTORY OF FLORENCE *4. 6; 5. 33. This combat, not named by Machiavelli, is that of Molinella (Mulinella).*

and after not much negotiation it was settled. Hence the Florentine exiles, deprived of all hope, left for various places. Messer Dietisalvi retired to Ferrara, where he was received and supported by the Marquis Borso; Niccolò Soderini went to Ravenna, where with a little pension supplied by the Venetians he grew old and died. He was considered a man just and courageous, but uncertain and slow in making up his mind. This caused him, when Gonfalonier of Justice, to lose that chance for victory which later, when he was deprived of it, he wished to regain and could not.

CHAPTER 21

[Partisan oppression by Piero's friends during his illness; the festivities for Lorenzo's marriage. 1468]

When peace had come, those Florentine citizens who were victorious—since they could not believe they had won unless with injuries of every sort they persecuted not merely their enemies but even those whom their party suspected—worked upon Bardo Altoviti, who was serving as Gonfalonier of Justice, to deprive many more citizens of their offices and many others of the privilege of living in the city. This policy added to their power and to the terror of their victims. This power they used without hesitation, conducting themselves as though God and Fortune had given them the city to be plundered. Of their actions Piero knew about only a few, and against those, since he was overcome by his chronic disease, he had no recourse; his body was so stiffened that he could make use of no member other than his tongue. So he could do nothing except admonish them and beseech them to live as good citizens and dwell in a city that was preserved rather than destroyed.

To cheer the city up, he determined to celebrate with splendor the marriage of his son Lorenzo, whom he had united with Clarice, of the Orsini family. This wedding exhibited the pomp of entertainment and every other splendor befitting so great a man; many days were spent in new sorts of dances, in banquets and in attending ancient dramas. Besides these things, in order to show further the greatness of the Medici house and of the state, there were two military spectacles. One, made up of men on horseback, represented a combat in the field; the other exhibited the storming of a town. These spectacles were carried out with the most extraordinary arrangement and excellence possible.

CHAPTER 22

[*Italian affairs; Sixtus IV becomes Pope. 1468–1471*]

While things were going on in this way in Florence, the rest of Italy lived quietly but in great fear of the power of the Turk, who in his campaigns continued to fight the Christians and had taken Negropont, with great disgrace and injury to the Christian name. At this time Borso Marquis of Ferrara died, and Ercole his brother succeeded him. Sigismondo of Rimini, a lifelong enemy of the Church, died and left as heir to his state Roberto, his natural son, then one of the most skilful generals in Italy.

Pope Paul died, and as his successor Sixtus IV was chosen, earlier known as Francesco da Savona, a man of very humble and lowly family, but because of his abilities he had become general of the Order of Saint Francis and then a cardinal. This Pontiff was the first to show what a Pope could do, and how many things earlier called sins could be hidden under the papal authority. He had in his household Piero and Girolamo, whom everybody believed to be his sons; nonetheless he cloaked them with other more decent names. Piero, because he was a priest, he brought to the dignity of the cardinalate, with the title of San Sisto. To Girolamo, Pope Sixtus gave the city of Forlì, taking her from Antonio Ordelaffi, whose ancestors had for a long time been rulers of that city. This ambitious way of acting made the Pope more esteemed by the princes of Italy, and everybody tried to make himself his friend; and for that reason the Duke of Milan gave his natural daughter Caterina to Girolamo as his wife, and for her dower the city of Imola, of which he had deprived Taddeo degli Alidosi.

Between this Duke and King Ferdinand a new marriage alliance was also made, for Elisabella, the daughter of Alfonso the King's oldest son, was united with Gian Galeazzo the Duke's oldest son.

CHAPTER 23

[Piero rebukes the rapacious rulers of Florence; his death. 1469]

Meanwhile life in Italy was very quiet, and the chief care of those princes was to watch one another and to make themselves secure against one another with marriages, new friendships, and alliances.

Nevertheless in the midst of peace Florence was severely tormented by her citizens, for Piero, hindered by his sickness, could not resist their ambition. Nonetheless, to unburden his conscience and to see if he could make them ashamed, he called them all to his house and spoke to them to this effect: "I would never have believed that there could come a time when the ways and habits of my friends would bring me to such a pass that I should love and mourn for my enemies, and victory would turn to defeat; because I thought I had as associates men who would set some limit or measure to their greed, and that it would be enough for them to live in their native city secure and honored and, besides, revenged on their enemies. But I know now that I have greatly deceived myself, since I little realized the natural ambition of all men, and still less yours. It does not suffice you to be leaders in so large a city, and for you who are so few to have those offices, dignities, and advantages with which earlier many citizens were wont to be honored; it does not suffice you to divide among yourselves the goods of your enemies; it does not suffice you to distress all the others with taxes, while you, free from them, have all the public profit, and distress everybody with every sort of injury. You plunder your neighbor of his goods, you sell justice, you escape civil lawsuits, you oppress peaceful men, and the arrogant you make powerful. I do not believe that in all Italy there are so many instances of violence and avarice as in this city. Then if this our native city has given us life, why do we take it from her? Has she made us victorious so that we can destroy her? Does she honor us so that we can disgrace her? I promise you, by that faith that ought to be given and received by good men, that if you continue to conduct yourselves in such a way that I am forced to repent having been victorious, I too will conduct myself in such a way that you will repent of having used your victory badly."

Those citizens according to the time and the place replied suitably; nonetheless, they did not draw back from their wicked actions. So

Piero secretly had Messer Agnolo Acciaiuoli come to Cafaggiuolo, and spoke with him at length on the conditions of the city. And it cannot at all be doubted that if he had not been interrupted by death, he would have brought back all the exiles to their native city, in order to restrain the greed of those within her.

But these his most honorable thoughts were thwarted by death. Overcome by the suffering of his body and the distress of his spirit, he died in the fifty-third year of his age. His ability and goodness his city did not have opportunity altogether to recognize, because he had been accompanied by Cosimo his father almost to the end of his life, and those few years during which he survived him were wasted in civil dissensions and in sickness. Piero was buried in the Church of San Lorenzo, near his father; and his funeral was conducted with the pomp that so great a citizen deserved. He left two sons, Lorenzo and Giuliano, who gave everybody hope that they were going to be men most useful to the republic, but nonetheless their youth dismayed everybody.

CHAPTER 24

[*Tommaso Soderini supports the young Medici. 1469*]

In Florence among the first citizens of the ruling party and by far superior to the others was Messer Tommaso Soderini, whose prudence and influence were known not merely in Florence but among all the princes of Italy. After Piero's death, the whole city rendered respect to Messer Tommaso, and many citizens visited him in his mansion as the head of the city; many princes wrote to him. But he, who was prudent and very well understood his fortune and that of his house, did not answer the letters of the princes, and gave the citizens to understand that they must visit not his mansion but that of the Medici.

To show with action what he had explained with his exhortations, he brought together all the leaders of the noble families in the convent of Sant' Antonio, where he had Lorenzo and Giuliano de' Medici also come. There in a long and serious speech he discussed the conditions of the city, those of Italy, and the dispositions of her princes. He ended by saying that if they wished Florence to live united and in peace, secure from divisions within and from wars without, they needed to respect these young men and to maintain the reputation of that house; men never complain about doing the things they are in the habit of doing; new things, as quickly they are taken up, so quickly they are dropped; to support a power that with length of time has suppressed envy is always easier than to raise up a new one that for many reasons can easily be superseded. After Messer Tommaso, Lorenzo spoke. Though young, he showed so much seriousness and modesty that he gave everybody hope of his being what he later became. So before they left that place, those citizens swore to take the young Medici as their sons, and the youths swore to take the citizens as fathers. Since, then, the citizens had come to this conclusion, Lorenzo and Giuliano were honored as the chief men in the government; and the citizens did not depart from the advice of Messer Tommaso.

CHAPTER 25

[Bernardo Nardi plans to cause rebellion in Prato and Pistoia. 1470]

While the Florentines were living very quietly inside and outside the city, without any war to disturb the common quiet, an unexpected disturbance came up, like a forewarning of future calamities. Among the families which fell with the party of Messer Luca Pitti was that of the Nardi, for Salvestro and his brothers, heads of that family, were first sent into exile and then, because of the war started by Bartolommeo Colleoni, were declared rebels. Among them was Bernardo, Salvestro's brother, a young man energetic and courageous. Unable to endure exile because of his poverty, and not seeing any way for his return when peace was made, he determined to attempt something that would give cause for a new war, knowing that many times a weak beginning brings forth mighty effects, since men are readier to carry along a thing already started than to start something themselves.

Bernardo was well acquainted in Prato and very well in the country around Pistoia, and especially with the members of the Palandra family, which though rural abounded in men and was, like the other Pistolese, brought up in arms and in blood. He knew they were discontented, because in their quarrels they had been badly treated by the Florentine magistrates. He knew besides this the dispositions of the Pratese, who felt that they were proudly and greedily governed; and he knew the ill will of some of them against the Florentine government. All these things, then, gave him hope that by making Prato rebel he could kindle a fire in Tuscany, around which so many men would assemble to keep it going that those attempting to put it out would not be sufficient. He imparted his idea to Messer Dietisalvi and asked what aid, if he should succeed in taking Prato, he could expect through his means from the princes. To Messer Dietisalvi the enterprise seemed very dangerous and al/most impossible of success. Nevertheless, seeing that through an/other man's peril he could again tempt Fortune, he encouraged him in the deed, promising him perfectly sure help from Bologna and Ferrara, if he could manage to hold and defend Prato for at least fifteen days. Bernardo, full of hope for success because of this prom/ise, thereupon went secretly to Prato; when he imparted the matter to several citizens, he found them strongly inclined to it. The same feeling and wish he found also in the Palandra family. So when they had agreed on the time and the method, Bernardo gave full information to Messer Dietisalvi.

CHAPTER 26

[Bernardo occupies Prato but cannot rouse the people. 1470]

The podestà of Prato for the people of Florence was Cesare Petrucci. Such governors of cities are in the habit of keeping the keys of the gates; then, especially in times when there is no suspicion, if anybody in the city asks for them to go out or to come in at night, they give them to him. Bernardo, who knew this custom, just before daybreak, with members of the Palandra family and about a hundred armed men, presented himself at the gate that looks toward Pistoia; those inside who knew about the matter were also armed. One of them asked the podestà for the keys, pretending that a citizen was asking for them in order to get in. The podestà, who on such a request could have no ground for suspicion, sent one of his servants with them. The conspirators took them away from him as soon as they were at some distance from the Palace. When the gate was open, Bernardo and his armed men were brought inside. According to their plan they then divided into two parts, one of which, guided by Salvestro Pratese, seized the citadel; the other, together with

Bernardo, took the Palace; Cesare with all his staff was given in charge to some of them. Then they raised an alarm and went through the city shouting the word "Liberty." Day had already appeared, and at that noise many of the people ran to the Public Square; when they heard that the Castle and the Palace had been seized and the podestà and his men made prisoners, they wondered what could have caused this event.

The eight citizens who held the highest rank in that city met in their palace to consult on what was to be done. But Bernardo with his followers, having once made a circuit through the city and seen that he was followed by nobody, when he heard that the Eight were meeting, went to them and said that the reason for his enterprise was that he wished to free them and their country from slavery, and that it would be a great glory to them if they took arms and went along with him in this glorious undertaking, from which they would gain lasting tranquillity and eternal fame. He reminded them of their ancient liberty and their present condition, and showed them that aid was certain if only for a very few days they would resist whatever forces the Florentines got together. He affirmed that he had support in Florence, which would appear as soon as news reached the city that Prato was united to follow him. The Eight were not moved by these words. They replied that they did not know whether Florence lived free or in slavery; to learn such a thing did not concern them; but they did know well that for their part they wished no other liberty than to serve those magistrates who ruled Florence, from whom they had never received such injury that they needed to take arms against them. Hence they exhorted him to liberate the podestà, free the city from his men, and withdraw speedily from that danger into which he had so imprudently entered.

Bernardo was not frightened by these words, but decided to see if fear would move the Pratese, since prayers did not move them; so to terrify them he decided to put Cesare to death; taking him from prison, he ordered him to be hanged at the windows of the Palace. Cesare was already near the windows, with the noose around his neck, when he saw Bernardo, who was urging on his death. Turning to him he said: "Bernardo, you are putting me to death, in the belief that then the Pratese will follow you; but it will come out the opposite for you, because the reverence of this people for the officials whom the Florentine people send here is so great that when they see this outrage done to me, such hatred will be roused against you that it will ruin you. So not my death but my life can be the cause of your victory, for if I order them to do what seems best to you, they will obey me more readily than you; when I carry out your designs, you secure your purpose." Since Bernardo had no plans, he ac/ cepted this advice as prudent; so he commanded him, going upon a balcony that overlooked the Public Square, to order the people to obey Bernardo. When Cesare had done this, he was put back in prison.

CHAPTER 27
[*Bernardo is defeated and captured. 1470*]

The weakness of the conspirators was already revealed. Hence many Florentines who lived in the city gathered together, among whom was Messer Giorgio Ginori, Knight of Rhodes. He was the first to use arms against the invaders. He attacked Bernardo, who was rushing about in the Public Square, now begging, now threat/ ening the people, if they did not follow and obey him. When he was attacked by many who followed Messer Giorgio, he was wounded and captured. When this was done, the podestà was easily freed and the other rebels overcome. Since they were few and divided into several parties, they were almost all captured or killed.

To Florence, in the meantime, a rumor of this event had come— much bigger than what had happened, since it reported Prato taken, the podestà and his staff killed, the town full of enemies, and Pistoia under arms, with many of its citizens in that conspiracy. Hence the Palace quickly was full of citizens, and they met with the Signoria for consultation. Roberto Sanseverino, a general of very high repu/ tation in war, was then in Florence; so they decided to send him, with as many men as he could assemble, to Prato; they charged him to approach the town and get special information on the affair, applying to it such remedies as occurred to his prudence. Roberto had gone only a little beyond the town of Campi when he was met by a messenger from Cesare, who announced that Bernardo was taken, his companions put to flight and killed, and all disturbance quieted. So he returned to Florence. A little later Bernardo was brought there. When he was examined by the magistrates on the facts and his undertaking was found weak, he said he had acted because, having decided rather to die in Florence than to live in exile, he wished that his death should at least be accompanied by some action worth remembering.

CHAPTER 28

[*Luxury in Florence; the visit of the Duke of Milan.* 1471]

After this disturbance had arisen and been put down almost at the same time, the citizens returned to their usual manner of living, thinking to enjoy without any reservation the government they had established and made firm. As a result there appeared in the city those evils that usually are generated in time of peace, for the young men, more unrestrained than had been customary, spent without measure on dress, on banquets, on similar luxuries; and being with⁄out occupation, they wasted on gambling and whores their time and their property. Their ambition was to appear magnificent in their clothing, and to use speech that was pithy and clever; he who most deftly nipped the others was the smartest and most highly regarded. Such habits as these gained added strength from the courtiers of the Duke of Milan, who with his wife and all his ducal court, to satisfy a vow as some said, came to Florence, where he was welcomed with the splendor befitting so great a prince and so great a friend of the city. Then people saw—a thing up to that time never before seen in our city—that although it was the Lenten season, in which the Church orders that there shall be fasting without the eating of meat, his entire court, without regard for the Church or for God, dined on meat. And because many pageants were arranged to honor him— among which, in the Church of Santo Spirito, was presented the giving of the Holy Spirit to the Apostles—and because, as a result of the many fires that are lighted during such a celebration, that church burned up, it was believed by many that God in anger against us had wished to show that sign of His wrath. If, then, that Duke found the city of Florence full of courtier⁄like luxury and of customs contrary to all well⁄ordered commonwealths, he left her much more so. Hence good citizens thought it was necessary to put a check to it; so with new laws they set a limit to clothing, to funerals, to banquets.

CHAPTER 29

[Trouble in Volterra over the alum mines. 1472]

In the midst of such great peace, a new and unexpected disturbance came about in Tuscany. In the territory of Volterra, some of the citizens found an alum mine. Realizing its value, they associated themselves with some citizens of Florence and made them sharers in the profits from the mine, in order to be aided with money and protected with influence. As usually happens in new undertakings, the people of Volterra paid little attention to this at the beginning, but in time, after its value was realized, they tried, too late and without result, to apply a remedy to a thing which at the right time could easily have been remedied. They discussed the matter in their councils, declaring that an industry situated on public lands could not properly be turned to private gain. They sent envoys to Florence about it. The case was referred to some citizens, who, either because they were bribed by the mine company or because they judged it right, ruled that the people of Volterra were unjust in attempting to deprive their citizens of their property and business; therefore those alum mines belonged to private persons, not to the people; yet it was proper that every year a certain amount of money should be paid, in sign of recognizing the people as superior.

This reply did not lessen the hatreds and disturbances in Volterra but made them grow greater; no other matter was discussed not merely in their councils but in the whole city; the generality asked for what they thought had been taken from them, and individuals wished to keep what they had earlier gained and what later had been confirmed to them by the judgment of the Florentines. Hence in these disputes one citizen of standing in that city, called Il Pecorino, was killed, and after him many others who took his side, and their houses were sacked and burned. Carried along by that same violence, the mob scarcely refrained from the death of the officials who were there on behalf of the Florentine people.

CHAPTER 30

[Force used against Volterra. 1472]

After this first insult, they decided before anything else to send envoys to Florence. These made it plain that if the Signors there would keep the old agreements, the Volterrani likewise would keep their city in her old subjection. The reply was much debated. Messer Tommaso Soderini advised that it would be best to welcome the Volterrani in whatever way they wished to return, since he believed it not the time to build a fire so close that it could burn our own house. For he feared the disposition of the Pope, and the power of the King, and did not rely on the friendship of the Venetians or on that of the Duke, because he did not know how much fidelity there was in one and how much strength in the other. He brought up that well-known saying: "Better a lean truce than a fat victory."[1] On the other hand Lorenzo de'Medici, believing he had an opportunity to show how much he could accomplish with advice and prudence—being greatly encouraged to do so by those who envied the influence of Messer Tommaso—advised that they undertake a campaign and punish the arrogance of the Volterrani with arms, declaring that if with some noteworthy punishment they were not penalized, others without any respect or fear would have no hesitation about doing the same thing for the slightest reasons. When the enterprise was decided on, then, the reply was given to the Volterrani that they could not ask for the observance of those conditions that they themselves had broken, and therefore they either must put themselves in the power of that Signoria or expect war.

When the ambassadors had returned to Volterra with this reply, then, the Volterrani prepared for defense, fortifying their city and sending to all the Italian princes to ask for help. But few listened to them; only the Sienese and the Lord of Piombino gave them any hope of assistance. The Florentines, on the other hand, thinking that the essential requirement for victory was speed, got together ten thousand infantry and two thousand cavalry, who, under the leader-ship of Frederick the Lord of Urbino, appeared in the rural territory of Volterra and easily took it all. They then laid siege to the city, which, being situated in a high place and almost cut off on every

1. *Cf.* DISCOURSES 2. 27.

side, could not be attacked except from the direction of the Church of Sant' Alessandro. The Volterrani had hired for their defense about a thousand soldiers, who, seeing the vigorous siege the Florentines were carrying on and having no hope that they could resist it, were slow in defense and very quick in the injuries they did every day to the Volterrani. So those poor citizens were attacked by their enemies from without and afflicted by their friends from within. Hence despairing of their safety, they considered negotiation; not achieving anything better, they gave themselves into the hands of the commissioners.

These had the gates opened, and having brought in the greater part of the army, went to the palace where the chief officials were and commanded them to return to their houses. On the way, one of the soldiers, in contempt, plundered one of them. From this beginning, since men are readier to evil than to good, came the devastation and sack of that city, which for all of one day was robbed and plundered. Neither women nor holy places were spared, and the soldiers, both those who had badly defended them and those who had attacked them, despoiled them of their property.

The news of this victory was received by the Florentines with very great pleasure; and because it had been altogether Lorenzo's undertaking, he rose to a very high reputation. So one of his more intimate friends reproved Messer Tommaso Soderini for his advice, asking him: "What do you say, now that Volterra is taken?" Messer Tommaso replied: "To me she seems lost, because if you had taken her on terms, you would have gained from her profit and security, but since you will have to keep her by force, in adverse times she will bring you weakness and trouble, and in peaceful times loss and expense."

CHAPTER 31

[*Rivalry and suspicions in Italy. Sixtus IV. 1473–1474*]

In these times the Pope, eager to keep the cities of the Church in subjection, had Spoleto sacked, since on account of factions within her she had rebelled. Later, because Città di Castello was likewise mutinous, he had her besieged. The prince in that city was Niccolò Vitelli; he was a close friend of Lorenzo de'Medici, so that from the latter he was not without aid, which was not enough to defend

Niccolò but quite enough to sow between Sixtus and the Medici the first seeds of enmity, which a little later brought forth very evil fruit.

The appearance of this fruit would not have been long delayed if Frate Piero, Cardinal of Santo Sisto, had not died, because when this cardinal made a circuit of Italy and visited Venice and Milan, with the excuse of paying his respects on the marriage of Ercole, Marquis of Ferrara, he kept testing the inclinations of those princes, to see how they were disposed to the Florentines. On his return to Rome, he died, not without suspicion that he had been poisoned by the Venetians, who feared the power of Sixtus as long as he could employ Frate Piero's courage and activity. For the latter, even though Nature produced him from humble stock and he was then humbly brought up within the limits of a monastery, as soon as he came to the cardinalate showed such great pride and ambition that the cardinalate and even the papacy itself would not have been sufficient to hold him. He did not hesitate to give in Rome a banquet that would have been thought marvelous for any king, spending on it more than twenty thousand florins. After Sixtus was deprived of this minister, then, he carried his schemes on more slowly.

Nonetheless, after the Florentines, the Duke and the Venetians renewed their league, leaving a place for the Pope and the King to enter it, Sixtus and the King also allied themselves, but left a place where the other princes could enter. And now Italy was divided into two factions, for every day things came up that caused hatred between these two leagues, such as the affair of the island of Cyprus; King Ferdinand aspired to it but the Venetians took it. Hence the Pope and the King kept drawing more closely together.

Frederick the ruler of Urbino, then considered the ablest general in Italy, had for a long time carried on wars for the Florentine people. The Pope and the King, therefore, in order that the hostile league might be without this leader, determined to get hold of Frederick, so the Pope advised him to visit the King in Naples and Ferdinand invited him. Frederick consented, to the wonder and displeasure of the Florentines, who believed he would fare as did Jacopo Piccinino. Nevertheless it came out differently, for Frederick returned from Naples and Rome with high honor and as general of Sixtus and Ferdinand's league.

The King and the Pope also did not fail to test the intentions of the rulers of Romagna and of the Sienese, in order to gain their alliance as a means for further injury to the Florentines. Learning this, the latter furnished themselves with every suitable defense against the ambition of the two. Having lost Frederick of Urbino, the Florentines employed Roberto Malatesta of Rimini; they renewed their league with the Perugians and made an alliance with the ruler of Faenza. The Pope and the King explained their enmity for Flor' ence by saying they wished that city to give up her league with Venice and to enter an alliance with themselves, because the Pope did not think the Church able to sustain her reputation or Count Girolamo able to hold the states of Romagna when the Florentines and the Venetians were united. The Florentines, however, feared that the two potentates were trying to make them enemies of the Venetians not in order to gain support from Florence but in order more easily to damage her. So in these suspicions and factional differences Italy lived two years before any disorder sprang up. The first to spring up, only a little one, was in Tuscany.

CHAPTER 32
[Carlo Braccio attacks Perugia. 1476]

Braccio of Perugia, a man who in war had the highest reputation, as we have many times remarked, left two sons: Oddo and Carlo. The latter was in his early years; the other was killed by the men of Val di Lamone, as we said above. But when Carlo came to military age, the Venetians, because of his father's memory and their hopes for him, appointed him one of the commanders of their republic. In these times the end of his term of service had come and he did not then wish that Senate to extend it. On the contrary, he determined to see if by means of his name and his father's reputation he could reoccupy his Perugian territories. To this the Venetians easily con' sented, since in the vicissitudes of affairs they were accustomed always to increase their power.

So Carlo came to Tuscany. Finding his Perugian attempt diffi' cult because that city was in league with the Florentines, and wishing his movement to produce something worth remembering, he attacked the Sienese, declaring that they were his debtors for services they had received from his father in the business of that republic, and that he wished to be paid. With such fury he assailed them that he turned almost all their territory upside down. Those citizens, seeing such an attack, since they easily believe ill of the Florentines, were convinced that it was all done with Florentine connivance; so they showered the Pope and the King with complaints. They also sent to Florence envoys who bewailed such great injury and cleverly demonstrated that, without being supported, Carlo could not with such impunity have injured them. Of this the Florentines tried to clear themselves, asserting that they were ready to do everything to make Carlo cease his attacks; so just as the envoys asked, they ordered Carlo to cease attacking the Sienese. Carlo complained about this, pretending that the Florentines through not supporting him had deprived themselves of great gain and had deprived him of great glory, because he could have promised them early possession of that city—so much cowardice he had found in her and such slight preparation for defense. Carlo went off, then, and returned to his usual salary from the Venetians. Yet the Sienese, though by Florentine aid liberated from such heavy afflictions, remained nonetheless full of anger against the Florentines, feeling no obligation to those who, first having caused them suffering, had then delivered them from it.

CHAPTER 33

[A conspiracy against Duke Galeazzo formed in Milan. 1476]

While these things were happening, in the ways related above, between the King and the Pope and in Tuscany, in Lombardy occurred an event of greater importance, a forewarning of greater ills. In Milan, Cola Montano, a lettered and ambitious man, taught the Latin language to youths from the leading families of that city. This man, whether he loathed the life and habits of the Duke, or whether some other reason stirred him, in all his discourses execrated life under a prince who was not good, calling those glorious and happy whom Nature and Fortune had permitted to be born and to live in a republic, and explaining that all famous men were brought up in republics and not under princes; republics cherished able men and princes destroyed them, since the first profited from the abilities of men, the second feared them. The youths with whom he was most intimate were Giovannandrea Lampognano, Carlo Visconti, and Girolamo Olgiato. With these he spoke many times of the evil nature of their prince and of the ill fortune of those governed by him. He came to have such trust in the courage and determination of those youths that he made them swear that when they were old enough they would free their native city from that prince's tyranny.

Since these youths, then, were filled with this desire, which kept growing with the years, the Duke's habits and ways, and still more the special injuries he had done to the young men, urged them to put it into effect. Galeazzo was lustful and cruel, and by frequent instances of these two qualities made himself greatly hated, because he was not satisfied merely to debauch noble women but also enjoyed making his successes public; he was not satisfied with putting men to death unless in some cruel way he killed them. He did not, moreover, escape the reproach of having killed his mother, because, since he felt that he was not prince when she was present, he conducted himself toward her in such a way that she wished to retire to her dower residence at Cremona. On this journey she was taken by a sudden illness and died; hence many judged that her death was caused by her son. This Duke had dishonored Carlo and Girolamo with regard to women, and to Giovannandrea he had not been willing to grant the possession of the Abbey of Miramondo, which had been turned over to a relative of his by the Pontiff. These private injuries strengthened the resolve of these young men to free their country—while getting their own revenge—from her great ills, for they hoped, if they succeeded in killing Duke Galeazzo, to be followed not merely by many of the nobles but by all the people.

Having determined then on this action, they often met together; their old friendship kept this from attracting attention. They were always discussing this matter, and to strengthen their courage for the deed, they struck one another in the sides and in the breast with the sheaths of the knives they had chosen for that exploit. They discussed the time and the place: they thought it unsafe in the Castle; on a hunt, uncertain and dangerous; at the times when the Duke walked through the city, difficult and not likely to succeed; at banquets uncertain. Hence they determined to attack him at some ceremony and public festival, where they would be sure he would come, and they with various pretexts could bring together their friends. They settled also that if any of them for some reason were kept from court, the others, in the midst of weapons and armed enemies, should be under obligation to kill the Duke.

CHAPTER 34

[*Duke Galeazzo murdered. 1476*]

It was the year 1476 and Christmas was approaching. Because on St. Stephen's day the Duke was accustomed to visit the church of that martyr with great pomp, the conspirators decided that that was the place and the time suited to carrying out their plan. When the morning of that saint came, then, they had some of their most faithful friends and servants armed, saying that they intended to aid Giovannandrea, who against the will of some enemies intended to divert a watercourse into his property. These who were so armed they led to the church, indicating that before going they wanted to take leave of the Duke. Also with various excuses they got many others of their friends and relatives to come to that place, hoping that when the deed was done all would follow them in the rest of the affair. They planned when the Duke was dead to unite with those armed men, go to the part of the city where they thought they could most easily stir up the people, and get them to arm against the Duchess and the leaders of the State. They believed that the people, who were afflicted with hunger, would easily follow them, because they planned to give them the houses of Messer Cecco Simonetta, Giovanni Botti and Francesco Lucani, all leaders in the government, to plunder, and in this way to make sure of them and to restore liberty to the people. Having made this plan and settled their courage for carrying it out thus, Giovannandrea with the others was at the church early. They heard Mass together, and after they had heard it, Giovannandrea turned to a statue of Saint Ambrose and said: "O patron of this city of ours, thou knowest our purpose and the reason for which we put ourselves into so many dangers; be favorable to this attempt of ours, and show, by favoring justice, that injustice is hateful to thee."

To the Duke, on the other hand, who was to go to the church, there appeared many signs of imminent death, for in the morning he put on a corselet, as he usually did, which he then at once took off, as if it were uncomfortable or injured his appearance; he wished to hear Mass in the Castle, and found that his chaplain had gone to St. Stephen's with all his chapel equipment; the Duke wished the Bishop of Como to celebrate Mass in place of his chaplain, and the Bishop

brought up certain proper objections. Hence, of necessity, he decided to go to the church. But first he had his sons Giovangaleazzo
and Ermes come to him, and embraced and kissed them many times
and did not seem able to part from them. At last, however, having
decided to go, he left the Castle, and placing himself between the
envoys from Ferrara and from Mantua, moved toward the church.

The conspirators, meanwhile, in order to cause less suspicion
of themselves and to escape the cold, which was very great, were in a
room belonging to the archpriest of the church, who was their friend.
When they heard that the Duke was coming, they went into the
church; and Giovannandrea and Girolamo put themselves on the
right side at the entrance of the church and Carlo on the left. First
those who preceded the Duke entered the church; then he entered,
surrounded by a great multitude, such as was fitting for a ducal
procession on that occasion. The first to act were young Lampognano
and Girolamo. These, pretending that they wanted room made for
the Duke and moving close to him, seized the weapons—short and
sharppointed—hidden in their sleeves, and attacked him. The
Lampognano youth gave him two wounds, one in the belly, the
other in the throat; Girolamo also struck him in the throat and in the
breast. Carlo Visconti, because he was stationed nearer the door
and the Duke had moved in front of him, was not able to strike him
in front when he was attacked by the others, but with two strokes
pierced his back and his shoulders. These six blows were so prompt
and swift that the Duke was on the floor before almost anybody
realized what had happened; he was not able to do or say anything,
except that when he fell he once only called for aid on the name of
Our Lady.

When the Duke had fallen to the floor, a great noise was made;
many swords were drawn, and as happens in events that have not
been foreseen, some fled from the church and some ran toward the
uproar, without feeling any certainty or knowing the reason for the
affair. Nevertheless those who were nearest to the Duke and saw
him fall and who recognized the slayers, pursued them. Of the
conspirators, Giovannandrea, trying to get outside the church, went
among the women, of whom many were sitting on the floor according to their custom, and being caught and held by their clothes, he
was overtaken and killed by a Moor, a sergeant of the Duke's. Carlo
was also killed by the bystanders. But Girolamo Olgiato, who got

out of the church by mixing with the people, seeing his companions dead and not knowing where else to escape, went home, where he was not received by his father and his brothers. Only his mother, having pity on her son, confided him to a priest, an old friend of their family, who put his own clothes on him and took him to his house. There he remained two days, not without hope that some disturbance rising in Milan would save him. Since this did not come about and he feared he would be found in that place, he attempted to flee in disguise, but was recognized and came into the power of justice, so that he revealed the whole course of the conspiracy. Girolamo was twenty-three years old; in dying he was not less courageous than he had been in acting, because when he was naked and the executioner in front of him with sword in hand to strike him, he said these words in the Latin tongue, for he was educated: "Death is bitter, fame everlasting; long will the memory of my deed endure."

This attempt by these unlucky young men was secretly planned and courageously executed; then they failed when those they hoped would follow and defend them did not defend or follow them. Yet princes should learn so to live and in such a way to make themselves revered and loved that nobody on killing them can hope to save himself. Subjects should observe how vain any hope is which makes them believe that a multitude, though disconcerted, will follow you or accompany you in your dangers.[1]

This event frightened all Italy, but much more terrifying were those that a little later happened in Florence, which broke the peace that had obtained in Italy for twelve years, as we shall show in the following book, which at its end will be sad and mournful and at its beginning bloody and terrifying.

1. *The shift to the second person such as occurs here is frequent in* THE PRINCE.

BOOK EIGHT

[FLORENCE FROM THE PAZZI CONSPIRACY TO THE DEATH OF LORENZO THE MAGNIFI- CENT. 1478–1492]

CHAPTER 1

[On conspiracies; Medici rule.]

Since the beginning of this eighth book lies between two conspiracies, one already related, which was carried on in Milan, and
the other to be related, which occurred in Florence, it seems proper
to follow our custom by speaking of the nature of conspiracies and
of their importance. I should gladly do so if in another place I had
not spoken of them, or if they were matters to be treated with brevity.
But since they require much consideration and I have already discussed them in another place,[1] I shall omit them.

So passing to another matter, we shall explain that after the
Medici party had overcome all the hostility that openly opposed it,
if that family were to take sole authority in the city and, through its
control of the state, detach itself from other families, it was under the
necessity of overcoming also those which secretly were scheming
against it. Earlier, while the Medici, on an equality in authority and
reputation with some of the other families, were carrying on their
struggle, citizens who envied their power could act openly against
them without fearing that in their first hostile acts they would be
crushed, because after the magistrates became free, none of the parties
had reason to fear except when defeated. But after the victory of
1466, the government was so completely limited to the Medici, who
had seized such great authority, that the discontented were forced
either with patience to bear that kind of government or, if they
did attempt to destroy it, to do so with conspiracies and secretly.

Such conspiracies, because unlikely to succeed, usually produce
ruin for those who form them, but greatness for those against whom
they are directed. Hence almost always the prince of a city, after he
is assailed with such a conspiracy, if he is not killed like the Duke of
Milan—which seldom happens—rises to greater power. Many times,

1. DISCOURSES 3. 6.

indeed, having been good, he becomes wicked, because these conspiracies, through their example, give him reasons for being afraid;
fear gives him reasons for making himself safe; making himself safe
gives him reasons for doing harm. Hence feelings of hatred result
from them, and in time often his downfall. So these conspiracies
destroy quickly those who carry them on and, in the course of time
at least, harm him against whom they are carried on.

CHAPTER 2

[Sixtus IV's enmity against Florence; the Pazzi hate the Medici. 1474]

At that time Italy, as we have shown, was divided into two
factions: the Pope and the King of Naples were on one side; on the
other were the Venetians, the Duke of Milan, and the Florentines.
Though as yet there had been no outbreak of war, nevertheless every
day there were new reasons for starting one. The Pontiff especially,
in all his activities, was trying to harm the state of Florence. Hence,
on the death of Filippo de'Medici Archbishop of Pisa, the Pope,
against the will of the Signoria of Florence, bestowed that archbish-
opric on Francesco Salviati, whom he knew to be an enemy of the
Medici family. Hence, because the Signoria did not consent to give
Francesco possession, between it and the Pope the dealings over this
affair produced new reasons for hatred.

Besides this, in Rome the Pope kept granting the Pazzi family the
greatest favors, but the Medici family in his every act he tried to
obstruct. At that time in Florence these Pazzi were for riches and
high position the most imposing of Florentine families. Their head
was Messer Jacopo, whom the people because of his wealth and
position had made a knight. He had no children except one natural
daughter but he did have many relatives in the families of Messer
Piero and Antonio his brothers: the most notable were Guglielmo,
Francesco, Rinato and Giovanni; after them came Andrea, Niccolò
and Galeotto. Now Cosimo de'Medici, on account of the Pazzi's
wealth and position, had wedded his granddaughter Bianca to
Guglielmo, hoping that the alliance would unite the families and get
rid of the feelings of enmity and hate so often caused by suspicion.
Nonetheless, so completely are human plans uncertain and deceptive
that the matter turned out differently, for Lorenzo's advisers showed

him that for any of the citizens to combine wealth and public office was dangerous and adverse to his authority.

As a result, to Messer Jacopo and his nephews Lorenzo did not grant those positions of honor which in comparison with the other citizens they seemed to deserve. This policy roused in the Pazzi their first anger and in the Medici their first fear; each of these passions gave its opposite matter for growing.

In every action, then, in which citizens might compete, the Pazzi were unfavorably regarded by the city officials. The magistracy of the Eight, when Francesco de' Pazzi was in Rome, without showing him the regard usually shown to great citizens, for a slight reason made him come to Florence on their orders. So the Pazzi with abusive and angry words everywhere kept complaining. These things increased other men's fear and their own feelings of injury. Giovanni de' Pazzi's wife was the daughter of Giovanni Buonromei, a very rich man, on whose death without other children, his daughter claimed his property as heir. Nonetheless Carlo his nephew took possession of part of his goods. When the affair came to court, a decree was made by virtue of which Giovanni de' Pazzi's wife was deprived of her father's estate and it was granted to Carlo. For this loss the Pazzi held the Medici entirely responsible. Over the affair Giuliano de' Medici many times expressed grief to his brother Lorenzo, saying that he feared that through wanting too many things they would lose everything.

CHAPTER 3

[The Pazzi conspiracy begun. 1478]

Nonetheless Lorenzo, hot with youth and with power, wished to attend to everything and to have all Florence admit that everything came from him. Since the Pazzi, then, with such a high position and so much wealth, could not bear such injuries, they began considering how to get revenge. The first who began to talk against the Medici was Francesco. He was more spirited and more sensitive than any of the others, so he determined either to get what he lacked or to lose what he had. Because he hated the rulers of Florence, he lived almost always in Rome, where, according to the custom of Florentine merchants, he had charge of a great sum of money. And because he was very friendly with Count Girolamo,[1] they often complained to each other about the Medici. So, after much complaint, they came to the opinion that if one were to live securely in his territories and the other in his city, they must change the government of Florence, but without the deaths of Giuliano and Lorenzo they thought no change could be made. They judged that the Pope and the King of Naples would easily consent to it, if only both of them could find out how easy it would be.

Having come to this conclusion, then, they imparted the whole to Francesco Salviati, Archbishop of Pisa, who, because he was ambitious and a little before had been injured by the Medici, gladly joined them. Having considered among themselves what could be done, they determined, in order that the affair might go more easily, to draw into their plan Messer Jacopo de' Pazzi, without whom they did not believe anything could be accomplished. They arranged, then, that Francesco de' Pazzi should go to Florence for this purpose, and the Archbishop and the Count remain at Rome to be with the Pope when it seemed time to impart it to him.

Francesco found Messer Jacopo more cautious and difficult than he would have wished; on his making this known at Rome, the plotters decided that greater authority was needed to influence him. Hence the Archbishop and the Count told everything to Giovan Battista da Montesecco, a military officer of the Pope's, a man highly reputed in war and under obligation to the Count and the Pope. He nevertheless demonstrated that the affair was difficult and dangerous. These dangers and difficulties the Archbishop tried to dispel: he set forth the assistance to be given by the Pope and the King, along with the hatred of the Medici by Florentine citizens and with the many relatives who would support the Salviati and the Pazzi; moreover the brothers could easily be killed because they went around the city without companions and without suspicion; as soon as they were dead the government could easily be changed. Giovan Battista did not altogether believe these assertions because he had heard many other Florentines speak differently.

1. *Girolamo Riario, made Count of Imola by the Pope, who feared that the Medici might get the city away from him.*

CHAPTER 4

[The Pazzi conspiracy; its planning. 1478]

While they were engaged in these discussions and debates, Carlo Fortebraccio, the ruler of Faenza, happened to fall sick, so that he was in danger of death. The Archbishop and the Count saw that his illness gave them a chance to send Giovan Battista to Florence and thence into Romagna with the excuse of repossessing certain cities that the ruler of Faenza was unjustly depriving them of. Moreover the Count charged Giovan Battista to speak with Lorenzo and to ask on the Count's behalf advice on the proper course for him in the affairs of Romagna. Then he was to speak with Francesco de' Pazzi, and they were to combine in attempting to influence Messer Jacopo de' Pazzi to support their plan. And so that Giovan Battista could use the Pope's influence to stir him, they decided that before his departure he should speak to the Pontiff, who made the largest offers he could in support of the attempt.

Having come to Florence, therefore, Giovan Battista spoke with Lorenzo, by whom he was very courteously received, and in the matters he asked about wisely and kindly advised; Giovan Battista was astonished, since it seemed to him that he had found a different man than had been represented to him; he judged him altogether courteous, wise and very friendly to the Count. Nonetheless he decided to speak with Francesco; not finding him there, because he had gone to Lucca, he spoke with Messer Jacopo, and found him in the beginning much adverse to the affair. Still, before Giovan Battista went away, the influence of the Pope stirred Messer Jacopo somewhat. He therefore told Giovan Battista to go to Romagna and return, and meanwhile Francesco would be in Florence, and then they would talk in more detail about the affair. So Giovan Battista went and returned. With Lorenzo de'Medici he continued his pretended discussion of the Count's business. Then he met with Messer Jacopo and Francesco de' Pazzi; and the two made such an effort that Messer Jacopo consented to the business.

They debated the method. Messer Jacopo believed it not feasible when both brothers were in Florence; therefore they needed to wait until Lorenzo went to Rome (for he was reported to be going there) and then carry out their plan. Francesco was glad that Lorenzo was to be in Rome. Nevertheless, if he did not go there, Francesco declared that at a wedding or at a game or in church both the brothers could be killed. And as to foreign aid, they thought the Pope could get soldiers together for the affair of the town of Montone, having a just cause to deprive Count Carlo Fortebraccio of it, for having made the disturbances already spoken of in the territories of Siena and Perugia.[1] Nonetheless, they did not make any other decision than that Francesco de' Pazzi and Giovan Battista should go to Rome, and there settle everything with Count Girolamo Riario and with the Pope. This matter was discussed again at Rome and finally it was settled, since the attempt on Montone had been decided on, that Giovan Francesco da Tolentino, a soldier of the Pope, should go into Romagna and Messer Lorenzo da Castello into his native district. Each of these, with the people of the country, should hold their companies in readiness to do whatever should be commanded by the Archbishop de' Salviati and Francesco de' Pazzi, who should go to Florence with Giovan Battista da Montesecco. There they were to provide whatever was needed for carrying out the attempt, to which King Ferdinand, through his envoy, promised some aid. When the Archbishop and Francesco de' Pazzi came in due course to Florence, they brought over to their view Jacopo, the son of Messer Poggio Bracciolini, a young man well educated but ambitious and very eager for revolution; they also persuaded two men both named Jacopo Salviati, one a brother, the other a relative of the Archbishop, and they gained Bernardo Bandini and Napoleone Franzesi, fiery young men and heavily obligated to the Pazzi family. As to non-Florentines, in addition to those already named, they were joined by Messer Antonio da Volterra and one Stefano, a priest, who lived in Messer Jacopo's house to teach his daughter the Latin language. Rinato de' Pazzi, a prudent and serious man, who very well knew the evil that can come from such undertakings, did not agree to the conspiracy. On the contrary, he loathed it and with any method he could honorably use he blocked it.

1. *See 7. 32, above.*

CHAPTER 5

[The final arrangements for the Pazzi conspiracy. 1478]

Up to this time the Pope had been keeping at the University of Pisa to learn canon law Raffaello de' Riario, Count Girolamo's nephew; still being there, he was by the Pope promoted to the dignity of the cardinalate. The conspirators therefore planned to take this Cardinal to Florence, so that his coming might cover up the conspiracy, since among his retinue they could conceal the conspirators they needed and thus get a chance for carrying out their plot.

Hence the Cardinal came and was received by Messer Jacopo de' Pazzi at Montughi, his villa near Florence. The conspirators hoped through him to bring together Lorenzo and Giuliano and then at once to kill them. They arranged, therefore, to give the Cardinal a banquet in their villa at Fiesole, where Giuliano, whether by chance or intention, was not present. After that, since their plan had failed, they judged that if they gave him a banquet in Florence, the two would of necessity be present. Having so decided, they selected for that banquet Sunday, 26 April 1478. The conspirators, then, supposing that in the midst of the banquet they could kill them, met on Saturday night, where they settled all that was to happen the morning following. But then when day came, Francesco was informed that Giuliano would not be at the banquet.

So the heads of the conspiracy again met and decided that they must not defer putting it into effect, for by no possibility could the plot, known to so many, escape discovery. They therefore determined to kill the Medici brothers in the Cathedral Church of Santa Reparata, to which, because of the Cardinal's presence, both Lorenzo and Giuliano would come according to their custom. The conspirators planned that Giovan Battista should be responsible for killing Lorenzo, and Francesco de' Pazzi and Bernardo Bandini for killing Giuliano. Giovan Battista refused to consider doing it, whether the contact he had had with Lorenzo had softened his purpose or some other cause moved him. He said that never would he have the courage to commit such an enormity in a church, thus accompanying treachery with sacrilege. From his refusal came the conspiracy's ruin because, time pressing, the plotters were forced to assign the murders in the church to Messer Antonio da Volterra and Stefano the priest, although these two were by nature and experience wholly unfit for such an act. Indeed if any actions require a spirit strong and firm and resolute in life and in death because of much experience, such a spirit is essential in actions of this kind, in which often men expert in arms and accustomed to blood have lost their courage. Having then made this decision, the conspirators determined that the signal for action should be the taking of communion by the priest who in the church was celebrating High Mass. Meanwhile Archbishop de' Salviati with his followers and with Jacopo, Messer Poggio Bracciolini's son, was to seize the Public Palace, so that the Signoria, whether willingly or under pressure, would be favorable to them after the deaths of the two young men.

CHAPTER 6
[*Giuliano is killed; Lorenzo escapes. 1478*]

After making this decision, they went to the Cathedral, to which Cardinal Riario had already come with Lorenzo de'Medici. The church was full of people and the divine office had begun, but as yet Giuliano de'Medici was not there. Thereupon Francesco de'Pazzi along with Bernardo, designated for Giuliano's murder, went to his house to get him and with prayers and craft brought him to the church. It truly is worth observing that so much hatred, so much attention to a crime so great, could with such rare courage and such firmness of mind be kept hidden by Francesco and Bernardo. Even when they were taking Giuliano to the Cathedral, both on the way and inside the building, with joking and youthful talk they kept him occupied; actually Francesco did not fail, under the appearance of caressing him, to press him with his hands and arms to see if he were wearing a corselet or some such protection. Giuliano and Lorenzo well understood the bitter feeling of the Pazzi against them and their intention of taking from the Medici the control of the state; but they did not at all fear for their lives, since they believed that if indeed the Pazzi were going to attempt something, they would do it according to law and not with violence. Therefore Lorenzo and Giuliano for their part, taking no precaution for their safety, pretended to be friends to the Pazzi.

When at last the assassins were ready, some by the side of Lorenzo, where because of the crowd in the Cathedral they could stand easily and without suspicion, and others with Giuliano, the appointed hour came. Bernardo Bandini, with a short weapon provided for that purpose, pierced the breast of Giuliano, who after a few steps fell to the floor. Francesco de' Pazzi, leaping on him, covered him with wounds; with such zeal he struck him that, blinded by the madness that carried him on, he severely wounded himself in one leg. Messer Antonio and Stefano on the other hand attacked Lorenzo, and after aiming many blows at him, with a slight wound did injure him in the neck; yet either their ineffectiveness or the courage of Lorenzo—who, seeing himself attacked, defended himself with his own weapon—or the aid of those who were with him, made useless every effort of theirs. Hence, in fright they fled and concealed themselves, but being later found, they were shamefully killed and dragged through all the city. Lorenzo on the other hand, forming a group with the friends he had around him, shut himself into the sacristy of the Cathedral. Bernardo Bandini, when he saw Giuliano dead, killed also Francesco Nori, a warm friend of the Medici, either because he had hated him for a long time or because Francesco tried to aid Giuliano. Yet not satisfied with these two homicides, Bernardo ran to find Lorenzo and to supply with his courage and readiness what the others through their sluggishness and impotence had lacked, but finding him withdrawn to the sacristy, he could do nothing.

In the midst of these perilous and confused events, which were so terrible that the Cathedral appeared to be falling, the Cardinal clung to the altar, where with difficulty the priests so protected him that the Signoria, after the confusion was over, could take him to the Palace, where he remained in the greatest fear until his liberation.

CHAPTER 7

[Events at the Palace of the Signoria. 1478]

There were in Florence at this time some Perugians, driven by factions from their home, whom the Pazzi, promising to restore them to their native city, had drawn into their way of thinking. Hence the Archbishop de' Salviati, who had gone to capture the Palace with Jacopo Messer Poggio's son and with some of the Salviati and their friends, had taken them with him. When he reached the Palace, he left part of his men below, with the order that when they heard a noise, they should hold the door, and he went up, with the greater part of the Perugians. Finding the Signoria eating, since the hour was late, after a short time, he was brought before Cesare Petrucci the Gonfalonier of Justice. So, entering with a few of his men, he left the rest outside. The greater part of these by their own doing shut themselves up in the Chancellery, because its door was so made that when it was shut it could not be opened except by using the key, from the inside as well as from the outside. The Archbishop meanwhile having gone into the Gonfalonier's room, with the excuse of wanting to say something to him on behalf of the Pope, spoke with broken and uncertain words, so that the agitation he showed in his face and his words aroused in the Gonfalonier so much suspicion that suddenly, shouting, he thrust him out of the room, and encountering Jacopo Messer Poggio's son, he seized him by the hair and put him in the hands of his officers. When the alarm was given, the Signors took such weapons as chance furnished, and with them killed all those who had come up with the Archbishop (some of whom were shut up and some of whom lost courage) or threw them still alive out of the windows of the Palace. Of those seized, the Archbishop, the two Jacopo Salviati and Jacopo Messer Poggio's son were hanged. Those who had remained below in the Palace had overpowered the guard and taken possession of the door and all the lower parts,[1] so that the citizens who on this alarm ran to the Palace could not, if armed, give aid or, if unarmed, give advice to the Signoria.

1. *Machiavelli assumes that his reader is familiar with the Palace of the Signoria (now called the Palazzo Vecchio). Those left below were on the ground floor; the Archbishop went up the long stairs to the more important rooms.*

CHAPTER 8

[Unsuccessful attempt to raise the people in the name of liberty. 1478]

Francesco de' Pazzi and Bernardo Bandini, meanwhile, seeing Lorenzo out of danger and one of themselves, in whom all the hope of the action rested, seriously wounded, were frightened. Hence, Bernardo, considering his own safety with that same courageous spirit with which he had considered harming the Medici, having seen that the business had failed, fled in security. Francesco, re-turning to his house wounded, experimented to see if he were able to handle himself on horseback, because the arrangement was that he was to make a circuit of the city with armed men and call the people to liberty and to arms, but he could not—so deep was the wound and so much blood he had lost from it. Hence, undressing, he threw himself naked on his bed, and begged Messer Jacopo to do what he himself could not do.

Messer Jacopo, though he was old and not experienced in such disturbances, in order to make that last test of their fortune, got on horseback with perhaps a hundred armed men who had been pre-pared for such an attempt, and went to the Public Square before the Palace, calling upon the people and liberty for aid. But because by the fortune and the liberality of the Medici the people had been made deaf and liberty was not known in Florence,[1] he got no reply from anybody. Nothing happened except that the Signors, who were masters of the upper part of the Palace, greeted him with the stones,[2] and with threats frightened him as much as they could. As Messer Jacopo stood uncertain, he was addressed by Giovanni Serristori his brother-in-law, who first rebuked him for the strife they had begun and then exhorted him to go home, asserting that the people and liberty were as much on the hearts of the other citizens as on his. Having lost all hope, then, Messer Jacopo, seeing the Palace hostile, Lorenzo alive, Francesco wounded, and nobody following him, not knowing what else to do, determined to save his life if he could by flight; so with the followers he had with him in the Piazza he went out of Florence to go to Romagna.

1. *A plain saying to put in a history written for the Medici. Moreover, Machiavelli did not close his eyes to Florentine defects in courage and patriotism.*

2. *Piles of stones were kept in readiness, to be dropped through holes provided in the over-hanging roof of the Palace.*

CHAPTER 9
[*The punishment of the conspirators. 1478*]

Meanwhile all the city was under arms, and Lorenzo de'Medici, accompanied by many armed men, had returned to his mansion. The Palace had been regained by the people, and those who had seized it were all either captured or dead. Already throughout the city people were shouting the name of the Medici, the limbs of the dead were to be seen either fixed on the points of weapons or scattered through the city, and everybody, with words full of anger and deeds full of cruelty, was hunting down the Pazzi. Already their houses were in the possession of the people, and Francesco, naked as he was, was dragged from his house and, taken to the Palace, was hanged beside the Archbishop and the others. And he could not be made to utter a word through whatever injury was done or spoken to him on the way or later, but looking fixedly at his captors, without making any further complaint, mutely he sighed. Guglielmo de' Pazzi, Lorenzo's brother-in-law, was sheltered in the latter's house, through his own innocence and the aid of Bianca his wife. There was not a citizen, armed or unarmed, who did not go to Lorenzo's house in that emergency, and everybody offered him himself and his prop erty—so great were the fortune and favor the Medici family had gained through its prudence and liberality.

Rinato de' Pazzi, when the event took place, had retired to his villa. Learning of its outcome, he tried to escape in disguise. Never theless, he was recognized on the road, seized and taken to Florence. Messer Jacopo was also seized when crossing the mountains, because, since the mountain people had learned what had happened in Flor ence and observed his flight, they attacked him and brought him to Florence; nor could he, though many times he begged them to do so, get them to kill him on the way. Messer Jacopo and Rinato were condemned to death, four days after the event. Among all the deaths inflicted in those days, when men's limbs filled the streets, only that of Rinato was looked on with pity, because he was thought a man wise and good, and not marked with the pride charged to the other members of his family.

That this affair should lack no sort of extraordinary happening, Messer Jacopo was first entombed in the sepulchre of his fathers; then, as excommunicated, he was taken from it and buried near the city walls. But there too being dug up, he was dragged naked through the city by the rope with which he was executed; and since on land there was no place for his burial, those who dragged him dumped him into the River Arno, whose waters were then at their highest. An example of Fortune's power truly very striking, that a man of such great wealth and so prosperous should fall into such great adversity, so destructive and shameful. We are told of some of his vices, among which were gambling and cursing more than might be expected even from a desperately wicked man; yet for those vices he compensated with many charities, because he gave large gifts to many who were in need and to many religious places. Another good thing to be said about him is that the Saturday before the Sunday set for so great a slaughter, in order not to make others share in his adverse fortune, with wonderful care he handed over to its owners all the merchandise belonging to any other man that he had in the customs house or in his own house.

Giovan Battista da Montesecco, after a long examination, was beheaded; Napoleone Franzesi escaped punishment by flight; Guglielmo de' Pazzi was banished, and his cousins who remained alive were imprisoned in the dungeon of the castle of Volterra.

When the tumults were quieted and the conspirators punished, funeral rites were celebrated for Giuliano, who was accompanied by all the citizens in tears, as having been more liberal and courteous than could be expected of anybody born to such fortune. He left a natural son, born a few months after his death, named Giulio, who abounded in the virtue and fortune recognized in these present times by all the world; when we come to present affairs, if God gives us life, we shall set them forth at length.

The soldiers under Messer Lorenzo da Castello in Val di Tevere and those under Giovan Francesco da Tolentino in Romagna united and set out for Florence to give aid to the Pazzi, but when they learned of the ruin of the undertaking, they turned back.

CHAPTER 10

[The Pope and the King of Naples begin war on Florence; Lorenzo de' Medici makes a patriotic speech. 1478]

Since in Florence there had not been the change in government which the Pope and King Ferdinand wished, they determined that what they had been unable to do by conspiracy they would do by war. So both of them with the utmost rapidity got their soldiers together to attack the state of Florence, proclaiming that they did not wish anything from that city except that it should rid itself of Lorenzo de' Medici, who alone of all the Florentines they held as an enemy. Already the King's soldiers had crossed the River Tronto, and the

Pope's were in the territory of Perugia; in order that in addition to
temporal wounds the Florentines should also feel spiritual ones, the
Pope excommunicated and cursed them. Hence the Florentines,
seeing such great armies coming against them, with the utmost care
prepared themselves for defense.

Lorenzo de'Medici decided before everything else, since by report the war was made against him, to bring together in the Palace
with the Signors all the qualified citizens, more than three hundred
in number, to whom he spoke to this effect:

"I do not know, exalted Signors, and you, honored citizens,
whether I lament with you because of the things that have happened
or whether I rejoice. And truly when I think with how much deceit,
with how much hate I have been attacked and my brother killed, I
cannot do other than grieve over it and with all my heart and with
all my mind lament it. When I consider then with what speed, with
what zeal, with what love, with what united agreement of the whole
city my brother has been avenged and I have been defended, it befits
me not merely to rejoice in it, but altogether to exult and glory.
Truly, if experience has made me realize that in this city I had more
enemies than I thought, it has also proved to me that I have here more
warm and ardent friends than I had believed. I am forced, then, to
lament with you over the injuries of others, and to rejoice in your
merits; but I am compelled to lament the more for the injuries as they
are more unusual, more without example, and less deserved by us.
Consider, honored citizens, that ill fortune had brought our family
to such a situation that among friends, among relatives, in the
Church, we were not safe. They who fear death are accustomed to
resort to their friends for aid; they are accustomed to resort to their
relatives. We found ours armed for our destruction. They who, for
public or private reasons, are persecuted are all accustomed to take
refuge in the churches. But if we do, we are killed by those who
defend others; where the parricides, the murderers are safe, the Medici
find their slayers.

"But God, who never in the past has deserted our house, has still
preserved us and taken up the defense of our just cause. What injuries justifying such great longing for revenge have we done to anyone? Truly those who have shown themselves so hostile to us, we
never have privately wronged; if we had wronged them, they would
not have been in a position to wrong us. If they attribute to us public

injuries, if any such have been inflicted—I know of none—they wrong rather you than us, rather this Palace and the majesty of this government than our house, making it appear that for our sake you without cause injure your citizens. This is utterly removed from all truth, because we, if we could have done so, and you, if we had wished you to, would not have done so, for he who carefully seeks out the truth will find that you have always raised our house on high with such complete agreement for no other reason than that it has striven to surpass everybody in courtesy, in liberality, in conferring benefits. If we, then, have honored strangers, how have we injured relatives?

"If they have been driven to this plot by the wish to rule, as is shown by their seizing the Palace and coming with armed men into the Public Square, their cause shows itself ugly, ambitious, and deserving of punishment, and condemns itself. If they have acted through hatred and envy of our power, they wrong you, not us, for you have given it to us. And truly those powers deserve to be hated which men usurp, not those which men gain through liberality, courtesy and generosity. You know that our house never rose to any level of greatness to which it was not impelled by this Palace and by your united consent. Not with arms and violence did my grand׳ father Cosimo return from exile, but with your agreement and union. My father, old and ill, did not himself defend his own position against many enemies, but you with your authority and good will defended it. Nor would I, after my father's death, when still a boy, as it were, have kept up the station of my house except for your advice and aid. My house could not have ruled and cannot rule this republic unless you together with us had ruled and now rule the state. I do not know, then, what reason for hate against us they can have, or what just reason for envy. Let them hate their own ancestors, who with pride and avarice deprived themselves of the reputation which ours have known how to gain with quite contrary efforts.

"But let us concede that the injuries we have done them are great and that with reason they wish our ruin. Why come to attack this Palace? Why make a league with the Pope and with the King against the liberty of this republic? Why break the long peace of Italy? For this they have no excuse, because they should harm those who harm them, and not mix private enmities with public injuries. This makes our danger more intense, though the Pazzi are destroyed, since for their sake the Pope and the King are coming to attack us with arms, in a war they declare they are making against me and my house. Would God it were true! The remedies would be quick and sure, for I would not be so wicked a citizen that I would rate my safety higher than your perils; on the contrary, gladly would I put out your fire with my ruin. But because the powerful always cover the injuries they do with something appearing less dishonorable, my enemies have taken this way for covering their dishonorable injury. Yet nevertheless, if you believe otherwise, I am in your hands; yours it is to control me or to abandon me; you are my fathers, you my defenders; and all that you may entrust to me to do, I shall always do gladly; nor shall I ever refuse, if so you wish, to end with my own blood this war begun with that of my brother."

While Lorenzo was speaking, the citizens could not restrain their tears, and with the same pity with which they listened to him, one of them assigned by the others replied, saying that the city recognized the many deserts of him and his, that he should be of good courage, for with the same speed as they had revenged his brother's death and preserved his life, they would preserve his reputation and his govern‑ ment, nor would he lose them sooner than they would be driven from their native city. That their deeds might fit with their words, for the protection of his body they provided at public expense a number of armed men to defend him from domestic plots.

CHAPTER 11

[The Florentines censure the Pope; they disregard the interdict. 1478]

Then the Florentines prepared for war, getting together men and money to the largest total they could. They sent for help, by virtue of the League, to the Duke of Milan and to the Venetians. And since the Pope had shown himself a wolf and not a shepherd, and they hoped not to be devoured as guilty, they showed in all the ways they could that their cause was just. They filled Italy with reports of the treachery carried on against their city, showing the Pontiff's impiety and his injustice, and declaring that as he had obtained the papacy wickedly, he had exercised his office wickedly, sending those whom he had put in the highest prelacies to commit treachery in the Cathedral, in the company of parricides and traitors, in the midst of the divine office, in the celebration of the Sacrament. Then, because he had not succeeded in killing the citizens, in changing the govern ment of their city and at his will plundering her, he had interdicted her and, with pontifical curses, threatened and wronged her. But if God is just and if acts of violence offend him, those of this vicar of his must offend him, and he must be glad when men who are injured and find no refuge with his vicar turn to himself.

Meanwhile the Florentines not merely did not receive the interdict and obey it, but they forced the clergy to celebrate the divine offices, and they called a council in Florence of all the Tuscan prelates who obeyed their authority, in which they appealed from the injuries of the Pope to the coming Council of the Church. The Pope also did not lack arguments for justifying his cause, declaring that it is a Pontiff's part to destroy tyranny, to put down the wicked and to raise up the good, and that he ought to carry on these duties with all fitting measures. But it is not the function of secular rulers to arrest cardi nals, to hang bishops, to murder, dismember and mangle priests, and to kill the innocent and the guilty without any distinction.

CHAPTER 12

[King Ferdinand's army in Florentine territory. 1478]

Nevertheless, among so many complaints and accusations, the Florentines sent the Cardinal Raffaello Riario, whom they had in their power, back to the Pontiff; this caused the Pope not to hesitate in attacking them with all his forces and those of the King of Naples. When the two armies, under Alfonso, King Ferdinand's eldest son and Duke of Calabria, with Frederick of Urbino as general, had come into the Chianti with the aid of the Sienese, who were of the hostile party, they took Radda and many other towns and laid waste the whole region. Then they led their army to Castellina.

The Florentines, learning of this attack, were in great terror, for they were without soldiers and the reinforcements sent by their allies were slow, because though the Duke of Milan sent help, the Vene tians denied that they were obligated to aid the Florentines in a private cause; in a war against individuals, they declared they were not obligated to give support because individual enmities cannot lay claim to public defense. Hence the Florentines, to influence the

Venetians to a saner view, sent to that Senate as an envoy Messer Tommaso Soderini. Meanwhile they hired soldiers and appointed as general of their armies Ercole the Marquis of Ferrara.

While these preparations were being made, the hostile army so hemmed in Castellina that the citizens, despairing of aid, surrendered after they had sustained forty days of siege. From there the enemy turned toward Arezzo and besieged Monte San Sovino. The Florentine army was by then in order; going against the enemy, it encamped three miles distant from them and gave them so much trouble that Federigo of Urbino asked a truce for some days. This was granted with such great disadvantage to the Florentines that those who asked it were astonished that it was granted, because if they had not obtained it, they would have been obliged to retreat in disgrace; but having had those days of opportunity to reorganize, when the time of the truce was over, in the face of our soldiers they took that town. By that time winter had come, so the enemy, in order to winter in suitable places, retired into Sienese territory. The Florentine soldiers also went into more suitable quarters, and the Marquis of Ferrara, having been of little value to himself and less to others, returned to his state.

CHAPTER 13

[Disturbances in Milan; revolution in Genoa. 1478–1479]

In these times Genoa rebelled against the government of Milan for these reasons. Since Duke Galeazzo was dead and Giovan Galeazzo his son was of an age unfit for rule, there rose strife between Sforza and Lodovico and Ottaviano and Ascanio his uncles, and Madonna Bona his mother—for each of them wished to take charge of the little Duke. In this dispute Madonna Bona, the old Duchess, through the advice of Messer Tommaso Soderini, then envoy for the Florentines in that state, and of Messer Cecco Simonetta, who had been secretary to Galeazzo, remained victor. Then as the Sforzas fled from Milan, Ottaviano was drowned in crossing the Adda, and the others were banished to various places along with Signor Roberto Sanseverino, who in those troubles had left the Duchess and sided with them. Then when the disturbances in Tuscany followed, those princes, hoping to find new fortune in new events, broke the bounds set for them, and each of them tried rebellion in order to return to his position.

King Ferdinand, who saw that the Florentines in their necessity had been aided only by the state of Milan, in order to take that help also away from them, planned to give the Duchess so much to think of in her own state that she could not furnish aid to the Florentines. And by means of Prospero Adorno and Signor Roberto Sanseverino and the Sforza rebels he got Genoa to revolt against Duke Galeazzo. Only the Castelleto remained in the Duke's power; hoping in that, the Duchess sent many soldiers to regain the city, but they were defeated. So seeing the danger that could come to the government of her son and to herself if that war went on—since Tuscany was upside down and the Florentines, in whom alone she was hoping, were in trouble—she determined to have Genoa as an ally if she could not have the city as a subject. Hence she made an agreement with Battistino Fregoso, the enemy of Prospero Adorno, to give him the Castelletto and make him prince in Genoa, if only he would drive out Prospero and would not give aid to the Sforza rebels. After this agreement, Battistino, with the help of the castle and of his party, became master of Genoa and, according to their custom, made himself doge. Hence the Sforzas and Signor Roberto, driven from Genoese territory, came with their followers into Lunigiana.

From this the Pope and the King of Naples, seeing that the troubles of Lombardy were quieted, took the opportunity offered by these men driven out from Genoa to upset Tuscany in the vicinity of Pisa, so that the Florentines, dividing their forces, would be weakened. To this end they so managed that Signor Roberto Sanseverino, since the winter was already over, left Lunigiana with his men and attacked Pisan territory. He stirred up a great deal of trouble and sacked and took many towns in the Pisan country, and raided as far as the city of Pisa herself.

CHAPTER 14
[*Attempts to save Pisa; Venetian aid. 1479*]

In these days envoys came to Florence from the Emperor and from the King of France and from the King of Hungary, who had been sent by their princes to the Pontiff, and they persuaded the Florentines to send ambassadors to the Pope, promising that they would make every effort with him to put an end to that war with a favorable peace. The Florentines did not refuse to make this experiment, in order in everybody's view to be excused, since for their part they loved peace. After going, however, the ambassadors came back without any decision. Hence the Florentines, to get honor for them/ selves from the reputation of the King of France, since by Italians they were partly attacked, partly deserted, sent to that King as an envoy Donato Acciaiuoli, a man thoroughly versed in Greek and Latin letters, whose ancestors had always held high positions in the city. But on the way, having reached Milan, he died. Hence, his native city, to reward his descendants and to honor his memory, buried him at public expense very honorably, and gave his sons exemptions and his daughters suitable dowers for their marriages. In his place as ambassador to the King, Florence sent Messer Guid/ antonio Vespucci, a man highly skilled in civil and canon law.

Signor Roberto Sanseverino's invasion of Pisan territory greatly upset the Florentines, as unexpected things do. Having in the direc/ tion of Siena a very serious war, they did not see how they could provide for places near Pisa, yet with conscripts and other like expedients they relieved the city of Pisa. To keep the Lucchese to their promises, so that they would not aid the enemy with either money or provisions, the Florentines sent there as envoy Piero di Gino di Neri Capponi. Because of the hatred of Lucca for the Florentine people—the result of ancient injuries and continual fear— he was received with great suspicion and many times was in danger of being killed by the people. Hence his visit gave cause for new hatreds rather than for new union. Thereupon the Florentines re/ called the Marquis of Ferrara, employed the Marquis of Mantua, and with great importunity gained from the Venetians Count Carlo, Braccio's son, and Deifebo, Count Jacopo Piccinino's son. These commanders were at last yielded by the Venetians after many objec/ tions; yet having made a truce with the Turk, and therefore not having an excuse that would shield them, they were ashamed not to keep their faith to the League.

Hence Count Carlo and Deifebo came with a large number of men/at/arms; with these they united all the men/at/arms they could detach from the army under the Marquis of Ferrara that was con/ fronting the Duke of Calabria's forces. They then moved toward

Pisa to attack Signor Roberto, who had his soldiers near the River Serchio. Though he had given the appearance of intending to wait for our forces, nevertheless he did not wait but retired to those quarters in Lunigiana which he had left when he entered Pisan territory. After his departure, Count Carlo recovered all those cities in the territory of Pisa that had been taken by the enemy.

CHAPTER 15
[Troubles within the Florentine army; the papal army defeated. 1479]

Then the Florentines, freed from attacks in the direction of Pisa, united all their soldiers between Colle and San Gimignano. But since in that army, through the coming of Count Carlo, there were followers of Sforza and of Braccio, at once their ancient enmities were revived, and it was believed that if they were long together they would come to blows. Hence, as the lesser evil, it was decided to divide the soldiers and send one part of them, under Count Carlo, into the territory of Perugia, and to keep the other part at Poggibonsi, where they were to prepare a fortified camp in order to block the enemy from entering the territory about Florence. They supposed that by this decision they would force the enemy also to divide his soldiers; because they believed either that Count Carlo would take Perugia, where they thought he had many partisans, or that the Pope would be obliged to send many soldiers there to defend her. They arranged also, in order to bring the Pope to greater necessity, that Messer Niccolò Vitelli—an exile from Città di Castello, where the ruler was Messer Lorenzo Vitelli his enemy—should approach that city with soldiers, to make an effort to drive out his adversary and take her from under the Pope's sway.

It seemed, when these movements began, that Fortune intended to favor Florentine affairs, because Count Carlo made great progress in the region of Perugia. Messer Niccolò Vitelli, though he did not succeed in entering Castello, had such superior forces that he plun-dered the open country around the city without any opposition. So also the soldiers left at Poggibonsi every day raided the country up to the walls of Siena. Nonetheless, at last all these hopes turned out fruitless. First, Count Carlo died, in the midst of hopes for victory. Yet his death improved the situation of the Florentines, if they had known how to use the victory that came from it, because the soldiers of the Church assembled at Perugia, learning of the Count's death, at once became confident of defeating the Florentine forces. Going into the field, they encamped near Lake Trasimene three miles from their enemies. On the Florentine side Jacopo Guicciardini, commissioner with the army—on the advice of His Excellency Roberto Malatesta of Rimini, who after Count Carlo's death was the ablest and most esteemed leader in that army—knowing the cause of the enemies' haughtiness, determined to wait for them. When they joined combat near the Lake, where once Hannibal the Carthaginian so memorably defeated the Romans, the soldiers of the Church were vanquished.

When this victory was reported in Florence, everybody rejoiced and praised the leaders. It would have made Florentine policy appear both honorable and profitable if disturbances in the army at Poggibonsi had not upset everything. So the good done by one army the other entirely destroyed, because after the soldiers at Poggibonsi had taken booty in Sienese territory, the Marquis of Ferrara and the Marquis of Mantua quarreled over its division. Then coming to blows, with every sort of outrage they assailed each other. Hence the Florentines, judging they could no longer make use of both, agreed that the Marquis of Ferrara and his men should go home.

CHAPTER 16

[Defeat of the Florentine army; fall of Colle. 1479]

Since this army then was weakened and leaderless and was in every way conducting itself with disorder, the Duke of Calabria, who had his army near Siena, took courage to attack it. And when he did as he planned, the Florentine soldiers, knowing they were to be attacked, showed no faith in their arms, none in their numbers, which were superior to those of the enemy, none in their position, which was very strong; without even so much as waiting to see their foes, they ran away at the sight of their dust, abandoning to the enemy their supplies, baggage and artillery. To such universal poltroonery and disorder were those mercenary armies then subject that a horse's turning its head or its tail determined defeat or victory in a campaign. This rout weighed down the King's soldiers with booty and the Florentines with terror. Their city was not merely at war, but also was distressed by a very severe pestilence, which so took over the city that all the citizens, to escape death, retired to their country houses. This condition made the defeat more terrifying, because immediately after it citizens who had gone to their estates in the Val di Pesa and Val d'Elsa, taking not merely their children and their property but their laborers, hurried to Florence as best they could, as though fearing that at any hour the enemy would appear before the city.

Those in charge of the war, seeing this confusion, commanded the soldiers who had been victorious in the Perugian territory to abandon their campaign against the Perugians and come to the Val d'Elsa to check the enemy, who, after the victory, without any opposition were looting the country. Although they had hemmed in the city of Perugia in such a way that at every hour they expected victory, nonetheless the Florentines preferred first to defend their own city rather than to capture that of others. Hence that army, taken from its successful actions, was brought to San Casciano, a town eight miles from Florence, since to resist elsewhere was thought impossible until the remnants of the routed army were brought together. The enemy, on the other hand—those who were at Perugia—set free by the departure of the Florentine soldiers, became so bold that every day they took quantities of booty in the territory of Arezzo and of Cortona. The enemy under Alfonso Duke of Calabria, who had conquered at Poggibonsi, first mastered Poggibonsi and later Vico, and sacked Certaldo. Having carried out these assaults and plunderings, they marched to the town of Colle, which in those times was considered very strong, and since its men were faithful to the state of Florence, it could hold the enemy off until soldiers could be brought together.

The Florentines, then, having assembled all their men at San Casciano, while the enemy were attacking Colle with all their might, decided to approach them, to give the men of Colle courage to defend themselves. And so that the enemy, having their adversaries near, would be more cautious in attacking the town, the Florentines, on making this decision, took their army from San Casciano and stationed it at San Gimignano, five miles from Colle; then with light cavalry and other light-armed soldiers they annoyed the army of the Duke every day. Nonetheless, for the people of

Colle this relief was not sufficient. Hence, since they lacked things necessary to them, on the thirteenth of November they surrendered, to the grief of the Florentines and to the great joy of their enemies and especially of the Sienese, who, besides their general hatred for the city of Florence, hated the men of Colle in particular.

CHAPTER 17

[The Florentines decide for peace; the nature of the Papacy; Lorenzo determines to visit King Alfonso. 1479]

It was already midwinter and the weather bad for war, so that the Pope and the King, moved either by the wish of giving hope for peace or wishing to enjoy more peacefully the victories they had won, offered the Florentines a truce for three months and gave ten days' time for their reply; the offer was accepted at once. But as it happens to everybody that when the blood grows cold, wounds are felt more than when they are received, this short repose made the Florentines realize more the troubles they had borne. The citizens, freely and without caution, blamed one another and pointed out the mistakes made in the war; they showed the money paid out in vain, the taxes unjustly laid; and these things they spoke of not merely in groups, among individuals, but boldly in the public councils. And one man gained so much courage that turning to Lorenzo de'Medici, he said to him: "This city is tired out and wants no more war"; therefore it was necessary for him to give attention to peace. So Lorenzo, understanding this necessity, consulted with the friends he thought most faithful and wisest. First of all they decided, seeing the Vene-tians cold and untrustworthy and the Duke of Milan a child and involved in civil disturbances, that they must seek new fortune with new allies. Yet they were doubtful in whose hands they should put themselves, those of the Pope or those of the King of Naples.

When they had examined everything, they approved alliance with the King as more stable and more secure. The short lives of the popes, the variations among those chosen, the Church's slight fear of the princes, the few scruples she has in making decisions, are reasons why a secular prince cannot wholly rely on a pontiff and cannot securely share his fortune with him. He who is the Pope's friend in wars and in dangers will in victory have a companion but in defeat

will be alone, since by his spiritual power and reputation the Pontiff
is supported and defended.

Having decided, then, that it was more to their advantage to gain
the King's support, they judged they could not better and with more
certainty do so than by Lorenzo de'Medici's presence, because in
dealing with the King, the more generous they were the more they
believed they could find correctives for past hostilities. So after
Lorenzo had determined on this journey, he gave over the city and
the government to Messer Tommaso Soderini, who was at that time
Gonfalonier of Justice, and at the beginning of December left Florence. On reaching Pisa, he wrote to the Signoria, giving the reason
for his leaving. And those Signors, to honor him and in order that
he could with more authority negotiate the treaty of peace with the
King, made him ambassador of the Florentine people and gave him
power to make an alliance with the King as he should think best
for their republic.

CHAPTER 18
[*Changes in Milan; war with Genoa. 1479*]

In these same times Signor Roberto Sanseverino together with
Lodovico and Ascanio Sforza, because Sforza their brother was
dead, once more attacked the state of Milan in order to return to its
control. And since they had taken Tortona, and Milan and all that
state were under arms, the Duchess Bona was advised to bring the
Sforzas back into the country and, in order to get rid of these civil
conflicts, to receive them into the government. The chief person of
this opinion was Antonio Tassino of Ferrara. Sprung from a humble family, he came to Milan and got into the service of Duke
Galeazzo, who gave him to the Duchess his wife as chamberlain.
Either because he was handsome or because of some secret ability,
after the death of the Duke he rose to such influence with the
Duchess that he almost ruled the state. This greatly vexed Messer
Cecco, a man of great prudence and long experience. Hence in
every way he could, both with the Duchess and with others in the
government, he strove to lessen Tassino's influence. On learning
this, Tassino, in an attempt to revenge himself for these injuries and
to have at hand somebody to protect him from Messer Cecco, encouraged the Duchess to bring back the Sforzas. Following his

advice, and without discussing the matter with Messer Cecco, she brought them back. Whereupon the latter said to her: "You have made a decision that will take away my life and your power." In a short time these things happened, because Lodovico put Messer Cecco to death, and some time after, when Tassino was driven from the dukedom, the Duchess was so angry that she left Milan and gave into Lodovico's hands the control of her son. After that, Lodovico Sforza, as sole ruler of the Dukedom of Milan, caused the ruin of Italy, as will be shown.

Already Lorenzo de'Medici had left for Naples, and the truce between the parties was in effect, when, against all expectation, Lodovico Fregoso, having a sure understanding with some Sarzanese, by stealth entered Sarzana with armed men, took the city and made the agent for the Florentine people a prisoner. This event gave great offense to the chief men in the government of Florence, who were convinced that everything had been done on the instance of King Ferdinand. So they complained to the Duke of Calabria, who was with the army at Siena, that during the truce they had been attacked in a new war. He gave every evidence, both through letters and through envoys, that such a thing had come about without his father's agreement or his own. Nevertheless, the Florentines realized that they were in a very bad situation, for they were out of money, the head of their republic was in the hands of the King, they had an old war with the King and with the Pope and a new one with the Genoese; and they were without friends, because they had no hope in the Venetians, and of the government of Milan they rather felt fear, since it was variable and unstable. Nothing was left to the Florentines except their one hope in what Lorenzo de'Medici was to negotiate with the King of Naples.

CHAPTER 19

[Lorenzo in Naples; his success: the Pope and the Venetians indignant. 1479–1480]

Already Lorenzo had arrived by sea in Naples, where not merely the King but all the city received him with honor and with great expectation because, since so important a war had been begun only to crush him, the greatness of his enemies had made him appear very great. Coming before the King, he so discussed conditions in Italy, the tendencies of her princes and peoples, and what could be hoped in peace and feared in war, that the King on hearing him wondered more at his mighty spirit, his dexterous intellect and his solid judgment than he had before wondered at his ability to carry on such a war alone. Hence he redoubled the marks of respect shown Lorenzo and soon decided that he had rather send him away as a friend than detain him as an enemy. Nonetheless for various reasons he kept him waiting from December to March, in order to make a double test not merely of Lorenzo but of Florence, for in that city Lorenzo did not lack enemies who hoped the King would imprison him and treat him like Jacopo Piccinino. Under cover of lamenting about it, they spoke of it throughout the city, and in public discussions they opposed whatever would help Lorenzo. With these methods they spread the rumor that if the King kept Lorenzo a long time in Naples, Florence would change her government. Hence the King for the time mentioned postponed Lorenzo's departure, to find out if in Florence any disturbance would come about. But having seen that things went on quietly, on 6 March 1479[1] he let him go. Yet first with every sort of favor and display of love Ferdinand gained Lorenzo's good will; and between them they made lifelong agreements for the preservation of both their states.

So at last Lorenzo returned to Florence exceedingly great, if he had left it great; and he was received by the citizens with such joy as his great qualities and his new deserts merited, since he had exposed his own life to bring his native city peace. Two days after his arrival, he announced the agreement made between the republic of Florence and the King. By this each one was bound to the preservation of their two states; as to the cities taken in the war from the Florentines, the King should follow his judgment about restoring them; the Pazzi imprisoned in the tower of Volterra should be freed; and to the Duke of Calabria, for a certain time, certain amounts of money should be paid. This peace, as soon as it was announced, greatly offended the Pope and the Venetians, because the Pope thought he had not been respected by the King, and the Venetians thought they had not been respected by the Florentines, so that, since both of them had been allies in the war, they complained at having no share in the peace. When the Florentines heard and credited the report of this

1. *According to the present reckoning, 6 March 1480.*

anger, they at once feared that from this peace would rise a greater war.

Hence the leaders of the Medici party decided to restrict the government, and to assign important decisions to a smaller number. So they made a council of seventy citizens, with the greatest authority in important matters that they could give. This new body checked the purpose of those who wished to attempt revolution. And to give themselves reputation, before anything else, the Seventy accepted the peace made by Lorenzo with the King; they assigned Messer Antonio Ridolfi and Piero Nasi as ambassadors to the Pope and to King Ferdinand.

Nonetheless, notwithstanding this peace, Alfonso Duke of Calabria, did not leave Siena with his army, pretending that he was detained by the dissensions of the citizens; these were so great that, though he had been camped outside the city, the Sienese took him inside and made him judge of their differences. The Duke, seizing this opportunity, punished many of the citizens with fines, condemned many of them to prison, many to exile and some to death, so that his methods led not merely the Sienese but the Florentines also to suspect him of intending to make himself prince of Siena. Nor was any remedy known for it, since Florence was in a new alliance with the King, and hostile to the Pope and the Venetians. This suspicion made its appearance not merely in the mass of the people of Florence, subtle interpreters of all things, but in the chiefs of the government; and everybody asserts our city never to have been in such great danger of losing her liberty. But God, who always in similar extremities has had special care of her, caused an unexpected event which gave the King, the Pope and the Venetians something to consider more serious than Tuscan affairs.

CHAPTER 20

[*The Turks capture Otranto. 1480*]

A little earlier Mahomet the Grand Turk had besieged Rhodes with a very large army and assailed the town for many months. Nonetheless, though his forces were great and his persistence in his attack on the city very great, he found still more in the besieged, who with such vigor defended themselves against so mighty an attack that Mahomet was obliged to leave the siege with disgrace. So when he left Rhodes, part of his fleet, under Achmet a Pashaw, went toward Valona; and whether he observed the ease of the undertaking or his lord actually gave him orders, as he coasted along Italy, he all at once put four thousand soldiers ashore; attacking the city of Otranto, he quickly took it and sacked it, and killed all the inhabitants. Then, with the best means he had at hand, he fortified himself both in the city and in the harbor; and having brought good cavalry there, he raided and plundered the surrounding country. The King, considering this attack and knowing how powerful a prince had undertaken it, sent agents everywhere to make it known and to ask for troops to assist him against the common enemy, and with great urgency called back the Duke of Calabria and his men who were at Siena.

CHAPTER 21

[The capture of Otranto relieves the Florentines; peace made with the Pope. 1480]

This attack, in proportion as it troubled the Duke and the rest of Italy, pleased Florence and Siena, since the latter believed she had regained her liberty, and the former that she had emerged from those dangers that made her fear losing it. This opinion was strengthened by the lamentation the Duke made in leaving Siena, blaming Fortune, who with an unexpected and unreasonable event had taken from him the lordship of Tuscany. This same event made the Pope change his plan; and whereas before he had never been willing to listen to any Florentine envoy, he became so much milder that he listened to anybody who spoke to him of universal peace. Hence the Florentines were assured that if they would bend to seek pardon from the Pope, they would get it.

It did not seem wise, then, to let this opportunity go by; so they sent the Pontiff twelve ambassadors. When they had reached Rome, the Pope, before he gave them audience, by various schemes kept them waiting. Yet at the end the parties decided how for the future they were going to live, and how much each was to contribute in peace and how much in war. The ambassadors then came to the feet of the Pontiff, who, in the midst of his cardinals, with exaggerated ceremony awaited them. The Florentines made excuses for the things that had happened, now blaming necessity, now the wickedness of others, now the fury of the people and their just anger; and pleading how unlucky they are who are obliged either to fight or to die. Yet because everything ought to be endured in order to escape death, they had endured war, the interdicts and the other hardships that past events had brought with them, in order that their republic might escape slavery, which is wont to be the death of free cities. Nevertheless, if, even though forced, they had committed any sin, they were ready to turn to repentance; and they trusted in His Clemency, who, after the example of the Supreme Redeemer, would be ready to receive them into his most merciful arms.

To these excuses the Pope replied with words full of pride and wrath, bringing up against them what in times past they had done against the Church. Nevertheless, in order to keep the precepts of God, he was glad to allow them that pardon they asked, but he gave them to understand that they would have to obey, and if they broke away from obedience, that freedom which they had been on the point of losing they would lose, and justly; for they are deservedly free who are engaged in good not evil works; for freedom badly used injures oneself and others; to be willing to show little respect for God and less for the Church is not the conduct of a free man but of a licentious one, more inclined to evil than to good, whose reproof is the duty not only of princes but of any Christian whatever. So that in relation to the past he complained of those who with evil deeds had given cause for the war and with very wicked ones had kept it going; it had been ended more through the goodness of others than through the deserts of those who caused it. He then read to them the formula of agreement and of blessing, to which the Pope added, beyond the things discussed and settled, that if the Florentines wished to enjoy the benefits of his blessing, they must furnish money for fifteen armed galleys as long as the Turk was assailing the Kingdom.

The ambassadors complained greatly of this burden, added to the agreement that had been made, but they were not able in any way, by any means or favor, or through any complaint, to lighten it. But after they returned to Florence, the Signoria, to make this peace reliable, sent to the Pope as envoy Messer Guidantonio Vespucci, who a short time before had returned from France. He through his prudence brought everything to endurable terms, and obtained from the Pontiff many favors—which was a sign of greater reconciliation.

CHAPTER 22

[*Florence recovers the Tuscan towns; Lorenzo regains his reputation; the Turks abandon Otranto; the Venetians prepare to conquer Ferrara. 1480–1482*]

At last, the Florentines had settled their affairs with the Pope and, with Siena, were freed from fear of the King through the Duke of Calabria's withdrawal from Tuscany, and the war with the Turks was continuing. Hence the Florentines pressed the King in every way for the restitution of their towns which the Duke of Calabria, on withdrawing, had left in the hands of the Sienese. As a result, the King feared that the Florentines in his great necessity would detach themselves from him and, by starting war against the Sienese, would hinder the assistance that he was hoping for from the Pope and the other Italians. Therefore he agreed to the restitution of the towns, and with new bonds again bound the Florentines to him. Force and necessity, therefore, not writings and obligations, make princes keep their agreements.

When the towns had been got back, and this new compact was established, Lorenzo de'Medici regained the reputation which first the war and then the peace, when there was fear of the King, had taken from him. There had not been lacking, in those times, men who had openly spoken evil of him, saying that to save himself he had sold his native city and that in war Florence lost towns, and in peace she would lose liberty. But when the cities were regained and an honorable agreement with the King established, and the city had recovered her old reputation, talk changed in Florence—for that city is greedy of speaking her mind and judges public matters according to their outcome and not according to their wisdom. So they praised Lorenzo to the sky, saying that his prudence won in the peace what wicked Fortune took from him in the war, and that his advice and judgment were stronger than the arms and forces of the enemy.

Recently the attacks by the Turk had delayed that war which, because the Pope and the Venetians were indignant over the peace, was ready to break out. But as the beginning of that attack was unhoped for and caused much good, so its end was unforeseen and caused much ill. For Mahomet the Grand Turk died, contrary to all expectation, and discord appeared among his sons. Hence the Turks in Apulia, abandoned by their lord, by treaty yielded Otranto to the King.

On the removal, then, of this fear, which kept the plans of the Pope and the Venetians at a standstill, everybody was afraid of new disturbances. On one side were leagued the Pope and the Venetians; with them were the Genoese, the Sienese, and other minor powers. On the other side were the Florentines, the King, and the Duke of Milan; with them were associated the Bolognese rulers and many others. The Venetians wished to make themselves masters of Ferrara, and thought they had a reasonable ground for such action and a certain hope of carrying it through. The ground was that the Marquis declared he was no longer bound to accept from them the *visdomine* and the salt,[1] for according to the agreement, after seventy years his city was to be free from both burdens. On the other hand, the Venetians answered that as long as he kept the Polesine, he must accept the *visdomine* and the salt. Since to this the Marquis would not agree, the Venetians believed they had just cause for taking up arms and a suitable time for doing so, because the Pope was very angry with the Florentines and the King. Still further to gain the Pope's favor, when Count Girolamo went to Venice,[2] they received him with the utmost respect, granting him the freedom of the city and their rank of gentleman—always a sign of the greatest honor to any man on whom they bestow it. In order to be ready for that war, they had levied new taxes and appointed as their general Signor Roberto Sanseverino who, angry with Duke Lodovico, ruler of Milan, had fled to Tortona, and after making some disturbance there had gone to Genoa. While there, he was summoned by the Venetians and made commander of their armies.

1. The *visdomine* *had jurisdiction in Ferrara over disputes involving Venetians. The Ferrarese were forbidden to make salt and obliged to buy it from Venice.*
2. *Girolamo Riario, nephew of Pope Sixtus IV; see 7. 22; 8. 3, above.*

CHAPTER 23

[Roberto Malatesta of Rimini wins at Campo Morto a victory for the Pope over the Duke of Calabria. 1482]

When these preparations for new movements were known, they caused the opposing League also to prepare for war. The Duke of Milan chose for his general Frederick of Urbino, and the Florentines Costanzo Sforza of Pesaro. In order to test the intention of the Pope and to make clear whether the Venetians with his consent were making war on Ferrara, King Ferdinand sent Alfonso Duke of Calabria with his army to the Tronto, and asked passage from the Pope in order to go into Lombardy for the relief of the Marquis of Ferrara. This the Pope absolutely refused. Hence, since the King and the Florentines felt they had made sure of the Pope's intention, they determined to hem him in with their forces, so that of necessity he would become their ally, or at least to impede him so much that he could not send the Venetians reinforcements. Already the latter were in the field and had started war against the Marquis, and had first plundered his territory and then laid siege to Ficarolo, a town very important to that lord's state. So then, the King and the Florentines having determined to attack the Pontiff, Alfonso Duke of Calabria raided toward Rome and with the aid of the Colonna family, who had joined him because the Orsini had sided with the Pope, did great damage in the country. On the other hand the Florentine people, with Messer Niccolò Vitelli, attacked Città di Castello, took that city and drove out Messer Lorenzo Vitelli, who held it for the Pope, and set up as its prince Messer Niccolò.

As a result, the Pope was in great distress, because Rome was disturbed inside by parties, and outside the country was overrun by the enemy. Nonetheless, being a spirited man, and one who intended to conquer and not to yield to the enemy, he engaged as general the Magnifico Roberto Malatesta of Rimini. And having him come to Rome, where the Pope had brought together all his men-at-arms, he showed Roberto how much honor he would gain if, against the troops of a king, he would free the Church from her present troubles, and the great obligation the Pope and all his successors would feel, and that not men only but even God must be grateful to him. The Magnifico Roberto, first having examined the Pope's men-at-arms and all his munitions, urged him to gather as many infantry as he could; this advice with all zeal and speed the Pope put into effect. At that time the Duke of Calabria was so near Rome that every day he raided and plundered up to the city gates. His conduct so angered the Roman people that many of their own free will offered to join with the Magnifico Roberto for the liberation of Rome. These were all thanked and accepted by that commander.

The Duke, knowing of these preparations, drew away from the city somewhat, thinking that if he were at a distance the Magnifico Roberto would not have courage to attack him. And in part he was expecting his brother Federigo, who with fresh troops had been sent him by his father. The Magnifico Roberto, seeing that he was almost equal to the Duke in men-at-arms and superior in infantry, went out from Rome with his forces in order, and made his camp about two miles from the enemy. The Duke, seeing his adversaries close to him, contrary to all his expectations, judged that he must either fight or run away as though defeated. Hence, almost compelled, in order not to do anything unworthy of the son of a king, he determined to fight. Turning their faces toward the enemy, each general arranged his soldiers in the order then usual, and led them to the combat, which lasted until midday. This battle was contested with more courage than any other that had been fought for fifty years in Italy, because on both sides together more than a thousand men were killed. The result was glorious for the Church, because the multi-tude of her infantry attacked the ducal cavalry in such a way that the latter were obliged to turn their backs; and the Duke would have been a prisoner if many Turks (some of those who had been at Otranto and now were fighting for him) had not rescued him.

After winning this victory, the Magnifico Roberto returned in triumph to Rome. His success he enjoyed but a short time because, drinking a large amount of water as a result of the day's labor, he was attacked by a diarrhea that in a few days killed him. His body was honored by the Pope with every sort of honor. When the Pontiff had won this victory, he at once sent Count Girolamo Riario against Città di Castello, to see about restoring that town to Messer Lorenzo, and partly to attempt the city of Rimini, because after the death of the Magnifico Roberto, since his little son was left in charge of his wife, the Pontiff supposed he could easily take the city. His plan would have succeeded if the Florentines had not defended the widow, opposing their armies to Count Girolamo in such a way that he could not effect anything either against Castello or against Rimini.

CHAPTER 24

[*The Venetian war on Ferrara. 1482*]

While in Romagna and at Rome these things were going on, the Venetians had taken Ficarolo and their soldiers had crossed the Po. And the army of the Duke of Milan and of the Marquis of Ferrara was in disorder because Frederick of Urbino fell sick and, after being taken to Bologna to be cared for, died. Hence the affairs of the Marquis kept going down, and in the Venetians the hope of taking Ferrara grew stronger every day.

On the other hand, the King and the Florentines made every effort to get the Pope where they wished him, and not having suc-ceeded in making him yield to arms, they threatened him with a Council, which already the Emperor had announced for Basel. Hence, through the King's ambassadors, who were at Rome, and through the leading cardinals, who wished peace, the Pope was persuaded and forced to think of peace and the union of Italy. Thereupon, through fear and also through seeing that the greatness of the Venetians was the ruin of the Church and of Italy, the Pontiff attempted to form a pact with the League; and he sent his nuncios to Naples, where a league for five years was made by the Pope, the King, the Duke of Milan, and the Florentines, who reserved a place for the Venetians if they accepted it. When this had been done, the Pope let the Venetians understand that they must desist from the war against Ferrara. To this the Venetians would not consent. On the contrary, with greater effort they prepared for war, and defeating the soldiers of the Duke of Milan and the Marquis of Ferrara at Argenta, they came so close to Ferrara that they put their tents in the Marquis' park.

CHAPTER 25

[*The war at Ferrara and in Venetian territory. 1483*]

Since the League believed it could no longer put off giving vigorous help to that lord, it had the Duke of Calabria go to Ferrara with his soldiers and those of the Pope, and likewise the Florentines sent there all their soldiers. In order better to arrange the plan of the war, the League held a meeting at Cremona, where the Pope's legate met with Count Girolamo, the Duke of Calabria, Signor Lodovico Sforza and Lorenzo de'Medici, with many other Italian princes. At this meeting, these princes divided among themselves all the activities of the future war. Because they judged that Ferrara could not be better relieved than by making a strong diversion, they wished Signor Lodovico to consent to undertake a war against the Venetians on behalf of the Duke of Milan's government, but Signor Lodovico would not consent, fearing that he would draw down on himself a war that he could not get rid of when he wished.

And therefore they decided to assemble their soldiers at Ferrara, and having got together four thousand men-at-arms and eight thou-sand infantry, they moved against the Venetians, who had twenty-two hundred men-at-arms and six thousand infantry. The League decided, as its first action, to assail the fleet the Venetians had in the Po, and having assailed it near Bondeno, they defeated it with the loss of more than two hundred boats; there they took prisoner Messer Antonio Giustinian, the overseer of the fleet.

The Venetians, when they saw Italy all united against them, to give themselves more prestige had hired the Duke of Lorraine with two hundred men-at-arms. So, having suffered this loss with their fleet, they sent him, with part of their army, to hold the enemy in check. And Signor Roberto Sanseverino with the remainder of their army they sent across the Adda and close to Milan, shouting the name of the Duke and of Madonna Bona his mother, for they be-lieved that in this way they would stir up rebellion in Milan, thinking that in the city Signor Lodovico and his government were hated. This attack at first roused great terror and put the city under arms. Nonetheless, it produced a result opposed to the Venetian plan, because what Signor Lodovico had not been willing to accept this injury drove him to accept. Therefore, leaving the Marquis of Fer-rara to the defense of his possessions with four thousand horsemen and two thousand infantry, the Duke of Calabria with twelve thousand cavalry and five thousand infantry entered the territory of Bergamo, next that of Brescia and finally that of Verona, and with-out possibility of defense by the Venetians, he deprived those three cities of almost all their country districts, for Signor Roberto and his soldiers were hardly able to save the cities themselves. On the other hand the Marquis of Ferrara also regained a great part of his territory, because the Duke of Lorraine, who was opposing him, was not able to resist, having not more than two thousand horsemen and a thousand infantry. So all that summer of the year 1483 the League fought successfully.

CHAPTER 26

[Venice regains by negotiation what she lost by war. 1484]

In the spring of the next year, then—for the winter went by quietly—the armies took the field. The League, in order more rapidly to overcome the Venetians, assembled its entire army as a unit. Easily, if the war had been carried on as in the preceding year, the League would have taken from the Venetians all the territory they held in Lombardy, because the Venetians sent out six thousand cavalry and five thousand infantry, and were opposed to thirteen thousand cavalry and six thousand infantry, because the Duke of Lorraine, having finished his year's contract, had gone home. But when many of equal authority are working together, it almost always happens that their disagreement gives victory to the enemy.

After the death of Federigo Gonzaga, Marquis of Mantua, whose influence kept the Duke of Calabria and Signor Lodovico united, differences came up between them, and from differences came jealousy. Giovangaleazzo, Duke of Milan, was now old enough to take over the government of his state, and since his wife was the daughter of the Duke of Calabria, the latter wanted not Lodovico but his son-law to rule the state. Knowing, then, this wish of the Duke's, Lodovico decided to preclude his effecting it. Knowing Lodovico's fear, the Venetians seized it as an opportunity; they judged that, as always, they could win with the treaty what they had lost with the war. So having secretly discussed a settlement between themselves and Lodovico, in August 1484 they confirmed it. When the other allies found this out, it disturbed them greatly, especially since they saw that they would have to restore to the Venetians the captured cities, to leave in their hands Rovigo and the Polesine, which they had taken from the Marquis of Ferrara, and even to let them have again all those powers over Ferrara which for many years they had enjoyed. So everybody realized that they had carried on a war in which they had spent much, and in waging it had gained honor, and in ending it, shame, since the captured towns were given back and the lost ones were not regained. But the allies were forced to accept it, being exhausted by the expense and unwilling, for the sake of the sins and ambition of others, to make any further trial of their fortune.

CHAPTER 27

[The Pope tries to regain Città di Castello; he puts down the Colonna family. 1484]

While things were being managed in this way in Lombardy, the Pope, by means of Messer Lorenzo, blockaded Città di Castello in order to drive out Niccolò Vitelli, whom the League, in order to draw the Pope to their way of thinking, had abandoned. And while the city was blockaded, those inside who were partisans of Niccolò made a sortie and, coming to blows with their enemies, defeated them. So the Pope recalled Count Girolamo Riario from Lombardy and had him come to Rome to renew his forces and return to that attempt. But then deciding that it was better to win Messer Niccolò's support with peace than again to attack him with war, he made an agreement with him; as well as he could, he reconciled him with Messer Lorenzo, his adversary.

To this he was forced more by fear of new disturbances than by love of peace, because he saw between the Colonna family and the Orsini family an outbreak of malevolent dissension. The King of Naples, in the war between him and the Pope, had taken from the Orsini the country of Tagliacozzo and had given it to the Colonnesi, who took his side. Then when peace was made between the King and the Pope, the Orsini, by virtue of the agreements, asked for it. Many times the Pope indicated to the Colonnesi that they should give it back, but neither for the requests of the Orsini nor for the threats of the Pope would they consent to its return. On the contrary, they did fresh injury to the Orsini with plundering and like damages. At last the Pope, since he could not bear them, assembled his forces and those of the Orsini against the Colonnesi; and he sacked the houses they had in Rome, killed and arrested those who tried to defend them, and deprived them of the greater part of their towns, so that those disturbances, not through peace but through the crushing of one party, were quieted.

CHAPTER 28

[Death of Sixtus IV; peace in Italy; the election of Pope Innocent VIII. 1484]

Not yet were affairs quiet at Genoa and in Tuscany; because the Florentines kept Count Antonio da Marciano with soldiers on the frontiers of Sarzana, and while the war lasted in Lombardy, with raids and similar light combats they annoyed the Sarzanese. In Genoa, Battistino Fregoso the doge of that city, confiding in Pagolo Fregoso the Archbishop, was with his wife and children captured by him; Pagolo made himself prince of the city. The Venetian fleet also had attacked the Kingdom and seized Gallipoli and harassed the other cities in the region. But when peace came in Lombardy, all the disturbances stopped, except in Tuscany and Rome. The Pope, after peace had been proclaimed, in five days died, whether because the limit for his life had come or because his sorrow at the peace that was made—for he was an enemy to peace—killed him. So at last this Pontiff left in peace that Italy which, while alive, he had always kept at war.

On his death, Rome was instantly under arms. Count Girolamo Riario retired with his soldiers to the Castle; the Orsini feared that the Colonna family would try to revenge their recent injuries; the Colonnesi again demanded their property and their towns; the result was that in a few days there were murders, robberies, and fires in many places in that city. But the cardinals having urged the Count to restore the Castle to the power of their College and to go to his estates and free Rome from his soldiers, he obeyed, since he wished to make the next pontiff well disposed to him; and restoring the Castle to the College of Cardinals, he went off to Imola.

Thereupon, since the cardinals were freed from this fear and the barons were deprived of the aid in their quarrels which they hoped for from the Count, the cardinals proceeded to the choice of a new pontiff. And after some differences they elected Giovanbattista Cibo, Cardinal of Malfetta, a Genoese, who called himself Innocent VIII. He, through his pliable nature, for he was a kindly and quiet man, had arms laid down and made Rome for the time peaceful.

CHAPTER 29

[The Florentines attack Sarzana; the Bank of San Giorgio in Genoa. 1484]

The Florentines, after the peace in Lombardy, could not remain quiet, since they thought it shameful and disgusting that a private gentleman had deprived them of the town of Sarzana.[1] And because the articles of the peace stated that not merely was it proper to ask again things that had been lost but to make war on anybody who hindered their acquisition, they quickly provided money and men for carrying on that expedition. Hence Agostino Fregoso, who had taken Sarzana, knowing that with his private forces he could not sustain so great a war, gave that city to San Giorgio.

Since of San Giorgio and the Genoese I shall many times make mention, it is not out of place to explain the organization and ways of that city, one of the chief in Italy. When the Genoese made peace with the Venetians, after that very important war between them many years ago, their republic, unable to repay those citizens who had lent her great sums of money, granted them the income of the customs house and decreed that, as the receipts permitted, every man, according to the amount of his principal sum, should share in that income until the commonwealth completely repaid him. And that they might meet together, the palace above the customs house was handed over to them. These creditors then organized a method of procedure, choosing among themselves a council of a hundred, which was to decide their affairs of business, and a magistracy of eight citizens which, as the head of all, was to carry them out. They divided their receipts into parts, which they called shares, and their entire body they named after San Giorgio. After in this way they had arranged their administration, new needs came upon the government of the commonwealth, which again applied for assistance to San Giorgio. Being rich and well managed, the company could give it. The commonwealth, on the other hand, as at first she granted the customs, later, as a pledge for the money she had had, granted San Giorgio some of her cities.

And the matter has gone so far, derived from the needs of the commonwealth and the services of San Giorgio, that it has under its

1. *See 8. 18, above.*

administration the greater part of the towns and cities subject to Genoese rule; these towns it governs and defends, and every year by public vote it sends its governors, without the commonwealth in any way taking any trouble. The result is that those citizens have aban-doned their affection for the commonwealth, as a tyrannical thing, and given it to San Giorgio, as a group that is well and fairly con-ducted. This permits easy and frequent changes in the city govern-ment, and sometimes they obey a citizen, sometimes a foreigner, because not San Giorgio but the commonwealth changes its gov-ernment.

Hence, when between the Fregosi and the Adorni there was a fight over the princedom, since they were fighting over the govern-ment of the commonwealth, the greater part of the citizens drew to one side and left it as the spoil of the conqueror. When anybody takes over the government, the company of San Giorgio simply makes him swear to observe its laws, which up to this time have not been changed. Because it has weapons and money and organiza-tion, they cannot be changed without danger of a sure and dangerous rebellion. A condition truly strange, and one that philosophers, among the many republics they have dreamed of and observed, never have found: that is, to see within the same wall, for the same citizens, liberty and tyranny, government fit for citizens and corrupt govern-ment, justice and disorder. That organization alone keeps that city full of ancient and venerable customs, and if it should come about— and with time it surely will come about—that San Giorgio should take over that entire city, she would be a republic memorable beyond the Venetian.

CHAPTER 30
[*War with Genoa. 1484*]

To this San Giorgio, then, Agostino Fregoso granted Sarzana. San Giorgio accepted her gladly and undertook her defense, at once sending a fleet to sea and dispatching soldiers to Pietrasanta in order to hinder anybody who tried to go to the Florentine army, already near Sarzana. On the other hand, the Florentines wished to take Pietrasanta, for without her, since she was between Sarzana and Pisa, the capture of Sarzana was less valuable. But they could not justly besiege Pietrasanta unless her people, or somebody in the town, hindered them in the capture of Sarzana. To bring this about, they sent from Pisa to the army a large amount of munitions and victuals, under a weak escort, in order that the men in Pietrasanta should fear less because of the small guard, and because of the large booty should be more eager to attack the convoy. The outcome was entirely according to plan, for the men in Pietrasanta, seeing so much booty before their eyes, took it. This gave the Florentines a lawful cause for undertaking the business; so abandoning Sarzana, they besieged Pietrasanta, which was full of soldiers who vigorously defended her. Stationing their artillery in the plain, the Florentines made a fort on the mountain, so they could close her in on that side. The commissioner of the army was Jacopo Guicciardini.

During the fighting at Pietrasanta, the Genoese fleet took and burned the castle of Vada, and their soldiers, stationed on land, raided and plundered the country round about. Against these Florence sent Messer Bongianni Gianfigliazzi, who with cavalry and infantry in part checked the insolence of the Genoese, so that they plundered with less freedom. But their fleet, continuing to annoy the Florentines, went to Livorno and with pontoons and other appliances approached the new tower and attacked it for many days with artillery, but since they made no progress, the assailants withdrew with shame.

CHAPTER 31
[*Pietrasanta taken; the Lucchese claim the town. 1484*]

Meanwhile the fighting at Pietrasanta was sluggish, so that the enemy, taking courage, attacked and captured the fort. This brought them such reputation and caused the Florentine army such fear that it was on the point of defeating itself. It withdrew four miles from the city and its leaders judged that since the month of October had come, they should go into winter quarters and put off the siege of Pietrasanta until spring.

This dereliction, when known in Florence, made the leaders of the state very angry. At once, in order to restore the army's reputation and power, they elected as new commissioners Antonio Pucci and Bernardo del Nero. With a large sum of money these two went to the army and reported to the generals the indignation of the Signoria, of the ruling party and of the entire city. They requested the generals to go back to the walls with their forces, and avoid being disgraced by the report that so many officers, with so large a force, having opposed to them only a small garrison, could not take a city so unimportant and weak. They showed the present profit and the future hope from such a capture, so that they stimulated the spirits of all the soldiers to return to the walls. First of all they determined on capturing the fort. Its capture revealed the effect of kindness, courtesy, and pleasant manners and words on soldiers' spirits, because Antonio Pucci, exhorting one soldier, promising something to another, extending his hand to another, embracing still another, got them to make that attack with such vigor that they gained the fort in a moment. Yet the gain was not without loss, for Count Antonio da Marciano was killed by a cannon shot. This victory so terrified those in the town that they began negotiations about surrender. Hence, in order that the affair might be finished with more acclaim, Lorenzo de' Medici decided to go to the army; after he arrived, in a few days the town was gained.

Winter had already come; hence the generals decided not to go on with the business but to wait until spring, especially because that autumn, on account of the bad air, the army had got sick, and many of the officers were seriously ill. Among them Antonio Pucci and Messer Bongianni Gianfigliazzi fell ill and died, lamented by everybody—such was the good opinion Antonio had gained by his actions at Pietrasanta.

After the Florentines had captured the town, the Lucchese sent envoys to Florence to claim her, as belonging to their republic, for they indicated as an article of their treaty with Florence that any city belonging to the other that one of them recovered from a third party must be restored to its first master. The Florentines did not deny the terms; but they answered that they did not know whether by the treaty under negotiation between them and the Genoese they would be obliged to restore that town. Therefore they could not before that time make a decision. If when the treaty was made, they did not have to restore her to Genoa, the Lucchese would need to consider repaying them for what they had spent and for the damage received from the deaths of so many Florentine citizens; and if the Lucchese would do this, they could well hope to have Pietrasanta back again.

All that winter, then, was spent in discussing the treaty of peace between the Genoese and the Florentines, which, with the mediation of the Pontiff, was done at Rome. Since the treaty was not con-cluded, the Florentines would in the spring have attacked Sarzana if Lorenzo de'Medici's sickness and the war that broke out between the Pope and King Ferdinand had not hindered them. Lorenzo was attacked not merely by the gout, which afflicted him as an inheritance from his father, but by severe stomach pains, so that he had to go to the baths to be cured.

CHAPTER 32
[*War between the Pope and the King of Naples. 1485–1486*]

But a more important cause was the war, which originated as follows. The city of Aquila was in such a way subject to the King-dom of Naples that it lived almost independent. The Count of Montorio had great influence in it. At that time, the Duke of Calabria, with his men-at-arms, was near the Tronto River, under the excuse that he wanted to quiet certain uprisings among the peasants in those regions. Planning to bring Aquila entirely into subjection to the King, he sent for the Count of Montorio, as if he wished to make use of him in what he then was doing. The Count obeyed without any suspicion; when he reached the Duke's camp, he was arrested and sent to Naples. When this was known at Aquila, it angered that entire city; the people took up arms and killed Antonio Concinello, the King's commissioner, and with him some citizens who were understood to be His Highness' partisans. And that the people of Aquila might have someone to protect them in their rebellion, they raised the banner of the Church, and sent envoys to the Pope to give him the city and themselves, begging that he would aid her, as his property, against kingly tyranny.

Courageously the Pontiff assumed their defense, for he hated the King for private and public reasons. Since Signor Roberto Sanse-verino was hostile to the state of Milan and without employment, the Pope engaged him as general and had him with the utmost haste come to Rome. He urged, in addition, all the friends and relatives of the Count of Montorio to rebel against the King; so the Princes of Altamura, of Salerno and of Bisignano took up arms against him. The King, seeing himself attacked so suddenly, applied to the Florentines and to the Duke of Milan for aid. At first the Florentines doubted what they ought to do, because they were reluctant to abandon their own affairs for those of another state, and to take up again arms against the Church seemed dangerous. Nonetheless, being in a league, they put their promise ahead of their convenience and their dangers, and hired the Orsini; in addition they sent all their soldiers, under the Count of Pitigliano, against Rome, to the assistance of the King.

So the King formed two armies: one, under the Duke of Calabria, he sent against Rome; this army, together with the Florentine soldiers, opposed the army of the Church; with the other, under his own command, he opposed the barons. In both places this war was carried on with varying fortune. At last, the King being everywhere superior, in August 1486, a treaty was settled by the intervention of the King of Spain's ambassadors. The Pope agreed, beaten down by Fortune and unwilling to tempt her further. In making peace all the potentates of Italy united, leaving out only the Genoese, as rebels against the state of Milan and in possession of Florentine cities.

Signor Roberto Sanseverino, when peace was restored—since in the war he had been to the Pope a friend little faithful, and to the others an enemy little dangerous—as though driven out by the Pope, left Rome. Being pursued by the soldiers of the Duke and the Florentines, when he had passed Cesena and saw that he was overtaken, he fled, and with fewer than a hundred cavalry got to Ravenna; of his other soldiers, part were taken into the Duke's service, part destroyed by the peasants. The King, when peace was made and he was reconciled with his barons, put to death Jacopo Coppola and Antonello d'Anversa with their children, because during the war they had revealed his secrets to the Pontiff.

CHAPTER 33

[The Pope becomes friendly to Florence; Lorenzo de'Medici receives in person the surrender of Sarzana. 1487]

The Pope, with this war as an object lesson, realized with what great promptness and zeal the Florentines observed their alliances, so that whereas earlier his love for the Genoese and the Florentine aid to the King had made him hate them, now he was ready to love the Florentines and showed more than accustomed favor to their ambassadors. This inclination Lorenzo de'Medici recognized and with every effort encouraged, because he judged it would give him a high reputation if to the alliance he had with the King he could add an alliance with the Pope. The Pontiff had a son named Francesco. Hoping to provide him with states and with friends through which he could maintain himself after his father's death, the Pope did not know with whom in Italy he could more securely unite him than with Lorenzo. Therefore he worked in such a way that Lorenzo gave Francesco one of his daughters as wife. Having made this alliance, the Pope urged the Genoese to cede Sarzana to the Floren⁄ tines by treaty, arguing that they could not retain what Agostino had sold and that Agostino could not give San Giorgio what was not his. Nevertheless he never had any success.

On the contrary the Genoese, while these matters were under discussion at Rome, armed a large number of ships and, before any report reached Florence, landed three thousand infantry and attacked the castle of Sarzanello, situated near Sarzana and held by the Floren⁄ tines; the adjacent village they sacked and burned. Next, placing their artillery before the castle, they assailed it with the utmost zeal. This attack was entirely unexpected by the Florentines, who quickly assembled their soldiers at Pisa under Virginio Orsini. They also complained to the Pope that while he was negotiating peace, the Genoese had begun war on them. Then they sent Piero Corsini to Lucca to keep that city to her agreement; they sent Pagolantonio Soderini to Venice, to test the intentions of that republic; they asked auxiliary forces from the King and from Signor Lodovico Sforza. They got none anywhere, because the King said he feared the Turk's fleet, and Lodovico, with various quibblings, put off sending any.

The Florentines in their wars almost always are alone, and do not find those who support them with that courage with which they aid others. But this time they were not bewildered when deserted by their allies, since it was not new to them. So having assembled a large army under Jacopo Guicciardini and Piero Vettori, they sent it against the enemy; the Florentines encamped on the River Magra. Meanwhile Sarzanello was hard pressed by the enemy, who besieged her with mines and every other method, so that the commissioners decided to relieve her. Nor did the enemy refuse battle, and when they came to blows, the Genoese were defeated; the Florentines took prisoner Messer Luigi dal Fiesco, with many other officers of the hostile army. This victory did not frighten the people of Sarzana to such an extent that they were willing to surrender. On the contrary, they stubbornly prepared for defense, and the Florentine commis‚ sioners for attack. Hence she was vigorously attacked and defended.

Since this siege was long drawn out, Lorenzo de' Medici de‚ cided that he should go to the army. When he got there, our soldiers took courage and the men of Sarzana lost it, because, seeing the stubbornness of the Florentines in attacking them and the coldness of the Genoese in aiding them, they put themselves, freely and with‚ out any conditions, in Lorenzo's hands. When they had come into Florentine power, all except a few responsible for the rebellion were humanely treated.

During that siege, Signor Lodovico Sforza sent men‚at‚arms to Pontremoli, to give the appearance of coming to our aid; but since he had a secret understanding in Genoa, the party opposed to those in power rebelled and, with the aid of those soldiers, put themselves in the hands of the Duke of Milan.

CHAPTER 34

[*War between the Venetians and the Germans; Count Girolamo Riario assassinated at Forlì; revenge by his widow. 1487*]

In those days the Germans started war against the Venetians. In the Marches, Boccolino da Osimo led a rebellion against the Pope and took sole authority in Osimo. After many strange events, he consented, on the persuasions of Lorenzo de' Medici, to surrender that city to the Pontiff. Coming to Florence under Lorenzo's pledge, for a long time he lived there very honorably; later he went to Milan where, not finding the same integrity, he was put to death by Signor Lodovico.

The Venetians, attacked by the Germans, were defeated near the city of Trent and their general, Signor Roberto Sanseverino, was killed. After that loss, the Venetians, in accord with their usual fortune, made a treaty with the Germans not as losers but as con‚ querors—so greatly was it to the republic's honor.

In those days very serious disturbances broke out also in Romag‚ na. Francesco d'Orso of Forlì, a man of great influence in that city, became an object of suspicion to Count Girolamo, who many times threatened him. Hence Francesco, living in great fear, was encouraged by his friends and relatives to forestall his danger and, since he feared to be killed by the Count, to kill him first and thus with another man's death to escape his own danger. Having, then, made this decision and settled their courage to this attempt, Francesco and his friends chose as the time the day of the fair of Forlì; since on that day many of their friends came into the city from the country, they thought that without having to ask them to come they could get help. It was the month of May and the greater part of the Italians have the custom of dining by daylight. So the conspirators decided that the suitable hour for killing him would be after his dinner, for at that time, while his servants were eating, he would be in his chamber almost alone. Having made this plan, Francesco at the hour set went to the Count's palace. Leaving his companions on the first floor, he came to the Count's chamber, where he had one of the chamberlains tell the Count that he wished to speak to him. Francesco was let in, and finding Count Girolamo alone, after a few words of pretended talk, he killed him. Then he called his companions, who killed the chamberlain also. By chance the Captain of the city came to speak with the Count, and coming into the hall with a few of his men, he also was killed by the Count's assassins. When these murders had been committed and a great outcry made, the head of the Count was thrown out of the window. Shouting "Church and Liberty," the assassins called to arms all the people, who hated the Count's avarice and cruelty; then they sacked his palace and made the Countess Caterina and all her children prisoners.

Only the fortress was left to take, if their attempt was to succeed. Since the castellan would not give it up, they asked the Countess to influence him. This she promised to do, if they would let her enter the fortress; as a pledge of her faith, they were to retain her children. The conspirators believed her talk and allowed her to enter. When she was inside, she threatened them with death and with every sort of punishment in revenge for her husband. When they threatened to kill her children, she answered that she had with her means for producing more. Then the conspirators became terrified, for they were not supported by the Pope and they heard that Signor Lodovico Sforza, the Countess' uncle, was sending men to aid her; so they took such property as they could carry and went to Città di Castello.

Then the Countess, reassuming power, with every sort of cruelty revenged her husband's death. When the Florentines heard of the Count's death, they took it as an opportunity to regain the castle of Piancaldoli, which in the past the Count had taken from them. Sending their soldiers there, with the death of Cecca, the famous architect, they regained it.

CHAPTER 35

[The murder of Galeotto Manfredi, ruler of Faenza; that city put in the hands of the Florentines. 1488]

To this disturbance in Romagna, another in that region, not of less importance, was added. Galeotto Manfredi ruler of Faenza had as his wife the daughter of Messer Bentivoglio, the chief man in Bologna. Either through jealousy or through her husband's bad treatment of her or through her wicked nature, she hated her husband. And in her hatred she went so far that she determined to take from him his position and his life. So pretending she was sick, she went to bed, arranging that when Galeotto came to visit her, certain of her confidants whom she concealed in her chamber should kill him. This woman shared her plan with her father, who hoped to become ruler of Faenza after his son-in-law's death. When the time planned for the murder came, Galeotto went into his wife's chamber according to his habit, and after he had talked with her a while, from the secret places in the chamber his murderers came out; since he found no way to escape, they killed him. After his death, there was great confusion. His wife, with her little son named Astorre, fled into the castle; the people took arms; Messer Giovanni Bentivoglio, together with one Bergamino, an officer of the Duke of Milan, first getting ready enough armed men, entered Faenza. Antonio Boscoli, a Florentine commissioner, was also there.

While in the midst of such disturbance the leaders just mentioned were meeting and talking about the government of the city, the men of the Val di Lamona, many of whom hastened to this scene of confusion, turned their weapons against Messer Giovanni and Bergamino; they killed Bergamino and took Messer Giovanni prisoner. Shouting the names of Astorre and of the Florentines, they entrusted the city to the Florentine commissioner. This event, when known at

Florence, greatly vexed everybody. Nevertheless, they had Messer Giovanni and his daughter set free, but with the approval of all the people, the Florentines assumed the guardianship of the city and of Astorre.

Besides these, after the chief wars between the greater princes were settled, there were for years many disturbances in Romagna, in the Marches and at Siena; since these were of little import, I judge it superfluous to relate them. It is true that those in Siena, from the time when the Duke of Calabria left after the war of 1478, were very frequent; after many changes, in which now the people, now the nobles were in power, the nobles were victorious. Among them Pandolfo and Jacopo Petrucci gained the greatest influence; these— one through his wisdom, the other through his courage—became virtually princes in that city.

CHAPTER 36
[*The death of Lorenzo de'Medici; his career. 1492*]

The Florentines, on ending the war over Sarzana, lived in the greatest happiness until 1492, when Lorenzo de'Medici died. When Italian arms, which through Lorenzo's wisdom and influence had been made inactive, were laid down, he turned his mind to strengthening himself and his city. To Piero, his eldest son, he married Alfonsina, daughter of the Cavaliere Orsino; then Giovanni, his second son, he brought to the dignity of the cardinalate. This was the more noteworthy in that contrary to all past examples, Giovanni— not fourteen years old—received so high a rank. This was a ladder to enable his house to rise to the skies, as in following years it did. For Giuliano his third son, because of his tender age and the short time that Lorenzo lived, he could not provide any extraordinary fortune. As to his daughters, he married one to Jacopo Salviati, another to Francesco Cibo, the third to Piero Ridolfi; the fourth, whom he married to Giovanni de'Medici in order to keep his house united, died.

In his private mercantile affairs he was very unlucky, since through the irregularities of his employees, who administered his affairs not as private persons but as princes, in many places much of his portable wealth was lost; hence his native city had to assist him with large sums of money. Therefore, in order not to tempt such a fortune further, laying aside mercantile activities, he turned to landed property as more fixed and solid wealth; so near Prato, near Pisa and in the Val di Pesa he formed estates which in income and in type of buildings and of magnificence were not those of a private citizen but kingly.

After this he turned to making his city more beautiful and larger; therefore, since she contained many spaces without dwellings, in them he planned new streets, to be filled with new buildings, so that the city might become more beautiful and larger. And in order that in his state he might live more quietly and safely and that his enemies could be fought or resisted at a distance, in the midst of the moun-tains toward Bologna he fortified the town of Firenzuola; toward Siena he started to erect Poggio Imperiale and make her very strong; toward Genoa, by the conquest of Pietrasanta and of Sarzana he closed the road to the enemy. In addition, with pensions and stipends he supported his friends the Baglioni in Perugia and the Vitelli in Città di Castello; of Faenza he had control in person. All these were like strong fortifications for his city.

Then in these peaceful times he kept his native city always cele-brating festivities, in which jousts and presentations of ancient deeds and triumphs were to be seen. His purpose was to keep the city rich, the people united, and the nobility honored. He greatly loved whoever was excellent in any profession. He favored men of letters, as Messer Agnolo da Montepulciano, Messer Cristofano Landino, and Messer Demetrio Chalcondylas the Greek bear strong witness. For this reason Count Giovanni Pico della Mirandola, a man al-most divine, rejected all the other parts of Europe he had visited and made his abode in Florence, because of Lorenzo's liberality. In architecture, in music, and in poetry Lorenzo took the greatest pleasure; many poetical compositions are extant which he not merely composed but commented on. That the Florentine youth might be trained in the study of letters, he opened in the city of Pisa a school in which he placed the most excellent men then in Italy. Because Fra Mariano da Ghinazzano of the order of Saint Augustine was a very excellent preacher, Lorenzo built him a monastery near Florence.

By Fortune and by God, Lorenzo was greatly loved; hence all his enterprises ended successfully and all those of his enemies were unsuccessful even though, in addition to the Pazzi, Battista Frescobaldi in the Carmine and Baldinetto da Pistoia in Lorenzo's villa attempted to murder him. But each of these, together with those who knew their secrets, suffered just penalties for their wicked conspiracies. His way of living and his prudence and good fortune were observed with admiration and highly respected not merely by the princes of Italy but by those at a distance. Matthias King of Hungary gave many signs of love for him; the Soldan sent him ambassadors and presented him with gifts; the Grand Turk put in his hands Bernardo Bandini, his brother's murderer. These things made Italy regard him as marvelous.

His reputation, because of his prudence, daily increased, since in discussing affairs he was eloquent and penetrating, in settling them wise, in carrying them out prompt and courageous. Nor can any vices be brought up against him that soiled his great virtues, even though in affairs of love he was wonderfully involved, and he delighted in witty and keen men and in childish plays more than seemed fitting for so great a man, so that he was often seen among his sons and daughters, taking part in their sports. Hence, observing both his frivolous and pleasure-seeking conduct and his serious conduct, we see in him two different persons joined in an almost impossible combination. He passed his last days in the severest suffering, caused by the disease that kept him incredibly distressed, because he was afflicted with unbearable stomach-pains, so violent that in April 1492 he died, in his forty-fourth year.

Never did any man die not merely in Florence but in all Italy who was so renowned for prudence and so deeply mourned by his native city. That his death would lead to the greatest calamities, the Heavens showed by many evident signs: among these, the very highest point of the Church of Santa Reparata was struck by lightning with such fury that a great part of the pinnacle fell, to the awe and wonder of everybody. His death was mourned, then, by all Florentines and by all the princes of Italy. Of this grief the princes gave clear signs, for there was not one who did not declare to Florence through his ambassadors the sorrow he felt at so great an event.

Whether they had just cause for mourning was soon after shown by the result, for when Italy was deprived of his advice, those who were left found no way either to satisfy or to check the ambition of Lodovico Sforza, the guardian of the Duke of Milan. No sooner was Lorenzo dead than Lodovico's ambition stimulated the growth of those evil seeds that not long after, since no living man could destroy them, devastated—and are still devastating—Italy.

THE NATURES OF FLORENTINE MEN

[*Generally supposed to have been intended for the* HISTORY OF FLOR⁄
ENCE, *after the eighth book; hence written in the 1520's.*
The four sections make up an autograph manuscript with the title: THE
NATURES OF FLORENTINE MEN AND IN WHAT PLACES I CAN
INSERT THEIR PRAISES. *The reference to insertion fits the title codas of
the sections on Giacomini and the two ambassadors. Evidently Machiavelli
did not compose in chronological order.*]

PIERO DI GINO CAPPONI

Thus died Piero Capponi, a man of high reputation because of
the abilities of his grandfather and great⁄grandfather, whose fame,
extinguished in his father, by his courage and his eloquence he had
for himself regained. In these two qualities he was of the highest
excellence. He was nevertheless varied in his actions, so much so
that, speaking of him, Lorenzo de'Medici said that Piero seemed to
him sometimes his father and sometimes his grandfather. His fortune
was not less varied than his nature, because by his fortune he was in
every sort of public office in various ways now raised up, now
brought down. One can praise him, above everything else, for this:
that he alone supported what all the other citizens had abandoned,
when before the King's face he tore up those articles of agreement
that took away the liberty of his native city; and he was not frightened
by the arrogance and power of the French, nor by the cowardice of
his fellows; and only through him it was that Florence did not live
as the slave of the French, as through Camillus it was that Rome
did not live by being bought from them.

ANTONIO GIACOMINI WHEN HE WAS CHOSEN COMMISSIONER FOR THE FIRST DEVASTATION

This man in his boyhood, on account of the parties of Messer
Luca and of Piero de'Medici the elder, had limits assigned to him

with his father,[1] outside the city. And having gone to a country house of his, his father sent him to Pisa into mercantile business, in which all the nobility of Florence labored as in a thing very profitable and very well regarded in their city. In this he did not remain long, because, having directed his thoughts to a higher fortune, he went to live in the courts of princes, and with Lord Roberto da Sanseverino, then the first general in Italy, he spent part of his youth.

He returned to Florence a little before 1494. With the help of Francesco Valori, he was, as an able man, early brought into public affairs; and in the first commissions that were given him he carried himself in such a way that he was constantly thought worthy of higher rank. Hence the people gave him all those offices at home and abroad which at his age could be given to the most honorable citizen.

Especially in matters of warfare Antonio was skilled far beyond all the other Florentine citizens: cautious in making his decisions, bold in carrying them out, an enemy to the wicked and cowardly, a lover and supporter of good and courageous men, strict in keeping the dignity of the government and—something that is admirable and unusual—he was very liberal with his own property and altogether refrained from that of others. Not even when he was in control of an army or a province did he ask from his subjects other than obedi⁄ence, yet on the disobedient he had no mercy. He was, in private life, without partisan feeling and without any ambition; when in public life, he was eager only for the glory of the city and for his own reputation. These qualities soon caused the people of Florence to believe that under other management they could neither attack their enemies nor defend themselves from them; nothing hard, bold, or dangerous was entrusted to any other than to him, nor did any other more willingly accept such a task. As a result his name grew great not only in Florence but in all Tuscany; and so Antonio, unknown at the beginning and obscure, gained esteem in that city where all the other important and esteemed citizens had lost it.

1. *In Florentine banishment, geographical limits were assigned which the banished man could not pass; he might be excluded from Florence; he might be required to live in some distant city, such as Bologna.*

OF MESSER COSIMO DE' PAZZI AND MESSER FRANCESCO PEPI, MADE AMBASSADORS TO THE EMPEROR

The ambassadors chosen were Messer Cosimo de' Pazzi, Bishop of Arezzo, and Messer Francesco Pepi, a lawyer. Besides being nobles, these men were distinguished and prudent; in them the new government had much confidence because it had given to the first his native city,[2] and to the second the government, and, though Messer Francesco was a mere advocate, had called him to that high place which in a free state, as a result of his ability, could not be denied to him.

OF FRANCESCO VALORI

Francesco Valori met this death unfitting his life and his goodness, because no country ever had a citizen who more desired her good than he did or who was so much and with fewer scruples her defender.[3] This, because it was not understood by many, made him hated by many. As a result, his special enemies determined to kill him. His courage and good character are proved by his always holding high office and dying poor, to such an extent that his grandchildren refused their inheritance from him.[4] They are proved by his never having been the cause or the originator of any revolution, but a staunch defender of the existing organization of the city. It was by no fault of his that the Medici government did not continue, for after the death of Lorenzo he defended it against its detractors. It was not his responsibility that the free government did not stand firm; and all its safeguards and laws must be attributed to his courage and resolution.

2. *His banishment was revoked.*

3. *He was one of those men Machiavelli admired for loving their native city more than their own souls.*

4. *They refused to accept a bequest burdened with debts*

WORDS TO BE SPOKEN ON THE LAW FOR APPROPRIATING MON- EY, AFTER GIVING A LITTLE IN- TRODUCTION AND EXCUSE

[*The date of this work has been considered fixed by a note in Machiavelli's hand on the autograph manuscript: "1503, March. Oration." He used the system of dating in which the year begins on March 25; hence this date refers to the end of March, 1503. It cannot refer to the earlier part of the month in 1504, as we now reckon, because Pope Alexander VI, mentioned as alive, died in 1503. On 1 April 1503 Machiavelli wrote a letter announcing the passage in the Great Council of a measure providing money for the army.[1]*

It is commonly assumed that this speech was written for delivery before some Florentine body, by a speaker other than Machiavelli. But the word for oration (concione *) used in his note is the same as he applies in the Dedication of his* HISTORY OF FLORENCE *to the invented speeches in that work. So closely does this speech resemble some of them as to indicate that it was pre- pared for some never-completed book of the* HISTORY; *the title-coda is, then, a note for its insertion. If so, though 1503 is the date of the events themselves, the composition of the speech was late in Machiavelli's life.*]

ALL THE CITIES THAT EVER AT ANY TIME HAVE BEEN ruled by an absolute prince, by aristocrats or by the people, as is this one, have had for their protection force combined with prudence, because the latter is not enough alone, and the first either does not produce things or, when they are produced, does not maintain them. Force and prudence, then, are the might of all the governments that ever have been or will be in the world. Hence any man who has considered change of kingdoms and the destruction of provinces and of cities has not seen them caused by anything other than failure in arms or in good sense. If Your Excellencies grant me this as true, as it is, of necessity I deduce that you desire in your city both of these two things, and that you try hard, if they are there, to maintain them, and if they are not there, to provide them.

1. *Canestrini,* SCRITTI INEDITI DI MACHIAVELLI, *1857, p. 49.*

And truly, up to two months ago I was very hopeful that you were moving toward this end, but then having seen how great is your obstinacy, I am much alarmed. And seeing that you can learn and see, and yet that you do not learn and see things about which even your enemies are astonished, I am convinced that God has not yet punished us as he intends, and that he is keeping us for greater chastisement. The cause that, up to two months ago, gave me reason for high hope, was the example you saw in the risk you ran a few months earlier, and the measure you took after it. Because I saw that after Arezzo and the other towns were lost and then regained, you gave a head to the city; and I believed you understood that, because there was among you neither force nor prudence, you had been in danger of losing Arezzo; so I judged that as you gave a place to prudence through the ability of that head, you were going also to give a place to force. This same belief was held by our exalted Signors; it was held also by all those citizens who so many times have striven in vain to make provision for you. I do not intend to debate whether that which is now current is good or bad, because I rely for it on him who is in a position to arrange it and on him who later has approved it. I hope strongly that you too may be of the same opinion and give credit in the matter to him who tells you that it is necessary.

Again I repeat that without forces cities are not preserved but come to an end. That end is either destruction or servitude. You have been close this year to both of them; and you will return to the same place if you do not change your opinion. I declare it to you. Do not say, then, "It was not said to me." And if you answer, "What need do we have for forces? We are under the King's protection; our enemies are destroyed; Valentino has no reason for attacking us," I answer you that no opinion could be rasher than yours, because every city, every state ought to consider as enemies all those who can hope to take possession of her territory and against whom she cannot defend herself. Never was princedom or republic wise that was willing to let her territory stand in the power of others or which, so letting it stand, thought she held it securely.

Let us not deceive ourselves deliberately; let us examine a bit, if you will, our situation; and let us begin by looking within. You find yourselves unarmed. You see your subjects without fidelity; and a few months ago you had experience with them. It is reasonable that it should be so, because men cannot be, and ought not to be, faithful servants of that master by whom they cannot be either de- fended or punished. How you have been able and are able to punish them is known to Pistoia, Romagna, Barga—places which have become nests and refuges for every sort of thief. How you have been able to defend them is known by all those places that have been attacked. And not seeing you now in better condition than in the past, they have not, you must believe, changed either opinion or purpose. You cannot call them your subjects, but rather those of the first who attacks them.

Leave home now, and observe whom you have around you. You find yourself in the midst of two or three cities that are more eager for your death than for their own lives. Go farther; leave Tuscany and consider all Italy: you see her controlled by the King of France, the Venetians, the Pope and Valentino.

Begin by observing the King. Here it is necessary to tell the truth and I am going to do so. As to him, either he will find no other obstacle or check in Italy than what you offer (and then there is no remedy, because all forces, all attempts at preparation, will not save you); or he will find some other obstacle, as it appears that he has, and in this instance there will be a remedy or no remedy, as you decide or do not decide. The remedy is to get your forces into such order that he will need in all his decisions to have regard for you as he does for others in Italy; you must not, by remaining unarmed, rouse the courage of some powerful man to ask you from the King as plunder; you must not give such an opportunity to the King that he can leave you among the abandoned, but must act in such a way that he has to respect you, and that nobody will suppose he can conquer you.

Observe now the Venetians. Here you do not need to take much trouble. Everybody knows their ambition, that they are to get from you a hundred and eighty thousand ducats, that they have waited a long time, and that it is better to spend the money in making war on them than to give it to them so that they will injure you with it.

Let us go on to the Pope and his Duke.[2] This side does not need comment. Everybody knows their nature and their ambition, of

2. Almost *"this Duke of his."* It is hard to feel that Machiavelli did not intend some con- tempt, at least such as appears in THE PRINCE 7: *"Duke Valentino gained his state with the*

what sort it is, their procedure, of what kind it is, and what fidelity can be given or received. I shall say this only, that nobody has up to now made any exact agreement with them; and I say further that it is not left for you to do so. But let us assume that one should be settled tomorrow. I have told you that these princes will be your friends when they cannot attack you; and again I say it to you, be-cause among private men laws, writings and agreements make them keep their word; but among princes nothing but arms makes them keep it. And if you say, "We shall apply to the King," it seems to me that already I have said to you this: that not on all occasions will the king be in a position to defend you, because not on all occasions are the times the same; it is not always possible to put your hand on another's sword, and therefore it is good to have a sword at your side and to gird it on when the enemy is at a distance, because afterward another man is too late and you have no resource.

Many of you can remember when Constantinople was taken by the Turks. That Emperor foresaw his ruin. He called upon his citizens, not being able with his organized forces to make proper provision. He showed them their dangers, showed them the pre-ventives; and they ridiculed him. The siege came on. Those citizens who had before had no respect for the exhortations of their lord, when they heard within their walls the thunder of artillery and the yells of the army of their enemies, ran weeping to the Emperor with their bosoms full of money; but he drove them away, saying: "Go to die with this money, since you have not wished to live with-out it." But it is not necessary that I go into Greece for instances, having them in Florence. In September 1500, Valentino with his soldiers left Rome; it was not known whether he was going to march into Tuscany or into Romagna. This whole city was in anxiety because she was unprepared, and everybody prayed God to give us time. But when he showed us his back by going in the direction of Pesaro, and the dangers did not seem immediate, you shifted to rash confidence, so that it was not possible to persuade you to pass any appropriation. There was no failure to bring before you and to name over and predict all the dangers that later came about, to which you stubbornly would not listen. Finally in this place, being assembled on 26 April 1501, you learned of the loss of Faenza and saw the tears

fortune of his father, and with that lost it." If this oration was written for the HISTORY OF FLORENCE, *it is one of Machiavelli's late expressions on Cesare.*

of your Gonfalonier, who wept over your unbelief and obstinacy and forced you to have mercy on yourselves.

But you were not in time because, though if the provision had passed earlier by six months it would have been effective, when it passed six days earlier, it could do little for your safety. Because, on the fourth day of May, you learned that Firenzuola had been reached by the hostile army; the city was in confusion; you began to find out the results of your obstinacy; you saw your houses burned, your goods plundered, your subjects killed, led prisoners, your women violated, your property laid waste, without being able to give any protection. And those who, six months before, had not wished to agree to pay twenty ducats had taken from them two hundred, and they had to pay the twenty just the same. And though you should have blamed your own unbelief and stubbornness, you blamed the maliciousness of the citizens and the ambition of the wealthy—for you are like those who, wrong all the time, do not admit that they have ever been wrong, and when you see the sun, do not believe that it is ever going to rain. So it happens now. For you do not consider that in eight days Valentino can be with his army in your territory, and the Venetians in two days; you do not take into account that the King is engaged with the Swiss in Lombardy; you do not take into account that he also does not have his affairs settled with Germany or with Spain, and that he is at a disadvantage in the Kingdom. You do not see your weakness when so placed, or the uncertainty of Fortune.

Other people often grow wise through the dangers of their neighbors; you do not grow wise through your own, you put no faith in yourselves, and you do not see the time that you are losing and that you have lost. That too you will weep for, and without result, if you do not change your views. Because I tell you that Fortune does not change her decision when there is no change in procedure; and the heavens do not wish or are not able to support a city that is determined to fall in any case. Such a fall I cannot believe in, when I see that you are free Florentines and that in your own hands rests your liberty. For that liberty I believe you will have such regard as they always have had who are born free and hope to live free.

THE DECENNALI

[Florentine contemporary history. 1494-1504]

[The first of these poems, dealing with the preceding ten years in Floren-tine affairs, was written in 1504. The second, left unfinished, was presumably written in 1514, though dealing with events only to 1509.

The FIRST DECENNALE was put on paper in fifteen days. It was, however, truly composed during ten years, while Machiavelli with intense interest followed the events of his time, and in some of them had a share. Such observation and brief characterization of current history were for him a neces-sary preoccupation. Moreover, poetry sometimes accepts chronicle, unless we are to reject the Roman chronicle in the sixth canto of Dante's PARADISE and the Hebrew chronicle in the last book of PARADISE LOST. A reader who frees himself from preconceptions about the subject of poetry will find here something of the artist. If the lines be taken merely as prose comment, they form a supplement to Machiavelli's other works; note, for example, his references to Cesare Borgia, Duke of Valence.]

FIRST DECENNALE
[Ten years of Florentine contemporary history]

Dedication*

Niccolò Machiavelli's greetings to Alamanno Salviati,
a pre-eminent man.

Read, Alamanno, since you wish to, the vexations of Italy for ten years and mine for fifteen days. I know that you will sorrow for her and for me, seeing her borne down by such misfortunes and me trying to include so many great things within such narrow limits. I am sure also that you will excuse us both: her because of fate's necessity and me because of the short time allowed me for such avocation. And since you, by preserving the liberty of one of her

---

* There is also a Latin form of this dedication, generally equivalent to the Italian here trans-lated. The Latin says, however, that the DECENNALE was written on Salviati's invitation: these words have been overlooked by those thinking Salviati unfriendly to Machiavelli. See the note on line 357.

chief members, have supported her, I am certain you will support me too as the narrator of her vexations, and will be willing to impart to these my verses so much spirit that they may be worthy of their serious subject and of your reading. Farewell.

8 November 1504

1 I shall sing Italian hardships for those two lustres now just over, under planets hostile to her good.

4 Of how many mountain paths, of how many swamps I shall tell, filled with blood and dead men by the vicissitudes of splendid states and kingdoms!

7 O Muse, hold up this harp of mine, and you, Apollo, come to give me aid, companioned by your sisters.

10 The swift sun over the surface of our world had run full a thousand, four hundred ninety-four courses

13 after the time when Jesus first visited our cities and, with the blood he spent, quenched the sparks of devilish fire,

16 when discordant Italy opened into herself a passage for the Gauls and suffered barbarian peoples to trample her down.

19 And because to comply with them your city was not prepared, he who held her reins was scourged by their violence.

22 So all Tuscany was in confusion; so you lost Pisa and those states the Medici family gave to the French.

25 Thus you could not rejoice as you should have done at being taken from under the yoke that for sixty years had been crushing you,

28 because you saw your state laid waste; you saw your city in great peril, and in the French arrogance and pride.

31 Nor was it your role, for escaping the talons of so great a king and not becoming his vassals, to show small courage or less wisdom.

34 The clangor of arms and of horses was not loud enough to keep unheard the voice of one capon among a hundred gamecocks;

37 so the proud King left, after he learned that the city, in maintaining her freedom, was united.

40 And when he had moved into the Sienese country, Alexander,

l. 19 *The words* your *and* you *refer to the Florentines, especially those in the government.*
l. 23 *To the French, Piero de' Medici gave up Sarzana and other places.*
l. 36 *Piero Capponi (Capon) defied the French (Galli, Cocks).*

making no account of shame, turned wholly against the Aragonese.

43 But the Gaul, who aspired to pass on securely, determined to have the Pope's son with him, not trusting Catalonia's promise.

46 So with his conquering army he moved upon the Kingdom like a falcon that swoops or a bird of swifter flight.

49 When the report of a victory so great and so easy came to the ears of that first mover of Italy's distress,

52 well he learned his folly clear, and afraid of falling into the trench that with so much sweat he had dug,

55 and aware that his own might did not suffice, that Duke, striving to save the whole, along with the Pope, the Empire and Saint Mark, formed a huge army.

58 Even with this he was not entirely safe, because Orléans by leaping into Novara gave him the first fruits from his seeds.

61 When that became known to Charles, over the Duke and over the Pope he greatly lamented, and over the Pope's son who escaped,

64 and not at all would he consent to remain in Apulia longer. Leaving many soldiers to guard the Kingdom, toward Tuscany with the rest he retreated.

67 You meanwhile, full of anger, sent troops into Pisa's country against that people filled with such hatred,

70 and after some dissension, you found new methods for your city government, and such they were that you set up a citizens' republic.

73 But being more than a little wearied of the French with their disgraceful ways and purposes, and the weights they had crushed you with,

76 when you learned of Charles's return, in your desire to avoid so great a throng, you furnished the city with arms and men.

79 And so, when with his host he reached Siena, being pushed on by a matter more urgent, he went off by the road which took him to Pisa,

82 where at once he heard of Gonzaga's ardor, and that to oppose him on the Taro he had brought the forces of Saint Mark.

l. 51 *Lodovico Sforza, called the Moor (Moro) because of his dark complexion and the pomegranate (moro) in his coat of arms. He invited the French invasion.*
l. 84 *Gonzaga led the forces opposing Charles VIII at Fornovo, on the Taro River.*

85 But those strong and ardent men with such vigor charged the Italic squadron that over its belly they marched onward.

88 A stream of blood the river seemed to beholders, full of men and arms and horses fallen under the Gallic sword.

91 So the Italians let them go, and without fearing hostile soldiers, the French reached Asti without further afflictions.

94 There they settled their treaty as though in a race, not regarding Orléans' outcry nor thinking of Novara's hunger.

97 And since the French returned to their own soil, after bringing you to new agreements, Ferdinand leaped into his pleasant nest.

100 From that resulted his compacts with the Venetians so they would aid him, and he granted them more than half Apulia and made them lord of her.

103 Then the League united itself afresh to resist the Gaul, and you all alone were left in Italy, as his ensign,

106 and in order to be good sons to France you did not object, as you followed her star, to enduring a thousand distresses and a thousand pains.

109 Yet while in the Kingdom there was strife between Saint Mark and France with undecided issue, until the French starved in Atella,

112 you stood here with open mouth to wait for someone coming from France who would bring you manna in the desert,

115 and would restore to you the castles in Pisa, Pietrasanta and the other towns, as many times the King had promised you.

118 At last there came Lanciaimpugno and he of Lille, Vitelli and many others, who deceived you in certain things it is better not to mention.

121 Only Beaumont gave you Livorno, but the others, traitors in revolt against Heaven, of all the other towns deprived you,

124 and from your Lion, the Wolf, along with Saint George and the Panther, tore away some fur. So much it seems that Fortune smites you!

127 After Italy drove the French troops from her, and without long delay became free through Fortune and Wisdom,

l. 94 In a race: with speed.
l. 124 The Lion (Marzocco) of Florence; the Wolf of Siena; St. George for Genoa; the Panther of Lucca.

130 she turned her breast and her face entirely against you, and said her reason was merely that she might take you from France.

133 You, favored only by right, against their skill and force for a time held erect your banner,

136 because you knew well that through hatred your debasement was sweet to your neighbors, and the others wanted you without expense.

139 Whoever feared your greatness was coming against you, and those others were deaf, since every man set high value on being lord of Pisa.

142 But as Heaven determined, among these gluttons ambition sprang up, and Saint Mark and the Moor on that acquisition were not of one mind.

145 This distrust that rose among them made the Empire come to your land and go away without result;

148 so that at last the Viper, in anger, encouraged you not to fear resisting Saint Mark and his armies;

151 and the latter brought against your walls your mighty exile; from this came burial for five citizens.

154 But that which to many was far more distressing and brought on disunion, was that sect under whose command your city lay.

157 I speak of that great Savonarola who, inspired with heavenly vigor, kept you closely bound with his words.

160 But many feared to see their country ruined, little by little, under his prophetic teaching;

163 hence no ground for your reunion could be discovered, unless his light divine continued to increase, or unless by a greater fire it was extinguished.

166 Nor of less moment at that time was King Charles's death, which made the Duke of Orléans that kingdom's master.

169 So because by himself alone the Pope had no strength to do anything great, he set out to win the new king's favor,

172 granted his divorce, and gave him Brittany; and in return the King promised him the lordship and the states of Romagna.

l. 148 *The Viper of Milan, from the arms of the Visconti.*

l. 151 *Piero de' Medici.*

l. 163 *Florentine factions could not be suppressed unless Savonarola was overthrown or obtained greater authority.*

175 And since Alexander lacked a man to hold his banner aloft after Candia's death and defeat,

178 he turned to his son who had a place among the great clerics and withdrew him from them, changing the cardinal's hat to the soldier's cap.

181 Meanwhile the Venetian, with those forces of men he had brought together in Pisa, moved his standard against you.

184 Hence when the Count's defeat at Santo Regolo followed, you were forced to give the truncheon and command to Vitello.

187 Then believing you were virile, strong and mighty through the force of those weapons, you moved your army against those unjust men;

190 and not lacking the help of Sforza, you determined to be seen on the wall of Pisa with the standard of Vitello.

193 But Saint Mark's soldiers, to keep your plan from succeeding, attacked Marradi first and then the Casentino.

196 You put the Calf on that road, so that under his banners were defeated the Bear and Urbino.

199 And still worse would have befallen them if you had not been divided by dissension between the Calf and the Cat.

202 After Saint Mark was so defeated, he made a treaty with Louis in France to get revenge for the blow he had suffered.

205 But because the Turk put his lance in rest against them, such great fear of making their balance squeak overcame them

208 that it drove them on to make peace with you, and in great confusion to abandon Pisa; and the Moor compelled you to approve a treaty,

211 to see if with this benefit he could regain Venetian friendship, judging other ways defective.

214 But this plan of his still was useless, because in secrecy they had partitioned Lombardy with the great Christian King.

l. 184 *Count Rinuccio da Marciano, Florentine general.*

l. 196 *Calf: the mercenary general Vitello, whose name means* calf. *Cf. lines 186, 201, 228, 347, 352, 386. His younger brother Vitellozzo is* Big Calf *or* Ugly Calf, *or the calf's other horn (line 402).*

l. 198 *The Bear (Orso) is Carlo Orsini, general for the Venetians. Others of the family are referred to in the same way (lines 321, 385, 400).*

l. 201 *The Cat is Count Rinuccio da Marciano, the Florentine general defeated at St. Regolo (line 184).*

l. 207 *A very heavy burden when weighed would make the balance squeak; cf.* INFERNO 23. 101.

217 So his shrewdness was mocked, and you without fear of any
thing surrounded Pisa with your army,

220 where you remained for the circuit of one moon without any
fruit, because to strong beginnings Fortune made violent op
position.

223 Long would it take to tell all the injuries, all the deceits en
countered in that siege, and all the citizens dead from fever.

226 So seeing no resource for her capture, you withdrew your army,
to escape the trouble of that campaign and Vitello's delay.

229 Soon after, for the trick he played, you took revenge in full,
inflicting death on him who had caused you such great harm.

232 At this time the Moor as well did not encounter better luck,
because the crown of France already was before his gates;

235 from which he fled to save his person, and Mark without any
hindrance planted his standards in Ghiaradadda and in Cre
mona.

238 And the Gaul, to keep his promises to the Pope, was forced to
yield Valentino some of his soldiers.

241 That duke, beneath the flag of the three lilies, mastered Imola
and Forlì and took away from them a woman and her sons.

244 But you found yourselves in great fear, having been a little
sluggish in complying with the victor Gaul.

247 Yet after his victory over the Lombards, he consented to receive
you, not without effort and cost as the price of your slackness.

250 Scarcely was he back in France when Milan recalled Lodo
vico—thus to follow the people's custom.

253 But the Gaul, swifter than I can tell, in less time than you can
say "Ecco" rose up against his enemy.

256 From Romagna, the French gamecocks turned their beaks
toward Milan to rescue their fellows, leaving the Pope and
Valentino high and dry.

259 And in order that then the Gaul might carry off, as he did, the
palm with the olive, you also did not fail to give him aid;

l. 231 *Vitello was executed.*

l. 243 *Cesare Borgia took Forlì from the widow of Girolamo Riario. See* THE PRINCE
20, *end.*

l. 252 *The populace is fickle.*

l. 256 *Cf. line 36.*

l. 260 *The palm indicates victory, the olive peace.*

262 so that the Moor, lacking all aid, at Mortara came to blows with the Gauls, and then went off into France wretched and captive.

265 Ascanio his brother, though he escaped from the mouths of the dogs, suffered greater injury when he tested the Venetians' fidelity.

268 Then the Gauls turned to enter your lands, solely to overcome the Pisans and bring them to render you homage.

271 So they came onward, and as he passed along with his soldiers, Beaumont pulled from the Saw more than one big tooth.

274 But when they confronted the Pisans, the Gauls, full of confusion, struck by fear, did not show their forces at all prepared,

277 but went away almost defeated and marked with severe disgrace; so the truth was known that the French can be conquered.

280 And it was not an affair to pass over lightly, because if it made you groveling and servile, upon the French was the chief reproach;

283 but you were not free from blame, although the Gaul tried to cover his shame with the failures of others;

286 and your government too did not understand how to make decisions, and while it stood between two opinions, not well pleased with the King,

289 Duke Valentino again spread his sails to the wind, and toward the Upper Sea turned his vessel's prow;

292 and with his soldiers did wonders, storming Faenza in short order and turning Romagna upside down.

295 After that, when he descended upon Bologna, with great effort the Saw sustained his soldiers' furious assault.

298 Leaving that place, he came into Tuscany, reclothing himself with your garments, while he kept his army opposed to yours.

301 Thereupon, to avoid so many distresses, since you could not do otherwise, you yielded in some part to his wishes.

304 And so his soldiers marched on, but as they marched by, it pleased him who rules Siena to remodel Piombino with a new master.

307 Behind these came a new horde that set its foot in your domain, not held back by restraint or by law.

l. 266 Turning to the Venetians for help, he was injured even more than by the French.
l. 271 The Saw is from the arms of the Bentivogli family, of Bologna.
l. 290 Toward the Adriatic Sea, that is, toward Romagna.

310 The King was sending these soldiers against the heir of Ferdinand, and to make sure of his flight, half of that Kingdom he
gave to Spain;

313 so that Frederick departed, after observing his men at the Capuan
test, and turned to put himself in the power of France.

316 Since at this time Rouen was in Lombardy, you bargained with
him about a new league to be made with the King.

319 You were unarmed and always in great terror of the horn that
was left to the Calf, and feared the Bear and the Pope.

322 And since you knew you were living quite haphazardly, and
feared to be undefended if there came upon you some bad luck,

325 after the circling of many days and months, not without heavy
spending, once more you gained the French king's protection.

328 Supported by his favor, you rashly expected to take from the
Pisans the grain in the leaf, and spread your banners abroad.

331 But Vitellozzo and his arrogant soldiers, bursting with anger
against you because of your bitter stroke at his brother,

334 by treachery broke the unbridled Stallion's bridle, and took
from you in a flash all Valdichiana and the other cities.

337 The war that had ruined Florence and the citizens' confusion
made this wound very ugly for you,

340 and to free yourself from so many injuries by your neighbors and
from such a savage attack, you summoned the Gauls to cross
your bounds.

343 Yet since Valentino halted at Nocera with his soldiers, and then
seized the duchy of Urbino at a single leap,

346 you stood with heart and soul in suspense lest he unite with
Vitello and come with him to distress you.

349 Whereupon the one was commanded to halt—through your
supplications—by the King of Saint Denis; for the other his
plans were useless.

352 Vitello marched away from Arezzo; the Duke appeared at
court in Asti to justify himself before King Louis.

l. 320 *Vitellozzo Vitelli, brother of the executed general (line 231).*

l. 329 *Capture the fields of the Pisans, on which they depended for food, before the grain
could form.*

l. 334 *The unbridled stallion rampant appears on the arms of Arezzo. The bridle indicates
Florentine rule.*

l. 350 *The King of France.*

355 Yet even such great aid would not have been in time, except for the effort of him who then was ruling your city.

358 Perhaps you would have come under another's power, because four mortal wounds you had, three of which were healed by that ruler.

361 Pistoia was in part rebellious, Florence was full of confusion, and you were not holding Pisa and Valdichiana.

364 That man placed a ladder leading up to the loftiest ensign, by which any soul worthy of such a climb could move upward;

367 that man brought Pistoia back to perfect peace; that man led Arezzo and all Valdichiana back beneath their ancient yoke.

370 The fourth wound of this body he could not heal, because when he tried to cure it, the climate was opposed to so skilful a hand.

373 On the coming, then, of that day so tranquil, on which your people, made bold, chose the bearer of its standard,

376 the two horns of a single deer were not so strong that on their solid rock you could erect your peace.

379 And if any man from such a decision draws back for any cause, he must be not a good surveyor of this world.

382 When Valentino had cleared himself and returned to Romagna, against Messer Giovanni he hoped to complete his campaign;

385 but when news of it was received, it seemed that the Bear and the Calf would not consent to join him in such an attack,

388 and, turned against one another, these serpents full of poison began to use their claws and with their talons to tear one another, and with their teeth,

l. 357 *Alamanno Salviati, to whom the* DECENNALE *is dedicated. He was officially only one of the Signoria. Yet Guicciardini says that* "he can be said to have controlled (governasse; Machiavelli's word is governava) everything," *and that* "he could be called head of the city" (HISTORY OF FLORENCE, 22, 23). *Machiavelli's account through line 369 is in agreement with the narrative of Guicciardini, who emphasizes Salviati's part in making the law that the Gonfalonier should hold office for life (lines 364–366). Guicciardini's concluding paragraph is similar to lines 367–369; to Salviati he gives three-fourths of the glory for making peace in Pistoia, regaining Arezzo, and reorganizing the government of Florence herself.*

l. 359 *For this figure of speech, see the* LEGATIONS, *8 November 1502.*

l. 364 *Salviati stabilized Florentine government by providing that the Gonfalonier, the chief city official, should hold office for life.*

l. 376 *Three horns, not two only, were required.* "Three horns of a white deer in a red field," (Tommasini, MACHIAVELLI 1, 310) *were the arms of Piero Soderini, in 1502 chosen Gonfalonier for life. Machiavelli puns also on his name; sodo means solid, and Piero, Peter, means rock; cf. Matthew* 16:18.

l. 384 *Giovanni Bentivoglio.*

391 and since Valentino could not escape, he was forced to cover
himself again with the shield of France, that he might avoid
the hazard,

394 and to catch his enemies with birdlime, and to get them into his
den, sweetly this basilisk whistled.

397 He did not lose much time in bringing them there, because the
traitor of Fermo and Vitellozzo and those Orsini who were so
hostile to him

400 rushed quickly into his snares, where the Bear left more than one
paw, and the Calf's second horn was cut off.

403 Perugia and Siena also felt the hydra's fire, and each of those
tyrants got away by fleeing before his fury.

406 And Cardinal Orsini could not escape the woes of his wretched
family, but lay dead after trying a thousand tricks.

409 In these times the Gauls, full of daring, turned their swords
against the Spanish, hoping to divide the Kingdom to their
liking,

412 and they would have destroyed the hostile soldiers and taken
every part of the Kingdom, if other forces had not come upon
them;

415 but having grown strong and powerful, the Spanish party with
hostile blood made Calabria and Apulia bloody.

418 Therefore the Gaul enraged turned against Italy, longing to
recover lost realm and honor.

421 The lord of Trémoille, a man of great reputation, rushed into
that land to avenge him by relieving Gaeta, which called him;

424 but not far forward he pushed his soldiers, because Valence and
his wily father raised his suspicions of their support.

427 They were seeking once again a companion who would give
them other states as booty, since with the Gaul they saw no
further winnings.

l. 394-402 See Machiavelli's DESCRIPTION OF THE METHOD USED BY DUKE
VALENTINO IN KILLING VITELLOZZO VITELLI, OLIVEROTTO DA FERMO, etc.
Cf. line 320, above.

l. 396 The basilisk was supposed to cause death by its whistle. Machiavelli seems to give it
the power of fascination or even of enticement. The latter fits Cesare Borgia's effect on Vitellozzo
Vitelli in the DESCRIPTION OF THE METHOD USED BY DUKE VALENTINO IN
KILLING VITELLOZZO VITELLI, etc.

l. 403 The hydra is Duke Valentino.

430 You, in order not to be Valentino's booty, as you had been
daily, and that he might not be Marzocco's heir,

433 had put on your payroll the Bailey of Can, with a hundred
lances and many men besides, believing yourself securer so.

436 With these soldiers, for a second time you took from Pisa any
hope that she might enjoy her harvest.

439 While Trémoille was coming, and between the Pope and France
concealed dissension and malicious ire were boiling up,

442 Valence fell sick, and the soul of splendid Alexander, that it
might have rest, departed to the blessed spirits;

445 his sacred footsteps were followed by his three dear and intimate
handmaids: Luxury, Simony, Cruelty.

448 But when in France he had the news, Ascanio Sforza, that
tricky fox, with speeches elaborate, sweet, and beautiful,

451 urged Rouen to go into Italy, promising him the mantle that
helps Christians mount to Heaven.

454 The Gauls at Rome were motionless meanwhile, and were not
willing to cross the honored river while the Holy Seat stood
empty.

457 And so Pope Pius was installed, but for a few days only he
supported the weight laid on his shoulders by God.

460 With full agreement, then, Julius the Second was made gate-
keeper of Paradise, to heal the world of its afflictions.

463 When Alexander was slain by Heaven, the state of his Duke of
Valence was broken and divided into many pieces.

466 Baglioni, Vitelli, Orsini, and the race of Montefeltro went back
to their homes, and Mark seized Rimini and Faenza.

469 Right into Rome, the Baglioni and the Orsini pursued Valentino, to make him suffer, and with his garments they reclothed
themselves.

472 Julius alone fed him with many hopes; and that Duke believed
he would find in another such pity as never he knew himself.

475 But after at Ostia he spent some days with the purpose of
escaping, the Pope made him come back to Rome and gave
him in charge to his soldiers.

l. 452 *The Pope's mantle.*
l. 472 *Compare Julius' conduct in* LEGATIONS, *4 November 1503, ff., especially the
Duke's belief that another man's promises will be surer than his own have been.*

478 Meanwhile the captains of the eager Gaul, having reached the banks of the Garigliano, made every effort to cross it,

481 but after spending there in vain many nights and days with great distress, afflicted by the cold and stung by ignominy,

484 and never being assembled in one body, but dispersed in various places and in many positions, by the weather and by their enemies they were defeated.

487 So having lost honor and money at Salsa, at Rome and there, the Gaul, full of sadness, bewailed his adverse fortunes.

490 And since the Spaniard knew that in this strife he had won the victory and he did not wish to wager the rest with the Gauls,

493 perhaps hoping more from a peace, he put a stop to war's confusion, and with the truce was entirely happy.

496 And you did not keep your valor hidden but with stronger weapons equipped yourself, so you could better oppose all outrage.

499 Nor did you desist from assailing the Pisans; instead, you took their third harvest away and attacked them by sea and by land.

502 And because they did not fear your swords, with various schemes you tried to turn Arno aside through different courses.

505 Then, to take the bitterness from spirits full of it, you opened your arms to every one who deigned to come asking pardon.

508 Meanwhile the Pope, after many attempts, gained Forlì and her castle, and Valence escaped by paths concealed;

511 and though Gonsalvo looked upon him with a pleasant face, he put on him the burden deserved by rebels against Christ,

514 and to make even such great pride submissive, he sent into Spain bound and chained the man who once forced you to tremble and Rome to shed tears.

517 For the second time the Sun has finished the fifth year's time above these happenings cruel and savage, and with blood has seen the world imbrued;

520 and now he is giving his coursers double barley that speedily speedily such a thing may be heard that these will seem to you slight.

523 By no means is Fortune yet satisfied; she has not put an end to Italian wars, nor is the cause of so many ills wiped out;

526 and the kingdoms and the powers are not united and cannot be, because the Pope is trying to cure the Church of its wounds;

529 the Emperor with his only son intends to present himself before
the successor of Peter; the Gaul feels pain from the blow received;

532 and Spain, who holds Apulia's scepter, keeps setting snares and
nets for his neighbors, in order that his projects may not move
backward;

535 Mark, full of fear and full of thirst, between peace and war is
wholly in suspense, and you for Pisa have too strong desire.

538 Hence easily we understand that as high as heaven the flame
will rise, if among these new fire is kindled.

541 Therefore my spirit is all aflame; now with hope, now with fear,
it is overwhelmed, so much that it wastes to nothing bit by bit;

544 because it seeks to know where your ship can sail, weighted with
such heavy weights, or into what harbor, with these winds.

547 Yet we trust in the skilful steersman, in the oars, in the sails, in
the cordage; but the voyage would be easy and short if you
would reopen the temple of Mars.

l. 547 The steersman is the Gonfalonier, Piero Soderini.

l. 550 Best explained as meaning that if Florence would form her own citizen army, instead
of relying on mercenaries, she would be more likely to prosper in her foreign policy.

SECOND DECENNALE

[Five years of Florentine contemporary history. 1504-1509]

1 The lofty events and insane actions that in ten succeeding years
have occurred since, falling silent, I laid down my pen,

4 the shifts in kingdoms, empires and states brought to pass in
Italian lands only, by divine wisdom foreordained,

7 I shall sing; and in singing, bold I shall be amid much weeping,
though I have become through pain almost bewildered.

10 Oh Muse, if ever I have trusted in you, lend me such favor that
my verse may rise to the greatness of the events themselves,

13 and from your fountain may I derive such powerful favor that
my song may content at least those now living.

16 The world was altogether in suspense; everyone was holding
slack in his hand the reins of his charger so greatly fatigued,

l. 2 This DECENNALE was planned to give events of 1504-1513; it breaks off in 1509.

19   when Bartolomeo, named from Alviano, with his company left the Kingdom, not well contented with the Great Captain,

22   and to give scope to his warlike nature, or for whatever cause it may have been, to enter Pisa was his plan;

25   and though with him he had small forces, nevertheless of the future game he was the first pawn moved.

28   But you, trying to put out this fire, made ready well and speedily; hence his plan was not achieved,

31   because when he came to Torre San Vincente, by the strength of your Giacomino his force was overthrown and defeated.

34   And Giacomino, through his virtue, through his fate, attained glory and renown as much as ever did private citizen.

37   For his native city this man bore much, and long he sustained with great justice your army's dignity.

40   Covetous of honor, generous with money, and capable of such virtue he is, that he merits honor much higher than I give him.

43   Now neglected and scorned he lies in his house, poor, old and blind. So greatly displeasing to Fortune is he who does well.

46   Then, if to my remembrance I bring quite everything, you moved against the Pisans with the hope which that defeat had brought with it,

49   but because Pisa feared little or nothing, no long time you kept the field there; thus it was the beginning of very evil seed.

52   And if you there lost money and honor by following the universal belief, you satisfied the popular desire.

55   Ascanio meanwhile had died, for whom great princes had risen in rivalry to put him back in his natural territory.

58   Dead was Ercole Duke of Ferrara, dead was Frederick, and, in Castile, Isabella the famous queen.

61   Hence the Gaul adopted the plan of making peace with Ferdinand, and granted to him as his consort di Foix's daughter,

64   and his part of Naples ceded as her dower, and to him the King of Spain made many large promises.

67   Meanwhile the Archduke had left Britain, and with him had taken many soldiers from Germany,

l. 21 *Gonsalvo of Cordova, the Spanish general in the Neapolitan kingdom.*

l. 34 *In the same strain, at greater length, Machiavelli speaks of Antonio Giacomini in the fragment called* THE NATURES OF FLORENTINE MEN.

l. 55 *Ascanio Sforza, a cardinal, eager to succeed his brother in the rule of Milan.*

l. 67 *Philip the Fair, Archduke of Burgundy and King of Spain.*

70 because he planned to seize control of the kingdom of Castile, which to him and not to his father-in-law of right belonged.

73 But when he reached the open sea, by the winds his fleet was battered; so he came into another's power,

76 because his ship, tossed by the winds, made shore in England— a thing that the Duke of Suffolk looked upon with displeasure.

79 Leaving that country with his soldiers, he arrived in Castile in person, where Ferdinand no longer resided;

82 for having entered the kingdom of Aragon, he departed with his galleys from Barcelona, to visit his state of Apulia.

85 Meanwhile Pope Julius, unable longer to hold in check his ardent spirit, gave to the winds his sacred banners,

88 and full of natural wrath and raging madness, against the usurpers of every one of his cities first poured out his first poison,

91 and, to throw all their tyrants to the ground, leaving unoccupied his holy throne, against Perugia and Bologna he carried on war.

94 But since the Baglioni yielded to his will, they remained in their dwelling, and only from Bologna's domain he drove the ancient house of Bentivoglio.

97 Meanwhile, too, a greater fire blazed up from that harsh dissen- sion arising between the nobles and the populace of Genoa.

100 In order to check this, the King of France determined to cross the mountains and aid the party that for his love lay prostrate and conquered,

103 and with cleverness and with force and with skill he brought the Genoese state entirely beneath his banners.

106 Then wholly to take from Pope Julius suspicion that he would attack him, to Savona he went at once,

109 where he awaited the coming of Ferdinand, who was going back to govern Castile, from which a little before he had departed,

112 because that kingdom already was in disorder, since Philip was dead; and on his way back he spoke with the King of France, where he was waiting for him.

115 The Emperor meanwhile, wishing to cross the mountains to Rome, in accord with the ancient custom, since he wished to be crowned,

118 had held a diet in Constance of all his barons, where he pre-

sented the injuries done by the Gaul, and those by the barons of France;

121 then he gave command that, without fail, everyone should be on horseback, with his men-at-arms and his infantry, on Saint Gall's day.

124 But France and Mark, who learned of this, brought together their soldiers, and uniting near Trent, they closed his road.

127 And Mark with defense did not rest satisfied, but struck him at home, and from the Empire took Gorizia and Trieste in a single moment.

130 Hence Maximilian wished to make a truce, seeing against his army so much opposition, and by agreement gave up the two cities,

133 which later were that repast, that bad morsel, that poisonous food that has spoiled Saint Mark's stomach,

136 because the Emperor, quite as I am writing for you, was offended, and to the good King of the Gauls he seemed to be the Venetians' credulous fool.

139 Hence, that Mark's intention might fail, the Pope and Spain both together joined with the Empire and the Yellow Lilies.

142 And they did not stop with truces between two, but quickly agreed at Cambrai that everyone might 'go for his own property.

145 Meanwhile you had made full preparations, because toward Pisa you kept your eyes turned always,

148 not being able to rest in any fashion if you did not have her; and by Ferdinand and Louis the road for reaching her had been blocked,

151 and your neighbors were following their tracks, making large their offers to them, starting with you every day a thousand disputes,

154 so if you wished to make your undertaking sure, you needed to fill every man's throat, and the mouth he was keeping open.

157 Then, since Pisa was left alone, suddenly you surrounded her, not letting anyone enter there save him who flew;

160 and four months you remained around her with great sufferings and much toil, and with much expense you starved her.

l. 157 *Though Machiavelli did not hold high office in Florence, the operations against Pisa were partly administered by him. Yet here and in* THE PRINCE *5 he shows sympathy for the conquered.*

163 And though she was a stubborn enemy, yet, by necessity compelled and conquered, she went back weeping to her ancient chain.

166 In France also the desire for making war was not ended, and according to the agreement made, she pushed a great host into Lombardy.

169 Pope Julius too came speedily into Romagna with his soldiers, and Brisighella he assailed and Faenza first of all.

172 But after France and Mark had had some slight encounters at Treviso and certain other towns, now with good, now with bad news,

175 Mark at last lay prostrate. Then when, wretched, he rose up at Vailà, he fell from his station that had been so high.

178 What will happen to the others if this one burned and froze in a few days only? And if justice and force and union for so great an empire did not avail?

181 Oh proud men, ever you have arrogant faces, you who hold the scepters and the crowns, and of the future do not know a single truth!

184 So blinded are you by your present greed which over your eyes holds a thick veil that things remote you cannot see.

187 From this it comes that heaven, shifting from this to that, shifts your states more often than the heat and the ice are changed,

190 because if you turned your prudence to learning the ill and finding its remedy, such great power from heaven would be taken.

193 I could not be so quick in telling you of it as after their defeat that Venetian domain was quick in vanishing.

196 Of Lombardy the great King of the Christians seized half, and the rest he who held in name alone the seat of the Romans;

199 and Romagna to the Great Shepherd passed without resistance, and the King of the Aragonese as well went to occupy his towns in Apulia.

202 But since into those countries the German had not yet come, Saint Mark at once retook both Padua and Treviso.

205 Hence Maximilian, learning this, with great assemblage of forces came soon to capture them and not to lose the rest.

208 But though he was helped by you and by France and by Spain, nonetheless he managed this like his other actions,

211 because after with courageous spirit he had remained at Padua some days, then, full of misery, he took his force away, worn out and tired;

214 and being deserted by the League and eager to return to Germany, he lost Vicenza as a greater injury.

EPIGRAMS

1. PIERO SODERINI

[*The playful tone of this epigram, sometimes incorrectly interpreted as full of bitter contempt, suggests composition during the prosperity of Soderini, before the return of the Medici in 1512.*]

That night when Piero Soderini died, his spirit went to the mouth of Hell. Pluto roared: "Why to Hell? Silly spirit,[1] go up into Limbo with all the rest of the babies."[2]

1. Dante, INFERNO 31. 70.
2. *As Dante knew, Limbo is the uppermost circle of Hell where no punishment is inflicted. There medieval belief put the souls of unbaptized infants. The Italian word for* babies *is* bambini, *a perfect rime for* Soderini *that Machiavelli could not resist.*

In his AI PALLESCHI (TO THE MEDICEANS) *Machiavelli suggests that Soderini might return, again to be important in the government of Florence.*

2. ARGUS

[*The dramatic speaker is Pope Clement VII, who has outwitted the Emperor Charles V and his viceroy, Lannoy, by getting them to release Francis I, captured at Pavia. The date must be after Francis received his freedom in 1526.*]

Understand that I am not Argus, as I seem, and these eyes that I have never belonged to Argus, but they are truly many eyes that from Christian princes everywhere I have extracted. And so it happens that brainless Charles King of the Romans and the Viceroy, because they cannot see, have released the King.

The End

INDEX

The index has been especially designed to supply cross references, so that all passages in which Machiavelli deals with any topic can easily be brought together. I have omitted factual matters of secondary importance in order to devote more space to the presentation of Machiavelli's thought.

A

ABILITY *cancels errors, brings success by any method 478f.; able man not blamed 935; sought in difficulty 468f.; versus Fortune 25; knowing one's own 554; feared by princes 622; prince dependent on others' ability 1236; honored by republics 622; of poor men recognized 486; tranquilizes countries 763; not friendly to Guinigi 554. See also* FORTUNE; WISDOM

ACCUSATIONS *legal a. necessary in state 211f.; by frightened citizens 1443*

ACCIAIUOLI, AGNOLO *banished for writing to Cosimo 1226; wishes revenge on Cosimo 1350f.; exile 1359; letter to Piero de'Medici 1360; secret interview with Piero de'Medici 1367*

ACTION *better than inaction 941, 998, 1161; not to be delayed 1084*

ADAPTATION *to times 896; defense against Fortune 91, 897, 1443; success requires 91; of battle array to conditions 617, 648f. See also* TIMES

ADMIRAL *See* GENERAL(S)

ADMONITION *factional weapon 1143f.; regulated 1155; dealt with by Ciompi 1164, of Guelfs 1171; by popular party 1178; of Medici and other friends of people 1185*

ADVERSITY *prepared for 39; causes republics to seek ability 386; ruins weak 498*

ADVICE *given indirectly 118; danger in giving 508ff.; from many 719; not to be judged by outcome 1193f.; selfish 1197*

ADVISER *duty to prince or city 509; to general 658. See also* MINISTER

AFFAIRS, HUMAN *do not remain fixed 210, 322, 534; contrary issue 900; gradual movement 924*

AFRICA *(on Mediterranean) few republics, few able men 622*

AGATHOCLES *wickedness and ability 35f.; invasion of Africa 353ff.*

AGE, OLD *effects 323; judgment of times 323; opinions on war 573*

AGITATOR *See* REFORMER

ALAMANNI, LODOVICO *letter to 966*

ALAMANNI, LUIGI *Art of War dedicated to 533f.; auditor in Art of War 569*

ALBERTI, BENEDETTO DEGLI *advises surrender to Ciompi 1165; almost prince 1169f.; love of liberty and power 1173; dislikes violence 1175; farewell speech 1177; above party 1177; slandered 1178*

ALBIZZI, MASO DEGLI *defects of his gov't 101; gonfalonier 1179; like head of Flor. 1181f.*

ALBIZZI, PIERO DEGLI *leader of Guelfs 1143; uses admonition against lower classes 1144; opposes Eight Saints 1150; advises conspirators to delay 1151f., 1154; ruin and death 1170; fortunate unfortunate 1170*

ALBIZZI, RINALDO DEGLI *fictitious speech 1028; aristocrat 1188; speech after*

C

CHANCE *Mach.'s enemy 757; injuries to Mach. 969; in Buondelmont~Amidei feud 1083; Ferdinand V uses 909; at gates of Fortune 747.* See also FORTUNE

CHANGE *according to times 896; in gov't dangerous 26, 1197f.* See also REFORM; TIMES

CHARACTER See NATURE

CHARITY *prince acts against 66; Ambition expels 736; of Giovanni de' Medici 1204; Mach. on 170ff.*

CHARLES V, EMPEROR *to be observed 119; ambition 990; not injured by bad decisions 992; tricky diplomacy 999f.; stupid? 992; will he release Francis I? 999f.; releases Francis I 1463; crazy to put Francis I in Italy (1526) 993; fails to reinforce army 1002; army does not observe Viceroy's treaty 1007, 1009; his Italian army (1527) 1008; what to learn about him 119*

CHARLES VIII, KING OF FRANCE *Italian expedition 45, 50, 103, 598, 708, 724, 779, 826, 1445f.; takes Italy with chalk 47; enters Flor. 1000*

CHARLES OF ANJOU *in Italy 1060; aids Flor. 1090; defeats Manfred 1088f.; Vicar of Tuscany 1091*

CHARLES OF CALABRIA *rescues and oppresses Flor. 1115f.*

CHARLES OF DURAZZO *feared as ally of Florentine exiles 1170; bribed by Flor. 1171; asks aid from Flor., retains Naples 1175*

CHIRON *centaur, educated Achilles 64*

CHOICE *inevitable 896*

CHRIST *example 422; example of mercy 1412; to watch over G. Vernacci 964, 967, 970*

CHRISTIANITY *effect of 191; mild 331; slothful interpretation 331; destroyed pagan records 340; mercy lessened need for defense 623; and patriotism 331.* See also RELIGION

CHURCH *how to keep influence 948; temporal power 19, 44, 50; bad example 228; failure in Italy 226ff.; corrupts Italy 228; divides Italy 228f.; made strong by France 20 ; lack of scruples 1406; Flor. under interdict 1100; Flor. does not observe interdict 1396, 1399; cry of conspirators in Forlì 1430; East and West union mooted 1254.* See also CHRISTIANITY; POPE; RELIGION

CIBO, CARDINAL *Mach. hopes aid from 1006*

CICERO *on people 203; on Caesar 266; hoist with his own petard 301; afflicted by Fortune 749; De Oratore 997; Familiar Letters 903f.*

CIOMPI *revolt of 1161~1169; demands of 1163f.; organize a gov't 1167; turn against Michele di Lando for favoring rich 1166f.; gains diminished 1169*

CIRCE *her animals once men 755, 765, 768*

CIRCUMSTANCES *determine value of fortresses 80, 397; alter rules 355f.* See also TIMES

CITIZEN(S) *three classes 107; should be poor 272ff.; should be content with any gov't 428; weak curse tyrant 431; uncorrupted, needed for army 722; ambitious rise to power 265f., 290f.; able but neglected seek revenge 469f.; foolish despise city 726; ready to sell Flor. 1221; support Lorenzo the Magnificent 1398; fellow, more rapacious than enemies 1243*

CITY *origin free or slavish 192ff.; free German 43; site barren or fertile 193; desirable for safety 1230; mixed body 1242; simple body 1242; six miles of territory ideal extent 762; of servile origin, freedom impossible 295f.; free, liberty hard to keep 295f.; corrupt cannot be reorganized 240f.; corrupt qualities 450; how to unite 489; divided, how unified 489; divided easily lost 491; great, not firm in decisions 975; to be loved which loves people equally 1242; capital does not fear destruction 624; system for defense 497; large, hard to defend 998; strong by nature or art 703; to be surrounded by unobstructed land 709f.; taken with difficulty when defended 1005; capture does not decide war 1272; in war to be abandoned or defended with whole army 513; preservation better than useless defense 1266; European, does not defend self 623f.; taken by stratagem 415; how captured by Romans 413; Flor. gains Tuscan cities by allowing independence or tyranny 1133, 1209; new, renown to founder 1080; native (see* COUNTRY*).   See also* REPUBLICS; STATE

CITY WALL   *See* WALL

CLASSES   *of people in Flor., enmity 107, 1141*

CLEMENT VII, POPE   *(Medici, Giulio de') supervises Flor. 111, 114; approves writing of Hist. Flor. 971; Mach.'s Hist. Flor. presented to 1027ff.; to feed flock 880; getting money from 985ff.; outwits Charles V 1463; can he hold Charles V? 998; on walls of Flor. 998; fears Imperial army 727; treaty with viceroy of Charles V 1008f.; wishes to fortify Flor. 995ff.; incapacity 1010; like a baby 1004; mistakes in war 1003f.; failure to raise money 1004; trust in ink rather than arms 1002*

CLERGY   *ambition 46; how estimated 255; bad influence 228; wickedness 422, 794.   See also* CHURCH; POPE

CLIZIA   See MACHIAVELLI, WORKS

COLLEONI, BARTOLOMMEO   *Venetian* condottiere *attacks Florentine territory 1362f.*

COLONIES   *value 1080f.; to hold conquests 14f., 19, 378; Roman 342f.*

COLONNA FAMILY   *mercenaries 29; pope's enemies 45; against Sixtus IV 1415; crushed by Sixtus IV 1420; demands on Sixtus IV's death 1421; Cardinals 46*

COLONNA, FABRIZIO   *speaker in* Art of War *568-726; military experience 569*

COMEDY   *theory of 814, 823f.; of Florentine life 928; by Mach. 1014; in Greece 725; staging 777*

COMMAND   *prolonged, dangerous to state 486; words of (see* ARMY*)*

COMMERCE   *prince encourages 84; price of wheat and spices (1512) 134; in German cities 43; in Flor. 871ff., 1159, 1437; labor troubles in Flor. 1158.   See also* POOR; RICH; VERNACCI

COMMODUS   *conspiracy against 437f.; assassination 446*

COMMON GOOD   *Mach.'s devotion to 1028; gov't for 1027; and patriotism 1145; arts and laws for 566; esteemed above private 572; of Italy 31, 38, 93; in free city 236, 329; sought in founding state 218f.; prince respects 506; esteemed above private feeling 1106; versus partisanship 458; desired by Salvestro de'Medici 1153; love for, basis of reputation 492; desired by Valori 1438; sought in reform 1158; officials love (1378) 1155; citizens loving (1382) 1172; advanced by Giovanni de'Medici 1204; served by historian 190; Borgia desires 149; not attacked 461, 1146; neglected in Flor. 296, 1140; opposed by Medici 1030; Alcibiades forgets 468; not sought in Flor. 103; individual passions oppose general interest 1276.   See also* PEOPLE; RULES, GENERAL

COMMYNES, PHILIP DE   *47*

COMPETENCE   *destroyed throughout world by Roman Empire 623; not understood 94f., 1363*

COMPROMISE   *See* HALFWAY MEASURES

CONCORD   *Ambition drives away 736*

CONDITIONS   *See* CIRCUMSTANCES

CONDOTTA   explained 51

CONDOTTIERE   See MERCENARIES

CONFIDENCE   *soldiers' causes for 662.   See also* HOPE

CONIO, ALBERIGO (LODOVICO) DA   *first* condottiere *50*

CONIO, LODOVICO DA   *his company of St. George 1074*

CONQUEROR   *advice for 13f., 426; writers subservient to 321; never disgraced 1160*

CONQUEST   *how retained 13f.; treatment 17; natural 18; new princedom 25; harmful* to weak republics 335, 377ff.; by peoples 344f.; by republics and princes 344; injured Rome 381; not the best way to gain subjects 1133; conquered to be destroyed or benefited 389ff.

CONSALVO   See GONSALVO

CONSCIENCE   should not frighten the oppressed 1160

CONSPIRACY   discussed 68f., 428-448; conditions for 1129; against prince 68f., 429-444; against republic 444ff.; by men of rank 432ff.; by weak men infrequent 431; by one man escapes danger 430; by many 433, 1184; rapidity of 785; courage of plotters 434f., 1390f.; dangers of 428, 430, 433, 438ff.; how to avoid discovery 435; to write is fatal 436f.; conspiracy against two, difficulty 441, 1391; how foiled 68, 446, 1382; ruins prince 1384; brings assailed prince power 1383; cannot long be secret 1389; how revealed 433f., 549, 1113, 1119, 1129, 1184, 1323, 1354; evil results 428, 442, 1383, 1388; usually unsuccessful 428; plotters flee 1185; in Bologna early success 1295; at Cennia by Alfonso successful 1301; in Cortona revealed 1277; Venetian in Cremona discovered 1299; in Faenza 1431; in Genoa 1429; in Genoa against Visconti rule 1240; in Forlì 1429ff.; in Prato fails 1369; in Pisa discovered 1217; in Sarzana against Flor. 1408; in Volterra successful 1206; against Maso degli Albizzi 1183; against Duke of Athens 1128ff.; by Bardi and Frescobaldi 1119; by Catiline 221, 445; against Caracalla 438; to receive Castruccio in Flor. 548; of Ciompi revealed 1161f.; against Commodus 74; against Iacopo Gabriegli 1118ff.; of Gambacorti thwarted 1324f.; by Guelfs (1378) 1151ff.; against Pagolo Guinigi 1216; by Duke of Milan and Florentine exiles 1184; Pazzi against Medici 1383-1395; of Stefano Porcari 1322f.; against Piero de' Medici 1351, 1354, 1356; against Galeazzo Sforza 1378ff.   See also RULES, GENERAL

CONSPIRATORS   cry "liberty" (1397) 1183; blinded by lust to rule 432

CONSTANTINOPLE   employs Turkish mercenaries 52; Emperor favors Flor. against Venice 1319; citizens too late with defense against Turks 1442

CONSTITUTIONS   See GOVERNMENT

CONTEMPT   prince must avoid 67ff., 74, 954, 957; for Emperor 75; avoided by able men 481; through poverty 61

CONVENIENCE   not to be broken for others' convenience 927

CORNO, DONATO DEL   900; eligibility for office 921, 931ff.; hopes for office 959; loan to Giuliano de' Medici 966

COSIMO   See MEDICI, COSIMO DE'

COUNCIL OF CHURCH   Flor. appeals to 1399

COUNCILS, FLOR.   109, 1091, 1152

COUNTRY   to be defended without regard to justice, cruelty or disgrace, without scruple 519; no sort of defense to be censured 1242.   See also CITY; PATRIOTISM

COUPLERS   put eligible names in bags 921; political use of 1237

COURAGE   against Fortune 92; loss of ruins conspiracy 440; failure in 441f.; in defending own property 1191f.; does not fear strange events 504; admired by enemies 1199; in executing decisions 1437; of Francesco Pazzi 1390; of the Bishop of Volterra against the mob 306; of Maffeo da Carrari in the Bardi rebellion 1120; of Biago del Melano at Monte Petroso 1199.   See also FORTUNE; RULES, GENERAL; VIRTÙ

COURTESY   prince's 84, 99, 926

COVETOUSNESS   See GREED

COWARDICE   bad result 540; is Sloth 737; in Italy 737; scorned 1199.   See also COURAGE; FEAR

CRIMES   not atoned for by good deeds 248

CROSSBOW   light cavalry weapon 625

CRUELTY   well used, badly used 38; dangers and benefits 61ff.; of generals 63, 474; injures ruler 75; weakens prince 236; price of prince's survival 254; of prince, of people 317;

E

F

872; bloodless revolution (1494) 448; servile origin 296; liberty in danger 1410; a slave 1177, 1184; slave to Cosimo or to Rinaldo degli Albizzi 1221; cannot keep liberty, cannot endure servitude 1128; suited for republic 107; never a true republic 296; lost liberty through Medici promises 461; wise lawgiver could give any form of rule 1141; citizens' republic 1446; complaints against aristocratic rulers 1193; difficulty of princedom 107; and popes (see name of pope); unarmed 276, 1440; military power in Cosimo's time 104; power in Italy 1233; unprepared for Charles VIII 1445; military difficulties 137; soldiers dis' posable 126f.; soldiers employed 129; defended by Robert of Naples 348; mercenaries 49; employs French auxiliaries 52; hampers generals 418; Mach.'s citizen army 3; citizen army imperfect 585, 590; citizen army bad showing 583f., 585, 725; failure in war 1002; destroys military virtues 1138; vigor, military 1032; to be defended (1527) 1008; weakly bought allies 409; usually alone in wars 1428; fruitless alliance with France 352; expects French aid 1447; makes King Robert of Naples lord 548; hates Orisini and Vitelli 164 (see also MERCENARIES); campaign against Uguccione 538; defeated at Serravalle 547; Castruccio near 548; Guelf aid against Castruccio (1328) 549; war on Visconti 355; repelled F. Visconti 399; war with Visconti 521; avarice 63; ambition 1366; fickle 278f., 1343; hesitating 361f.; subtle 1410; ungrateful 740; free speech in 1128, 1413; people's good opinion of themselves 226; citizens thinking themselves wise 78, 392; cannot learn by experience 1147; in necessity respected ability 470; produces few lion'like men 765; weak at heart 411; life of a sober citizen 835f.; discontent at war (1479) 1406; over' confidence (1512) 403; ability of citizens 1032; vigor, financial 1032; great in spite of factions 1032; power and stubbornness 1243; population (1298) 1097; weak (1435) 1243; dress 872; defeat (1479) 1404; cost of Visconti war 1032; poorer through Visconti war 1203; peace treaty with F. Visconti (1435) 1238f.; deceived by French and Germans at Pisa against Visconti 521f.; fears union of Sforza and Visconti 1251; alliance with Sforza 1316ff.; devotion to in Tuscany 1211; gentleness and reluctance win subjects 1133, 1209; name shouted by men of Val di Lamona 1431; bad policy in Tuscany 385, 460; foolish mercy to rebels 61; hostility of neighbors 1448; does not instruct Mach. 150; halfway measures at Arezzo 390; cruelty and avarice toward Lucca 1248; failure to gain Lucca 1252f.; loss of Pisa 278; tried to hold Pisa with fortresses 396; folly about Pisa and Arezzo 276f.; war with Pisa 782; popular support for foolish siege of Pisa 304; roused hatred of Pisa, Lucca, Siena 385; two wounds: Pisa, Vitellozzo 131; four wounds: Pisa, Pistoia, Valdichiana, internal trouble 1453; effect of Pistolese factions 490f.; like brothers to Pistolese 385; wise policy in disunited Pistoia 399; weaker by her conquests 380; danger in expansion 763; threatened by Ambition 739; fortifications visited, from San Niccolò Gate going down the Arno, back to start (names of gates, etc., are not indexed) 727'734; walls to be more or less extensive 995ff.   See also BAGS; BALÍA; DISSENSIONS IN FLOR.; DIVISIONS IN CITY; FACTIONS; MEDICI; WALL; etc.

FOIX, DE   killed by steel 371; speedy action 397; promptness with Marquis of Mantua 523f.
FOLCHI, GIOVANNI   740
FORCE   versus fraud 65, 357; gains wealth 1160; keeps princes to agreements 1413; kingdoms gained by 11; to be used by strong ruler 480; force does not hold people down 393, 1181; brings trouble to conqueror 1375; preserves states 1440.   See also ARMS
FOREIGN AID   good laws make unnecessary 214; dangerous in domestic trouble 212, 214, 489
FOREIGN RELATIONS   of conqueror 15ff., 68, 82f.; aggression 81; of unarmed 352; internal importance 68, 1032, 1336; Flor. with Borgia 121'162; in Italy 1232'1335, 1444'1461. See also ALLIES; CHARLES VIII; FLOR.; NEUTRALITY; etc.
FORESIGHT   of prince 14, 16f., 32f., 39, 42, 54, 56, 90, 264f.; brings success 1161; takes power from heaven 1461; of dangers to state 16, 242, 264ff., 911, 1189, 1218f., 1358;

FRIEND   *old, new enemy 13, 20, 543, 558, 744, 1333; haughty, bend whom enemies cannot 1289; unrewarded, enemies saved 1289.   See also* ALLIES

FRIENDSHIP   *mercenary 62; ancient, stronger than money 1171; among rivals, difficult 1295*

G

GAETA   *Abbot of, mock triumph 766*

GAIN   *hope for political results 204ff.; men moved by hope of g. rather than fear of loss 1204*

GARIGLIANO   *campaign on (1503) 120, 702f., 909, 1456*

GATES, CITY   *when locked 1369; how defended 707*

GATTAMELATA   *Venetian* condottiere *1235, 1257*

GAULS   *See* FRENCH

GENERAL(S)   *advice to 459-472, 566-647, 648-662, 718-721; qualities and conduct of 503, 512-519; dignity of 305; methods and devices of 648ff., 695; followed by philosophers 1232; anxieties of 262; able, successful by any method 478f., 565; foresight of 472, 656; successful, feared by prince 257ff.; becomes prince 49, 541; victorious envied and hated 540; g.'s double glory of training and winning 464; victorious with trained army 722; Roman, prolonged command ruinous 485, 593; good and bad, with army bad and good 462ff.; popularity dangerous to state 483; needs full power 417f.; more than one damaging 467f.; must adapt methods to enemy 472, 658, 674f.; must be inventive 721; must think enemy intelligent 673f.; his reputation makes soldiers confident 662; must be orator 504, 539, 648, 660f.; gets advice 658; must have maps 674; prompt (see* SPEED*); observes justice 701; harshness versus kindness 479ff.; competent not recognized in Italy 94f., 1363; lack opportunity in Italy 620; abilities needed in Italy 722; goes easily from sea to land 586; unsuccessful Roman 261f.   See also* ARMY; LEADERS; MERCENARIES; PRINCE; WAR

GENOA   *granted self-gov't by French 384; rebellion against Louis XII 705; civil wars 1240; successful rebellion 1241; stubborn defense (1436) 1244; Bank of San Giorgio and gov't 1422*

GENTLEMEN   *defined 308; accomplishments and manners 536; in Rome, Naples, Romagna, Lombardy 308f.; hostile to free gov't 308f.; essential to prince 309; Venetian 310*

GERMAN AFFAIRS, REPORT ON   *See* MACHIAVELLI, WORKS

GERMANS   *infantry at Ravenna 95; honest 307; have kept same qualities from antiquity 521f.; wise gov't of 90, 322f.; free cities of 379, 762; good armies of 582*

GHIARADADDA   *See* VAILÀ

GHIBELLINES   *in Flor. 1085, 1088f., 1090f., 1105f., 1142f.; in Lombard cities 78; Castruccio champion of 542*

GIACOMINI, ANTONIO   *Florentine general 782; ability and character 470; ruined by one failure 305; Mach. writes to 163; military skill, virtues, misfortunes 1436f., 1458*

GILDS   *in Flor. (1266) 1089; organization (1378) 1158; power of 1169*

GIOTTO   *builds Tower 1118*

GIROLAMO, RAFFAELO   *ambassador, Mach. advises 116ff.*

GLORY   *See* FAME

GOD   *Mach. prays to 899; invoked by Mach. 938; thanked by Mach. 898; has not abandoned Mach. 915; saved Mach.'s life 913f.; gives Mach. life 1395; assists Flor. 1410; Flor. begs to defend her 1442; wrath against Flor. 1372; chastises Flor. 1440; inspires Savonarola 886ff.; defends Medici 1396; made to share Medici treachery 1362; loved Lorenzo the Mag. 1433; to aid Italy against Spain 1005; will punish Sforza's treachery 1309; saves Lucca 1247; grateful to papal* condottiere *1415; given share in gov't 1340f.; procession by partisans to thank 1359; citizens arrested and tortured during thanks to 1359; fear of*

L

M

N

allow succession of able rulers 246; varied talents of citizens 452f.; reorganization dangerous 196; must be brought back to origins 419ff.; degenerate to tyranny or license 1187; ancient, good laws gave long life 1187; for freedom need steady foresight 527; prudent think victory enough 401; use citizens as soldiers 48, 261, 580; good, reject professional soldiers 576; good, reject auxiliary troops 383; must estimate forces 388; good form of gov't 196f.; where they are possible 106; growth of 3, 379; discussed 11, 195; cherish able men 1378; encourage beneficial actions suppressing tyranny 493; strong, do not buy friends 409f.; loyalty in danger 318f.; how to make great 335, 378; move slowly 268, 318, 360ff., 444, 453, 924; irresolute 275, 277f., 490; emergencies dangerous to 268; make bad decisions 303; use fraud 357f.; lawful authority does not harm 270; impossible where there is inequality 309; should reward good deeds 251f.; should appear liberal 299; not permanent 471; unarmed cannot form empires 339; small cannot sustain empire 335, 378; when inferior to princedom 310; ingratitude 318; more grateful than princes 259; corrupt employ good men only in distress 385, 468ff.; corrupt subject to conspiracy 444; should not give office to injured man 471; conspiracies against 444; do not adapt to times 453; strong, alliance sought 409; weak buy allies 409f.; foolish to build fortresses 396; must punish properly 404; should be rich 272ff.; Roman methods necessary 378; get subjects 336; slavery to 333; composed of many states 338f., 1336. See also CITY; STATE

REPUTATION prince's 36, 59f., 68, 73, 79, 81ff., 96, 909; of citizens, essential to state 492; in cities how gained 1337; how increased in city 1204; by service to state 1337; to be gained early 506f.; derived from habits, associates, deeds 505; maintained by new wonders 506; dangerous to state, how gained 493; by public means, by private means 492f.; from deeds, not quickly lost 505f.; secured by striking conduct 897; general's lost with loss of what he defends 513; lost by failure in office 515; extraordinary, damaging to new official 1355; ally needs more than 352

RESERVES essential in battle 551, 627, 642, 719; Greek method 627f.; Roman practice 627; Roman and Greek 633; Swiss method 628; modern failure in 365, 641; at Anghiari 1280

RESULT men judge by 67, 508, 1413; political affairs judged by 895; policy not to be judged by 1193f.; good may excuse evil deed 218

RETIREMENT impossible for man of rank 424

REVENGE more powerful than gratitude 1197; brings profit and pleasure 1197; heavy injury does not fear 15; of old injuries 34; for brother's death 74; ruins states 212; satisfied in spite of danger 406; for injuries by princes or states 405; private reason for killing tyrant 1379; possible to destitute 430; by neglected or injured citizen 469ff.; in revolution terrifying 448f.; for liberty, horrible 1132; on Guelfs desired (1378) 1156; by mob 1162. See also ENVY

REVOLUTION injurious 12, 115, 235, 428; opposed by patriot 1438; men naturally discontented 477; conditions favoring 451; bloody or not 448; cannot be regulated 1154; slanders used in inciting 217; in small city 547; through return of exiles 545; with foreign aid 544; typical in Italian city 538ff.; in Flor. (1378) 1154ff.; result of idleness 1352; suppressed in Rome 493

REWARDS excessive, expected by supporters of new prince 79; for good citizens 251; for public service 493; for good citizens and soldiers 493, 690

RIARIO, GIROLAMO lord of Forlì 1365, 1377, 1450; in Pazzi conspiracy 1386ff.; fears Medici 1386; alarm on Sixtus IV's death 1421; makes threats, dangerous to himself 1429f.; assassinated 444, 1430

RICH support prince 39; shrewdness 40; ruined by prince 40; in gov't 70; prince secures himself against 40, 70, 88; party of 203f.; fears 206; unruly under tyrant 237; conspiracies by 432; their ambition ruins city 274; economic importance 1157; not better than poor 1160;

RULES, GENERAL *(representative instances)*

Conspiracies usually fail 1323; for conspiracies, few men not enough, many reveal 1184; prince should avoid assassination by being loved 1382; all men have power to conspire 428; assassination requires men resolute in bloodshed 1390

When men able to conquer do so, they are praised 18; states must be organized by one man 218; men change ruler, believing they will gain 12; a conqueror must damage his new subjects 12; injuries to be done all together, benefits slowly 38; the new master of a free city must destroy her or be destroyed 24; conqueror best supported by former enemies 79; conquerors never disgraced 1160

Better disgraceful peace than dangerous war 1234; no truce so bad as to lack all value 403; good defenses depend on yourself 89; strong prince can fight any attacker 42; princes able to keep army are secure 88f.; allies by disagreement give victory to enemy 1419; union of many against one difficult 953; durable alliances advantage both sides 135; powerful states betray weak allies 1121; the forcer must be stronger than the forced 283; forces get names; names do not get forces 267; expansion poisons weak states 210; traitor to country traitor elsewhere 1240; fools fall, hoping to be raised 89; war made through greed, through fear 210

Fortune mistress of half our actions 90; Fortune is a woman 92; Fortune friends the bold 92; Fortune varies 497; Fortune matches bad and good 1116; the good man displeases Fortune 1458; there is never a perfect time 1152; time harms the right time 1151; who lets time pass, regrets 879; Time drives along good and bad 17; time awaits no one 487; delay dangerous 1152

Prudence uses men according to times 1196; prudence is to choose the least evil 84, 954; the less evil is a good 276; plans reveal themselves to the active, not to the slothful 1299; choose the course having fewest evils 209; do not judge a plan by its outcome 1193; do not accept too dangerous a plan 301; human plans deceptive and uncertain 1384; under necessity rashness is prudence 1161; an injury must be such that it does not fear revenge 15; human affairs always in motion 210; affairs move gradually 924; human affairs cannot be balanced 211; no blame or praise deserved for necessary acts 1247; he cannot keep who does not gain 206; who wishes to learn must tell 117; falling man allowed to fall 1354; a pushed man is supported by others 1354; where there are men there is a way 131; everyone helps man who helps self 1006; better to act and repent than not to act 941; he who stands at last must fall 759; good men always poor 1160; goodness not enough 497; malice cannot be mastered or placated 425, 497; desperation comes back on him who despairs 146; no escape from danger without danger 1161; what cannot be resisted must be dodged 641; weak start may produce big result 1368; opposites clarify each other 888; riches come from force or fraud 1160; the weakest fare worst 1160; little faults punished, big ones rewarded 1159f.; new things soon dropped 1368; what has pleased cannot displease 879; to run away from things the way to get them 1133; the best gift the means of learning from another's experience 10; discord produces good laws 203; verifying takes time 133; truth wars on its teller 760; a firm gov't either a princedom or a republic 106; to keep old gov't easier than to form new one 1368; states go from good to bad, from bad to good 1232; backward-looking law dangerous 1143; be content with half a political victory 1202; there are no secure courses 84

Men desire the impossible 1355; thinking to gain, men lose 399; those promising benefit believed 751; men moved by hope of gain rather than fear of loss 1207; men want what they cannot get 1117; not satisfied to get own, men covet more 1156; men do not limit their hopes 404; men feel obligation for benefits they confer 44; men blind to own vice, persecute vices of others 934; men readier to ill than good 1375; everybody avoids evil 888, 1374; men bad except by necessity 88; the inexperienced deceived 386; showy things feared at distance 1057; men in fear try to gain safety 289; revenge preferred to gratitude 1197; revenge seems profitable 257; gratitude a burden 257; no gratitude to him giving up convenience for others 927; those ungrateful to God are unfriendly to their neighbors 173; men not insane about life and property 431; the proud and base are haughty in prosperity, abject in adversity 1306; man wise by day not held foolish by night 557, 935; necessity makes men good 201; men do not return to old habits 105; free man respects God and Church 1412; the more authority, the worse use 1120; courage admired cowardice scorned 1199; no one can promise certainty in courage 441; men yield to those not eager to take 385; good to be praised by praised man 903f.

No defense of country to be censured 1242; country loved more than soul 1010, 1150, 1438; common good esteemed above private friendship 1106

Free men do good, not evil 1412; desires of free people aid liberty 203; men deceived in generalities, not in particulars 292; where religion is, arms easily brought 224f.; multitude fickle 26, 994, 1172, 1173, 1450; masses set in motion by accident 1315; weak men hesitate 361; decisions find words 360f.; crowd readier to take other's property than to defend own 1207; vexation at failure to gain as great as at loss 1252f.; property is more esteemed than honor 274; victory causes thirst for more 952; men better suited to keeping than to devising improvements 1148; necessity drives men to the unintended 924; those who attempt more than victory often lose 1202; men follow policy without knowing hidden perils 54; bad men abandon right through fear 1125; people will not follow liberator 1382; dangerous to try to free men preferring slavery 1184; men never complain of habitual 1368; regainers of liberty more savage than preservers 256; the good ruined among the many wicked 1177; two able kings in succession exalt a state 244; after strong prince weak one can survive 245; individual passions act against public good 1276; powerful mask evil with justice 1398; rivals easily make marriages but not friendship 1295

Men well ruled seek no other liberty 428; ruler's best fortress not to be hated 80; princes lose positions when they break laws 427; gov't is to make subjects unable to harm or not to wish to 389; princes who do not punish are held worthless 390; prince must have policy not needing change 39; the strong prince can rely on his people 41; wise princes take thought for future discords 16; he who has his own arms gets good effects 137; good arms mean good gov't 202; only freely given authority durable 1125; do not defer liberality 263; ruler must not make men despair 1096; do not risk all of fortune, part of forces 248f., 950; to gain dominion without strength ruinous 380; no wise prince puts himself in another's power 1299; without necessity, prince should not endanger everything 904; limbs of state follow head, not the reverse 1334; people wish what kings do 949; a lawgiver sup-poses all men evil 201; unexpected favors secure peoples' support 41; the powerful easily deceive weak 1347; do not take what cannot be held 133; do not spend your own money 61; foolishly cruel princes cannot last 38; force and necessity keep princes to agreements 1258, 1413, 1442; benefits do not erase injuries 34, 426; new benefits erase old injuries 917; he who makes another power-ful is destroyed by him 20; prince-maker feared by prince 1240; a prince dependent on others falls without support 1236; a prince attacked can hope for aid 1354; great men ashamed to lose, not to gain by trickery 1304; men forestall rulers' ingratitude 1175; great men must be either untouched or destroyed 1225; great men not arrested to be released 1270; do not injure a prince, then trust him 166; subjects do not forget loss of property 484; rulers defend own property with most courage 1191f.; princes give new favors after old 987; not prudent to wish complete victory 1096; do not negotiate the same thing in two places 139; a prince needs nobles 107; what the ruler does his subjects do 494

Gov't firm when all have parts 115; a citizen has right to offer, uninjured, new laws 296; good laws, good armies 47; a free state keeps citizens poor 486; pernicious in a republic to consult non-officials 109; after emergency laws changed 1113; people and rich cannot agree 1093f.; no tyrants rise in armed republic 48; cities surrender after experiencing tyrannical rule 1209; when present desire satisfied, future ills not imagined 383; certain peace better than doubtful victory 1289; offices do not renown men, men renown offices 515; power seized, not power given, causes hate 1204; if no foreign enemy, one appears at home 379; to test security of peace, find the discontented 917; one magistrate must not block public business 112; perilous to undertake office with high reputation 1355; objectionable customs hard to remove 594; republics are slow 924

By penitence men rise to Heaven 171; those fearing hunger and prison need not to fear Hell 1160; pope's ally is abandoned in defeat 1406; those ungrateful to God are ungrateful to their neighbors 173; one must imitate Saint Francis and Saint Jerome 174; men have interpreted our religion according to sloth and not according to vigor 331; the prelates do the worst they can, not fearing God's punishment 422

    Good man does not become tyrant 243; a wicked tyrant will not rule well 243; hostile damage ends, tyrant's oppression never 1242; people more injured by domestic than by enemy's oppression 1243

    Many rules for warfare 718ff.; mercenary armies dangerous 47; mercenaries give slow gains, rapid losses 50; mercenaries live by war 1234; mercenaries can be bribed 1215; wise princes choose to lose with their own soldiers 52; he who plans not to conquer should employ auxiliaries 52; princes and republics with own arms make advances 48; best armies are those of peoples 925; where there are men there are soldiers 247; wars begun but not ended at will 1148; victory not to be lost in hope of greater 402; victorious army formidable 387; do not give up certain victory for uncertain good 1294; war won by defeating hostile army 1272; army brave through discipline 611; necessary wars just 94, 1241; war made where hostile army is 1272; fortresses useful or not according to times 80, 392; infantry is the strength of an army 374; good infantry beaten only by infantry 375f.; stubbornness brings victory 363; movements succeed that enemy thinks impossible 1266; army with reserves must have Fortune unfavorable thrice 365; delay takes away opportunity 1106; speed takes away strength 1106; best remedy to do willingly what enemy tries to compel 656; leader to be obeyed must know how to command 480; artillery useless without valor 372; is attack or defense better? 1191f.; who gives cause for arms causes strife 1358. See also PROVERB

RULER   See PRINCE

RUSCELLI, GIROLAMO   editor of Mandragola 789, 805

S

SAINT DOMINIC   reformer 422; his order 1058
SAINT FRANCIS   penance 174; reformer 422; trod in muddy places 972; his order 1058
SAINT JEROME   penance 174
SAINT MARK   See VENICE
SALI   able sultan 245
SALLUST   Jugurtha 344
SALVIATI, ALAMANNO   requests Decennale 1444; preserved Florentine liberty 1444; healed Flor.'s wounds 1453
SALVIATI, GIOVANNI DE'   (Cardinal) Mach.'s friend 967
SAN CASCIANO   topography 1330
SAMNITES   turn to religion in distress 233f.; religion fails 234; halfway measure after Caudine Forks 391
SAN GIORGIO, BANK   history, organization 1422f.
SAN GIOVANNI GUALBERTO   his mantle 874
SAN LEO   loyal to Montefeltro 137; captured from Borgia 123, 141, 164; strong by rock and height 703
SAN MINIATO   hill to be fortified 996f., 999
SAN PIERO AD VINCULA   See JULIUS II; POPE
SAN SEVERINO, RUBERTO DA   condottiere 50, 145, 1437; Florentine condottiere 1371; condottiere at Genoa and Pisa 1400ff.; Venetian commander 1414; condottiere for Innocent VIII against Naples 1426; flight to Ravenna 1427; killed 1429
SAN SISTO, CARDINAL   See RIARIO
SANT' ANDREA IN PERCUSSINA   Mach.'s farm 915, 929, 1330
SAN ZANOBI   his skull 874
SARACENS   crusades against 1054; in Italy 1049, 1052; in service of Frederick II 1059; attack Genoa 1081.   See also TURKS

STORM in Tuscany, destruction by 1329ff.

STRATAGEM in battle 651, 653f.; for dividing hostile forces 697; and deception 694-698; ancient examples 699f. See also FRAUD; WAR

STRATEGY See GENERAL(S); TACTICS; etc.

STROZZI, LORENZO Art of War dedicated to 566f.

SUBJECTS gained by liberality 1133; faithful when defended and punished 1441; unfaithful 1440; not able to do harm, not wishing to 389f.; injured by successful war 1284; dependent on prince 79; dissatisfied 79; as soldiers 51; to be disarmed? 77f.; of republics 336f.; conciliation 1375; Flor. acquires by running from them 1133, 1209. See CITIZENS

SUCCESS requires adaptation to times 90f.; from ability, not method 481; no method for 896f.; many s. wiped out by one failure 305, 743

SULTAN depends on soldiers 75; sought Lorenzo the Magnificent's favor 1434; to invade Italy 880. See also TURK

SUPERSTITION army kept from battle by 658; modern and ancient 699. See also PORTENT

SURPRISE success of 653; precautions against 674; capture of city 712

SUSPICION by conspirators 442; mother of Ingratitude 740; awake in city 741; causes hate 1384. See also FEAR

SWISS armed and free 48; gained freedom 379ff.; poor 597, 916; army 52; why mercenaries 338; hired as mercenaries by Louis XI 53f.; no Roman empire 925; good soldiers 723; infantry 378, 598; phalanx 596, 628; arms 597; halberds with pikes 629; length of pikes 641; punishment of guilty soldier 690; like Romans 919; order of battle 638f.; firmness before artillery 638; masters of modern war 366; selection 589; victory at Novara 376; will gain tributaries 952; beaten at Marignano 387; defeated by Carmignuola at Arbedo 599ff.; insult Italy 50; power in Lombardy 918f., 1443; danger to Italy 920, 924ff., 952; will bridle Italy 924; capture Milan 386; power in Milan 942f.; save Ferdinand after Ravenna 905; system of gov't 952; league 335f.; brutal, victorious, proud 922; greedy 917; ambitious 951; how Church would affect 229. See also GERMANS

SYRACUSE freedom 238; hesitation in policy 361; Agathocles 35

T

TACITUS CORNELIUS Annals 54; men should endure bad rulers 428; on severity 474

TACTICS adaptability 648f.; military, new 95f.; variations 651; superior force applied 650; infantry 95f.; Castruccio's 546ff., 551; Roman 539; battalion 611-619. See also ARMY; etc.

TARO RIVER battle at Fornovo 95, 826f., 1446f.

TAUNTS See INSULTS

TAXES reasonable 59ff., 84; cause complaints against rulers (1442) 1191; decreased for poor, to get favor 1197; inequality in 1201f.; Medici weapon 1238; property (1427) revived 1339; heavier for rich, laid on property 1201; heavy for rich 1194; violently collected 1194f.; objections to 1194f.; on rich 299; excessive, caused by mercenary soldiers 1285; after successful war 1284; Mach.'s 943. See also CATASTO

TEACHING good man's duty 324; by history 56, 1031

TEGRIMI Life of Castruccio 533-559

TEMERITY See RASHNESS

TEMPERAMENT See NATURE

TEMPORIZING about ills in state 265f., 1219; unavoidable evils 275; bad when weak 16. See also DELAY; TIME

WORLD   *See* AFFAIRS, HUMAN

WRITERS   *fame 220; on gov't 374; on lives of princes 1346; praise ability of republics 622f.; on warfare 374, 581, 587, 606, 626.   See also* DE REGIMINE PRINCIPUM; HIS-
TORIANS

X

XENOPHON   Life of Cyrus *57, 357, 476, 482, 516;* On Tyranny *329*

Y

YOUNG MEN   *able, approved 265; war their business 626; in Venice speak first 626; favored by Fortune 746*
YOUTH   *See* AGE